The Ultimate
Ninja Foodi
Cookbook

500 Easy Ninja Foodi Recipes for Beginners to Air Fry, Dehydrate, Pressure Cook, Slow Cook, and More.

George Juarez

Table of Contents

Beef, Pork & Lamb 80

Introduction

If you haven't heard about the Ninja Foodi, you should start reading this book, because not only will it offer some of the most sumptuous recipes that you can ever stumble into, but it will also offer you useful information that will help you understand the function of this new cooking appliance. So, if you are a Newbie in the use of Ninja Foodies, don't get frustrated, because, in this book, you will just find everything you need and enough information that will help you understand this cooking appliance better.

The Ninja Foodi is not just for cooking food for adults. If you have a little one at home, you can use the Foodi to make healthy and delicious baby food, so you know exactly what you're feeding your child.

It is a single machine that can do the work of four machines. It can do everything that is done by an Instant Pot. It can even do much more than that. Also, the Ninja Foodi costs you less than the amount you have to pay for buying all other machines individually.

Sometimes the ease you feel at things is due to how friendly they behave towards you. It means that the more comfortable it is to use, the more you enjoy using it. Ninja Foodi is very easy to use, and you don't need to put in a lot of effort into understand how it works. It's easy to learn its usage and does not bother you much. There is a digital display given in Ninja Foodi whereas there is no such kind of technologically developed approach in an Instant Pot.

As the pressure keeps rising within Ninja Foodi, it continuously becomes visible at the digital display. Ninja Foodi is reliable because everything is visible on the digital display while in the case of Instant Pot it is not like that. Its all about how accurately you can guess.

Apart from other aspects comes the cleaning of Ninja Foodi. It's easy to clean Ninja Foodi and clear it from the food particles and oily content of your food. One who uses it can quickly get the trick of its efficient cleaning.

How to Use the Ninja Foodi Pressure Cooker

Before using the device, it is essential to check all its components, if the power cord is intact, all the valves are in their position, and the sealing ring is properly fixed, etc. If any of the components are not properly set, the device will not function well. Now that everything is in place, you can plug in your device. Once plugged in, the LED screen of the control panel lights up.

1. Add Ingredients to the Ninja Foodi Cooking Pot:

To start with the cooking, you can either remove the cooking pot from the vessel and add ingredients to it or leave it in the vessel to cook a meal in which we need to start by sautéing the ingredients; the inner pot is left inside of the vessels and ingredients are added gradually to the pot. The inner markings of the pot provide a good measurement for the food, and it also marks the limit, do not add anything above its 2/3 full limit. There must be enough space above the food so that it could easily boil or expand.

2. . Seal and Secure the Lid:

For pressure cooking, the pressure lid with the valve attached needs to be installed, sealed, and locked on top of the vessel. For that, simply place the lid over the vessel and rotate it until it sounds clicks. When the arrow on the vessel aligns with the close marking of the lid, it means your lid is sealed. Whenever the lid is not properly closed, the timer does not initiate. This is one of the security features of the Ninja Foodi, which does not initiate cooking without proper locking of the lid. For Air Crisping, use the crisping lid.

3. . Select the Appropriate Cooking Mode:

As a multipurpose Ninja Foodi cooker offers you several different cooking modes, each of these modes has its own preset or integrated settings to adjust both the time and pressure according to the requirement. To start the cooking process, select any of the desired programs by pressing their respective buttons or keys. Remember that each mode has its own settings; to make changes in time and pressure, use the adjustment keys. Every standard control panel of a Ninja Foodi pressure cooker gives you these many options:

- Steam
- Air Crisp
- Sear/Sauté
- Pressure

- Slow Cook
- Bake/Roast
- Broil
- Dehydrate
- Keep Warm

Once the mode is selected, the Ninja Foodi will immediately switch to a Preheating State, which continues for 10 seconds. During this stage, the cooker sets its internal temperature and the internal pressure; then, it finally switches to the cooking state. Once the food is all cooked, the Ninja Foodi automatically switches to a standby mode where it is kept warm at low temperatures. The Keep Warm key allows you to either stop or cancel the operation or switch the appliance to the Warm mode. Once set, the warm mode will continue until the button is pressed again.

Once the mode is selected, use the time and temperature keys to increase or decrease the values. Then pressure the START/STOP button to initiate the cooking or stop it.

Accessories to Help with Your Ninja Foodi Pressure Cooker

In addition to the accessories that came with your Ninja Foodi Pressure Cooker, there are a few additional accessories you can purchase so that you can truly get the most out of your Ninja Foodi.

1. Dehydrate Rack – This rack is specifically designed to expand the amount of food you can dehydrate at once. Arrange ingredients in a single layer and carefully place the rack in the cooking pot. Follow the Dehydrate Chart to create your own custom jerky, vegetable chips, dried fruit snacks, and more.

2. Glass Lid – With this new accessory, there is no second guessing with how your food is cooking. The glass allows you to check on your food as it steams and slow cooks without removing the lid. I also love using the glass lid with the Keep Warm setting as a buffet. Great for holidays or keeping dinner warm until the whole family is home to enjoy together!

3. Loaf Pan – This specially designed loaf pan fits perfectly on the Reversible Rack. The ideal baking accessory for quick breads, it works equally as well for your favorite meatloaf recipe. Plus, the loaf pan has ceramic coating and is nonstick for easy cleaning.

4. Multi-Purpose Pan – Perfect for baking everything from desserts to casseroles, the Multi-Purpose Pan is the must-have accessory for any Ninja Foodi fanatic and can be used across most Ninja Foodi products.

5. Multi-Purpose Sling – Aluminum foil is a hack used in many recipes for removing accessories and roasts from pressure cookers. The multi-purpose sling is a more durable, reusable option, and is great for that whole roasted chicken or the Multi-Purpose Pan.

6. Tube Pan – A tube pan is very similar to a Bundt pan but it has detachable sides like a springform pan, making it easy to remove foods. Use this pan for everything from cheesecakes and delicate desserts to cornbread and casseroles.

Tips and Tricks for the Perfect TenderCrisp

It's the TenderCrisp Technology that sets the Ninja Foodi apart from every other product out there. Here are seven basic, simple steps to get that tender and crispy finish every time you use your Ninja Foodi.

1. Heat it up. When using the Sear/Sauté, Air Crisp, or Broil functions, always preheat the Ninja Foodi for 5 minutes before adding food. This will ensure that you have reached the correct temperature before you begin to cook.

2. Shake it up. It is recommended to always shake (or toss with tongs) food that is layered on top of itself in the Cook & Crisp Basket at least once or twice during crisping. But the more you shake or toss, the more even and crispy the result will be.

3. Spritz with oil. Use a bottle with a nozzle or a cooking spray can to evenly coat large proteins and veggies with oil. You can also use a brush if you're applying thick sauces and marinades.

4. Keep it consistent. Foods that are the same size cook more evenly. Be sure to cut foods into similar-size pieces when prepping a recipe.

5. Rinse the rice. When using Pressure to cook rice and grains, for best results be sure to rinse them thoroughly, until the water runs clear.

6. Keep it separate. When following recipes for a 360 Meal, you will layer meats over veggies and rice using the Reversible Rack. This builds flavor and keeps the meal in one pot, all while maintaining texture. If you prefer to keep the meat drippings separate, place aluminum foil over the Revesible Rack before adding the meat.

7. Utensils matter. Keep your Ninja Foodi looking and performing its best by only using wooden, silicone, or silicone-tipped utensils.

Frequently Asked Questions

1. Why does the Ninja Foodi come with two lids?

The Ninja Foodi is the only pressure cooker that crisps. For this reason, it comes with a Pressure Lid for the Pressure, Steam, Slow Cook, and Sear/Sauté functions, as well as a Crisping Lid for the Air Crisp, Bake/Roast, Broil, and Dehydrate functions. Use the lids individually or one right after the other to unlock a world of recipes you never knew you could make at home.

2. How do I convert my favorite recipes to the Ninja Foodi?

You can easily convert a number of your favorite recipes to the Ninja Foodi. When converting recipes from a conventional oven, use the Bake/Roast setting and reduce the temperature of the recipe by 25°F or 5°C. So if a recipe is baked in the oven at 375°For 190°C, you would set the Ninja Foodi for 350°F or 185°C. You will also likely be able to cut down the cook time. Check the food frequently to avoid overcooking.

You can also cook your favorite slow cooker recipes using Pressure so that they cook much quicker. A good rule of thumb is that recipes that slow cook for 8 hours on Low or 4 hours on High should take 25 to 30 minutes in the pressure cooker. It is also important to check your liquid level and ensure that your recipe includes ½ to 1 cup of liquid for the cooker to get to pressure. And as always, make sure the pressure release valve is in the Seal position.

A number of the recipes throughout this book are staples that my husband, Julien, and I have been cooking for years, but with the Ninja Foodi we no longer need to turn on a bunch of appliances and use numerous pots and pans. Instead, recipes like Crispy Chicken Thighs with Roasted Carrots are all made in one pot while maintaining their own unique textures. However, every recipe is different, and there is no one rule for doubling or halving all recipes in the book. I recommend trying the recipes as they are and then experimenting with ingredient swaps, cutting recipes in half, or doubling recipes. Note that cook times may change, too.

3. What is the difference between quick release and natural release?

Quick release is when you manually switch the pressure release valve to the Vent position. Quick release is used in the majority of this book's recipes. Natural release occurs when you let the Ninja Foodi decrease in pressure naturally after cooking is complete. This technique is most commonly used when cooking beans.

4. When doing a Tender Crisp recipe, should I remove the liquid after using the Pressure Lid, before switching to the Crisping Lid?

If you are following one of the Tender Crisp recipes in this book, there is no need to remove the liquid before switching to the Crisping Lid. These recipes are specifically designed to work with the amount of liquid in the bottom of the pot.

If you are creating your own recipe and would like to make sure the bottom of your food is browned in the Cook & Crisp™ Basket, make sure not to exceed the 3-cup mark (located on the inside of the pot) with liquid.

5. Can I cook frozen food in the Ninja Foodi?

Yes! One of the best things about the Ninja Foodi is that you can cook frozen food straight from the freezer without the need to defrost. Use Pressure to turn frozen chicken breasts into shredded chicken or ground beef into chili, or use the combination of Pressure and the Crisping Lid to roast a whole chicken from frozen or cook the perfect medium-rare steak.

Snacks, Appetizers & Sides

Rosemary Potato Fries

Servings: 4

Cooking Time: 30 Min

Ingredients:

- 4 russet potatoes, cut into sticks
- 2 garlic cloves, crushed
- 2 tbsp butter, melted /30ml
- 1 tsp fresh rosemary; chopped /5g
- Salt and pepper, to taste

Directions:

1. Add butter, garlic, salt, and pepper to a bowl; toss until the sticks are well-coated. Lay the potato sticks into the Ninja Foodi's basket. Close the crisping lid and cook for 15 minutes at 370 °F or 185°C. Shake the potatoes every 5 minutes.
2. Once ready, check to ensure the fries are golden and crispy all over if not, return them to cook for a few minutes.
3. Divide standing up between metal cups lined with nonstick baking paper, and serve sprinkled with rosemary.

Fried Beef Dumplings

Servings: 8

Cooking Time: 45 Min

Ingredients:

- 8 ounces ground beef /240g
- 20 wonton wrappers
- 1 carrot, grated
- 1 large egg, beaten
- 1 garlic clove, minced
- ½ cup grated cabbage /65g
- 2 tbsps olive oil /30ml
- 2 tbsps coconut aminos /30g
- ½ tbsp melted ghee /7.5ml
- ½ tbsp ginger powder /7.5g
- ½ tsp salt /2.5g
- ½ tsp freshly ground black pepper/2.5g

Directions:

1. Put the Crisping Basket in the pot. Close the crisping lid, choose Air Crisp, set the temperature to 400°F or 205°C, and the time to 5 minutes; press Start/Stop. In a large bowl, mix the beef, cabbage, carrot, egg, garlic, coconut aminos, ghee, ginger, salt, and black pepper.
2. Put the wonton wrappers on a clean flat surface and spoon 1 tbsp of the beef mixture into the middle of each wrapper.
3. Run the edges of the wrapper with a little water; fold the wrapper to cover the filling into a semi-circle shape and pinch the edges to seal. Brush the dumplings with olive oil.
4. Lay the dumplings in the preheated basket, choose Air Crisp, set the temperature to 400°F or 205°C, and set the time to 12 minutes. Choose Start/Stop to begin frying.
5. After 6 minutes, open the lid, pull out the basket and shake the dumplings. Return the basket to the pot and close the lid to continue frying until the dumplings are crispy to your desire.

Green Vegan Dip

Servings: 4

Cooking Time: 20 Min

Ingredients:

- 10 ounces canned green chiles, drained with liquid reserved /300g
- 2 cups broccoli florets /260g
- ¼ cup raw cashews /32.5g
- ¼ cup soy sauce /62.5ml
- 1 cup water /250ml
- ¾ cup green bell pepper; chopped /98g
- ¼ tsp garlic powder /1.25g
- ½ tsp sea salt /2.5g
- ¼ tsp chili powder /1.25g

Directions:

1. In the cooker, add cashews, broccoli, green bell pepper, and water. Seal the pressure lid, choose Pressure, set to High, and set the timer to 5 minutes. Press Start. When ready, release the pressure quickly.
2. Drain water from the pot; add reserved liquid from canned green chilies, sea salt, garlic powder, chili powder, soy sauce, and cumin.
3. Use an immersion blender to blend the mixture until smooth; set aside in a mixing bowl. Stir green chilies through the dip; add your desired optional additions.

Pull Apart Cheesy Garlic Bread

Servings:6

Cooking Time: 25 Minutes

Ingredients:

- ½ pound store-bought pizza dough
- 3 tablespoons unsalted butter, melted
- 4 garlic cloves, minced
- ¼ cup shredded Parmesan cheese
- ¼ cup shredded mozzarella cheese
- ¼ cup minced parsley
- ½ teaspoon kosher salt
- ½ teaspoon garlic powder
- Cooking spray
- Marinara sauce, for serving

Directions:

1. Cut the pizza dough into 1-inch cubes. Roll each cube into a ball. Place the dough balls in a large bowl. Add the butter, garlic, Parmesan cheese, mozzarella cheese, parsley, salt, and garlic powder. Toss, ensuring everything is evenly coated and mixed. Set aside.
2. Close crisping lid. Select BAKE/ROAST, set temperature to 325°F or 165°C, and set time to 30 minutes. Select START/STOP to begin. Let preheat for 5 minutes.
3. Coat the Ninja Multi-Purpose Pan with cooking spray. Place the dough balls in the pan and place pan on Reversible Rack, making sure it is in the lower position.
4. Once unit has preheated, open lid and insert the rack in pot. Close lid and cook for 25 minutes.
5. Once cooking is complete, open lid and let the bread cool slightly. Serve with marinara sauce for dipping.

Nutrition:

- InfoCalories: 182,Total Fat: 10g,Sodium: 514mg,Carbohydrates: 20g,Protein: 6g.

Pistachio Stuffed Mushrooms

Servings: 8
Cooking Time: 20 Minutes
Ingredients:

- 16 large mushrooms
- 1 tbsp. olive oil
- ½ onion, diced fine
- ¼ cup unsalted pistachios, chopped
- 1/3 cup pretzels, crushed
- 2 tbsp. sour cream, fat free
- 2 tbsp. fresh parsley, chopped
- ¼ tsp pepper
- 1/8 tsp hot pepper sauce

Directions:

1. Remove stems from mushrooms and dice them.
2. Set cooker to sauté on medium heat. Add oil and let it get hot.
3. Add the chopped mushrooms, onions, and pistachios and cook, until vegetables are tender, about 2-4 minutes. Transfer to a large bowl.
4. Add the remaining ingredients to the mushroom mixture and mix well.
5. Wipe out the cooking pot and add the rack to it. Select the air fryer function on 350°F or 175°C.
6. Stuff the mushroom caps with the filling. Lay a sheet of parchment paper over the top of the rack and place mushrooms on it.
7. Add the tender-crisp lid and bake 20-25 minutes or until mushrooms are tender. Serve.
8. Preheat oven to 350 °F or 175°C. Remove mushroom stems from caps; finely chop stems.

Nutrition:

- InfoCalories 84,Total Fat 4g,Total Carbs 11g,Protein 3g,Sodium 26mg.

Cheesy Fried Risotto Balls

Servings:6
Cooking Time: 45 Minutes
Ingredients:

- ½ cup extra-virgin olive oil, plus 1 tablespoon
- 1 small yellow onion, diced
- 2 garlic cloves, minced
- 5 cups vegetable broth
- ½ cup white wine
- 2 cups arborio rice
- ½ cup shredded mozzarella cheese
- ½ cup shredded fontina cheese
- ½ cup grated Parmesan cheese, plus more for garnish
- 2 tablespoons chopped fresh parsley
- 1 teaspoon sea salt
- 1 teaspoon freshly ground black pepper
- 2 cups fresh bread crumbs
- 2 large eggs

Directions:

1. Select SEAR/SAUTÉ and set to MD:HI. Select START/STOP to begin. Allow the pot to preheat for 5 minutes.
2. Add 1 tablespoon of oil and the onion to the preheated pot. Cook until soft and translucent, stirring occasionally. Add the garlic and cook for 1 minute.

3. Add the broth, wine, and rice to the pot; stir to incorporate. Assemble the pressure lid, making sure the pressure release valve is in the SEAL position.
4. Select PRESSURE and set to HI. Set the time to 7 minutes. Press START/STOP to begin.
5. When pressure cooking is complete, allow pressure to naturally release for 10 minutes. After 10 minutes, quick release any remaining pressure by turning the pressure release valve to the VENT position. Carefully remove the lid when the unit has finished releasing pressure.
6. Add the mozzarella, fontina, and Parmesan cheeses, the parsley, salt, and pepper. Stir vigorously until the rice begins to thicken. Transfer the risotto to a large mixing bowl and let cool.
7. Meanwhile, clean the pot. In a medium mixing bowl, stir together the bread crumbs and the remaining ½ cup of olive oil. In a separate mixing bowl, lightly beat the eggs.
8. Divide the risotto into 12 equal portions and form each one into a ball. Dip each risotto ball in the beaten eggs, then coat in the breadcrumb mixture.
9. Arrange half of the risotto balls in the Cook & Crisp Basket in a single layer.
10. Close the crisping lid. Select AIR CRISP, set the temperature to 400°F or 205°C, and set the time to 10 minutes. Select START/STOP to begin.
11. Repeat steps 9 and 10 to cook the remaining risotto balls.

Nutrition:

- InfoCalories: 722,Total Fat: 33g,Sodium: 1160mg,Carbohydrates: 81g,Protein: 23g.

Chicken Lettuce Wraps

Servings: 6
Cooking Time: 30 Minutes
Ingredients:

- 8 ounces chicken fillet
- ¼ cup tomato juice
- 5 tablespoon sour cream
- 1 teaspoon black pepper
- 8 ounces lettuce leaves
- 1 teaspoon salt
- ½ cup chicken stock
- 1 teaspoon butter
- 1 teaspoon turmeric

Directions:

1. Chop the chicken fillet roughly and sprinkle it with sour cream, tomato juice, black pepper, turmeric, and salt.
2. Mix up the meat mixture. Put the chicken spice mixture in the Ninja Foodi's insert and add chicken stock.
3. Close the Ninja Foodi's lid and cook the dish in the "Sauté" mode for 30 minutes.
4. Once the chicken is done, remove it from the Ninja Foodi's insert and shred it well.
5. Add the butter and blend well. Transfer the shredded chicken to the lettuce leaves.
6. Serve the dish warm.

Nutrition:

- InfoCalories: 138; Fat: 7.4g; Carbohydrates: 12.63g; Protein: 6g

Chicken Meatballs With Dill Dipping Sauce

Servings: 8
Cooking Time: 15 Minutes

Ingredients:

- Nonstick cooking spray
- 1 lb. lean ground chicken
- 1 tsp oregano
- 1 cup whole wheat panko bread crumbs
- 1 egg, beaten
- 1/3 cup milk
- 2 cloves garlic, diced fine
- 1/3 cup red onions, diced fine
- 1/3 cup fresh parsley, chopped fine
- ¾ tsp salt, divided
- ¼ tsp black pepper
- 1 cup plain Greek yogurt, low fat
- 1/3 cup fresh dill, chopped fine
- 1 lemon, zest and juice
- ½ tsp cumin
- 1/8 tsp cayenne pepper

Directions:

1. Lightly spray the fryer basket with cooking spray.
2. In a large bowl, combine chicken, oregano, bread crumbs, egg, milk, garlic, onions, parsley, ½ teaspoon salt, and black pepper until thoroughly combined. Form into 1-inch meatballs.
3. Place meatballs in the basket in a single layer, do not over crowd. Add the tender crisp lid and set to air fry on 400°F or 205°C. Cook meatballs 10-15 minutes until cooked through, turning over halfway through cooking time.
4. In a small bowl, stir together yogurt, dill, lemon zest and juice, remaining salt, cumin, and cayenne pepper until combined.
5. Serve meatballs with sauce for dipping.

Nutrition:

- InfoCalories 174,Total Fat 7g,Total Carbs 13g,Protein 14g,Sodium 386mg.

Mexican Street Corn

Servings:3
Cooking Time: 14 Minutes

Ingredients:

- 3 ears corn, husked, rinsed, and dried
- Olive oil spray
- ¼ cup sour cream
- ¼ cup mayonnaise
- ¼ cup crumbled cotija cheese, plus more for garnish
- 1 teaspoon freshly squeezed lime juice
- ½ teaspoon garlic powder
- ¼ teaspoon chili powder, plus more as needed
- Fresh cilantro leaves, for garnish
- ½ teaspoon salt
- ½ teaspoon freshly ground black pepper

Directions:

1. Select AIR CRISP, set the temperature to 400°F or 205°C, and set the time to 5 minutes to preheat. Select START/STOP to begin.
2. Lightly mist the corn with olive oil and place the corn in the Cook & Crisp Basket. Close the crisping lid.
3. Select AIR CRISP, set the temperature to 400°F or 205°C, and set the time to 12 minutes. Select START/STOP to begin. After 7

minutes, flip the corn. Close the crisping lid and cook for 5 minutes more.
4. While the corn cooks, in a small bowl, stir together the sour cream, mayonnaise, cotija cheese, lime juice, garlic powder, and chili powder until blended.
5. When cooking is complete, carefully remove the corn and brush or spoon the sauce onto it. Sprinkle with cilantro, cotija cheese, and more chili powder.
6. If desired, return the corn to the basket. Close the crisping lid. Select BROIL and set the time for 2 minutes. Select START/STOP to begin.
7. Serve hot, seasoned with salt and pepper, as needed.

Nutrition:

- InfoCalories: 280,Total Fat: 15g,Sodium: 701mg,Carbohydrates: 35g,Protein: 7g.

Broccoli Turmeric Tots

Servings: 8
Cooking Time: 8 Minutes

Ingredients:

- 1-pound broccoli
- 3 cups of water
- 1 teaspoon salt
- 1 egg
- 1 cup pork rind
- ½ teaspoon paprika
- 1 tablespoon turmeric
- ⅓ cup almond flour
- 2 tablespoons olive oil

Directions:

1. Wash the broccoli and chop it roughly.
2. Put the broccoli in the Ninja Foodi's insert and add water.
3. Set the Ninja Foodi's insert to "Steam" mode and steam the broccoli for 20 minutes.
4. Remove the broccoli from the Ninja Foodi's insert and let it cool.
5. Transfer the broccoli to a blender. Add egg, salt, paprika, turmeric, and almond flour.
6. Blend the mixture until smooth. Add pork rind and blend the broccoli mixture for 1 minute more.
7. Pour the olive oil in the Ninja Foodi's insert.
8. Form the medium tots from the broccoli mixture and transfer them to the Ninja Foodi's insert.
9. Set the Ninja Foodi's insert to "Sauté" mode and cook for 4 minutes on each side.
10. Once the dish is done, remove the broccoli tots from the Ninja Foodi's insert.
11. Allow them to rest before serving.

Nutrition:

- InfoCalories: 147; Fat: 9.9g; Carbohydrates: 4.7g; Protein: 11.6g

Italian Pita Crisps

Servings: 8
Cooking Time: 15 Minutes

Ingredients:

- 4 whole wheat pita breads
- 1/3 cup finely chopped parsley
- 1 teaspoon Italian herb seasoning
- 1/3 cup finely grated fresh parmesan cheese

Directions:

1. With a sharp knife, cut away the outside edge of each pita. Open the pitas up into 2 halves. Cut each half into 4 wedges.
2. In a small bowl, combine parsley, seasoning, and parmesan.
3. Place pita wedges, in a single layer in the fryer basket, these will need to be cooked in batches. Sprinkle with some of the parmesan mixture.
4. Add the tender-crisp lid and set to air fryer function on 350°F or 175°C. Bake 12-15 minutes or until golden brown. Repeat with remaining pitas and seasoning.

Nutrition:

- InfoCalories 103,Total Fat 4g,Total Carbs 18g,Protein 4g,Sodium 303mg.

Herbed Cauliflower Fritters

Servings: 7
Cooking Time: 13 Minutes

Ingredients:

- 1-pound cauliflower
- 1 medium white onion
- 1 teaspoon salt
- ½ teaspoon ground white pepper
- 1 tablespoon sour cream
- 1 teaspoon turmeric
- ½ cup dill, chopped
- 1 teaspoon thyme
- 3 tablespoons almond flour
- 1 egg
- 2 tablespoons butter

Directions:

1. Wash the cauliflower and separate it into the florets.
2. Chop the florets and place them in a blender.
3. Peel the onion and dice it. Add the diced onion to a blender and blend the mixture.
4. When you get the smooth texture, add salt, ground white pepper, sour cream, turmeric, dill, thyme, and almond flour.
5. Add egg blend the mixture well until a smooth dough form.
6. Remove the cauliflower dough from a blender and form the medium balls.
7. Flatten the balls a little. Set the Ninja Foodi's insert to" Sauté" mode.
8. Add the butter to the Ninja Foodi's insert and melt it.
9. Add the cauliflower fritters in the Ninja Foodi's insert, and sauté them for 6 minutes.
10. Flip them once. Cook the dish in" Sauté" stew mode for 7 minutes.
11. Once done, remove the fritters from the Ninja Foodi's insert.
12. Serve immediately.

Nutrition:

- InfoCalories: 143; Fat: 10.6g; Carbohydrates: 9.9g; Protein: 5.6g

Chili Chicken Dip

Servings: 8
Cooking Time: 20 Minutes

Ingredients:

- 1 tbsp. olive oil
- 1 sweet onion, chopped fine
- 2 cloves garlic, chopped fine
- 2 jalapeño peppers, seeded & chopped
- 1 Poblano pepper, seeded & chopped

- 1 cup Greek yogurt
- 8 oz. cream cheese, fat free, soft
- ½ cup cheddar cheese, reduced fat, grated
- 4 oz. green chilies, diced
- 1 tsp salt
- 2 cups chicken breasts, cooked & shredded
- 1 tbsp. chili powder
- 2 tsp cumin
- ½ tsp pepper
- 1 tsp oregano
- Nonstick cooking spray
- ¼ cup cilantro, chopped

Directions:

1. Set the cooker to sauté on medium heat. Add oil and let it get hot.
2. Add the onion, garlic, jalapeno, and poblano peppers. Cook, stirring frequently, until vegetables are tender, about 3-5 minutes. Transfer to a bowl and let cool completely.
3. In a medium bowl, beat together yogurt, and cream cheese until smooth.
4. Turn the mixer to low and add onion mixture along with remaining ingredients, except cilantro. Beat until all ingredients are combined.
5. Spray a casserole dish with cooking spray. Spread dip evenly in the dish.
6. Place the rack in the cooking pot and put the dish on it. Add the tender-crisp lid and select bake on 400°F or 205°C. Bake 15 minutes until bubbly. Sprinkle with cilantro and serve.

Nutrition:

- InfoCalories 189,Total Fat 7g,Total Carbs 15g,Protein 19g,Sodium 1004mg.

Honey-garlic Chicken Wings

Servings:4
Cooking Time: 43 Minutes

Ingredients:

- 2 pounds fresh chicken wings
- ¾ cup potato starch
- Cooking spray
- ¼ cup unsalted butter
- 4 tablespoons minced garlic
- ¼ cup honey
- ¼ teaspoon sea salt

Directions:

1. Insert Cook & Crisp Basket into pot and close crisping lid. Select AIR CRISP, set temperature to 390°F or 200°C, and set time to 5 minutes. Select START/STOP to begin preheating.
2. Pat the chicken wings dry. In a large bowl, toss the chicken wings with potato starch until evenly coated.
3. Once unit has preheated, place the wings in the basket. Close lid.
4. Select AIR CRISP, set temperature to 390°F or 200°C, and set time to 30 minutes. Select START/STOP to begin.
5. After 15 minutes, open lid, then lift the basket and shake the wings. Coat with cooking spray. Lower basket back into the pot. Close lid and continue cooking until the wings reach your desired crispiness.
6. Cooking is complete when the internal temperature of the meat reads at least 165°F or 75°C on a food thermometer.

7. Remove basket from pot. Cover with aluminum foil to keep warm.
8. Select SEAR/SAUTÉ and set to MD:LO. Select START/STOP to begin.
9. Add the butter and garlic and sauté until fragrant, about 3 minutes. Add the honey and salt and simmer for about 10 minutes, adding water as needed to thin out the sauce.
10. Place the wings in a large bowl. Drizzle with the sauce and toss the chicken wings to coat. Serve.

Nutrition:

- InfoCalories: 654,Total Fat: 33g,Sodium: 302mg,Carbohydrates: 53g,Protein: 39g.

Cheesy Stuffed Mushroom

Servings: 7

Cooking Time: 7 Minutes

Ingredients:

- 12 ounces Parmesan cheese
- 7 mushroom caps
- 2 teaspoons minced garlic
- ¼ sour cream
- 1 teaspoon butter
- 1 teaspoon ground white pepper
- 2 teaspoons oregano

Directions:

1. Mix the minced garlic, sour cream, ground white pepper, and oregano, and stir the mixture.
2. Add grated parmesan to the minced garlic mixture.
3. Blend the mixture until smooth.
4. Stuff the mushrooms with the cheese mixture and place the dish in the Ninja Foodi's insert.
5. Set the Ninja Foodi's insert to "Pressure" mode, add butter, and close the Ninja Foodi's lid.
6. Cook the dish for 7 minutes.
7. Once done, remove it from the Ninja Foodi's insert, let it rest briefly, and serve.

Nutrition:

- InfoCalories: 203; Fat: 7.6g; Carbohydrates: 8.35g; Protein: 8g

Spicy Turkey Meatballs

Servings: 8

Cooking Time: 15 Minutes

Ingredients:

- 1 lb. lean ground turkey
- 1 onion, chopped fine
- ¼ cup shredded wheat cereal, crushed
- 2 egg whites
- ½ tsp garlic powder
- ½ tsp salt
- ¼ tsp pepper
- Nonstick cooking spray
- ¼ cup jalapeno pepper jelly

Directions:

1. In a large bowl, combine all ingredients, except pepper jelly, and mix well. Form into 24 1-inch meatballs.
2. Lightly spray the fryer basket with cooking spray. Place meatballs in a single layer in the basket, these will need to be cooked in batches.
3. Add the basket to the cooking pot and secure the tender crisp lid. Set to air fry on 400°F or 205°C. Cook meatballs 12-15 minutes, until no longer pink inside, turning halfway through cooking time.

4. Place the pepper jelly in a medium, microwave safe bowl. Microwave in 30 second intervals until the jelly is melted.
5. Toss cooked meatballs in the melted pepper jelly and serve immediately.
6. In a medium bowl, combine the turkey, onion, cereal, egg whites, garlic powder, salt, and black pepper. Shape into 24 one-inch meatballs.

Nutrition:

- InfoCalories 113,Total Fat 5g,Total Carbs 6g,Protein 12g,Sodium 199mg.

Bacon Wrapped Scallops

Servings: 8

Cooking Time: 10 Minutes

Ingredients:

- 1/3 cup ketchup
- 2 tbsp. vinegar
- 1 tbsp. brown sugar
- ¼ tsp hot pepper sauce
- 13 slices turkey bacon, cut in half
- 1 lb. scallops, rinse & pat dry
- Nonstick cooking spray

Directions:

1. In a large bowl, whisk together ketchup, vinegar, brown sugar, and hot pepper sauce until smooth.
2. Wrap each scallop with a piece of bacon and use a toothpick to secure. Add to the sauce and toss to coat. Cover and refrigerate 20 minutes.
3. Place the rack in the cooking pot. Spray a small baking sheet with cooking spray. Working in batches, place scallops in a single layer on the tray and place on the rack.
4. Add the tender-crisp lid and set to air fry on 450°F or 230°C. Cook scallops 4-5 minutes, then flip over and cook another 4-5 minutes or until cooked through. Serve immediately.

Nutrition:

- InfoCalories 100,Total Fat 2g,Total Carbs 6g,Protein 13g,Sodium 525mg.

Horseradish Roasted Carrots

Servings:4

Cooking Time: 10 Minutes

Ingredients:

- 1 pound carrots, peeled and cut into 1-inch pieces
- ½ cup vegetable stock
- 2 tablespoons grated horseradish
- ¾ cup mayonnaise
- ½ teaspoon kosher salt
- ½ teaspoon freshly ground black pepper
- Minced parsley, for garnish

Directions:

1. Place the carrots and stock in the pot. Assemble pressure lid, making sure the pressure release valve is in the SEAL position.
2. Select PRESSURE and set to HI. Set time to 2 minutes. Select START/STOP to begin.
3. When pressure cooking is complete, quick release the pressure by turning the pressure release valve to the VENT position. Carefully remove lid when unit has finished releasing pressure.

4. In a small bowl, combine the horseradish, mayonnaise, salt, and pepper. Add mixture to the cooked carrots and stir carefully. Close crisping lid.
5. Select BROIL and set time to 6 minutes. Select START/STOP to begin.
6. After 3 minutes, open lid to check doneness. If further browning desired, close lid and continue cooking.
7. When cooking is complete, garnish with parsley and serve immediately.

Nutrition:

- InfoCalories: 323,Total Fat: 30g,Sodium: 632mg,Carbohydrates: 13g,Protein: 1g.

Cheesy Onion Dip

Servings: 8
Cooking Time: 15 Minutes

Ingredients:

- 8 oz. cream cheese, soft
- 1 cup Swiss cheese, grated
- 1 cup mayonnaise
- 1 cup onion, grated

Directions:

1. In a medium bowl, combine all ingredients and mix thoroughly. Transfer to a small baking dish and cover tightly with foil.
2. Place the trivet in the cooking pot along with 1 cup of water. Place the dish on trivet.
3. Secure the lid and select pressure cooking on high. Set timer for 15 minutes.
4. When timer goes off, use quick release to remove the lid.
5. Remove the foil and add the tender-crisp lid. Set to air fryer on 400°F or 205°C cook 1-2 minutes until the top is golden brown. Serve warm.

Nutrition:

- InfoCalories 352,Total Fat 35g,Total Carbs 3g,Protein 6g,Sodium 290mg.

Loaded Potato Skins

Servings:4
Cooking Time: 45 Minutes

Ingredients:

- 2 large Russet potatoes, cleaned
- 1 tablespoon extra-virgin olive oil
- Kosher salt
- Freshly ground black pepper
- ¾ cup shredded sharp Cheddar cheese
- 3 tablespoons unsalted butter
- ¼ cup milk
- ¼ cup sour cream, plus more for serving
- 1 bunch chives, sliced
- 4 slices of ham, cubed

Directions:

1. Using a fork, poke holes in each potato. Rub each potato with the olive oil and season the skin with salt and pepper. Place the potatoes on the Reversible Rack in the lower position and place in the pot. Close the crisping lid.
2. Select AIR CRISP, set temperature to 390°F or 200°C, and set time to 35 minutes. Select START/STOP to begin.
3. When cooking is complete, open lid and use tongs to transfer the potatoes to a cutting board.

4. Cut the potatoes in half lengthwise. Using a spoon, scoop out the flesh into a large bowl, leaving about ¼ inch of flesh on the skins. Set aside.
5. Sprinkle the hollowed-out potato skins with ¼ cup of cheese and place them back in the pot on the rack. Close crisping lid.
6. Select BROIL and set time to 5 minutes. Select START/STOP to begin.
7. Add the butter, milk, and sour cream to the bowl with the flesh. Season with salt and pepper and mash together. Use a spatula to fold in ¼ cup of cheese, one-quarter of the chives, and ham into the potato mixture.
8. When cooking is complete, open lid. Using tongs, carefully transfer the potato skins to the cutting board. Evenly distribute the mashed potato mixture into each potato skin and top with the remaining ¼ cup of cheese. Return the loaded potato skins to the rack. Close crisping lid.
9. Select BROIL and set time to 5 minutes. Select START/STOP to begin.
10. When cooking is complete, open lid. Carefully remove the potatoes. Cut them in half and garnish with the remaining chives. Serve with additional sour cream, if desired.

Nutrition:

- InfoCalories: 402,Total Fat: 24g,Sodium: 561mg,Carbohydrates: 32g,Protein: 14g.

Crispy Delicata Squash

Servings:4
Cooking Time: 15 Minutes

Ingredients:

- 1 large delicata squash, seeds removed and sliced
- 1 tablespoon extra-virgin olive oil
- ¼ teaspoon sea salt

Directions:

1. Place Cook & Crisp Basket in pot. Close crisping lid. Select AIR CRISP, set temperature to 390°F or 200°C, and set time to 5 minutes. Select START/STOP to begin preheating.
2. In a large bowl, toss the squash with the olive oil and season with salt.
3. Once unit has preheated, place the squash in the basket. Close crisping lid.
4. Select AIR CRISP, set temperature to 390°F or 200°C, and set time to 15 minutes. Select START/STOP to begin.
5. After 7 minutes, open the lid, then lift the basket and shake the squash. Lower the basket back into pot. Close lid and continue cooking until the squash achieves your desired crispiness.

Nutrition:

- InfoCalories: 75,Total Fat: 4g,Sodium: 117mg,Carbohydrates: 10g,Protein: 2g.

Enchilada Bites

Servings: 12
Cooking Time: 25 Minutes

Ingredients:

- ½ lb. ground turkey
- ¾ cup mild red enchilada sauce
- ½ cup black beans, drained & rinsed
- ½ tsp cumin

- 1 tbsp. cilantro, chopped
- Nonstick cooking spray
- 6 whole wheat tortillas, 6-inch
- 1 cup cheddar cheese, reduced fat, grated fine

Directions:

1. Add turkey to the cooking pot and set cooker to sauté on medium heat. Cook 8-10 minutes until no longer pink.
2. Add enchilada sauce, beans, cumin, and cilantro, stir to mix. Reduce heat to low and simmer 5 minutes. Transfer to a bowl.
3. Lightly spray fryer basket with cooking spray.
4. Spray both sides of the tortillas. Spread 2 tablespoons turkey mixture over each tortilla and top with 4 teaspoons cheese. Roll up tightly and secure with a toothpick. Cut each roll in half and place them in a single layer in the basket.
5. Add the tender-crisp lid and set to air fryer on 375°F or 190°C. Bake 8-10 minutes, or until cheese has melted. Cut each roll in half and serve.

Nutrition:

- InfoCalories 135,Total Fat 4g,Total Carbs 15g,Protein 9g,Sodium 465mg.

Garlicky Tomato

Servings: 5

Cooking Time: 5 Minutes

Ingredients:

- 5 tomatoes
- ¼ cup chives, chopped
- ⅓ cup garlic clove, minced
- ½ teaspoon salt
- ½ teaspoon black pepper
- 1 tablespoon olive oil
- 7 ounces Parmesan cheese

Directions:

1. Wash the tomatoes and slice them into thick slices.
2. Place the sliced tomatoes in the Ninja Foodi's insert.
3. Combine the grated cheese and minced garlic and stir the mixture.
4. Sprinkle the tomato slices with chives, black pepper, and salt.
5. Then sprinkle the sliced tomatoes with the cheese mixture.
6. Close the Ninja Foodi's lid and cook the dish in the "Pressure" mode for 5 minutes.
7. Once done, remove the tomatoes carefully and serve.

Nutrition:

- InfoCalories: 224; Fat: 14g; Carbohydrates: 12.55g; Protein: 13g

Mexican Rice & Beans

Servings: 4

Cooking Time: 3 Hours

Ingredients:

- 1 cup rice, rinsed
- 1 jar salsa
- 1 can black beans, drained & rinsed
- 1 packet taco seasoning
- 1 cup vegetable broth
- 2 cloves garlic, diced fine
- 1 jalapeno, seeded & chopped

Directions:

1. Place all ingredients in the cooking pot and stir to mix.

2. Add the lid and select slow cooking on high. Set timer for 3 hours.
3. Cook until rice is tender and dip is heated through. Stir well then serve immediately.

Nutrition:

- InfoCalories 274,Total Fat 2g,Total Carbs 56g,Protein 9g,Sodium 1462mg.

Almond Lover's Bars

Servings: 20

Cooking Time: 30 Minutes

Ingredients:

- 2 cups almond flour, sifted
- 1 ½ cups flour
- 1 tsp baking powder
- ½ tsp salt
- 10 tbsp. butter, soft
- 1 cup sugar
- 2 eggs
- 2 tsp vanilla
- 1 tbsp. powdered sugar

Directions:

1. Line an 8-inch square baking dish with parchment paper.
2. In a medium bowl, whisk together both flours, baking powder, and salt.
3. In a large bowl, beat butter and sugar until creamy.
4. Beat in eggs and vanilla. Then stir in dry ingredients until combined. Press firmly in prepared pan.
5. Place the rack in the cooking pot and place the pan on it. Add the tender-crisp lid and set to bake on 325°F or 165°C. Bake 25-30 minutes until lightly browned and the bars pass the toothpick test.
6. Let cool before cutting into bars. Sprinkle with powdered sugar before serving.

Nutrition:

- InfoCalories 207,Total Fat 11g,Total Carbs 23g,Protein 3g,Sodium 83mg.

Three-layer Taco Dip

Servings:6

Cooking Time: 15 Minutes

Ingredients:

- 2 cans pinto beans, rinsed and drained
- 1 white onion, chopped
- 8 garlic cloves, chopped
- 1 can diced tomatoes
- 1 serrano chile, seeded and chopped
- 1 teaspoon kosher salt
- 2 teaspoons ground cumin
- 2 teaspoons chili powder
- 2 cups shredded Mexican blend cheese
- 1 cup shredded iceberg lettuce

Directions:

1. Place the beans, onions, garlic, tomatoes, chile, salt, cumin, and chili powder in the pot. Assemble pressure lid, making sure the pressure release valve is in the SEAL position.
2. Select PRESSURE and set to HI. Set time to 5 minutes. Select START/STOP to begin.

3. When pressure cooking is complete, quick release the pressure by moving the pressure release valve to the VENT position. Carefully remove lid when unit has finished releasing pressure.
4. Using a silicone spatula, stir the mixture in the pot. Sprinkle shredded cheese across the top of the bean mixture. Close crisping lid.
5. Select BROIL and set time to 10 minutes. Select STOP/START to begin.
6. When cooking is complete, open lid. Let cool for 5 minutes, then add the shredded lettuce. Serve immediately.

Nutrition:

- InfoCalories: 327,Total Fat: 14g,Sodium: 612mg,Carbohydrates: 33g,Protein: 19g.

Spicy Honey Wings

Servings: 6
Cooking Time: 2 Hours

Ingredients:

- 2 tbsp. brown sugar
- 1 ½ tsp salt
- 1 tsp pepper
- 1 ½ tsp garlic powder
- 1 ½ tsp onion powder
- 1 tsp smoked paprika
- 1 tsp chili powder
- 1 tsp cumin
- 1 tsp parsley
- Nonstick cooking spray
- 4 lbs. chicken wings, pat dry
- ¾ cup hot sauce
- ½ cup honey
- 1 tbsp. butter, melted
- 1 tbsp. molasses

Directions:

1. In a small bowl, stir together brown sugar, salt, pepper, garlic powder, onion powder, paprika, chili powder, cumin, and parsley.
2. Spray the cooking pot with cooking spray. Place the wings in the pot. Sprinkle the spice mix over the chicken and rub the spices into the wings.
3. In the same bowl, whisk together hot sauce, honey, butter, and molasses. Pour over wings and toss to coat.
4. Add the lid and select slow cooking on high. Set timer for 2 hours. Cook until chicken wings are cooked through.
5. Add the tender-crisp lid and set to air fry on 450°F or 230°C. Cook until wings are nicely caramelized, stirring every few minutes. Serve.

Nutrition:

- InfoCalories 389,Total Fat 10g,Total Carbs 23g,Protein 50g,Sodium 781mg.

Apricot Snack Bars

Servings: 16
Cooking Time: 25 Minutes

Ingredients:

- Butter flavored cooking spray
- ¾ cup oats
- ¾ cup flour
- ¼ cup brown sugar
- ¾ tsp vanilla
- ¼ cup butter
- ¾ cup apricot preserves, sugar free

Directions:

1. Lightly spray an 8-inch baking pan with cooking spray. Place the rack in the cooking pot.
2. In a large bowl, combine oats, flour, sugar, and vanilla until combined.
3. With a pastry blender or a fork, cut the butter in until mixture is crumbly. Press half the mixture in the bottom of the pan.
4. Spread the preserves over the top of the oat mixture and sprinkle the remaining oat over the top, gently press down.
5. Place the pan on the rack and add the tender-crisp lid. Set to air fry on 350°F or 175°C. Bake 25-30 minutes until golden brown and bubbly.
6. Transfer to a wire rack and let cool before cutting.

Nutrition:

- InfoCalories 100,Total Fat 3g,Total Carbs 18g,Protein 2g,Sodium 3mg.

Chipotle-lime Chicken Wings

Servings:4
Cooking Time: 28 Minutes

Ingredients:

- ½ cup water
- 2 pounds frozen chicken wings
- ¼ cup extra-virgin olive oil
- 2 tablespoons chipotle chiles in adobo sauce, chopped
- Juice of 2 limes
- Zest of 1 lime
- 1 tablespoon minced garlic
- Sea salt
- Freshly ground black pepper

Directions:

1. Pour the water in the pot. Place the wings in the Cook & Crisp Basket and insert basket in pot. Assemble pressure lid, making sure the pressure release valve is in the SEAL position.
2. Select PRESSURE and set to HI. Set time to 5 minutes. Select START/STOP to begin.
3. In a large bowl mix together the olive oil, chipotles in adobo sauce, lime juice, lime zest, and garlic. Season with salt and pepper.
4. When pressure cooking is complete, quick release the pressure by turning the pressure release valve to the VENT position. Carefully remove lid when unit has finished releasing pressure.
5. Transfer the chicken wings to the large bowl and toss to coat. Place the wings back in the basket. Close crisping lid.
6. Select AIR CRISP, set temperature to 375°F or 190°C, and set time to 15 minutes. Select START/STOP to begin.
7. After 7 minutes, open lid, then lift the basket and shake the wings. Lower the basket back into pot. Close lid and continue cooking until the wings reach your desired crispiness.

Nutrition:

- InfoCalories: 560,Total Fat: 45g,Sodium: 942mg,Carbohydrates: 2g,Protein: 38g.

Sweet Potato And Beetroot Chips

Servings:1
Cooking Time: 8 Hours
Ingredients:

- ½ small beet, peeled and cut into ⅛-inch slices
- ½ small sweet potato, peeled and cut into ⅛-inch slices
- ½ tablespoon extra-virgin olive oil
- ½ teaspoon sea salt

Directions:

1. In a large bowl, toss the beet slices with half the olive oil until evenly coated. Repeat, in a separate bowl, with the sweet potato slices and the rest of the olive oil (if you don't mind pink sweet potatoes, you can toss them together in one bowl). Season with salt.
2. Arrange the beet slices flat in a single layer in the bottom of the pot. Arrange the sweet potato slices flat in a single layer on the Reversible Rack in the lower position. Place rack in pot and close crisping lid.
3. Select DEHYDRATE, set temperature to 135°F or 55°C, and set time to 8 hours. Select START/STOP to begin.
4. When dehydrating is complete, remove rack from pot. Transfer the beet and sweet potato chips to an airtight container.

Nutrition:

- InfoCalories: 221,Total Fat: 7g,Sodium: 1057mg,Carbohydrates: 36g,Protein: 4g.

Rosemary And Garlic Mushrooms

Servings: 4
Cooking Time: 20 Min
Ingredients:

- 12 oz. button mushrooms /360g
- 2 rosemary sprigs
- 3 garlic cloves, minced
- ¼ cup melted butter /62.5ml
- ½ tsp salt /2.5g
- ¼ tsp black pepper /1.25g

Directions:

1. Wash and pat dry the mushrooms and cut them in half. Place in a large bowl. Add the remaining Ingredients to the bowl and toss well to combine.
2. Transfer the mushrooms to the basket of the Ninja Foodi. Close the crisping lid and cook for 12 minutes on Air Crisp mode, shaking once halfway through; at 350 °F or 175°C.

Popcorn Chicken

Servings: 4
Cooking Time: 15 Minutes
Ingredients:

- Nonstick cooking spray
- 1 cup cornflakes, crushed
- ½ cup Bisquick baking mix, reduced fat
- ½ tsp garlic powder
- ½ tsp salt
- ¼ tsp pepper
- ½ tsp paprika
- ¾ lb. chicken breasts, boneless, skinless & cut in 1-inch pieces

Directions:

1. Lightly spray fryer basket with cooking spray.
2. In a large Ziploc bag, combine cornflakes, baking mix, garlic powder, salt, pepper, and paprika, shake to mix.
3. Add chicken and shake to coat.

4. Place chicken in basket in single layer, spray lightly with cooking spray.
5. Add the tender-crisp lid and set to air fry on 400°F or 205°C. Cook chicken 12-15 minutes until crispy on the outside and no longer pink on the inside, turning over halfway through cooking time. Serve immediately.

Nutrition:

- InfoCalories 179,Total Fat 3g,Total Carbs 17g,Protein 21g,Sodium 596mg.

Honey Bourbon Wings

Servings: 6
Cooking Time: 11 Minutes
Ingredients:

- ¾ cup ketchup
- 1 tbsp. Liquid Smoke
- ½ cup brown sugar
- ¼ cup onion, chopped fine
- 2 cloves garlic, chopped fine
- ½ cup water
- ¼ cup bourbon
- 3 tbsp. honey
- 2 tsp paprika
- ¼ tsp cayenne pepper
- 1 tsp salt
- ½ tsp pepper
- 4-5 lb. chicken wings

Directions:

1. Set cooker to sauté on medium heat.
2. Add ketchup, liquid smoke, brown sugar, onion, and garlic to the cooking pot. Cook, stirring often, until sauce starts to thicken, about 5 minutes. Turn off the cooker.
3. Stir in water, bourbon, honey, and seasonings until combined.
4. Add the wings and stir to coat.
5. Secure the lid and set to pressure cooking on high for 5 minutes. When the timer goes off use quick release to remove the lid.
6. Line the fryer basket with foil.
7. Transfer the wings to the basket. Set cooker to sauté on medium again and cook sauce until thickened. Pour sauce into a large bowl.
8. Place the basket in the cooking pot and add the tender-crisp lid. Set to air fry on 400°F or 205°C. Cook wings 6 minutes. Dunk in sauce to coat the wings, then air fry another 6 minutes. Serve with any remaining sauce for dipping.

Nutrition:

- InfoCalories 636,Total Fat 13g,Total Carbs 36g,Protein 84g,Sodium 972mg.

Hand-cut French Fries

Servings:4
Cooking Time: 25 Minutes
Ingredients:

- 1 pound Russet or Idaho potatoes, cut in 2-inch strips
- 3 tablespoons canola oil

Directions:

1. Place potatoes in a large bowl and cover with cold water. Let soak for 30 minutes. Drain well, then pat with a paper towel until very dry.

2. Place Cook & Crisp Basket in pot. Close crisping lid. Select AIR CRISP, set temperature to 390°F or 200°C, and set time to 5 minutes. Select START/STOP to begin preheating.
3. In a large bowl, toss the potatoes with the oil.
4. Once unit is preheated, open lid and add the potatoes to the basket. Close lid.
5. Select AIR CRISP, set temperature to 390°F or 200°C, and set time to 25 minutes. Select START/STOP to begin.
6. After 10 minutes, open lid, then lift basket and shake fries or toss them with silicone-tipped tongs. Lower basket back into pot and close lid to continue cooking.
7. After 10 minutes, check for desired crispness. Continue cooking up to 5 minutes more, if necessary.
8. When cooking is complete, serve immediately with your favorite dipping sauce.

Nutrition:

- InfoCalories: 171,Total Fat: 11g,Sodium: 7mg,Carbohydrates: 18g,Protein: 2g.

Turkey Scotch Eggs

Servings: 6
Cooking Time: 20 Min

Ingredients:

- 10 oz. ground turkey /300g
- 4 eggs, soft boiled, peeled
- 2 garlic cloves, minced
- 2 eggs, lightly beaten
- 1 white onion; chopped
- ½ cup flour /65g
- ½ cup breadcrumbs /65g
- 1 tsp dried mixed herbs /5g
- Salt and pepper to taste
- Cooking spray

Directions:

1. Mix together the onion, garlic, salt, and pepper. Shape into 4 balls. Wrap the turkey mixture around each egg, and ensure the eggs are well covered.
2. Dust each egg ball in flour, then dip in the beaten eggs and finally roll in the crumbs, until coated. Spray with cooking spray.
3. Lay the eggs into your Ninja Foodi's basket. Set the temperature to 390 °F or 200°C, close the crisping lid and cook for 15 minutes. After 8 minutes, turn the eggs. Slice in half and serve warm.

Sweet Potato Skins

Servings: 4
Cooking Time: 20 Minutes

Ingredients:

- 2 sweet potatoes, baked & halved lengthwise
- 1 tsp olive oil
- 2 cloves garlic, diced fine
- 1 tbsp. fresh lime juice
- 2 cups baby spinach
- ½ cup chicken, cooked & shredded
- 1 tsp oregano
- 1 tsp cumin
- 2 tsp chili powder
- ½ cup mozzarella cheese, grated
- ¼ cup cilantro, chopped

Directions:

1. Scoop out the center of the potatoes, leaving some on the side to help keep the shape.
2. Set the cooker to sauté on med-high heat and add the oil.
3. Once the oil is hot, add garlic, lime juice, and spinach. Cook 2-3 minutes until spinach is wilted.
4. In a large bowl, mash the sweet potato centers until almost smooth.
5. Stir in chicken, oregano, cumin, and chili powder. Stir in spinach until combined.
6. Place the rack in the cooking pot and top with parchment paper.
7. Spoon the potato mixture into the skins and top with cheese. Place on the rack.
8. Add the tender-crisp lid and set to bake on 400°F or 205°C. Bake 15-20 minutes until cheese is melted and lightly browned. Let cool slightly then cut each skin in 4 pieces and serve garnished with cilantro.

Nutrition:

- InfoCalories 132,Total Fat 2g,Total Carbs 20g,Protein 9g,Sodium 155mg.

Parmesan Stuffed Mushrooms

Servings: 5
Cooking Time: 15 Minutes

Ingredients:

- 1 lb. button mushrooms, wash & remove stems
- 2 tbsp. olive oil, divided
- ¼ cup parmesan cheese, fat free
- 2 cloves garlic, diced fine
- ¼ cup cream cheese, fat free, soft
- ¼ cup whole wheat panko bread crumbs

Directions:

1. Place the rack in the cooking pot and top with a piece of parchment paper.
2. Brush the mushrooms with 1 tablespoon oil.
3. In a small bowl, combine parmesan, garlic, and cream cheese until smooth. Spoon 1 teaspoon of the mixture into each mushroom. Place mushrooms on parchment paper.
4. In a separate small bowl, stir together bread crumbs and remaining oil. Sprinkle over tops of mushrooms.
5. Add the tender-crisp lid and select bake on 375°F or 190°C. Cook mushrooms 15 minutes, or until tops are nicely browned and mushrooms are tender. Serve immediately.

Nutrition:

- InfoCalories 121,Total Fat 6g,Total Carbs 10g,Protein 7g,Sodium 191mg.

Asian Chicken Nuggets

Servings: X
Cooking Time: 20 Minutes

Ingredients:

- 1 lb. chicken breasts, boneless, skinless & cut in 1-inch pieces
- 1 tsp salt
- ½ tsp pepper
- 2 eggs
- 1 cup Panko bread crumbs
- ¼ cup lite soy sauce
- ¼ cup honey

mixture is flat, then cover top with remaining 1 cup of cheese. Sprinkle the nuts over the cheese. Close crisping lid.
8.   Select BROIL and set time to 5 minutes. Select START/STOP to begin.
9.   When cooking is complete, open lid and let the gratin cool for 10 minutes before serving.

Nutrition:
- InfoCalories: 536,Total Fat: 47g,Sodium: 409mg,Carbohydrates: 20g,Protein: 10g.

South Of The Border Corn Dip

Servings: 8
Cooking Time: 2 Hours

Ingredients:
- 33 oz. corn with chilies
- 10 oz. tomatoes & green chilies, diced
- 8 oz. cream cheese, cubed
- ½ cup cheddar cheese, grated
- ¼ cup green onions, chopped
- ½ tsp garlic, diced fine
- ½ tsp chili powder

Directions:
1.   Place all ingredients in the cooking pot and stir to mix.
2.   Add the lid and set to slow cooking function on low heat. Set timer for 2 hours. Stir occasionally.
3.   Dip is done when all the cheese is melted and it's bubbly. Stir well, then transfer to serving bowl and serve warm.

Nutrition:
- InfoCalories 225,Total Fat 13g,Total Carbs 24g,Protein 7g,Sodium 710mg.

Hot Crab Dip

Servings: 8
Cooking Time: 30 Minutes

Ingredients:
- 8 oz. cream cheese, fat free, soft
- ¼ lb. crabmeat, flaked
- ½ tsp fresh lemon juice
- ½ tsp onion powder
- 1 tbsp. fresh dill, chopped
- ¼ tsp garlic powder

Directions:
1.   Set to air fryer on 350°F or 175°C. Place the rack in the cooking pot.
2.   In a medium bowl, combine all ingredients until smooth. Transfer to a small baking dish.
3.   Place the dish on the rack and add the tender-crisp lid. Bake 30-35 minutes until heated through and lightly browned on top. Serve warm.

Nutrition:
- InfoCalories 78,Total Fat 1g,Total Carbs 8g,Protein 10g,Sodium 201mg.

Caribbean Chicken Skewers

Servings: 8
Cooking Time: 30 Minutes

Ingredients:
- 2 tsp jerk seasoning
- 1 lime, juiced
- 1 tbsp. extra virgin olive oil
- 1 lb. chicken, boneless, skinless & cut in 1-inch cubes
- 1 red onion, cut in 1-inch pieces
- 1 cup cherry tomatoes
- 1 cup fresh pineapple, cut in 1-inch cubes
- 1 very ripe plantain, peel on, sliced
- ½ tsp salt
- ½ tsp pepper
- Nonstick cooking spray

Directions:
1.   If using wood skewers, soak them in water for 30 minutes.
2.   In a large bowl, combine jerk seasoning, lime juice, and olive oil.
3.   Add the chicken, onions, and tomatoes and toss to coat. Cover and refrigerate 20 minutes.
4.   Thread skewers with chicken, onion, tomatoes, pineapple, and plantains, leaving a little space at both ends. Sprinkle skewers with salt and pepper.
5.   Lightly spray the rack with cooking spray and place in the cooking pot. Place the skewers on top.
6.   Add the tender-crisp lid and set to air fry on 400°F or 205°C. Cook skewers 25-30 minutes until chicken is cooked through. Baste with marinade and turn over halfway through cooking time. Serve.

Nutrition:
- InfoCalories 127,Total Fat 3g,Total Carbs 11g,Protein 13g,Sodium 173mg.

Cheesy Tangy Arancini

Servings: 6
Cooking Time: 105 Min

Ingredients:
- ½ cup olive oil, plus 1 tbsp /140ml
- 2 large eggs
- 2 garlic cloves, minced
- 1 small white onion; diced
- ½ cup apple cider vinegar /125ml
- 2 cups short grain rice /260g
- 2 cups fresh panko bread crumbs /260g
- 5 cups chicken stock /1250ml
- 1½ cups grated Parmesan cheese, plus more for garnish /195g
- 1 cup chopped green beans /130g
- 1 tsp salt /5g
- 1tsp freshly ground black pepper /5g

Directions:
1.   Choose Sear/Sauté on the pot and set to Medium High. Choose Start/Stop to preheat the pot. Add 1 tbsp of oil and the onion, cook the onion until translucent, add the garlic and cook further for 2 minutes or until the garlic starts getting fragrant.
2.   Stir in the stock, vinegar, and rice. Seal the pressure lid, choose pressure, set to High, and set the time to 7 minutes; press Start.
3.   After cooking, perform a natural pressure release for 10 minutes, then a quick pressure release and carefully open the pressure lid.
4.   Stir in the Parmesan cheese, green beans, salt, and pepper to mash the rice until a risotto forms. Spoon the mixture into a bowl and set aside to cool completely.

5. Clean the pot and in a bowl, combine the breadcrumbs and the remaining olive oil. In another bowl, lightly beat the eggs.
6. Form 12 balls out of the risotto or as many as you can get. Dip each into the beaten eggs, and coat in the breadcrumb mixture.
7. Put half of the rice balls in the Crisping Basket in a single layer. Close the crisping lid, hit Air Crisp, set the temperature to 400°F or 205°C, and set the time to 10 minutes; press Start. Leave to cool before serving.

Dill Butter

Servings: 7
Cooking Time: 5 Minutes

Ingredients:
- 1 cup butter
- 1 teaspoon minced garlic
- 1 teaspoon dried oregano
- 1 teaspoon dried cilantro
- 1 tablespoon dried dill
- 1 teaspoon salt
- ½ teaspoon black pepper

Directions:
1. Set "Sauté" mode and place butter inside the Ninja Foodi's insert.
2. Add minced garlic, dried oregano, dried cilantro, butter, dried dill, salt, and black pepper.
3. Stir the mixture well and sauté it for 4-5 minutes or until the butter is melted.
4. Then switch off the cooker and stir the butter well.
5. Transfer the butter mixture into the butter mould and freeze it.

Nutrition:
- InfoCalories: 235; Fat: 26.3g; Carbohydrates: 0.6g; Protein: 0.4g

Zesty Meatballs

Servings: 12
Cooking Time: 15 Minutes

Ingredients:
- Nonstick cooking spray
- 1 lb. ground pork
- ½ cup plain bread crumbs
- ¼ cup water
- 1 onion, chopped
- ¼ cup fresh parsley, chopped
- 1 tsp fennel seed, crushed
- ½ tsp garlic powder
- ¼ tsp cayenne pepper
- ½ tsp salt
- ½ tsp black pepper

Directions:
1. Set to air fryer on 350°F or 175°C. Lightly spray fryer basket with cooking spray and put in the cooking pot.
2. In a large bowl, combine all ingredients thoroughly. Form into 1-inch balls.
3. Place meatballs in a single layer in the fryer basket, these will need to be cooked in batches.
4. Add the tender-crisp lid and bake 15 minutes, or until no longer pink. Turn meatballs over halfway through cooking time. Transfer to serving plate.

Nutrition:
- InfoCalories 109, Total Fat 8g, Total Carbs 2g, Protein 7g, Sodium 127mg.

Spicy Black Bean Dip

Servings: 12
Cooking Time: 20 Minutes

Ingredients:
- 2 16 oz. cans black beans, rinsed & drained, divided
- 1 cup salsa, divided
- 1 tsp olive oil
- ¾ onion, diced fine
- 1 red bell pepper, diced fine
- 3 cloves garlic, diced fine
- 1 tbsp. cilantro
- 2 tsp cumin
- ¼ tsp salt
- ¼ cup cheddar cheese, reduced fat, grated
- 1 tomato, chopped

Directions:
1. Add 1 can beans and ¼ cup salsa to a food processor or blender. Pulse until smooth.
2. Set cooker to sauté on medium heat. Add oil and let it get hot.
3. Add the onion, pepper, and garlic and cook, stirring occasionally, 5-7 minutes, or until vegetables are tender.
4. Add the pureed bean mixture along with remaining ingredients except cheese and tomatoes, mix well. Reduce heat to low and bring to a simmer. Let cook 5 minutes, stirring frequently.
5. Transfer dip to serving bowl and top with cheese and tomato. Serve immediately.

Nutrition:
- InfoCalories 100, Total Fat 2g, Total Carbs 16g, Protein 6g, Sodium 511mg.

Crispy Spiced Cauliflower Bites

Servings: 12
Cooking Time: 15 Minutes

Ingredients:
- Nonstick cooking spray
- 1 egg
- 1 tbsp. water
- 1 cup whole wheat panko bread crumbs
- 1 tbsp. garlic powder
- ½ tsp onion powder
- 1 tbsp. fresh parsley, chopped
- 6 cups cauliflower florets
- ¼ cup light mayonnaise
- 2 tbsp. sweet chili sauce
- 2 tbsp. hot sauce

Directions:
1. Lightly spray the fryer basket with cooking spray and place in the cooking pot.
2. In a small bowl, whisk together egg and water.
3. In a separate small bowl, stir together bread crumbs, garlic powder, onion powder, and parsley.
4. Dip each floret first in egg then in bread crumbs. Place in fryer basket, in batches.
5. Add the tender-crisp lid and set to air fry on 400°F or 205°C. Bake cauliflower 15 minutes or until golden brown and crispy.

6. In a small bowl, whisk together mayonnaise, chili sauce, and hot sauce. When all the cauliflower is done, drizzle sauce over the top and serve.

Nutrition:
- InfoCalories 77,Total Fat 3g,Total Carbs 11g,Protein 3g,Sodium 177mg.

Louisiana Crab Dip

Servings:8
Cooking Time: 50 Minutes

Ingredients:
- 2 tablespoons unsalted butter
- 3 garlic cloves, minced
- ½ cup mayonnaise
- 1 pound whipped or room temperature cream cheese
- 2 teaspoons Worcestershire sauce
- 3 teaspoons hot sauce
- 3 teaspoons freshly squeezed lemon juice
- 2 teaspoons Creole seasoning
- ¾ cup Parmesan cheese
- 1 pound lump crab meat

Directions:
1. Select SEAR/SAUTÉ and set to MED. Select START/STOP to begin. Let preheat for 3 minutes.
2. Add the butter and garlic and sauté for 2 minutes.
3. Add the mayonnaise, cream cheese, Worcestershire sauce, hot sauce, lemon juice, Creole seasoning, and Parmesan cheese. Stir well.
4. Add the crab meat and lightly fold to incorporate. Close crisping lid.
5. Select BAKE/ROAST, set temperature to 350°F or 175°C, and set time to 40 minutes. Select START/STOP to begin
6. When cooking is complete, open lid. Let cool for 10 minutes before serving.

Nutrition:
- InfoCalories: 391,Total Fat: 39g,Sodium: 976mg,Carbohydrates: 4g,Protein: 16g.

Spinach Hummus

Servings: 12
Cooking Time: 1 Hr 10 Min

Ingredients:
- 2 cups spinach; chopped /260g
- ½ cup tahini /65g
- 2 cups dried chickpeas /260g
- 8 cups water /2000ml
- 5 garlic cloves, crushed
- 5 tbsp grapeseed oil /75ml
- 2 tsp salt; divided /10g
- 5 tbsp lemon juice /75ml

Directions:
1. In the pressure cooker, mix 2 tbsp oil, water, 1 tsp or 5g salt, and chickpeas. Seal the pressure lid, choose Pressure, set to High, and set the timer to 35 minutes. Press Start. When ready, release the pressure quickly. In a small bowl, reserve ½ cup of the cooking liquid and drain chickpeas.
2. Mix half the reserved cooking liquid and chickpeas in a food processor and puree until no large chickpeas remain; add remaining cooking liquid, spinach, lemon juice, remaining tsp salt, garlic, and tahini.

3. Process hummus for 8 minutes until smooth. Stir in the remaining 3 tbsp or 45ml of olive oil before serving.

Chicken And Vegetable Egg Rolls

Servings:16
Cooking Time: 10 Minutes Per Batch

Ingredients:
- 2 tablespoons sherry
- 2 tablespoons soy sauce
- 2 tablespoons beef broth
- 2 tablespoons cornstarch
- ½ teaspoon salt
- ½ teaspoon granulated sugar
- ½ teaspoon ground ginger
- 3 tablespoons canola oil
- 8 scallions, chopped
- ½ cup chopped mushrooms
- 3 cups shredded cabbage
- ½ cup shredded carrot
- ½ cup bean sprouts, washed
- 2 cups chopped cooked chicken
- 1 package egg rolls wrappers
- 1 egg, beaten
- Cooking spray
- Hot mustard, for dipping
- Sweet and sour sauce, for dipping

Directions:
1. In a small bowl, stir together the sherry, soy sauce, beef broth, cornstarch, salt, sugar, and ginger until combined and the sugar dissolves. Set aside.
2. Select SEAR/SAUTÉ and set temperature to HI. Select START/STOP to begin and allow to preheat for 5 minutes.
3. Add the canola oil to the cooking pot and allow to heat for 1 minute. Add the scallions and mushrooms and sauté for 2 to 3 minutes, stirring well, until the vegetables just begin to soften.
4. Add the cabbage, carrot, and bean sprouts, stirring to incorporate well. Decrease the temperature to MD:LO. Cook the vegetables for about 7 minutes, until cabbage and carrots are softened.
5. Stir in the chicken. Add the sauce and cook, stirring constantly, until the sauce thickens the filling, about 3 minutes. Select START/STOP to end the function. Transfer the filling to a bowl to cool. Wash the pot and return it to the cooker.
6. Place the Cook & Crisp Basket in the Foodi pot.
7. Select AIR CRISP, set the temperature to 390°F or 200°C, and set the time to 5 minutes to preheat. Select START/STOP to begin.
8. Working one at a time, using a small silicone spatula, moisten the 4 sides of an egg roll wrapper with the beaten egg. Place 3 tablespoons of the filling on the center of the egg roll wrapper. Fold an edge over the mixture and tuck it under the point. Fold the edges in and continue rolling. Press the end point over the top of the roll to seal. Continue with the remaining wrappers and filling.
9. Place 3 egg rolls in the basket, making sure they don't touch each other. Coat the egg rolls in on cooking spray, then close the crisping lid.
10. Select AIR CRISP, set the temperature to 390°F, and set the time to 10 minutes. After 5 minutes, open the crisping lid, flip the egg rolls, and spritz the other side with

cooking spray. Close the crisping lid and cook for the remaining 5 minutes.

11. Using tongs, carefully transfer the egg rolls to a wire rack to cool for least 6 minutes before serving.

12. Repeat step 8 with the remaining egg rolls. Keep in mind that the unit is already hot, which may decrease the cooking time. Monitor closely for doneness.

13. Serve with the hot mustard and sweet and sour sauce for dipping.

Nutrition:

- InfoCalories: 166,Total Fat: 6g,Sodium: 364mg,Carbohydrates: 20g,Protein: 9g.

Jalapeno Salsa

Servings: 10

Cooking Time: 7 Minutes

Ingredients:

- 8 ounces jalapeno pepper
- ¼ cup Erythritol
- 5 tablespoon water
- 2 tablespoons butter
- 1 teaspoon paprika

Directions:

1. Wash the jalapeno pepper and remove the seeds.
2. Slice it into thin circles. Sprinkle the sliced jalapeno pepper with paprika and Erythritol.
3. Put the butter and jalaeno mixture into the Ninja Foodi's insert and add water.
4. Set the Ninja Foodi's insert to" Sauté" mode.
5. Once the butter melts, add the sliced jalapeno in the Ninja Foodi's insert.
6. Close the Ninja Foodi's lid and sauté the dish for 7 minutes.
7. Once done, remove the dish from the Ninja Foodi's insert.
8. Cool it and serve.

Nutrition:

- InfoCalories: 28; Fat: 2.5g; Carbohydrates: 7.5g; Protein: 0.4g

Zesty Brussels Sprouts With Raisins

Servings: 4

Cooking Time: 45 Min

Ingredients:

- 14 oz. Brussels sprouts, steamed /420g
- 2 oz. toasted pine nuts /60g
- 2 oz. raisins /60g
- 1 tbsp olive oil/15ml
- Juice and zest of 1 orange

Directions:

1. Soak the raisins in the orange juice and let sit for about 20 minutes. Drizzle the Brussels sprouts with the olive oil, and place them in the basket of the Ninja Foodi.
2. Close the crisping lid and cook for 15 minutes on Air Crisp mode at 370 °F or 185°C. Remove to a bowl and top with pine nuts, raisins, and orange zest.

Saucy Chicken Wings

Servings: 6

Cooking Time: 35 Minutes

Ingredients:

- 1-pound chicken wings
- 1 teaspoon black pepper

- 1 teaspoon tomato paste
- 1 tablespoon garlic, minced
- ⅓ teaspoon soy sauce
- 3 tablespoons olive oil
- 1 teaspoon red pepper
- 1 teaspoon cilantro, chopped
- 1 tablespoon tomato sauce

Directions:

1. Combine the black pepper, red pepper, and cilantro together in a mixing bowl and stir the mixture.
2. Place the chicken wings in a separate bowl and sprinkle the meat with the black pepper mixture.
3. Add tomato paste, minced garlic, soy sauce, and tomato sauce.
4. Coat the chicken completely using your hands.
5. Transfer the meat to the Ninja Foodi's insert.
6. Close the Ninja Foodi's lid and cook the dish in the" Sauté" mode for 35 minutes.
7. Once done, remove the dish from the Ninja Foodi's insert.
8. Serve the chicken wings hot.

Nutrition:

- InfoCalories: 165; Fat: 9.5g; Carbohydrates: 2.02g; Protein: 17g

Cumin Baby Carrots

Servings: 4

Cooking Time: 25 Min

Ingredients:

- 1 ¼ lb. baby carrots /562.5g
- 1 handful cilantro; chopped
- 2 tbsp olive oil /30ml
- ½ tsp cumin powder /2.5g
- ½ tsp garlic powder /2.5g
- 1 tsp cumin seeds /5g
- 1 tsp salt /5g
- ½ tsp black pepper /2.5g

Directions:

1. Place the baby carrots in a large bowl. Add cumin seeds, cumin, olive oil, salt, garlic powder, and pepper, and stir to coat them well.
2. Put the carrots in the Ninja Foodi's basket, close the crisping lid and cook for 20 minutes on Roast mode at 370 °F or 185°C. Remove to a platter and sprinkle with chopped cilantro, to serve.

Caramelized Cauliflower With Hazelnuts

Servings: 4

Cooking Time: 15 Minutes

Ingredients:

- 1 head cauliflower, cut in ½-inch thick slices
- 2 cups cold water
- 2 tbsp. olive oil
- 1 tbsp. honey
- ½ tsp fresh lemon juice
- ½ tsp salt
- ¼ tsp pepper
- 1 tbsp. fresh sage, chopped
- 1 tbsp. hazelnuts, toasted & chopped

- ¼ cup parmesan cheese, reduced fat

Directions:
1. Remove any core from the cauliflower slices. Lay them in a single layer in the cooking pot.
2. Add enough water to come halfway up the sides of the cauliflower. Add oil, honey, lemon, salt, and pepper.
3. Set cooker to sauté on high. Cover and cook cauliflower until the water has evaporated, about 6-8 minutes. When it begins to brown reduce heat to low.
4. Once water has evaporated, flip cauliflower over and cook another 5 minutes, or until bottom is golden brown.
5. Transfer to serving plates and top with sage, hazelnuts, and parmesan cheese. Serve.

Nutrition:
- InfoCalories 112,Total Fat 8g,Total Carbs 9g,Protein 3g,Sodium 407mg.

Cheesy Jalapeno Boats

Servings: 12
Cooking Time: 25 Minutes

Ingredients:
- 8 oz. cream cheese, reduced fat, soft
- 1 cup cheddar cheese, reduced fat, grated
- 1 tsp garlic powder
- 2 eggs
- 2 tbsp. skim milk
- 1 cup panko bread crumbs
- ½ tsp paprika
- ½ tsp chili powder
- ½ tsp salt
- ¼ tsp pepper
- 12 jalapeno peppers, halved lengthwise, stems & seeds removed

Directions:
1. Place the rack in the cooking pot and line with parchment paper.
2. In a medium bowl, beat together cream cheese, cheddar, and garlic powder.
3. In a small bowl, whisk together eggs and milk.
4. In a shallow dish, stir together bread crumbs, paprika, chili powder, salt, and pepper.
5. Spread a tablespoon of cheese mixture in each jalapeno. Dip in egg mixture then coat with bread crumbs. Place on the parchment paper.
6. Add the tender-crisp lid and set to bake on 350°F or 175°C. Cook 20-25 minutes or until golden brown. Serve immediately.
7. Bake 30 to 35 minutes, or until golden.

Nutrition:
- InfoCalories 107,Total Fat 5g,Total Carbs 9g,Protein 6g,Sodium 326mg.

Glazed Walnuts

Servings: 4
Cooking Time: 4 Minutes
Ingredients:
- ⅓ cup of water
- 6 ounces walnuts
- 5 tablespoon Erythritol

- ½ teaspoon ground ginger
- 3tablespoons psyllium husk powder

Directions:
1. Combine Erythritol and water together in a mixing bowl.
2. Add ground ginger and stir the mixture until the erythritol is dissolved.
3. Transfer the walnuts to the Ninja Foodi's insert and add sweet liquid.
4. Close the Ninja Foodi's lid and cook the dish in the "Pressure" mode for 4 minutes.
5. Remove the walnuts from the Ninja Foodi's insert.
6. Dip the walnuts in the Psyllium husk powder and serve.

Nutrition:
- InfoCalories: 286; Fat: 25.1g; Carbohydrates: 10.4g; Protein: 10.3g

Honey Mustard Hot Dogs

Servings: 4
Cooking Time: 22 Min
Ingredients:
- 20 Hot Dogs, cut into 4 pieces
- ¼ cup honey /62.5ml
- ¼ cup red wine vinegar /62.5ml
- ½ cup tomato puree /125ml
- ¼ cup water /62.5ml
- 1½ tsp soy sauce /7.5ml
- 1 tsp Dijon mustard /5g
- Salt and black pepper to taste

Directions:
1. Add the tomato puree, red wine vinegar, honey, soy sauce, Dijon mustard, salt, and black pepper in a medium bowl. Mix them with a spoon.
2. Put sausage weenies in the crisp basket, and close the crisping lid. Select Air Crisp mode. Set the temperature to 370 °F or 185°C and the timer to 4 minutes. Press Start/Stop. At the 2-minute mark, turn the sausages.
3. Once ready, open the lid and pour the sweet sauce over the sausage weenies.
4. Close the pressure lid, secure the pressure valve, and select Pressure mode on High for 3 minutes. Press Start/Stop. Once the timer has ended, do a quick pressure release. Serve and enjoy.

Cheesy Smashed Sweet Potatoes
Servings: 4
Cooking Time: 70 Min
Ingredients:
- 2 slices bacon, cooked and crumbled
- 12 ounces baby sweet potatoes /360g
- ¼ cup shredded Monterey Jack cheese /32.5g
- ¼ cup sour cream /62.5ml
- 1 tbsp chopped scallions /15g
- 1 tsp melted butter /5ml
- Salt to taste

Directions:

1. Put the Crisping Basket in the pot and close the crisping lid. Choose Air Crisp, set the temperature to 350°F or 175°C, and the time to 5 minutes. Press Start/Stop to begin preheating.
2. Meanwhile, toss the sweet potatoes with the melted butter until evenly coated. Once the pot and basket have preheated, open the lid and add the sweet potatoes to the basket. Close the lid, Choose Air Crisp, set the temperature to 350°F or 175°C, and set the time to 30 minutes; press Start.
3. After 15 minutes, open the lid, pull out the basket and shake the sweet potatoes. Return the basket to the pot and close the lid to continue cooking. When ended, check the sweet potatoes for your desired crispiness, which should also be fork tender.
4. Take out the sweet potatoes from the basket and use a large spoon to crush the soft potatoes just to split lightly. Top with the cheese, sour cream, bacon, and scallions, and season with salt.

Breakfast

Poached Egg Heirloom Tomato

Servings: 4

Cooking Time: 10 Min

Ingredients:

- 4 large eggs
- 2 large Heirloom ripe tomatoes; halved crosswise
- 4 small slices feta cheese
- 1 cup water /250ml
- 2 tbsp grated Parmesan cheese /30g
- 1 tsp chopped fresh herbs, of your choice /5g
- Salt and black pepper to taste
- Cooking spray

Directions:

1. Pour the water into the Ninja Foodi and fit the reversible rack. Grease the ramekins with the cooking spray and crack each egg into them.
2. Season with salt and pepper. Cover the ramekins with aluminum foil. Place the cups on the trivet. Seal the lid.
3. Select Steam mode for 3 minutes on High pressure. Press Start/Stop.Once the timer goes off, do a quick pressure release. Use a napkin to remove the ramekins onto a flat surface.
4. In serving plates, share the halved tomatoes, feta slices, and toss the eggs in the ramekin over on each tomato half. Sprinkle with salt and pepper, parmesan, and garnish with chopped herbs.

Stuffed Baked Tomatoes

Servings: 4

Cooking Time: 25 Minutes

Ingredients:

- 4 large tomatoes
- 4 slices turkey bacon, chopped
- ¼ cup green pepper, chopped
- 3 tbsp. mushroom, chopped
- 2 eggs
- 4 egg whites
- 2 tbsp. skim milk
- ¼ tsp salt
- ½ cup cheddar cheese, reduced fat, grated

Directions:

1. Cut off the tops of the tomatoes and scoop out the inside, do not cut the bottom or sides. Set aside.
2. Set cooker to sauté on medium heat. Add bacon and cook until almost crisp.
3. Add the peppers and mushrooms and cook until bacon is crisp and peppers are tender. Spoon into tomatoes.
4. In a medium bowl, whisk together eggs, egg whites, milk, and salt. Pour into tomatoes leaving ¼ inch space at the top.
5. Place tomatoes in the cooking pot and top with cheese. Set to air fryer function on 350°F or 175°C. Secure the tender-crisp lid and bake 15-20 minutes or until eggs are cooked through. Let rest 5 minutes before serving.

Nutrition:

- InfoCalories 165,Total Fat 8g,Total Carbs 9g,Protein 15g,Sodium 483mg.

Hearty Breakfast Muffins

Servings: 12

Cooking Time: 20 Minutes

Ingredients:

- ½ cup brown sugar
- 3 eggs
- 1/3 cup coconut oil, melted
- 1/3 cup applesauce, unsweetened
- ¼ cup orange juice
- 1 tsp vanilla
- 2 cups whole wheat flour
- 2 tsp baking soda
- 2 tsp cinnamon
- ¼ tsp salt
- 1 ½ cup carrots, grated
- 1 cup apple, grated
- ¼ cup pecans, chopped

Directions:

1. Set to bake function on 375°F or 190°C. Line 2 6-cup muffin tins with paper liners.
2. In a large bowl, whisk together sugar, eggs, oil, applesauce, orange juice, and vanilla.
3. Stir in flour, baking soda, cinnamon, and salt just until combined.

4. Fold in carrots, apple, and pecans and mix well. Divide evenly among prepared muffin tins.
5. Place tins, one at a time, in the cooker and add the tender-crisp lid. Bake 20-25 minutes, or until muffins pass the toothpick test. Repeat.
6. Let cool in pan 10 minutes, then transfer to wire rack to cool completely.

Nutrition:

- InfoCalories 206,Total Fat 9g,Total Carbs 28g,Protein 5g,Sodium 288mg.

Waffle Bread Pudding With Maple-jam Glaze

Servings:6

Cooking Time: 25 Minutes

Ingredients:

- 2 whole eggs
- 4 egg yolks
- 1 cup heavy (whipping) cream
- ½ teaspoon ground cinnamon
- ¼ cup granulated sugar
- 1 teaspoon vanilla extract
- 20 waffles, cut in sixths
- 1 cup water
- ⅓ cup desired jam
- raspberry)
- ⅓ cup maple syrup

Directions:

1. In a large mixing bowl, combine the eggs, egg yolks, cream, cinnamon, sugar, and vanilla. Whisk well to combine. Add the waffle pieces and toss very well to incorporate. The waffles should be completely soaked through with cream sauce, with some extra residual cream sauce at the bottom of the bowl.
2. Place the waffle mixture in the Ninja Multi-Purpose Pan or 8-inch round baking dish. Press down gently to ensure ingredients are well packed into the pan. Cover the pan tightly with plastic wrap.
3. Add the water to the pot. Place the pan on the Reversible Rack and place rack in pot. Assemble pressure lid, making sure the pressure release valve is in the SEAL position.
4. Select PRESSURE and set to HI. Set time to 15 minutes. Select START/STOP to begin.
5. Place the jam and maple syrup in a small bowl and mix well to combine.
6. When pressure cooking is complete, quick release the pressure by moving the pressure release valve to the VENT position. Carefully remove lid when unit has finished releasing pressure.
7. Remove rack from pot, then remove the plastic wrap from the pan. Pour the jam and syrup mixture over top of waffles. Place rack and pan back in pot. Close crisping lid.
8. Select BROIL and set time to 10 minutes. Select START/STOP to begin.
9. When cooking is complete, open lid and remove rack from pot. Serve the bread pudding warm.

Nutrition:

- InfoCalories: 640,Total Fat: 30g,Sodium: 765mg,Carbohydrates: 82g,Protein: 12g.

Cranberry Vanilla Oatmeal

Servings: 6

Cooking Time: 8 Hours

Ingredients:

- Nonstick cooking spray
- 1 ½ cups steel cut oats
- 4 ½ cups water
- 1 ½ tsp cinnamon
- 2 ½ tsp vanilla
- 1 ½ cups cranberries, dried

Directions:

1. Spray the cooking pot with cooking spray.
2. Add the oats, water, cinnamon, and vanilla and stir to combine.
3. Secure the lid and set to slow cooker on low heat. Set timer for 8 hours.
4. When timer goes off stir in cranberries and serve.

Nutrition:

- InfoCalories 250,Total Fat 3g,Total Carbs 51g,Protein 7g,Sodium 2mg.

Carrot Cake Oats

Servings:8

Cooking Time: 13 Minutes

Ingredients:

- 2 cups oats
- 1 cup water
- 4 cups unsweetened vanilla almond milk
- 2 apples, diced
- 2 cups shredded carrot
- 1 cup dried cranberries
- ½ cup maple syrup
- 2 teaspoons cinnamon
- 2 teaspoons vanilla extract

Directions:

1. Place all the ingredients in the pot. Assemble pressure lid, making sure the pressure release valve is in the SEAL position.
2. Select PRESSURE and set to LO. Set time to 3 minutes. Select START/STOP to begin.
3. When pressure cooking is complete, allow pressure to naturally release for 10 minutes. Then quick release remaining pressure by moving the pressure release valve to the VENT position. Carefully remove lid when unit has finished releasing pressure.
4. Stir oats, allowing them to cool, and serve with toppings such as chopped walnuts, diced pineapple, or shredded coconut, if desired.

Nutrition:

- InfoCalories: 252,Total Fat: 3g,Sodium: 112mg,Carbohydrates: 54g,Protein: 4g.

Breakfast Burritos

Servings:4

Cooking Time: 30 Minutes

Ingredients:

- 1 pound ground chorizo
- ½ onion, diced
- ½ red bell pepper, diced
- 1 small jalapeño, minced
- ½ cup canned black beans, rinsed and drained
- Kosher salt
- Freshly ground black pepper

- 6 eggs, beaten
- 4 flour tortillas
- 1 cup shredded Mexican blend cheese
- 1 cup cilantro, minced
- Guacamole, for serving
- Pico de gallo, for serving

Directions:
1. Select SEAR/SAUTÉ and set temperature to MED. Let preheat for 5 minutes.
2. Add the chorizo, breaking up the meat with a silicone spatula until cooked through, 3 to 5 minutes. Add the onions, bell pepper, jalapeño, black beans, and season with salt and pepper. Cook until onions are translucent, about 3 minutes.
3. Add the eggs and cook, stirring frequently, until they have reached your desired consistency. When cooking is complete, transfer the mixture to a large bowl.
4. Lay a tortilla on a flat surface and load with ¼ cup of cheese, ¾ cup of egg mixture, and ¼ cup of cilantro. Roll the burrito by folding the right and left sides over the filling, then roll the tortilla over itself from the bottom forming a tight burrito. Repeat this step three more times with the remaining tortillas, cheese, egg mixture, and cilantro.
5. Place two burritos seam-side down in the Cook & Crisp Basket and place basket in pot. Close crisping lid.
6. Select AIR CRISP, set temperature to 390°F or 200°C, and set time to 16 minutes. Select START/STOP to begin.
7. After 8 minutes, open lid and remove the burritos from basket. Place the remaining two burritos seam-side down in the basket. Close lid and continue cooking for the remaining 8 minutes.
8. When cooking is complete, let the burritos cool for a few minutes. Serve with the guacamole and pico de gallo.

Nutrition:
- InfoCalories: 693,Total Fat: 36g,Sodium: 1732mg,Carbohydrates: 48g,Protein: 44g.

Flaxseeds Granola

Servings: 16
Cooking Time: 2½ Hours
Ingredients:
- ½ cup sunflower kernels
- 5 cups mixed nuts, crushed
- 2 tablespoons ground flax seeds
- ¼ cup olive oil
- ½ cup unsalted butter
- 1 teaspoon ground cinnamon
- 1 cup choc zero maple syrup

Directions:
1. Grease the Ninja Foodi's insert.
2. In the greased Ninja Foodi's insert, add sunflower kernels, nuts, flax seeds, oil, butter, and cinnamon and stir to combine.
3. Close the Ninja Foodi's lid with a crisping lid and select "Slow Cooker."
4. Set on "High" for 2½ hours.
5. Press the "Start/Stop" button to initiate cooking.
6. Stir the mixture after every 30 minutes.
7. Open the Ninja Foodi's lid and transfer the granola onto a large baking sheet.
8. Add the maple syrup and stir to combine.
9. Set aside to cool completely before serving.
10. You can preserve this granola in an airtight container.

Nutrition:

- InfoCalories: 189; Fat: 10 g; Carbohydrates: 7.7 g; Protein: 4.6 g

Cinnamon Apple Bread

Servings: 10
Cooking Time: 55 Minutes
Ingredients:
- Butter flavored cooking spray
- ½ cup coconut flour
- 1 ½ cup almond flour, sifted
- ¾ cup Stevia
- 1 tsp baking soda
- 2 tbsp. cinnamon
- 5 eggs
- 1 cup applesauce, unsweetened

Directions:
1. Set to bake function on 350°F or 175°C. Lightly spray a loaf pan with cooking spray.
2. In a large bowl, combine both flours, Stevia, cinnamon, and baking soda.
3. In a medium bowl, whisk the eggs and applesauce together. Add to dry ingredients and stir to combine.
4. Pour into prepared pan and place in the cooker. Add the tender-crisp lid and bake 45-55 minutes, or until bread passes the toothpick test.
5. Let cool 15 minutes, then invert onto serving plate and slice.

Nutrition:
- InfoCalories 189,Total Fat 10g,Total Carbs 30g,Protein 7g,Sodium 162mg.

Strawberry Muffins

Servings: 12
Cooking Time: 25 Minutes
Ingredients:
- 1 ¼ cups white whole wheat flour
- 1/3 cup oats
- ½ tsp cinnamon
- ½ tsp baking soda
- 1 tsp baking powder
- ½ tsp salt
- 2/3 cup Stevia
- 3/4 cup Greek yogurt
- 1 egg
- 1/3 cup coconut oil, melted
- 1 cup strawberries, chopped

Directions:
1. Set to air fryer function on 375°F or 190°C. Line 2 6-cup muffin tins with paper liners.
2. In a large bowl, combine dry ingredients.
3. In a medium bowl, whisk together yogurt, egg, and oil. Stir in berries and add to dry ingredients. Stir just until combined.
4. Fill prepared muffin tins 2/3 full. Place pans, one at a time, in the cooker and secure the tender-crisp lid. Bake 25 minutes, or until muffins pass the toothpick test. Repeat.
5. Let cool in the pan 10 minutes, then transfer to wire rack to cool completely.

Nutrition:
- InfoCalories 131,Total Fat 8g,Total Carbs 27g,Protein 4g,Sodium 163mg.

Cinnamon Bun Oatmeal

Servings:6
Cooking Time: 26 Minutes

Ingredients:

- 1 cup gluten-free steel-cut oats
- 3½ cups water
- ¼ teaspoon sea salt
- 1 teaspoon nutmeg
- 2 teaspoons cinnamon, divided
- ½ cup all-purpose flour
- ½ cup rolled oats
- ⅔ cup brown sugar
- ⅓ cup cold unsalted butter, cut into pieces
- 2 tablespoons granulated sugar
- ¾ cup raisins
- 2 ounces cream cheese, at room temperature
- 2 tablespoons confectioners' sugar
- 1 teaspoon whole milk

Directions:

1. Place the steel-cut oats, water, salt, nutmeg, and 1 teaspoon of cinnamon in the pot. Assemble pressure lid, making sure the pressure release valve is in the SEAL position.
2. Select PRESSURE and set to HI. Set time to 11 minutes. Select START/STOP to begin.
3. In a medium bowl, combine the flour, rolled oats, brown sugar, butter, remaining 1 teaspoon of cinnamon, and granulated sugar until a crumble forms.
4. When pressure cooking is complete, allow pressure to naturally release for 5 minutes. After 5 minutes, quick release any remaining pressure by moving the pressure release valve to the VENT position. Carefully remove lid when unit has finished releasing pressure.
5. Stir the raisins into the oatmeal. Cover and let sit 5 minutes to thicken.
6. Evenly spread the crumble topping over the oatmeal. Close crisping lid.
7. Select AIR CRISP, set temperature to 400°F or 205°C, and set time to 10 minutes. Select START/STOP to begin.
8. In a small bowl, whisk together the cream cheese, confectioners' sugar, and milk. Add more milk or sugar, as needed, to reach your desired consistency.
9. When crumble topping is browned, cooking is complete. Open lid and serve the oatmeal in individual bowls topped with a swirl of cream cheese topping.

Nutrition:

- InfoCalories: 454,Total Fat: 16g,Sodium: 117mg,Carbohydrates: 73g,Protein: 8g.

Apple Pie Oatmeal

Servings: 8
Cooking Time: 8 Hours

Ingredients:

- 2 cups steel cut oats
- 7 cups water
- 2 apples peel, core & chop
- ¾ tsp vanilla
- ½ tsp cinnamon
- ¼ tsp ginger
- ¼ tsp nutmeg

Directions:

1. Add all the ingredients to the cooking pot and stir to combine.

2. Add the lid and set to slow cooking on low heat. Cook 6-8 hours, stirring occasionally.
3. When oatmeal is done, stir well before serving.

Nutrition:

- InfoCalories 172,Total Fat 3g,Total Carbs 31g,Protein 7g,Sodium 1mg.

Butternut Squash Cake Oatmeal

Servings: 4
Cooking Time: 35 Min

Ingredients:

- 1 cup steel-cut oats /130g
- ⅓ cup honey /84ml
- 3 ½ cups coconut milk /875ml
- ¼ cup toasted walnuts; chopped /32.5g
- 1 cup shredded Butternut Squash /250ml
- ½ cup sultanas /65g
- ¼ tsp ground nutmeg /1.25g
- 1 tsp ground cinnamon /5g
- ½ tsp vanilla extract /2.5ml
- ½ tsp fresh orange zest /2.5g
- ¾ tsp ground ginger /3.75g
- ½ tsp salt /2.5g
- ½ tsp sugar /2.5g

Directions:

1. In the pressure cooker, mix sultanas, orange zest, ginger, milk, honey, squash, salt, oats, and nutmeg.
2. Seal the pressure lid, choose Pressure, set to High, and set the timer to 12 minutes; press Start. When ready, do a natural pressure release for 10 minutes. Into the oatmeal, stir in the vanilla extract and sugar. Top with walnuts and serve.

Maple Dipped Asparagus

Servings: 4
Cooking Time: 15 Minutes.

Ingredients:

- 2-pounds asparagus, trimmed
- 1/2 teaspoon black pepper
- 1 teaspoon salt
- 1/4 cup choc zero maple syrup
- 2 tablespoons olive oil
- 4 tablespoons tarragon, minced

Directions:

1. Toss asparagus with salt, oil, choc zero maple syrup, black pepper, and tarragon. Toss well.
2. Take Ninja Foodi Grill, set it over your kitchen platform, and open the Ninja Foodi's lid.
3. Set the grill grate and close the Ninja Foodi's lid.
4. Select "Grill" mode and select the "MED" temperature.
5. Set the cooking time to about 8 minutes, and then press the "Start/Stop" button to initiate preheating.
6. Set the asparagus over the grill grate.
7. Close the Ninja Foodi's lid and cook for 4 minutes.
8. Now open the Ninja Foodi's lid, flip the asparagus.
9. Close the Ninja Foodi's lid and cook for 4 more minutes.
10. Serve warm.

Nutrition:

- InfoCalories: 241; Fat: 15g; Carbohydrates: 31g; Protein: 7.5g

Bacon And Sausage Cheesecake

Servings: 6

Cooking Time: 25 Min

Ingredients:

- 8 eggs, cracked into a bowl
- 8 oz. breakfast sau sage; chopped /240g
- 4 slices bread, cut into ½ -inch cubes
- 1 large green bell pepper; chopped
- 1 large red bell pepper; chopped
- 1 cup chopped green onion /130g
- ½ cup milk /125ml
- 2 cups water /500ml
- 1 cup grated Cheddar cheese /130g
- 3 bacon slices; chopped
- 1 tsp red chili flakes /5g
- Salt and black pepper to taste

Directions:

1. Add the eggs, sausage chorizo, bacon slices, green and red bell peppers, green onion, chili flakes, cheddar cheese, salt, pepper, and milk to a bowl and use a whisk to beat them together.
2. Grease a bundt pan with cooking spray and pour the egg mixture into it. After, drop the bread slices in the egg mixture all around while using a spoon to push them into the mixture.
3. Open the Ninja Foodi, pour in water, and fit the rack at the center of the pot. Place bundt pan on the rack and seal the pressure lid. Select Pressure mode on High pressure for 6 minutes, and press Start/Stop.
4. Once the timer goes off, press Start/Stop, do a quick pressure release. Run a knife around the egg in the bundt pan, close the crisping lid and cook for another 4 minutes on Bake/Roast on 380 °F or 195°C.
5. When ready, place a serving plate on the bundt pan, and then, turn the egg bundt over. Use a knife to cut the egg into slices. Serve with a sauce of your choice.

Banana Coconut Loaf

Servings: 8

Cooking Time: 35 Minutes

Ingredients:

- Nonstick cooking spray
- 1 ¼ cup whole wheat flour
- ½ cup coconut flakes, unsweetened
- 2 tsp baking powder
- ½ tsp baking soda
- ½ tsp salt
- 1 cup banana, mashed
- ¼ cup coconut oil, melted
- 2 tbsp. honey

Directions:

1. Select the bake function on heat cooker to 350°F or 175°C. Spray an 8-inch loaf pan with cooking spray.
2. In a large bowl, combine flour, coconut, baking powder, baking soda, and salt.
3. In a separate bowl, combine banana, oil, and honey. Add to dry ingredients and mix well. Spread batter in prepared pan.
4. Secure the tender-crisp lid and bake 30-35 minutes or until loaf passes the toothpick test.
5. Remove pan from the cooker and let cool 10 minutes. Invert loaf to a wire rack and cool completely before slicing.

Nutrition:

- InfoCalories 201,Total Fat 11g,Total Carbs 26g,Protein 3g,Sodium 349mg.

Breakfast Pies

Servings: 4

Cooking Time: 20 Minutes

Ingredients:

- 1 ½ cup mozzarella cheese, grated
- 2/3 cup almond flour, sifted
- 4 eggs, beaten
- 4 tbsp. butter
- 6 slices bacon, cooked crisp & crumbled

Directions:

1. Select air fryer function and heat cooker to 400°F or 205°C.
2. In a microwave safe bowl, melt the mozzarella cheese until smooth.
3. Stir in flour until well combined.
4. Roll the dough out between 2 sheets of parchment paper. Use a sharp knife to cut dough into 4 equal rectangles.
5. Heat the butter in a skillet over medium heat. Add the eggs and scramble to desired doneness.
6. Divide eggs evenly between the four pieces of dough, placing them on one side. Top with bacon.
7. Fold dough over filling and seal the edges with a fork. Poke a few holes on the top of the pies.
8. Place the pies in the fryer basket in a single layer. Secure the tender-crisp lid and bake 20 minutes, turning over halfway through. Serve immediately.

Nutrition:

- InfoCalories 420,Total Fat 33g,Total Carbs 3g,Protein 28g,Sodium 663mg.

Quinoa Protein Bake

Servings: 4

Cooking Time: 30 Minutes

Ingredients:

- Nonstick cooking spray
- 1 cup white quinoa, cooked
- 3 egg whites, lightly beaten
- ½ tsp salt
- ¼ cup red bell pepper, chopped
- ¼ cup spinach, chopped
- ½ cup mozzarella cheese, grated

Directions:

1. Spray the cooking pot with cooking spray.
2. In a large bowl, combine all ingredients thoroughly. Pour into pot.
3. Add the tender-crisp lid and select air fry on 350°F or 175°C. Bake 25-30 minutes until lightly browned on top and eggs are completely set.
4. Let cool a few minutes before serving.

Nutrition:

- InfoCalories 191,Total Fat 3g,Total Carbs 28g,Protein 13g,Sodium 441mg.

Mediterranean Quiche

Servings: 6
Cooking Time: 45 Minutes
Ingredients:
- Nonstick cooking spray
- 2 cups potatoes, grated
- ¾ cup feta cheese, fat free, crumbled
- 1 tbsp. olive oil
- 1 cup grape tomatoes, halved
- 3 cups baby spinach
- 2 eggs
- 2 egg whites
- ¼ cup skim milk
- ½ tsp salt
- ¼ tsp pepper

Directions:
1. Select bake function and heat to 375°F or 190°C. Spray an 8-inch round pan with cooking spray.
2. Press the potatoes on the bottom and up sides of the prepared pan. Place in the cooker. Secure the tender-crisp lid and bake 10 minutes.
3. Remove pan from the cooker and sprinkle half the feta cheese over the bottom of the crust.
4. Set cooker to sauté function on medium heat. Add the oil and heat until hot.
5. Add the tomatoes and spinach and cook until spinach has wilted, about 2-3 minutes. Place over the feta cheese.
6. In a medium bowl, whisk together eggs, milk, salt, and pepper. Pour over spinach mixture and top with remaining feta cheese.
7. Place the pan back in the cooking pot and secure the tender-crisp lid. Set temperature to 375°F or 190°C and bake 30 minutes or until eggs are completely set and starting to brown. Let cool 10 minutes before serving.

Nutrition:
- InfoCalories 145,Total Fat 8g,Total Carbs 12g,Protein 7g,Sodium 346mg.

Cinnamon Sugar French Toast Bites

Servings: 4
Cooking Time: 10 Minutes
Ingredients:
- Butter flavored cooking spray
- 1/3 cup Stevia
- 1 tsp cinnamon
- 4 slices sourdough bread, sliced thick, remove crust
- 2 eggs
- 2 tbsp. milk
- 1 tsp vanilla

Directions:
1. Set to air fryer function on 350°F or 175°C. Spray the fryer basket with cooking spray.
2. In a small bowl, combine Stevia and cinnamon.
3. In a medium bowl, whisk together eggs, milk, and vanilla until smooth.
4. Slice bread into bite-size cubes, about 8 pieces per slice. Dip in egg mixture to coat. Place in a single layer in the fryer basket and spray lightly with cooking spray.
5. Secure the tender-crisp lid and cook 3-5 minutes until golden brown, turning over halfway through cooking time.
6. Roll French toast bites in cinnamon mixture and serve. Repeat with remaining bread and egg mixture.

Nutrition:
- InfoCalories 219,Total Fat 4g,Total Carbs 34g,Protein 10g,Sodium 424mg.

Southwest Tofu Scramble

Servings: 4
Cooking Time: 10 Minutes
Ingredients:
- 1 tbsp. olive oil
- 4 oz. extra firm tofu, cut in small cubes
- ¼ cup red bell pepper, diced fine
- ¼ cup red onion, diced fine
- 1 cup kale, chopped
- ½ tsp cumin
- 1 tsp chili powder
- 6 egg whites, lightly beaten
- 2 tbsp. cilantro, chopped

Directions:
1. Select sauté function on med-high heat. Add oil and heat until hot.
2. Add the tofu, pepper, onion, and kale and cook, stirring frequently, until onion is soft and kale has wilted.
3. Stir in spices. Slowly add egg whites, stirring frequently to scramble. Cook until egg whites are set, but not brown. Sprinkle with cilantro and serve immediately.

Nutrition:
- InfoCalories 91,Total Fat 5g,Total Carbs 3g,Protein 10g,Sodium 97mg.

Chocolate Chip And Banana Bread Bundt Cake

Servings:8
Cooking Time: 40 Minutes
Ingredients:
- 2 cups all-purpose flour
- 1 teaspoon baking soda
- ¼ teaspoon cinnamon
- ¼ teaspoon sea salt
- 1 stick (½ cup) unsalted butter, at room temperature
- ½ cup dark brown sugar
- ¼ cup granulated sugar
- 2 eggs, beaten
- 1 teaspoon vanilla extract
- 3 ripe bananas, mashed
- 1 cup semisweet chocolate chips
- Cooking spray

Directions:
1. Close crisping lid. Select BAKE/ROAST, set temperature to 325°F or 165°C, and set time to 5 minutes. Select START/STOP to begin preheating.
2. In a medium bowl, stir together the flour, baking soda, cinnamon, and salt.
3. In a large bowl, beat together the butter, brown sugar, and granulated sugar. Stir in the eggs, vanilla, and bananas.
4. Slowly add the dry mixture to wet mixture, stirring until just combined. Fold in chocolate chips.
5. Use cooking spray to grease the Ninja Tube Pan or a 7-inch Bundt pan. Pour the batter into the pan.
6. Once preheated, place pan on the Reversible Rack in the lower position. Close crisping lid.

7. Select BAKE/ROAST, set temperature to 325°F or 165°C, and set time to 40 minutes. Select START/STOP to begin.
8. After 30 minutes, open lid and check doneness by inserting a toothpick into the cake. If it comes out clean, it is done. If not, continue baking until done.
9. When cooking is complete, remove pan from pot and place on a cooling rack for 30 minutes before serving.

Nutrition:

- InfoCalories: 484,Total Fat: 21g,Sodium: 238mg,Carbohydrates: 70g,Protein: 6g.

Walnut Orange Coffee Cake

Servings: 8

Cooking Time: 25 Minutes

Ingredients:

- Butter flavor cooking spray
- 1 cup Stevia
- 1/4 cup butter, unsalted, soft
- 1 egg
- 2 tsp orange zest, grated
- ½ tsp vanilla
- 1/8 tsp cinnamon
- 2 cups whole wheat flour
- 1 tsp baking soda
- ½ cup orange juice, fresh squeezed
- ½ cup water
- ½ cup walnuts, chopped

Directions:

1. Select bake function and heat cooker to 350°F or 175°C. Spray a 7-inch round pan with cooking spray.
2. In a medium bowl, beat Stevia and butter until smooth.
3. Add egg, zest, vanilla, and cinnamon and mix until combined.
4. In a separate bowl, combine dry ingredients. Add to butter mixture and mix until thoroughly combined. Stir in nuts.
5. Spread batter in prepared pan and place in the cooker. Secure the tender-crisp lid and bakke 20-25 minutes, or until it passes the toothpick test.
6. Let cool in pan 10 minutes, then invert onto wire rack. Serve warm.

Nutrition:

- InfoCalories 203,Total Fat 10g,Total Carbs 53g,Protein 6g,Sodium 170mg.

Savory Custards With Ham And Cheese

Servings: 4

Cooking Time: 40 Min

Ingredients:

- 4 large eggs
- 1 ounce cottage cheese; at room temperature /30g
- 2 serrano ham slices; halved widthwise
- ¼ cup caramelized white onions /32.5g
- ¼ cup half and half /62.5ml
- ¼ cup grated Emmental cheese /32.5g
- ¼ tsp salt /1.25g
- Ground black pepper to taste

Directions:

1. Preheat the inner pot by choosing Sear/Sauté and adjust to Medium; press Start. Put the serrano ham in the pot and cook for 3 to 4 minutes or until browned, turning occasionally.
2. Remove the ham onto a paper towel-lined plate. Next, use a brush to coat the inside of four 1- cup ramekins with the ham fat.

Set the cups aside, then, empty and wipe out the inner pot with a paper towel, and return the pot to the base.
3. Crack the eggs into a bowl and add the cottage cheese, half and half, salt, and several grinds of black pepper. Use a hand mixer to whisk the Ingredients until co cheese lumps remain.
4. Stir in the grated emmental cheese and mix again to incorporate the cheese. Lay a piece of ham in the bottom of each custard cup. Evenly share the onions among the cups as well as the egg mixture. Cover each cup with aluminum foil.
5. Pour 1 cup or 250ml of water into the inner pot and fix the reversible rack in the pot. Arrange the ramekins on top. Lock the pressure lid in Seal position; choose Pressure, adjust to High, and set the timer to 7 minutes. Press Start.
6. After cooking, perform a quick pressure release. Use tongs to remove the custard cups from the pressure cooker. Cool for 1 to 2 minutes before serving.

Baked Eggs & Kale

Servings: 4

Cooking Time: 25 Minutes

Ingredients:

- 1 tbsp. olive oil
- 6 cups kale, remove stems & chop
- 2 cloves garlic, diced fine
- ¼ cup ricotta cheese, fat free
- ¼ cup feta, fat free, crumbled
- 4 eggs
- 1/3 cup grape tomatoes, halved
- ¼ tsp pepper
- ½ tsp salt

Directions:

1. Add oil to the cooking pot and select sauté on medium heat.
2. Add the kale and garlic and cook until kale is wilted, about 2-3 minutes.
3. In a small bowl, combine ricotta and feta cheeses.
4. Make 4 small indents in the kale mixture and crack an egg into each one.
5. Drop the cheese mixture by tablespoons around the eggs.
6. Top with tomatoes, pepper, and salt. Secure the tender-crisp lid, set to air fryer function at 350°F or 175°C and bake 20-25 minutes or until egg whites are cooked through. Serve immediately.

Nutrition:

- InfoCalories 154,Total Fat 12g,Total Carbs 7g,Protein 7g,Sodium 410mg.

Broccoli, Ham, And Cheddar Frittata

Servings:6

Cooking Time: 40 Minutes

Ingredients:

- 1 head broccoli, cut into 1-inch florets
- 1 tablespoon canola oil
- Kosher salt
- Freshly ground black pepper
- 12 large eggs
- ¼ cup whole milk

- 1½ cups shredded white Cheddar cheese, divided
- 3 tablespoons unsalted butter
- ½ medium white onion, diced
- 1 cup diced ham

Directions:

1. Place Cook & Crisp Basket in the pot. Close crisping lid. Select AIR CRISP, setting temperature to 390°F or 200°C, and set time to 5 minutes. Select START/STOP to begin preheating.
2. In a large bowl, toss the broccoli with the oil and season with salt and pepper.
3. Once unit is preheated, open lid and add the broccoli to basket. Close crisping lid.
4. Select AIR CRISP, set temperature to 390°F or 200°C, and set time to 15 minutes. Select START/STOP to begin.
5. In a separate large bowl, whisk together the eggs, milk, and 1 cup of cheese.
6. After 7 minutes, open lid. Remove basket and shake the broccoli. Return basket to pot and close lid to continue cooking.
7. After 8 minutes, check the broccoli for desired doneness. When cooking is complete, remove broccoli and basket from pot.
8. Select SEAR/SAUTÉ and set to HI. Select START/STOP to begin.
9. After 5 minutes, add the butter. Melt for 1 minute, then add the onion and cook for 3 minutes, stirring occasionally.
10. Add the ham and broccoli and cook, stirring occasionally, for 2 minutes.
11. Add the egg mixture, season with salt and pepper, and stir. Close crisping lid.
12. Select BAKE/ROAST, set temperature to 400°F or 205°C, and set time to 15 minutes. Select STOP/START to begin.
13. After 5 minutes, open lid and sprinkle the remaining ½ cup of cheese on top. Close lid to continue cooking.
14. When cooking is complete, remove pot from unit and let the frittata sit for 5 to 10 minutes before serving.

Nutrition:

- InfoCalories: 404, Total Fat: 30g, Sodium: 671mg, Carbohydrates: 10g, Protein: 27g.

Spinach Casserole

Servings: 4
Cooking Time: 5 Minutes

Ingredients:

- 4 whole eggs
- 1 tablespoons milk
- 1 tomato, diced
- ½ cup spinach
- ¼ teaspoon salt
- ¼ teaspoon black pepper

Directions:

1. Take a baking pan small enough to fit Ninja Foodi and grease it with butter.
2. Take a medium bowl and whisk in eggs, milk, salt, pepper, add veggies to the bowl and stir.
3. Pour egg mixture into the baking pan and lower the pan into the Ninja Foodi .
4. Close Air Crisping lid and Air Crisp for 325 degrees for 7 minutes.
5. Remove the pan from eggs, and enjoy hot.

Nutrition:

- InfoCalories: 78; Fat: 5g; Carbohydrates: 1 g; Protein: 7 g

Strawberry Oat Breakfast Bars

Servings: 16
Cooking Time: 25 Minutes

Ingredients:

- 2 cups oats
- ¼ cup oat flour
- 1 cup coconut flakes, unsweetened
- 2 tbsp. chia seeds, ground
- ½ cup almonds, chopped
- ¼ salt
- 2 bananas, mashed
- 2 tbsp. honey
- ¼ cup coconut oil, melted
- 1 cup strawberries, chopped
- 1 tsp vanilla

Directions:

1. Set to bake function on 350°F or 175°C. Line an 8-inch baking dish with parchment paper.
2. In a large bowl, combine dry ingredients.
3. Stir in remaining ingredients until thoroughly combined.
4. Press mixture into prepared pan and place in cooker. Add the tender-crisp lid and bake 25 minutes until golden brown.
5. Let cool before slicing into 2-inch squares.

Nutrition:

- InfoCalories 179, Total Fat 8g, Total Carbs 24g, Protein 5g, Sodium 53mg.

Sausage & Egg Stuffed Peppers

Servings: 4
Cooking Time: 6 Hours

Ingredients:

- ½ lb. breakfast sausage
- 4 bell peppers
- ½ cup water
- 6 eggs
- ½ cup cheddar Jack cheese, grated
- 4 oz. green chilies, diced
- ¼ tsp salt
- 1/8 tsp pepper
- 2 tbsp. green onion, diced

Directions:

1. Set cooker to sauté on med-high heat.
2. Add sausage and cook, breaking up with spatula, until no longer pink. Transfer to a bowl and drain off the grease.
3. Cut the tops off the peppers and remove the seeds and ribs. Place in the cooking pot and pour the water around them.
4. In a medium bowl, whisk eggs until smooth. Stir in cheese, chilies, salt, and pepper until combined. Fill the peppers with the egg mixture.
5. Secure the lid and set to slow cooker function on high. Set the timer for 4 hours.
6. Casserole is done when the eggs are set, if not done when the timer goes off, cook another 1-2 hours. Garnish with green onions and serve.

Nutrition:

- InfoCalories 364, Total Fat 22g, Total Carbs 15g, Protein 27g, Sodium 874mg.

Savory Oatmeal

Servings: 2
Cooking Time: 10 Minutes
Ingredients:

- 2 cups chicken broth, low sodium
- ¾ cup old-fashioned oats
- ¼ tsp salt, divided
- 1 tbsp. olive oil
- 1 tbsp. butter, unsalted
- 8 oz. baby bella mushrooms, sliced
- ¼ tsp pepper
- 1 cup fresh baby spinach
- 2 eggs
- ½ cup cherry tomatoes, halved

Directions:

1. Add the broth, oats, and 1/8 teaspoon salt to the cooking pot, stir to combine.
2. Secure the lid and select pressure cooking function on high. Set timer to 5 minutes.
3. Heat oil and butter in a medium skillet over low heat until butter has melted.
4. Add mushrooms and season with salt and pepper. Cook 4-5 minutes, or until mushrooms are tender.
5. Stir in spinach and cook until it wilts, about 2 minutes. Transfer to a plate.
6. In the same skillet, crack 2 eggs and fry them the way you like them.
7. When the timer goes off, use quick release to remove the lid. Stir the oatmeal and ladle into bowls.
8. Top each bowl with spinach mixture, an egg, and tomatoes. Serve immediately.

Nutrition:

- InfoCalories 511,Total Fat 21g,Total Carbs 59g,Protein 25g,Sodium 1268mg.

Cinnamon Roll Monkey Bread

Servings:8
Cooking Time: 20 Minutes
Ingredients:

- 4 eggs
- ¼ cup whole milk
- 1 teaspoon vanilla extract
- ½ teaspoon cinnamon
- Cooking spray
- 2 tubes refrigerated cinnamon rolls with icing, quartered

Directions:

1. In a medium bowl, whisk together the eggs, milk, vanilla, and cinnamon.
2. Lightly coat the pot with cooking spray, then place the cinnamon roll pieces in the pot. Pour the egg mixture over the dough. Close crisping lid.
3. Select BAKE/ROAST, set temperature to 350°F or 175°C, and set time to 20 minutes. Select START/STOP to begin.
4. When cooking is complete, remove pot from unit and place it on a heat-resistant surface. Remove lid. Let cool for 5 minutes, then top with the icing from the cinnamon rolls and serve.

Nutrition:

- InfoCalories: 327,Total Fat: 12g,Sodium: 710mg,Carbohydrates: 46g,Protein: 7g.

Pepperoni Omelets

Servings: 4
Cooking Time: 5 Minutes
Ingredients:

- 4 tablespoons heavy cream
- 15 pepperoni slices
- 2 tablespoons butter
- Black pepper and salt to taste
- 6 whole eggs

Directions:

1. Take a suitable and whisk in eggs, cream, pepperoni slices, salt, and pepper.
2. Set your Ninja Foodi to "Sauté" mode and add butter and egg mix.
3. Sauté for 3 minutes, flip.
4. Lock and secure the Ninja Foodi's lid and Air Crisp for 2 minutes at 350 °F or 175°C.
5. Transfer to a serving plate and enjoy.

Nutrition:

- InfoCalories: 141; Fat: 11g; Carbohydrates: 0.6g; Protein: 9g

Swiss Bacon Frittata

Servings: 6
Cooking Time: 23 Minutes
Ingredients:

- 1 small onion, chopped
- 1/2 lb. of raw bacon, chopped
- 1 lb. of frozen spinach
- 10 eggs
- 1 cup cottage cheese
- 1/2 cup half and half cream
- 1 tsp salt
- 1 cup shredded swiss cheese

Directions:

1. Preheat your Ninja Foodi for 5 minutes at 350 °F or 175°C on Saute Mode.
2. Add bacon, and onion to the Foodi and saute for 10 minutes until crispy.
3. Stir in spinach and stir cook for 3 minutes.
4. Whisk eggs with cottage cheese, salt and half and half cream in a bowl.
5. Pour this mixture into the Ninja Foodi cooking pot.
6. Drizzle swiss cheese over the egg mixture.
7. Secure the Ninja Foodi lid and switch the Foodi to Bake/Roast mode for 20 minutes at 350 °F or 175°C.
8. Serve warm.

Nutrition:

- InfoCalories 139; Total Fat 10.1g; Total Carbs 2.3g; Protein 10.1 g

Omelets In The Jar

Servings: 5
Cooking Time: 8 Minutes
Ingredients:

- 10 eggs
- 1/3 cup heavy cream
- 2/3 cup of shredded cheese
- 1 green pepper, chopped
- 1 ham steak, chopped

- 1/2 lb. bacon, cooked and chopped
- 5 mason jars or other jars
- 1 cup of water

Directions:
1. Grease the mason jars with canola spray.
2. Whisk 2 eggs with 1 tbsp cream in a bowl then pour it into a jar.
3. Add 1 tbsp of ham, green peppers, and cheese to the same jar.
4. Repeat the same steps to fill remaining jars.
5. Pour 1 cup water in the Ninja Food pot and place trivet over it.
6. Set all the mason jars over the trivet.
7. Secure the Ninja Foodi lid and turn its pressure handle to 'Closed' position.
8. Select Pressure mode for 8 minutes at 350 °F or 175°C.
9. Once done, release the steam naturally then remove the lid.
10. Drizzle bacon and cheese over each jar.
11. Serve fresh.

Nutrition:
- InfoCalories 111; Total Fat 8.3 g; Total Carbs 1.9 g; Protein 7.4 g

Bacon And Gruyère Egg Bites

Servings:6
Cooking Time: 26 Minutes

Ingredients:
- 5 slices bacon, cut into ½-inch pieces
- 5 eggs
- 1 teaspoon kosher salt
- ¼ cup sour cream
- 1 cup shredded Gruyère cheese, divided
- Cooking spray
- 1 cup water
- 1 teaspoon chopped parsley, for garnish

Directions:
1. Select SEAR/SAUTÉ and set temperature to HI. Select START/STOP and let preheat for 5 minutes.
2. Add the bacon and cook, stirring frequently, about 5 minutes, or until the fat is rendered and bacon starts to brown. Transfer the bacon to a paper towel-lined plate to drain. Wipe the pot clean of any remaining fat.
3. In a medium bowl, whisk together the eggs, salt, and sour cream until well combined. Fold in ¾ cup of cheese and the bacon.
4. Spray egg molds or Ninja Silicone Mold with the cooking spray. Ladle the egg mixture into each mold, filling them halfway.
5. Pour the water in the pot. Carefully place the egg molds in the pot. Assemble pressure lid, making sure the pressure release valve is in the SEAL position.
6. Select PRESSURE and set to LO. Set time to 10 minutes. Select START/STOP to begin.
7. When pressure cooking is complete, natural release the pressure for 6 minutes, then quick release the remaining pressure by moving the pressure release valve to the VENT position.
8. Carefully remove the lid. Using mitts or a towel, carefully remove egg molds. Top with the remaining ¼ cup of cheese, then place the mold back into the pot. Close the crisping lid.
9. Select AIR CRISP, set temperature to 390°F or 200°C, and set time to 5 minutes. Select START/STOP to begin.
10. Once cooking is complete, carefully remove the egg molds and set aside to cool for 5 minutes. Using a spoon, carefully remove the egg bites from the molds. Top with chopped parsley and serve immediately.

Nutrition:

- InfoCalories: 230,Total Fat: 18g,Sodium: 557mg,Carbohydrates: 2g,Protein: 16g.

Kale-egg Frittata

Servings: 6
Cooking Time: 20 Min

Ingredients:
- 1 ½ cups kale; chopped /195g
- 6 large eggs
- ¼ cup grated Parmesan cheese /32.5g
- 1 cup water /250ml
- 2 tbsp heavy cream /30ml
- ½ tsp freshly grated nutmeg /2.5g
- cooking spray
- Salt and black pepper to taste

Directions:
1. In a bowl, beat eggs, nutmeg, pepper, salt, and cream until smooth; stir in Parmesan cheese and kale. Apply a cooking spray to a cake pan. Wrap aluminum foil around outside of the pan to cover completely.
2. Place egg mixture into the prepared pan. Add water into the pot of your Foodi. Set your Foodi's reversible rack over the water. Gently lay the pan onto the reversible rack.
3. Seal the pressure lid, choose Pressure, set to High, and set the timer to 10 minutes. Press Start. When ready, release the pressure quickly.

Glazed Lemon Muffins

Servings: 12
Cooking Time: 20 Minutes

Ingredients:
- 1 cup flour
- 1 tsp baking powder
- ½ tsp baking soda
- ¼ tsp salt
- ½ cup of coconut oil, melted
- 2 eggs
- 2 tbsp. Stevia
- ¼ cup honey
- 1 cup Greek yogurt, low-fat
- 1 ¼ tsp vanilla, divided
- 3 tbsp. + 2 tsp fresh lemon juice, divided
- 1 ½ tsp lemon zest
- 2 tbsp. Stevia powdered sugar

Directions:
1. Select bake function and heat to 350°F or 175°C. Line 2 6- cup muffin tins with paper liners.
2. In a medium bowl, stir together flour, baking powder, baking soda, and salt.
3. In a large bowl, whisk together oil and eggs until smooth.
4. Add Stevia, honey, and yogurt and mix until combined.
5. Whisk in 1 teaspoon vanilla, 3 tablespoons lemon juice, and 1 teaspoon zest. Fold in dry ingredients just until combined.
6. Pour batter evenly into prepared muffin tins. Place tins, one at a time in the cooker. Secure the tender-crisp lid and bake 20 minutes or until muffins pass the toothpick test. Remove to wire rack to cool.

7.   In a small bowl, whisk together Stevia confectioner's sugar and remaining vanilla, lemon juice, and zest until smooth. Drizzle over the tops of the muffins and serve.

Nutrition:

- InfoCalories 164,Total Fat 10g,Total Carbs 15g,Protein 4g,Sodium 120mg.

Maple Giant Pancake

Servings: 6

Cooking Time: 30 Min

Ingredients:

- 3 cups flour /390g
- ⅓ cup olive oil /84ml
- ⅓ cup sparkling water /84ml
- ¾ cup sugar /98g
- 5 eggs
- 2 tbsp maple syrup /30ml
- ⅓ tsp salt /1.67g
- 1 ½ tsp baking soda /7.5g
- A dollop of whipped cream to serve

Directions:

1.   Start by pouring the flour, sugar, eggs, olive oil, sparkling water, salt, and baking soda into a food processor and blend until smooth. Pour the batter into the Ninja Foodi and let it sit in there for 15 minutes. Close the lid and secure the pressure valve.
2.   Select the Pressure mode on Low pressure for 10 minutes. Press Start/Stop.
3.   Once the timer goes off, press Start/Stop, quick-release the pressure valve to let out any steam and open the lid.
4.   Gently run a spatula around the pancake to let loose any sticking. Once ready, slide the pancake onto a serving plate and drizzle with maple syrup. Top with the whipped cream to serve

Blueberry Muffins

Servings: 12

Cooking Time: 20 Minutes

Ingredients:

- 2 ½ cups oats
- 1 ½ cups almond milk, unsweetened
- Nonstick cooking spray
- 1 egg, lightly beaten
- 1/3 cup pure maple syrup
- 2 tbsp. coconut oil, melted
- 1 tsp vanilla
- 1 tsp cinnamon
- 1 tsp baking powder
- ¼ tsp salt
- 1 tsp lemon zest, grated
- 1 cup fresh blueberries

Directions:

1.   In a large bowl, combine oats and milk. Cover and refrigerate overnight.
2.   Select bake function and heat to 375°F or 190°C. Spray 2 6-cup muffin tins with cooking spray.
3.   Stir remaining ingredients into the oat mixture. Spoon into muffin tins.
4.   Place the rack in the cooking pot and place muffin tin on it, these will need to be baked in 2 batches.
5.   Secure the tender crisp lid and bake 20 minutes or until tops are golden brown. Serve warm.

Nutrition:

- InfoCalories 122,Total Fat 4g,Total Carbs 19g,Protein 3g,Sodium 108mg.

Zucchini Pancakes

Servings: 6

Cooking Time: 10 Minutes

Ingredients:

- 1 cup almond milk, unsweetened
- 1 egg
- 2 tbsp. honey
- 1 tbsp. coconut oil, melted
- 1 tsp vanilla
- ½ cup zucchini, grated
- 1 ½ cup oat flour
- 2 tsp cinnamon
- 1 tsp baking powder
- ¼ tsp salt
- Nonstick cooking spray

Directions:

1.   In a large bowl, combine milk, egg, honey, oil, vanilla, and zucchini.
2.   In a separate bowl, stir together remaining ingredients. Add to zucchini mixture and mix just until combined.
3.   Spray the cooking pot with cooking spray. Set to sauté on medium heat.
4.   Pour batter, ¼ cup at a time, into cooking pot. Cook 3-4 minutes or until bubble form in the middle. Flip and cook another 2-3 minutes. Repeat with remaining batter. Serve immediately with your favorite toppings.

Nutrition:

- InfoCalories 188,Total Fat 7g,Total Carbs 27g,Protein 6g,Sodium 132mg.

Spinach Turkey Cups

Servings: 4

Cooking Time: 23 Minutes

Ingredients:

- 1 tablespoon unsalted butter
- 1-pound fresh baby spinach
- 4 eggs
- 7 ounces cooked turkey, chopped
- 4 teaspoons unsweetened almond milk
- Black pepper and salt, as required

Directions:

1.   Select the "Sauté/Sear" setting of Ninja Foodi and place the butter into the pot.
2.   Press the "Start/Stop" button to initiate cooking and heat for about 2-3 minutes.
3.   Add the spinach and cook for about 3 minutes or until just wilted.
4.   Press the "Start/Stop" button to pause cooking and drain the liquid completely.
5.   Transfer the spinach into a suitable and set aside to cool slightly.
6.   Set the "Air Crisp Basket" in the Ninja Foodi's insert.
7.   Close the Ninja Foodi's lid with a crisping lid and select "Air Crisp."
8.   Set its cooking temperature to 355 °F or 180°C for 5 minutes.
9.   Press the "Start/Stop" button to initiate preheating.

10. Divide the spinach into 4 greased ramekins, followed by the turkey.
11. Crack 1 egg into each ramekin and drizzle with almond milk.
12. Sprinkle with black pepper and salt.
13. After preheating, Open the Ninja Foodi's lid.
14. Place the ramekins into the "Air Crisp Basket."
15. Close the Ninja Foodi's lid with a crisping lid and select "Air Crisp."
16. Set its cooking temperature to 355 °F or 180°C for 20 minutes.
17. Press the "Start/Stop" button to initiate cooking.
18. Open the Ninja Foodi's lid and serve hot.

Nutrition:
- InfoCalories: 200; Fat: 10.2g; Carbohydrates: 4.5g; Protein: 23.4g

Almond Quinoa Porridge

Servings: 6
Cooking Time: 1 Minute

Ingredients:
- 1¼ cups water
- 1 cup almond milk
- 1½ cups uncooked quinoa, rinsed
- 1 tablespoon choc zero maple syrup
- 1 cinnamon stick
- Pinch of salt

Directions:
1. In the Ninja Foodi's insert, add all ingredients and stir to combine well.
2. Close the Ninja Foodi's lid with the pressure lid and place the pressure valve in the "Seal" position.
3. Select "Pressure" mode and set it to "High" for 1 minute.
4. Press the "Start/Stop" button to initiate cooking.
5. Now turn the pressure valve to "Vent" and do a "Quick" release.
6. Open the Ninja Foodi's lid, and with a fork, fluff the quinoa.
7. Serve warm.

Nutrition:
- InfoCalories: 186; Fat: 2.6 g; Carbohydrates: 4.8 g; Protein: 6 g

Bell Pepper Frittata

Servings: 2
Cooking Time: 18 Minutes

Ingredients:
- 1 tablespoon olive oil
- 1 chorizo sausage, sliced
- 1½ cups bell peppers, seeded and chopped
- 4 large eggs
- Black pepper and salt, as required
- 2 tablespoons feta cheese, crumbled
- 1 tablespoon fresh parsley, chopped

Directions:
1. Select the "Sauté/Sear" setting of Ninja Foodi and place the butter into the pot.
2. Press the "Start/Stop" button to initiate cooking and heat for about 2-3 minutes.
3. Add the sausage and bell peppers and cook for 6-8 minutes or until golden brown.
4. Meanwhile, in a suitable bowl, add the eggs, salt, and black pepper and beat well.

5. Press the "Start/Stop" button to pasue cooking and place the eggs over the sausage mixture, followed by the cheese and parsley.
6. Close the Ninja Foodi's lid with a crisping lid and select "Air Crisp."
7. Set its cooking temperature to 355 °F or 180°C for 10 minutes.
8. Press the "Start/Stop" button to initiate cooking.
9. Open the Ninja Foodi's lid and transfer the frittata onto a platter.
10. Cut into equal-sized wedges and serve hot.

Nutrition:
- InfoCalories: 398; Fat: 31g; Carbohydrates: 8g; Protein: 22.9g

Very Berry Puffs

Servings: 3
Cooking Time: 20 Min

Ingredients:
- 3 pastry dough sheets
- 2 cups cream cheese /260g
- 1 tbsp honey /15ml
- 2 tbsp mashed raspberries /30g
- 2 tbsp mashed strawberries /30g
- ¼ tsp vanilla extract /1.25ml

Directions:
1. Divide the cream cheese between the dough sheets and spread it evenly. In a small bowl, combine the berries, honey, and vanilla. Divide the mixture between the pastry sheets. Pinch the ends of the sheets, to form puff.
2. You can seal them by brushing some water onto the edges, or even better, use egg wash. Lay the puffs into a lined baking dish.
3. Place the dish into the Ninja Foodi, close the crisping lid and cook for 15 minutes on Air Crisp mode at 370 °F or 185°C. Once the timer beeps, check the puffs to ensure they're puffed and golden. Serve warm.

Chicken Omelet

Servings: 2
Cooking Time: 16 Minutes

Ingredients:
- 1 teaspoon butter
- 1 small yellow onion, chopped
- ½ jalapeño pepper, seeded and chopped
- 3 eggs
- Black pepper and salt, as required
- ¼ cup cooked chicken, shredded

Directions:
1. Select the "Sauté/Sear" setting of Ninja Foodi and place the butter into the pot.
2. Press the "Start/Stop" button to initiate cooking and heat for about 2-3 minutes.
3. Add the onion and cook for about 4-5 minutes.
4. Add the jalapeño pepper and cook for about 1 minute.
5. Meanwhile, in a suitable, add the eggs, salt, and black pepper and beat well.
6. Press the "Start/Stop" button to pause cooking and stir in the chicken.
7. Top with the egg mixture evenly.
8. Close the Ninja Foodi's lid with a crisping lid and select "Air Crisp."

9. Set its cooking temperature to 355 °F or 180°C for 5 minutes.
10. Press the "Start/Stop" button to initiate cooking.
11. Open the Ninja Foodi's lid and transfer the omelette onto a plate.
12. Cut into equal-sized wedges and serve hot.

Nutrition:

- InfoCalories: 153; Fat: 9.1g; Carbohydrates: 4g; Protein: 13.8g

Pumpkin Steel Cut Oatmeal

Servings: 4

Cooking Time: 25 Min

Ingredients:

- ½ cup pumpkin seeds, toasted /65g
- 1 cup pumpkin puree /250ml
- 2 cups steel cut oats /260g
- 3 cups water /750ml
- 1 tbsp butter /15g
- 3 tbsp maple syrup /45ml
- ¼ tsp cinnamon /1.25g
- ½ tsp salt /2.5g

Directions:

1. Melt butter on Sear/Sauté. Add in cinnamon, oats, salt, pumpkin puree and water. Seal the pressure lid, choose Pressure, set to High, and set the timer to 10 minutes; press Start. When cooking is complete, do a quick release.
2. Open the lid and stir in maple syrup and top with toasted pumpkin seeds to serve.

Sweet Potato Hash And Eggs

Servings:6

Cooking Time: 35 Minutes

Ingredients:

- 3 pounds sweet potatoes, diced
- 2 cups water
- 2 tablespoons unsalted butter
- 1 yellow onion, diced
- 3 garlic cloves, minced
- 1 red bell pepper, diced
- 1 green bell pepper, diced
- 1 bunch scallions, sliced
- 2 teaspoons smoked paprika
- Kosher salt
- Freshly ground black pepper
- 6 brown eggs

Directions:

1. Place the sweet potatoes in the Cook & Crisp Basket. Pour the water in pot and insert basket. Assemble the pressure lid, making sure the pressure release valve is in the SEAL position.
2. Select PRESSURE and set to HI. Set timer for 2 minutes. Select START/STOP to begin.
3. When pressure cooking is complete, quick release the pressure by turning the pressure release valve to the VENT position. Carefully remove lid when the unit has finished releasing pressure.
4. Remove basket with sweet potatoes. Pour out any remaining water from the pot.
5. Select SEAR/SAUTÉ and set to MED. Let preheat for 3 minutes.
6. Add the butter, onion, garlic, and bell peppers. Cook for 5 minutes. Add the sweet potatoes, scallions, and paprika and stir. Cook for 5 minutes, stirring occasionally. Season with salt and

pepper. Crack the eggs on top of the hash, equally spaced apart. Close crisping lid.
7. Select AIR CRISP, set temperature to 325°F or 165°C, and set time to 10 minutes. Select START/STOP to begin.
8. When cooking is complete, open lid and serve immediately.

Nutrition:

- InfoCalories: 376, Total Fat: 13g, Sodium: 304mg, Carbohydrates: 51g, Protein: 16g.

Chocolate Hazelnut Toaster Pastries

Servings:4

Cooking Time: 14 Minutes

Ingredients:

- All-purpose flour
- 1 refrigerated piecrust, at room temperature
- ¼ cup chocolate hazelnut spread
- Cooking spray
- Vanilla icing, for frosting
- Chocolate sprinkles, for topping

Directions:

1. Place the Cook & Crisp Basket in the pot and close crisping lid. Select AIR CRISP, set temperature to 350°F or 175°C, and set time to 5 minutes. Press START/STOP to preheat.
2. On a lightly floured surface, roll out the piecrust into a large rectangle. Cut the dough into 8 rectangles.
3. Spoon 1 tablespoon of chocolate hazelnut spread into the center of each of 4 dough rectangles, leaving a ½-inch border. Brush the edges of the filled dough rectangles with water. Top each with one of the remaining 4 dough rectangles. Press the edges with a fork to seal.
4. Once unit is preheated, carefully place two pastries in the basket in a single layer. Coat each pastry well with cooking spray. Close crisping lid.
5. Select AIR CRISP, set temperature to 350°F or 175°C, and set time to 7 minutes. Select START/STOP to begin.
6. Once cooking is complete, check for your desired crispiness. Place the pastries on a wire rack to cool. Repeat steps 4 and 5 with the remaining 2 pastries.
7. Frost the pastries with vanilla icing, then top with sprinkles.

Nutrition:

- InfoCalories: 334, Total Fat: 17g, Sodium: 271mg, Carbohydrates: 43g, Protein: 1g.

Morning Pancakes

Servings: 4

Cooking Time: 10 Minutes

Ingredients:

- 2 cups cream cheese
- 2 cups almond flour
- 6 large whole eggs
- 1/4 teaspoon salt
- 2 tablespoons butter
- ¼ teaspoon ground ginger
- ½ teaspoon cinnamon powder

Directions:

1. Take a large bowl and add cream cheese, eggs, 1 tablespoon butter. Blend on high until creamy.
2. Slow add flour and keep beating.

3. Add salt, ginger, cinnamon.
4. Keep beating until fully mixed .
5. Select "Sauté" mode on your Ninja Foodi and grease stainless steel insert.
6. Add butter and heat it up.
7. Add ½ cup batter and cook for 2-3 minutes, flip and cook the other side.
8. Repeat with the remaining batter. Enjoy.

Nutrition:
- InfoCalories: 432; Fat: 40g; Carbohydrates: 3g; Protein: 14g

Peaches & Brown Sugar Oatmeal

Servings: 8
Cooking Time: 8 Hours
Ingredients:
- Nonstick cooking spray
- 2 cups steel cut oats
- 8 cups water
- 1 tsp cinnamon
- ½ cup brown sugar
- 1 tsp vanilla
- 1 cup peaches, cubed

Directions:
1. Spray cooking pot with cooking spray.
2. Add the oats, water, cinnamon, sugar, and vanilla to the pot, stir to combine.
3. Secure the lid and select slow cooker function on low. Set timer for 8 hours.
4. Stir in peaches and serve.

Nutrition:
- InfoCalories 231,Total Fat 3g,Total Carbs 46g,Protein 7g,Sodium 7mg.

Sausage Wrapped Scotch Eggs

Servings: 4
Cooking Time: 55 Min
Ingredients:
- 12 ounces Italian sausage patties /360g
- 4 eggs
- 1 cup water /250ml
- 1 cup panko bread crumbs /130g
- Nonstick cooking spray; for preparing the rack
- 2 tbsps melted unsalted butter /30ml

Directions:
1. Pour 1 cup of water into the inner pot. Put the reversible rack in the pot at the bottom, and carefully place the eggs on top. Seal the pressure lid, choose Pressure, set the pressure to High, and the cook time to 3 minutes. Press Start.
2. While cooking the eggs, fill half a bowl with cold water and about a cup full of ice cubes to make an ice bath.
3. After cooking, perform a quick pressure release, and carefully open the lid. Use tongs to pick up the eggs into the ice bath. Allow cooling for 3 to 4 minutes; peel the eggs.
4. Pour the water out of the inner pot and return the pot to the base. Grease the reversible rack with cooking spray, fix the rack in the upper position, and place in the pot.
5. Cover the crisping lid; choose Air Crisp, set the temperature to 360°F or 180°C and the timer to 4 minutes. Press Start to preheat.
6. While preheating the pot, place an egg on each sausage patty. Pull the sausage around the egg and seal the edges.

7. In a small bowl, mix the breadcrumbs with the melted butter. One at a time, dredge the sausage-covered eggs in the crumbs while pressing into the breadcrumbs for a thorough coat.
8. Open the crisping lid and place the eggs on the rack. Close the crisping lid; choose Air Crisp, adjust the temperature to 360°F or 180°C, and the cook time to 15 minutes. Press Start.
9. When the timer has ended, the crumbs should be crisp and a deep golden brown color. Remove the eggs and allow cooling for several minutes. Slice the eggs in half and serve.

Banana Custard Oatmeal

Servings: 6
Cooking Time: 40 Minutes
Ingredients:
- Butter flavored cooking spray
- 1 2/3 cups vanilla almond milk, unsweetened
- 2 large bananas, mashed
- 1 cup bananas, sliced
- 1 cup steel cut oats
- 1/3 cup maple syrup
- 1/3 cup walnuts, chopped
- 2 eggs, beaten
- 1 tbsp. butter, melted
- 1 ½ tsp cinnamon
- 1 tsp baking powder
- 1 tsp vanilla extract
- ½ tsp nutmeg
- ¼ teaspoon salt
- 2 ½ cups water

Directions:
1. Spray a 1 1/2 –quart baking dish with cooking spray.
2. In a large bowl, combine all ingredients thoroughly. Transfer to prepared baking dish.
3. Pour 1 ½ cups water into the cooking pot and add the trivet. Place dish on the trivet and secure the lid.
4. Select pressure cooking on high and set timer for 40 minutes.
5. When timer goes off, release pressure naturally for 10 minutes, then use quick release. Stir oatmeal well then serve.

Nutrition:
- InfoCalories 349,Total Fat 10g,Total Carbs 56g,Protein 10g,Sodium 281mg.

Pumpkin Coconut Breakfast Bake

Servings: 8
Cooking Time: 1 Hour 15 Minutes
Ingredients:
- Butter flavored cooking spray
- 5 eggs
- ½ cup coconut milk
- 2 cups pumpkin puree
- 1 banana, mashed
- 2 dates, pitted & chopped
- 1 tsp cinnamon
- 1 cup raspberries
- ¼ cup coconut, unsweetened & shredded

Directions:

1. Lightly spray an 8-inch baking dish with cooking spray.
2. In a large bowl, whisk together eggs and milk.
3. Whisk in pumpkin until combined.
4. Stir in banana, dates, and cinnamon. Pour into prepared dish.
5. Sprinkle berries over top.
6. Place the rack in the cooking pot and place the dish on it. Add the tender-crisp lid and select bake on 350°F or 175°C. Bake 20 minutes.
7. Sprinkle coconut over the top and bake another 20-25 minutes until top is lightly browned and casserole is set. Slice and serve warm.

Nutrition:

- InfoCalories 113,Total Fat 5g,Total Carbs 14g,Protein 6g,Sodium 62mg.

Applesauce Pumpkin Muffins

Servings: 8

Cooking Time: 15 Minutes

Ingredients:

- 4 eggs
- ½ cup applesauce, unsweetened
- ½ cup pumpkin
- ½ cup coconut flour
- 2 tbsp. cinnamon
- ¼ tsp cloves
- ¼ tsp ginger
- 1/8 tsp nutmeg
- ¼ tsp salt
- 1 tsp baking soda
- 2 tsp vanilla
- 4 tbsp. coconut oil, melted
- 1 tbsp. honey

Directions:

1. Set cooker to air fryer function on 375°F or 190°C. Line 2 6-cup muffin tins with paper liners.
2. Add all ingredients to a blender or food processor and blend on low just until combined.
3. Pour batter evenly into prepared tins. Place muffin pans, one at a time, in the cooker and secure the tender-crisp lid. Bake 12-15 minutes or until muffins pass the toothpick test.
4. Let cool in pans 10 minutes, then transfer to wire rack to cool completely.

Nutrition:

- InfoCalories 122,Total Fat 9g,Total Carbs 11g,Protein 3g,Sodium 264mg.

Banana Nut Muffins

Servings: 12

Cooking Time:x

Ingredients:

- 1 ½ cups flour
- 1 tsp baking powder
- 1 tsp baking soda
- ½ tsp salt
- ½ tsp cinnamon
- 1 egg
- 3 bananas, mashed
- ¾ cup Stevia
- 1/3 cup coconut oil, melted
- 1 tsp vanilla
- ½ cup walnuts, chopped

Directions:

1. Set cooker to air fryer function on 350°F or 175°C. Line 2 6-cup muffin tins with paper liners.
2. In a medium bowl, combine flour, baking powder, baking soda, salt, and cinnamon.
3. In a large bowl, whisk together egg, banana, Stevia, oil, and vanilla until smooth.
4. Stir in dry ingredients just until combined. Fold in nuts and pour into prepared tins.
5. Add one at a time to the cooker and secure the tender-crisp lid. Bake 12-15 minutes or until muffins pass the toothpick test. Repeat.
6. Let cool in pan 10 minutes then transfer to wire rack to cool completely.

Nutrition:

- InfoCalories 174,Total Fat 10g,Total Carbs 34g,Protein 3g,Sodium 209mg.

Ham, Egg, And Cheese Breakfast Pockets

Servings:4

Cooking Time: 29 Minutes

Ingredients:

- 5 large eggs, divided
- 1 tablespoon extra-virgin olive oil
- Sea salt
- Freshly ground black pepper
- 1 tube refrigerated crescent rolls
- 4 ounces thinly sliced ham
- 1 cup shredded Cheddar cheese
- Cooking spray

Directions:

1. Select SEAR/SAUTÉ and set to MD:HI. Select START/STOP and let preheat for 5 minutes.
2. Lightly whisk 4 eggs in a medium bowl.
3. Once unit has preheated, add the oil and beaten eggs. Season with salt and pepper. Whisk the eggs until they just begin to set, cooking until soft and translucent, 3 to 5 minutes. Remove the eggs from the pot and set aside.
4. In a small bowl, whisk the remaining egg.
5. Remove the crescent rolls from the tube and divide them into 4 rectangles. Gently roll out each rectangle until it is 6-by-4 inches. Top one half of each rectangle with ham, cheese, and scrambled eggs, leaving about a ½-inch border.
6. Brush the edges of the filled dough with water. Fold over the rectangle and press firmly to seal. Brush the top of each pocket with the egg.
7. Place Cook & Crisp Basket in pot. Coat 2 pastries well on both sides with cooking spray and arrange them in the basket in a single layer. Close crisping lid.
8. Select AIR CRISP, set temperature to 375°F or 190°C, and set time to 12 minutes. Select START/STOP to begin.
9. After 6 minutes, open lid, remove basket, and use silicone-tipped tongs to flip the breakfast pockets. Lower basket back into pot and close lid to continue cooking, until golden brown.
10. When cooking is complete, check for your desired crispiness. Place the pockets on a wire rack to cool. Repeat steps 7, 8, and 9 with the remaining 2 pastries.

Nutrition:

- 2 tbsps red wine vinegar; divided /30ml
- 3 tbsps olive oil /45ml
- ¼ tsp freshly ground black pepper /1.25g
- 1 tsp salt; divided, plus more as needed 5g

Directions:

1. Pour the water into the inner pot and set the reversible rack. Place the potatoes on the rack. Lock the pressure lid into place and set to Seal. Choose Pressure; adjust the pressure to High and the cook time to 4 minutes. Press Start/Stop.
2. After pressure cooking, perform a quick pressure release and carefully open the pressure lid. Take out the rack, empty the water in the pot, and return the pot to the base.
3. Arrange the potatoes and asparagus on the Crisping Basket. Drizzle the half of olive oil on them, and season with salt.
4. Place the basket in the pot. Close the crisping lid; choose Air Crisp, adjust the temperature to 375°F or 190°C, and the cook time to 12 minutes. Press Start.
5. After 8 minutes, open the lid, and check the veggies. The asparagus will have started browning and crisping. Gently toss with the potatoes and close the lid. Continue cooking for the remaining 4 minutes.
6. Take out the basket, pour the asparagus and potatoes into a salad bowl. Sprinkle with 1 tbsp of red wine vinegar and mix to coat.
7. In a bowl, pour the remaining oil, remaining vinegar, salt, and pepper. Whisk to combine.
8. To the potatoes and asparagus, add the roasted red peppers, olives, parsley, and tuna. Drizzle the dressing over the salad and mix to coat. Adjust the seasoning and serve immediately.

Kung Pao Shrimp

Servings: 4

Cooking Time: 15 Minutes

Ingredients:

- 1 tbsp. olive oil
- 1 red bell pepper, seeded & chopped
- 1 green bell pepper, seeded & chopped
- 3 cloves garlic, chopped fine
- 1 lb. large shrimp, peeled & deveined
- ¼ cup soy sauce
- 1 tsp sesame oil
- 1 tsp brown sugar
- 1 tsp Sriracha
- 1/8 tsp red pepper flakes
- 1 tsp cornstarch
- 1 tbsp. water
- ¼ cup peanuts
- ¼ cup green onions, sliced thin

Directions:

1. Add oil to the cooking pot and set to sauté on med-high heat.
2. Add the bell peppers and garlic and cook, 3-5 minutes, until pepper is almost tender.
3. Add the shrimp and cook until they turn pink, 2-3 minutes.
4. In a small bowl, whisk together soy sauce, sesame oil, brown sugar, Sriracha, and pepper flakes until combined.
5. In a separate small bowl, whisk together cornstarch and water until smooth. Whisk into sauce and pour over shrimp mixture. Add the peanuts.
6. Cook, stirring, until the sauce has thickened, about 2-3 minutes. Serve garnished with green onions.

Nutrition:

- InfoCalories 212,Total Fat 11g,Total Carbs 10g,Protein 20g,Sodium 1729mg.

Caramelized Salmon

Servings: 4

Cooking Time: 10 Minutes

Ingredients:

- 1 tbsp. coconut oil, melted
- 1/3 cup Stevia brown sugar, packed
- 3 tbsp. fish sauce
- 1 ½ tbsp. soy sauce
- 1 tsp fresh ginger, peeled & grated
- 2 tsp lime zest, finely grated
- 1 tbsp. fresh lime juice
- ½ tsp pepper
- 4 salmon fillets
- 1 tbsp. green onions, sliced
- 1 tbsp. cilantro chopped

Directions:

1. Add the oil, brown sugar, fish sauce, soy sauce, ginger, zest, juice, and pepper to the cooking pot. Stir to mix.
2. Set to sauté on medium heat and bring mixture to a simmer, stirring frequently. Turn heat off.
3. Add the fish to the sauce making sure it is covered. Add the lid and set to pressure cooking on low. Set the timer for 1 minute.
4. When the timer goes off let the pressure release naturally for 5 minutes, the release it manually. Fish is done when it flakes with a fork.
5. Transfer fish to a serving dish with the caramelized side up.
6. Set cooker back to sauté on medium and cook sauce 3-4 minutes until it's thickened. Spoon over fish and garnish with chopped green onions and scallions. Serve.

Nutrition:

- InfoCalories 316,Total Fat 18g,Total Carbs 5g,Protein 35g,Sodium 1514mg.

Italian Flounder

Servings: 4

Cooking Time: 70 Min

Ingredients:

- 4 flounder fillets
- 3 slices prosciutto; chopped
- 2 bags baby kale /180g
- ½ small red onion; chopped
- ½ cup whipping cream /125ml
- 1 cup panko breadcrumbs /130g
- 2 tbsps chopped fresh parsley /30g
- 3 tbsps unsalted butter, melted and divided /45g
- ¼ tsp fresh ground black pepper /1.25g
- ½ tsp salt; divided /2.5g

Directions:

1. On the Foodi, choose Sear/Sauté and adjust to Medium. Press Start to preheat the inner pot. Add the prosciutto and cook until crispy, about 6 minutes. Stir in the red onions and cook for about 2 minutes or until the onions start to soften. Sprinkle with half of the salt.
2. Fetch the kale into the pot and cook, stirring frequently until wilted and most of the liquid has evaporated, about 4-5 minutes. Mix in the whipping cream.

3.   Lay the flounder fillets over the kale in a single layer. Brush 1 tbsp or 15ml of the melted butter over the fillets and sprinkle with the remaining salt and black pepper.
4.   Close the crisping lid and choose Bake/Roast. Adjust the temperature to 300°F or 150°C and the cook time to 3 minutes. Press Start.
5.   Combine the remaining butter, the parsley and breadcrumbs in a bowl.
6.   When done cooking, open the crisping lid. Spoon the breadcrumbs mixture on the fillets.
7.   Close the crisping lid and Choose Bake/Roast. Adjust the temperature to 400°F or 205°Cand the cook time to 6 minutes. Press Start.
8.   After about 4 minutes, open the lid and check the fish. The breadcrumbs should be golden brown and crisp. If not, close the lid and continue to cook for an additional two minutes.

Buttered Fish

Servings: 4
Cooking Time: 6 Minutes
Ingredients:
- 1-pound fish chunks
- 1 tablespoon vinegar
- 2 drops liquid stevia
- 1/4 cup butter
- Black pepper and salt to taste

Directions:
1.   Select "Sauté" mode on your Ninja Foodi.
2.   Stir in butter and melt it.
3.   Add fish chunks, Sauté for 3 minutes.
4.   Stir in stevia, salt, pepper, stir it.
5.   Close the crisping lid.
6.   Cook on "Air Crisp" mode for 3 minutes to 360 °F or 180°C.
7.   Serve and enjoy.

Nutrition:
- InfoCalories: 274g; Fat: 15g; Carbohydrates: 2g; Protein: 33g

Tuna Zoodle Bake

Servings: 4
Cooking Time: 20 Minutes
Ingredients:
- Nonstick cooking spray
- 2 zucchini, cut in noodles with a spiralizer
- 1tsp olive oil
- ¼ cup onion, chopped fine
- 6 oz. tuna, drained
- ½ tbsp. tomato paste
- ½ cup tomatoes, diced & drained
- ¼ cup skim milk
- ½ tsp thyme
- ¼ tsp salt
- ¼ tsp pepper
- 1/8 cup parmesan cheese, fat free
- 1/4 cup cheddar cheese, reduced fat, grated

Directions:
1.   Spray an 8x8-inch baking pan with cooking spray.
2.   Place the zucchini in an even layer in the prepared pan.
3.   Add the oil to the cooking pot and set to sauté on med-high heat. Once the oil is hot, add the onion and cook 2 minutes, or until soft.

4.   Stir in the tuna and tomato paste and cook 1 minute more. Add the tomatoes, milk, thyme, salt, and pepper and bring to a low simmer. Stir in parmesan cheese and cook until it melts.
5.   Pour the tuna mixture over the zucchini and sprinkle cheddar cheese over the top. Wipe out the pat and place the baking pan in it.
6.   Add the tender-crisp lid and set to bake on 400°F or 205°C. Bake 15 minutes until cheese is melted and bubbly. Serve.

Nutrition:
- InfoCalories 80,Total Fat 3g,Total Carbs 2g,Protein 11g,Sodium 371mg.

Blackened Tilapia With Cilantro-lime Rice And Avocado Salsa

Servings:4
Cooking Time: 12 Minutes
Ingredients:
- 2 cups white rice, rinsed
- 2 cups water
- ¼ cup blackening seasoning
- 4 tilapia fillets
- 2 tablespoons freshly squeezed lime juice, divided
- 1 bunch cilantro, minced
- 1 tablespoon extra-virgin olive oil
- 2 avocados, diced
- 1 large red onion, diced
- 2 Roma tomatoes, diced
- Kosher salt
- Freshly ground black pepper

Directions:
1.   Place the rice and water in the pot and stir. Assemble pressure lid, making sure the pressure release valve is in the SEAL position.
2.   Select PRESSURE and set to HI. Set time to 2 minutes. Select START/STOP to begin.
3.   Place the blackening seasoning on a plate. Dredge the tilapia fillets in the seasoning.
4.   When pressure cooking is complete, allow pressure to naturally release for 10 minutes. After 10 minutes, quick release remaining pressure by turning the pressure release valve to the VENT position. Carefully remove lid when unit has finished releasing pressure.
5.   Transfer the rice to a large bowl and stir in 1 tablespoon of lime juice and half the cilantro. Cover the bowl with aluminum foil and set aside.
6.   Place the Reversible Rack in the pot and arrange tilapia fillets on top. Close crisping lid.
7.   Select BROIL and set time to 10 minutes. Select START/STOP to begin.
8.   In a medium bowl, stir together the remaining cilantro, remaining 1 tablespoon of lime juice, olive oil, avocado, onion, tomato, and season with salt and pepper.
9.   When cooking is complete, open lid and lift the rack out of the pot. Serve the fish over the rice and top with avocado salsa.

Nutrition:
- InfoCalories: 637,Total Fat: 19g,Sodium: 108mg,Carbohydrates: 89g,Protein: 30g.

Sweet Sour Fish

Servings: 4

Cooking Time: 6 Minutes

Ingredients:

- 1-pound fish chunks
- 1 tablespoon vinegar
- 2 drops liquid stevia
- 1/4 cup butter
- Black pepper and salt to taste

Directions:

1. Select "Sauté" mode on your Ninja Foodi.
2. Stir in butter and melt it.
3. Add fish chunks, sauté for 3 minutes.
4. Stir in stevia, salt, pepper, stir it.
5. Close the crisping lid.
6. Cook on "Air Crisp" mode for 3 minutes to 360°F or 180°C.
7. Serve and enjoy.

Nutrition:

- InfoCalories: 274g; Fat: 15g; Carbohydrates: 2g; Protein: 33g

Lemon Cod Goujons And Rosemary Chips

Servings: 4

Cooking Time: 100 Min

Ingredients:

- 4 cod fillets, cut into strips
- 2 potatoes, cut into chips
- 4 lemon wedges to serve
- 2 eggs
- 1 cup arrowroot starch /130g
- 1 cup flour /130g
- 2 tbsps olive oil /30ml
- 3 tbsp fresh rosemary; chopped /45g
- 1 tbsp cumin powder /15g
- ½ tbsp cayenne powder /7.5g
- 1 tsp black pepper, plus more for seasoning /5g
- 1 tsp salt, plus more for seasoning /5g
- Zest and juice from 1 lemon
- Cooking spray

Directions:

1. Fix the Crisping Basket in the pot and close the crisping lid. Choose Air Crisp, set the temperature to 375°F or 190°C, and the time to 5 minutes. Choose Start/Stop to preheat the pot.
2. In a bowl, whisk the eggs, lemon zest, and lemon juice. In another bowl, combine the arrowroot starch, flour, cayenne powder, cumin, black pepper, and salt.
3. Coat each cod strip in the egg mixture, and then dredge in the flour mixture, coating well on all sides. Grease the preheated basket with cooking spray. Place the coated fish in the basket and oil with cooking spray.
4. Close the crisping lid. Choose Air Crisp, set the temperature to 375°F or 190°C, and the time to 15 minutes; press Start/Stop. Toss the potatoes with oil and season with salt and pepper.
5. After 15 minutes, check the fish making sure the pieces are as crispy as desired. Remove the fish from the basket.
6. Pour the potatoes in the basket. Close the crisping lid; choose Air Crisp, set the temperature to 400°F or 205°C, and the time to 24 minutes; press Start/Stop.

7. After 12 minutes, open the lid, remove the basket and shake the fries. Return the basket to the pot and close the lid to continue cooking until crispy.
8. When ready, sprinkle with fresh rosemary. Serve the fish with the potatoes and lemon wedges.

Speedy Clams Pomodoro

Servings: 4

Cooking Time: 10 Minutes

Ingredients:

- 2 dozen clams
- 14 ½ oz. stewed tomatoes, chopped & undrained
- ¼ cup dry white wine
- 2 tbsp. fresh basil, chopped
- ¼ tsp pepper
- 1 lemon, cut in wedges

Directions:

1. Set cooker to sauté on med-high heat.
2. Add all the ingredients to the cooking pot and stir to mix.
3. Add the lid and bring mixture to a boil. Reduce heat to low and simmer 6-8 minutes or until the clams open.
4. Discard any unopened clams and serve immediately with lemon wedges.

Nutrition:

- InfoCalories 123,Total Fat 1g,Total Carbs 12g,Protein 14g,Sodium 715mg.

Caribbean Catfish With Mango Salsa

Servings: 4

Cooking Time: 10 Minutes

Ingredients:

- 1 red pepper, roasted & chopped
- 1 mango, peeled & chopped
- 1 orange, peeled & chopped
- ¼ cup cilantro, chopped fine
- ¼ cup green onion, chopped fine
- 1 tsp jalapeno, chopped
- 1 tbsp. olive oil
- 1 tsp salt, divided
- ½ tsp pepper, divided
- ½ cup panko bread crumbs
- ½ cup coconut, shredded
- 4 catfish fillets
- Nonstick cooking spray

Directions:

1. In a medium bowl, combine red pepper, mango, orange, cilantro, green onion, jalapeno, olive oil, ¼ tsp salt, and ¼ tsp pepper. Cover and let sit until ready to use.
2. In a shallow dish, stir together bread crumbs and coconut until combined.
3. Season catfish with salt and pepper. Dredge in bread crumbs coating both sides thoroughly.
4. Spray the fryer basket with cooking spray. Lay the catfish in the basket in a single layer. Add the tender-crisp lid and set to air fry on 375°F or 190°C. Cook fish 8-10 minutes per side until golden brown and fish flakes easily with a fork.
5. Transfer fish to serving plates and top with mango salsa. Serve immediately.

- InfoCalories 357,Total Fat 12g,Total Carbs 34g,Protein 30g,Sodium 534mg.

Sweet & Spicy Shrimp Bowls

Servings: 8
Cooking Time: 5 Minutes

Ingredients:

- ½ cup green onions, chopped
- 1 jalapeno pepper, seeded & chopped
- 1 tsp red chili flakes
- 8 oz. crushed pineapple, drained
- 2 tbsp. honey
- 1 lime, zested & juiced
- 1 tbsp. olive oil
- 2 lbs. large shrimp, peeled & deveined
- ¼ tsp salt
- 2 cups brown rice, cooked

Directions:

1. In a small bowl, combine green onions, jalapeno, chili flakes, pineapple, honey, lime juice, and zest and mix well.
2. Add the oil to the cooking pot and set to saute on medium heat.
3. Sprinkle the shrimp with salt and cook, 3-5 minutes or until they turn pink.
4. Add the shrimp to the pineapple mixture and stir to coat.
5. Spoon rice into bowls and top with shrimp mixture. Serve immediately.

Nutrition:

- InfoCalories 188,Total Fat 3g,Total Carbs 23g,Protein 17g,Sodium 644mg.

Paella Señorito

Servings: 5
Cooking Time: 25 Min

Ingredients:

- 1 pound frozen shrimp, peeled and deveined /450g
- 2 garlic cloves, minced
- 1 onion; chopped
- 1 lemon, cut into wedges
- 1 red bell pepper; diced
- 2 cups fish broth /500ml
- ¼ cup olive oil /62.5ml
- 1 cup bomba rice /130g
- ¼ cup frozen green peas /32.5g
- 1 tsp paprika /5g
- 1 tsp turmeric /5g
- salt and ground white pepper to taste
- chopped fresh parsley

Directions:

1. Warm oil on Sear/Sauté. Add in bell pepper and onions and cook for 5 minutes until fragrant. Mix in garlic and cook for one more minute until soft.
2. Add paprika, ground white pepper, salt and turmeric to the vegetables and cook for 1 minute.
3. Stir in fish broth and rice. Add shrimp in the rice mixture. Seal the pressure lid, choose Pressure, set to High, and set the timer to 5 minutes; press Start. When ready, release the pressure quickly.
4. Stir in green peas and let sit for 5 minutes until green peas are heated through. Serve warm garnished with parsley and lemon wedges.

Salmon Florentine

Servings: 4
Cooking Time: 15 Minutes

Ingredients:

- 2 tbsp. olive oil, divided
- 4 salmon filets
- ½ tsp salt
- ¼ tsp pepper
- 4 cloves garlic, chopped fine
- 10 oz. fresh spinach
- ½ tbsp. lemon juice
- ¼ tsp basil

Directions:

1. Add 1 tablespoon oil to the cooking pot and set to sauté on medium heat.
2. Season salmon with salt and pepper and add to the pot. Cook 8-10 minutes or until fish flakes easily with a fork, turning over halfway through cooking time. Transfer to a plate.
3. Add remaining oil and let heat up. Add remaining ingredients and cook 2-3 minutes until spinach is wilted.
4. Place fish on serving plates and top with spinach mixture. Serve immediately.

Nutrition:

- InfoCalories 436,Total Fat 30g,Total Carbs 4g,Protein 37g,Sodium 448mg.

Poached Flounder With Mango Salsa

Servings: 6
Cooking Time: 10 Minutes

Ingredients:

- 1 mango, peeled, pitted & chopped
- 1 red bell pepper, seeded & chopped
- ½ red onion, chopped fine
- 8 ¼ oz. pineapple tidbits, drain & reserve juice
- ¼ tsp salt, divided
- ½ tsp red pepper, divided
- 6 flounder filets
- ½ cup water

Directions:

1. In a medium bowl, combine mango, bell pepper, onion, pineapple, 1/8 teaspoon salt, and ¼ teaspoon pepper, mix well. Cover and refrigerate at least one hour.
2. Season fish with remaining salt and pepper and place in the cooking pot. Pour reserved pineapple juice and water over the fish.
3. Add the lid and set to sauté on med-high heat. Bring to a boil then reduce heat to low and cook 7-8 minutes or until fish flakes easily with a fork.
4. Transfer to fish to serving plates and top with mango salsa. Serve immediately.

Nutrition:

- InfoCalories 200,Total Fat 4g,Total Carbs 17g,Protein 24g,Sodium 1092mg.

Simple Salmon & Asparagus

Servings: 4
Cooking Time: 15 Minutes

Ingredients:

- 4 salmon filets
- 1 tsp rosemary
- ½ tsp pepper, divided
- 14 oz. vegetable broth, low sodium
- 1 tbsp. lemon juice
- ½ lb. asparagus, trimmed & cut in 2-inch pieces

Directions:

1. Season the fish with rosemary and ¼ teaspoon pepper and add to cooking pot.
2. In a small bowl, whisk together broth, lemon juice, and remaining pepper until smooth. Pour over fish.
3. Add the lid and set to sauté on medium heat. Once mixture reaches a boil, reduce heat to low and simmer 5 minutes.
4. Add the asparagus around the salmon, recover, and cook another 5 minutes until asparagus is fork-tender and fish flakes easily. Serve immediately..

Nutrition:

- InfoCalories 163,Total Fat 5g,Total Carbs 3g,Protein 25g,Sodium 454mg.

Shrimp And Chorizo Potpie

Servings:6

Cooking Time: 23 Minutes

Ingredients:

- ¼ cup unsalted butter
- ½ large onion, diced
- 1 celery stalk, diced
- 1 carrot, peeled and diced
- 8 ounces chorizo, fully cooked, cut into ½-inch wheels
- ¼ cup all-purpose flour
- 16 ounces frozen tail-off shrimp, cleaned and deveined
- ¾ cup chicken stock
- 1 tablespoon Cajun spice mix
- ½ cup heavy (whipping) cream
- Sea salt
- Freshly ground black pepper
- 1 refrigerated store-bought pie crust, at room temperature

Directions:

1. Select SEAR/SAUTÉ and set to MD:HI. Select START/STOP to begin. Let preheat for 5 minutes.
2. Add the butter. Once melted, add the onion, celery, carrot, and sausage, and cook until softened, about 3 minutes. Stir in the flour and cook 2 minutes, stirring occasionally.
3. Add the shrimp, stock, Cajun spice mix, and cream and season with salt and pepper. Stir until sauce thickens and bubbles, about 3 minutes.
4. Lay the pie crust evenly on top of the filling, folding over the edges if necessary. Make a small cut in center of pie crust so that steam can escape during baking. Close crisping lid.
5. Select BROIL and set time to 10 minutes. Select START/STOP to begin.
6. When cooking is complete, open lid and remove pot from unit. Let rest 10 to 15 minutes before serving.

Nutrition:

- InfoCalories: 528,Total Fat: 37g,Sodium: 776mg,Carbohydrates: 19g,Protein: 28g.

Salmon Kale Meal

Servings: 4

Cooking Time: 4 Minutes

Ingredients:

- 1 lemon, juiced
- 2 salmon fillets
- 1/4 cup extra virgin olive oil
- 1 teaspoon Dijon mustard
- 4 cups kale, sliced, ribs removed
- 1 teaspoon salt
- 1 avocado, diced
- 1 cup pomegranate seeds
- 1 cup walnuts, toasted
- 1 cup goat parmesan cheese, shredded

Directions:

1. Season salmon with salt and keep it on the side.
2. Place a trivet in your Ninja Foodi.
3. Place salmon over the trivet.
4. Release pressure naturally over 10 minutes.
5. Transfer salmon to a serving platter.
6. Take a suitable and stir in kale, season with salt.
7. Season kale with dressing and add diced avocado, pomegranate seeds, walnuts and cheese.
8. Toss and serve with the fish.
9. Enjoy.

Nutrition:

- InfoCalories: 234; Fat: 14g; Carbohydrates: 12g; Protein: 16g

Haddock With Sanfaina

Servings: 4

Cooking Time: 40 Min

Ingredients:

- 4 haddock fillets
- 1 can diced tomatoes, drained /435g
- ½ small onion; sliced
- 1 small jalapeño pepper, seeded and minced
- 2 large garlic cloves, minced
- 1 eggplant; cubed
- 1 bell pepper; chopped
- 1 bay leaf
- ⅓ cup sliced green olives /44g
- ¼ cup chopped fresh chervil; divided /32.5g
- 3 tbsps olive oil /45ml
- 3 tbsps capers; divided/45g
- ½ tsp dried basil /2.5g
- ¼ tsp salt /1.25g

Directions:

1. Season the fish on both sides with salt, place in the refrigerator, and make the sauce. Press Sear/Sauté and set to Medium. Press Start. Melt the butter until no longer foaming. Add onion, eggplant, bell pepper, jalapeño, and garlic; sauté for 5 minutes.
2. Stir in the tomatoes, bay leaf, basil, olives, half of the chervil, and half of the capers. Remove the fish from the refrigerator and lay on the vegetables in the pot.
3. Seal the pressure lid, choose Pressure; adjust the pressure to Low and the cook time to 3 minutes; press Start. After cooking, do a quick pressure release and carefully open the lid. Remove and discard the bay leaf.
4. Transfer the fish to a serving platter and spoon the sauce over. Sprinkle with the remaining chervil and capers. Serve.

Cod Cornflakes Nuggets

Servings: 4

Cooking Time: 25 Min

Ingredients:

- 1 ¼ lb. cod fillets, cut into chunks /662.5g
- 1 egg
- 1 cup cornflakes /130g
- ½ cup flour /65g
- 1 tbsp olive oil/15ml
- 1 tbsp water /15ml
- Salt and pepper, to taste

Directions:

1. Add the oil and cornflakes in a food processor, and process until crumbed. Season the fish chunks with salt and pepper.
2. Beat the egg along with 1 tbsp or 15ml water. Dredge the chunks in flour first, then dip in the egg, and coat with cornflakes. Arrange on a lined sheet. Close the crisping lid and cook at 350 °F or 175°C for 15 minutes on Air Crisp mode.

New England Lobster Rolls

Servings:4

Cooking Time: 20 Minutes

Ingredients:

- 4 lobster tails
- ¼ cup mayonnaise
- 1 celery stalk, minced
- Zest of 1 lemon
- Juice of 1 lemon
- ¼ teaspoon celery seed
- Kosher salt
- Freshly ground black pepper
- 4 split-top hot dog buns
- 4 tablespoons unsalted butter, at room temperature
- 4 leaves butter lettuce

Directions:

1. Insert Cook & Crisp Basket into the pot and close the crisping lid. Select AIR CRISP, set temperature to 375°F or 190°C, and set time to 15 minutes. Select START/STOP to begin. Let preheat for 5 minutes.
2. Once unit has preheated, open lid and add the lobster tails to the basket. Close the lid and cook for 10 minutes.
3. In a medium bowl, mix together the mayonnaise, celery, lemon zest and juice, and celery seed, and add salt and pepper.
4. Fill a large bowl with a tray of ice cubes and enough water to cover the ice.
5. When cooking is complete, open lid. Transfer the lobster into the ice bath for 5 minutes. Close lid to keep unit warm.
6. Spread butter on the hot dog buns. Open lid and place the buns in the basket. Close crisping lid.
7. Select AIR CRISP, set temperature to 375°F or 190°C, and set time to 4 minutes. Select START/STOP to begin.
8. Remove the lobster meat from the shells and roughly chop. Place in the bowl with the mayonnaise mixture and stir.
9. When cooking is complete, open lid and remove the buns. Place lettuce in each bun, then fill with the lobster salad.

Nutrition:

- InfoCalories: 408,Total Fat: 24g,Sodium: 798mg,Carbohydrates: 22g,Protein: 26g.

Farfalle Tuna Casserole With Cheese

Servings: 4

Cooking Time: 60 Min

Ingredients:

- 6 ounces farfalle /180g
- 1 can full cream milk; divided /360ml
- 2 cans tuna, drained /180g
- 1 medium onion; chopped
- 1 large carrot; chopped
- 1 cup vegetable broth /250ml
- 2 cups shredded Monterey Jack cheese /260g
- 1 cup chopped green beans /130g
- 2½ cups panko bread crumbs /325g
- 3 tbsps butter, melted /45ml
- 1 tbsp olive oil/ 15ml
- 1 tsp salt/ 5g
- 2 tsp s corn starch /10g

Directions:

1. On the Foodi, Choose Sear/Sauté and adjust to Medium. Press Start to preheat the pot.
2. Heat the oil until shimmering and sauté the onion and carrots for 3 minutes, stirring, until softened.
3. Add the farfalle, ¾ cup or 188ml of milk, broth, and salt to the pot. Stir to combine and submerge the farfalle in the liquid with a spoon.
4. Seal the pressure lid, choose pressure; adjust the pressure to Low and the cook time to 5 minutes; press Start. After cooking, do a quick pressure release and carefully open the pressure lid.
5. Choose Sear/Sauté and adjust to Less for low heat. Press Start. Pour the remaining milk on the farfalle.
6. In a medium bowl, mix the cheese and cornstarch evenly and add the cheese mixture by large handfuls to the sauce while stirring until the cheese melts and the sauce thickens. Add the tuna and green beans, gently stir. Heat for 2 minutes.
7. In another bowl, mix the crumbs and melted butter well. Spread the crumbs over the casserole. Close the crisping lid and press Broil. Adjust the cook time to 5 minutes; press Start. When ready, the topping should be crisp and brown. If not, broil for 2 more minutes. Serve immediately.

Sweet & Spicy Shrimp

Servings: 4

Cooking Time: 5 Minutes

Ingredients:

- ¾ cup pineapple juice, unsweetened
- 1 red bell pepper, sliced
- 1 ½ cups cauliflower, grated
- ¼ cup dry white wine
- ½ cup water
- 2 tbsp. soy sauce
- 2 tbsp. Thai sweet chili sauce
- 1 tbsp. chili paste
- 1 lb. large shrimp, frozen
- 4 green onions, chopped, white & green separated
- 1 ½ cups pineapple chunks, drained

Directions:

1. Add ¾ cup pineapple juice along with remaining ingredients, except the pineapple chunks and green parts of the onion, to the cooking pot. Stir to mix.
2. Add the lid and set to pressure cook on high. Set timer for 2 minutes. When the timer goes off, release pressure 10 minutes before opening the pot.
3. Add the green parts of the onions and pineapple chunks and stir well. Serve immediately.

Nutrition:

- InfoCalories 196,Total Fat 1g,Total Carbs 22g,Protein 26g,Sodium 764mg.

Salmon, Cashew & Kale Bowl

Servings: 6

Cooking Time: 15 Minutes

Ingredients:

- 12 oz. salmon filets, skin off
- 2 tbsp. olive oil, divided
- ½ tsp salt
- ¼ tsp pepper
- 2 cloves garlic, chopped fine
- 4 cups kale, stems removed & chopped
- ½ cup carrot, grated
- 2 cups quinoa, cooked according to package directions
- ¼ cup cashews, chopped

Directions:

1. Place the rack in the cooking pot and set to bake on 400°F or 205°C. Place a sheet of parchment paper on the rack.
2. Brush the salmon with 1 tablespoon of oil and season with salt and pepper. Place the fish on the parchment paper.
3. Add the tender-crisp lid and cook 15 minutes or until salmon reaches desired doneness. Transfer the fish to a plate and keep warm.
4. Set the cooker to sauté on medium heat and add the remaining oil. Once the oil is hot, add garlic, kale, and carrot and cook, stirring frequently, until kale is wilted and soft, about 2-3 minutes.
5. Add the quinoa and cashews and cook just until heated through. Spoon mixture evenly into bowl and top with a piece of salmon. Serve immediately.

Nutrition:

- InfoCalories 294,Total Fat 17g,Total Carbs 18g,Protein 17g,Sodium 243mg.

Seafood Minestrone

Servings: 14

Cooking Time: 20 Minutes

Ingredients:

- 3 14 oz. cans beef broth, low sodium
- 28 oz. tomatoes, crushed
- 19 oz. garbanzo beans, undrained
- 15 ¼ oz. red kidney beans, undrained
- 16 oz. pkg. frozen mixed vegetables, thawed
- 16 oz. frozen spinach, thawed, chopped & drained
- 1 onion, chopped
- 1 tsp garlic powder
- ½ tsp pepper
- ½ cup elbow macaroni, uncooked
- 1 lb. cod, cut in 1-inch pieces
- 1 lb. shrimp, peeled & deveined

Directions:

1. Set cooker to sauté on med-high. Add the broth, tomatoes, garbanzo beans, kidney beans, vegetables, spinach, onion, and seasonings to the cooking pot, stir to mix. Bring to a boil.
2. Stir in the macaroni and cook until tender, about 8 minutes.
3. Reduce the heat to med-low and add the fish and shrimp. Cook 5-7 minutes until shrimp turn pink and fish flakes easily. Serve immediately.

Nutrition:

- InfoCalories 292,Total Fat 3g,Total Carbs 42g,Protein 25g,Sodium 645mg.

Air Fried Scallops

Servings: 4

Cooking Time: 5 Minutes

Ingredients:

- 12 scallops
- 3 tablespoons olive oil
- Black pepper and salt, to taste

Directions:

1. Rub the scallops with salt, pepper and olive oil.
2. Transfer it to Ninja foodi.
3. Place the insert in your Ninja foodi.
4. Close the air crisping lid.
5. Cook for 4 minutes to 390°F or 200°C.
6. Flip them after 2 minutes.
7. Serve and enjoy.

Nutrition:

- InfoCalories: 372g; Fat: 11g; Carbohydrates: 0.9g; Protein: 63g

Roasted Bbq Shrimp

Servings: 2

Cooking Time: 7 Minutes

Ingredients:

- 3 tablespoons chipotle in adobo sauce, minced
- 1/4 teaspoon salt
- 1/4 cup BBQ sauce
- 1/2 orange, juiced
- 1/2-pound large shrimps

Directions:

1. Toss shrimp with chipotles and rest of the ingredients in a suitable bowl.
2. Preheat Ninja Foodi by pressing the "Bake/Roast" mode and setting it to "400 °F or 205°C" and timer to 7 minutes.
3. Let it preheat until you hear a beep.
4. Set shrimps over Grill Grate and lock lid, cook until the timer runs out.
5. Serve and enjoy.

Nutrition:

- InfoCalories: 173; Fat: 2g; Carbohydrates: 21g; Protein: 17g

Glazed Salmon

Servings: 4

Cooking Time: 25 Minutes

Ingredients:

- 1-2 Coho salmon filets

- 1 cup of water
- 1/4 cup of soy sauce
- 1/4 cup brown erythritol
- 1 tablespoon choc zero maple syrup
- 1 and 1/2 tablespoons ginger roots, minced
- 1/2 teaspoon white pepper
- 2 tablespoons cornstarch
- 1/4 cup of cold water

Directions:

1. Preheat Ninja Foodi by pressing the "GRILL" option and setting it to "HIGH" for 15 minutes.
2. Take a medium saucepan over medium heat, combine sauce ingredients. except for salmon, cornstarch and cold water and bring to a low boil.
3. Then add cornstarch and water in another bowl, whisk cornstarch mixture slowly into sauce until it thickens.
4. Stir in one chunk of pecan wood to the hot coal of your grill.
5. Brush sauce onto the salmon filet.
6. Place on the grill grate, then close the hood.
7. Cook for 15 minutes.
8. Brush the salmon with another coat of sauce.
9. Serve and enjoy.

Nutrition:

- InfoCalories: 163; Fat: 0g; Carbohydrates: 15g; Protein: 0g

Cheesy Crab Pie

Servings: 8
Cooking Time: 40 Minutes

Ingredients:

- 1 cup cheddar cheese, grated
- 1 pie crust, uncooked
- 1 cup crab meat
- 3 eggs
- 1 cup half and half, fat free
- ½ tsp salt
- ¼ tsp pepper
- ½ tsp lemon zest

Directions:

1. Place the rack in the cooking pot.
2. Spread the cheese in an even layer in the bottom of the pie crust. Top with crab.
3. In a medium bowl, whisk together remaining ingredients until combined. Pour over crab.
4. Place the pie on the rack and add the tender-crisp lid. Set to bake on 325°F or 165°C. Bake 40 minutes until filling is set and the top is lightly browned. Let cool 10 minutes before serving.

Nutrition:

- InfoCalories 246,Total Fat 14g,Total Carbs 18g,Protein 11g,Sodium 469mg.

Garlic Shrimp And Veggies

Servings:4
Cooking Time: 5 Minutes

Ingredients:

- 2 tablespoons unsalted butter
- 1 shallot, minced
- 3 garlic cloves, minced
- ¼ cup white wine
- ½ cup chicken stock
- Juice of ½ lemon

- ½ teaspoon sea salt
- ½ teaspoon freshly ground black pepper
- 1½ pounds frozen shrimp, thawed
- 1 large head broccoli, cut into florets

Directions:

1. Add the butter. Select SEAR/SAUTÉ and set to MED. Select START/STOP to begin.
2. Once the butter is melted, add the shallots and cook for 3 minutes. Add the garlic and cook for 1 minute.
3. Deglaze the pot by adding the wine and using a wooden spoon to scrape the bits of garlic and shallot off the bottom of the pot. Stir in the chicken stock, lemon juice, salt, pepper, and shrimp.
4. Place the broccoli florets on top of the shrimp mixture. Assemble pressure lid, making sure the pressure release valve is in the SEAL position.
5. Select PRESSURE and set to HI. Set time to 0 minutes. Select START/STOP to begin.
6. When pressure cooking is complete, quick release the pressure by moving the pressure release valve to the VENT position. Carefully remove lid when the unit has finished releasing pressure. Serve immediately.

Nutrition:

- InfoCalories: 281,Total Fat: 8g,Sodium: 692mg,Carbohydrates: 9g,Protein: 39g.

Crab Cakes With Spicy Dipping Sauce

Servings: 4
Cooking Time: 20 Minutes

Ingredients:

- Nonstick cooking spray
- 1/3 cup + ¼ cup mayonnaise, divided
- 1 tbsp. + 2 tsp spicy brown mustard, divided
- 1 tsp hot sauce
- ¼ cup + 1 tbsp. celery, chopped fine, divided
- ¼ cup + 1 tbsp. red bell pepper, chopped fine, divided
- 4 tsp Cajun seasoning, divided
- 2 tbsp. fresh parsley, chopped, divided
- 8 oz. jumbo lump crab meat
- ¼ cup green bell pepper, chopped fine
- 2 tbsp. green onions, chopped fine
- ¼ cup bread crumbs

Directions:

1. Spray the fryer basket with cooking spray.
2. In a small bowl, combine 1/3 cup mayonnaise, 2 teaspoons mustard, hot sauce, 1 tablespoon celery, 1 tablespoon red bell pepper, 2 teaspoons Cajun seasoning, and 1 tablespoon parsley, mix well. Cover and refrigerate until ready to use.
3. In a large bowl, combine all remaining ingredients with the crab, green bell pepper, onions, and bread crumbs, mix well. Form into 8 patties.
4. Place the patties in the fryer basket and add the tender-crisp lid. Set to air fry on 400 °F or 205°C. Cook 20 minutes, or until golden brown, turning over halfway through cooking time.
5. Serve with prepared sauce for dipping.

Nutrition:

- InfoCalories 166,Total Fat 8g,Total Carbs 11g,Protein 11g,Sodium 723mg.

Shrimp Egg Rolls

Servings: 10
Cooking Time: 10 Minutes
Ingredients:
- Nonstick cooking spray
- ¼ cup soy sauce, low sodium
- 2 tbsp. brown sugar
- 1 tsp ginger, grated
- 1 tsp garlic powder
- 5 cups coleslaw mix
- 2 green onions, sliced thin
- 3 tbsp. cilantro, chopped
- 1 cup small shrimp, chopped
- 10 egg roll wrappers

Directions:
1. Spray the fryer basket with cooking spray.
2. In a small bowl, whisk together, soy sauce, brown sugar, ginger, and garlic powder until combined.
3. In a large bowl, combine coleslaw, green onions, cilantro, and shrimp and mix well.
4. Pour the soy sauce over the coleslaw and toss well to coat. Let sit 15 minutes. After 15 minutes, place in a colander and squeeze to remove as much liquid as possible.
5. Place egg roll wrappers on a work surface. Spoon about 1/3 cup of shrimp mixture in the center of each wrapper. Fold opposite sides over filling, then one corner and roll up egg roll fashion. Place seam side down in fryer basket and spray lightly with cooking spray.
6. Add the tender-crisp lid and set to air fry on 425°F or 220°C. Cook 8-10 minutes until golden brown and crisp, turning over halfway through cooking time.

Nutrition:
- InfoCalories 138,Total Fat 1g,Total Carbs 24g,Protein 7g,Sodium 532mg.

Fish Broccoli Stew

Servings: 4
Cooking Time: 20 Minutes
Ingredients:
- 1-pound white fish fillets, chopped
- 1 cup broccoli, chopped
- 3 cups fish stock
- 1 onion, diced
- 2 cups celery stalks, chopped
- 1 cup heavy cream
- 1 bay leaf
- 1 and 1/2 cups cauliflower, diced
- 1 carrot, sliced
- 2 tablespoons butter
- 1/4 teaspoon garlic powder
- 1/2 teaspoon salt
- 1/4 teaspoon black pepper

Directions:
1. Select "Sauté" mode on your Ninja Foodi.
2. Add butter, and let it melt.
3. Stir in onion and carrots, cook for 3 minutes.
4. Stir in remaining ingredients.
5. Close the Ninja Foodi's lid.
6. Cook for 4 minutes on High.
7. Release the pressure naturally over 10 minutes.
8. Remove the bay leave once cooked.

9. Serve and enjoy.
Nutrition:
- InfoCalories: 298g; Fat: 18g; Carbohydrates: 6g; Protein: 24g

Stir Fried Scallops & Veggies

Servings: 6
Cooking Time: 15 Minutes
Ingredients:
- 2 tbsp. peanut oil
- 3 cloves garlic, chopped fine
- 1 tsp crushed red pepper flakes
- 1 lb. bay scallops
- 2 tbsp. sesame seeds
- 1 ½ tsp ginger
- 1 head bok choy, trimmed and chopped
- 16 oz. stir-fry vegetables
- 1 tbsp. soy sauce, low sodium

Directions:
1. Add the oil to the cooking pot and set to saute on med-high heat.
2. Add the garlic, red pepper flakes, and scallops and cook until scallops are golden brown and cooked. Transfer scallops to a bowl and keep warm.
3. Add the sesame seeds and ginger and cook, stirring, 1-2 minutes until all the liquid is gone.
4. Add the cabbage and vegetables and cook 4-5 minutes, stirring occasionally.
5. Add the soy sauce and return the scallops to the pot. Cook 1-2 minutes more until heated through. Serve immediately.

Nutrition:
- InfoCalories 172,Total Fat 5g,Total Carbs 17g,Protein 15g,Sodium 485mg.

Drunken Saffron Mussels

Servings:4
Cooking Time: 25 Minutes
Ingredients:
- 2 tablespoons vegetable oil
- 2 shallots, sliced
- 3 garlic cloves, minced
- 1 cup cherry tomatoes, halved
- 2 pounds fresh mussels, washed with cold water, strained, scrubbed, and debearded, as needed
- 2 cups white wine (chardonnay or sauvignon blanc)
- 2 cups heavy cream
- 1½ teaspoons cayenne pepper
- 1½ teaspoons freshly ground black pepper
- ½ teaspoon saffron threads
- 1 loaf sourdough bread, cut into slices, for serving

Directions:
1. Select SEAR/SAUTÉ and set the temperature to HI. Select START/STOP to begin and allow to preheat for 5 minutes.
2. Add oil to the pot and allow to heat for 1 minute. Add the shallots, garlic, and cherry tomatoes. Stir to ensure the ingredients are coated and sauté for 5 minutes.
3. Add the mussels, wine, heavy cream, cayenne, black pepper, and saffron threads to the pot.

4. Assemble the pressure lid, making sure the pressure release valve is in the VENT position.
5. Select STEAM and set the temperature to HI. Set the time to 20 minutes. Select START/STOP to begin.
6. When cooking is complete, carefully remove the lid.
7. Transfer the mussels and broth to bowls or eat straight from the pot. Discard any mussels that have not opened.
8. Serve with the bread and enjoy!

Nutrition:
- InfoCalories: 882,Total Fat: 54g,Sodium: 769mg,Carbohydrates: 61g,Protein: 20g.

Low Country Boil

Servings:6
Cooking Time: 10 Minutes

Ingredients:
- 2 pounds Red Bliss potatoes, diced
- 3 ears corn, cut crosswise into thirds
- 1 package smoked sausage or kielbasa, sliced into 1-inch pieces
- 4 cups water
- 2½ tablespoons Creole seasoning
- 1 pound medium shrimp, peeled and deveined

Directions:
1. Place the potatoes, corn, sausage, water, and Creole seasoning into the pot and stir. Assemble pressure lid, making sure the pressure release valve is in the SEAL position.
2. Select PRESSURE and set to HI. Set time to 5 minutes. Select START/STOP to begin.
3. When pressure cooking is complete, quick release the pressure by turning the pressure release valve to the VENT position. Carefully remove lid when unit has finished releasing pressure.
4. Stir in the shrimp.
5. Select SEAR/SAUTÉ and set to MD:LO. Simmer for about 5 minutes, until the shrimp is cooked through.
6. When cooking is complete, serve immediately.

Nutrition:
- InfoCalories: 445,Total Fat: 20g,Sodium: 1251mg,Carbohydrates: 40g,Protein: 28g.

Coconut Shrimp

Servings: 2
Cooking Time: 30 Min

Ingredients:
- 8 large shrimp
- ½ cup orange jam /65g
- ½ cup shredded coconut /65g
- ½ cup breadcrumbs /65g
- 8 oz. coconut milk /240ml
- 1 tbsp honey /15ml
- ½ tsp cayenne pepper/2.5g
- ¼ tsp hot sauce /1.25ml
- 1 tsp mustard /5g
- ¼ tsp salt /1.25g
- ¼ tsp pepper /1.25g

Directions:
1. Combine the breadcrumbs, cayenne pepper, shredded coconut, salt, and pepper in a small bowl. Dip the shrimp in the coconut milk, first, and then in the coconut crumbs.
2. Arrange in the lined Ninja Foodi basket, close the crisping lid and cook for 20 minutes on Air Crisp mode at 350 °F or 175°C.

3. Meanwhile whisk the jam, honey, hot sauce, and mustard. Serve the shrimp with the sauce.

Coconut Shrimp With Pineapple Rice

Servings:4
Cooking Time: 45 Minutes

Ingredients:
- 2 tablespoons canola oil
- 1 can diced pineapple
- 1 yellow onion, diced
- 1 cup long-grain white rice
- 1½ cups chicken stock
- ½ cup freshly squeezed lime juice
- ¾ cup all-purpose flour
- 1 tablespoon kosher salt
- ½ teaspoon freshly ground black pepper
- 2 large eggs
- ½ cup coconut flakes
- ½ cup plain panko bread crumbs
- 10 ounces, deveined shrimp, tails removed
- Cooking spray

Directions:
1. Select SEAR/SAUTÉ and set temperature to HI. Select START/STOP to begin. Let preheat for 5 minutes.
2. Add the oil and heat for 1 minute. Add the pineapple and onion. Cook, stirring frequently, for about 8 minutes, or until the onion is translucent.
3. Add the rice, chicken stock, and lime juice. Assemble pressure lid, making sure the pressure release valve is in the SEAL position.
4. Select PRESSURE and set to HI. Set time to 2 minutes. Select START/STOP to begin.
5. When pressure cooking is complete, allow press to naturally release for 10 minutes. After 10 minutes, quick release remaining pressure by turning the pressure release valve to the VENT position. Carefully remove lid when unit has finished releasing pressure.
6. Transfer the rice mixture to a bowl and cover to keep warm. Clean the cooking pot and return to the unit.
7. Create a batter station with three medium bowls. In the first bowl, mix together the flour, salt and pepper. In the second bowl, whisk the eggs. In the third bowl, combine the coconut flakes and bread crumbs. Dip each shrimp into the flour mixture. Next dip it in the egg. Finally, coat in the coconut mixture, shaking off excess as needed. Once all the shrimp are battered, spray them with cooking spray.
8. Place Cook & Crisp Basket into pot. Place the shrimp in basket and close crisping lid.
9. Select AIR CRISP, set temperature to 390°F or 200°C, and set time to 10 minutes. Select START/STOP to begin.
10. After 5 minutes, open lid, then lift basket and shake the shrimp. Lower basket back into the pot and close the lid to continue cooking until the shrimp reach your desired crispiness.
11. When cooking is complete, serve the shrimp on top of the rice.

Nutrition:
- InfoCalories: 601,Total Fat: 15g,Sodium: 784mg,Carbohydrates: 88g,Protein: 28g.

Shrimp & Sausage Gumbo

Servings: 8
Cooking Time: 1 Hour 30 Minutes

Ingredients:

- ½ cup peanut oil
- ½ cup flour
- 1 green bell pepper, chopped
- 1 onion, chopped
- 3 stalks celery, chopped
- 4 cloves garlic, chopped fine
- 1 tbsp. Cajun seasoning
- 1 quart chicken broth, low sodium
- 1 cup water
- 2 tsp Worcestershire sauce
- ¼ tsp pepper
- ½ tsp salt
- 12 oz. smoked andouille sausage, sliced ¼-inch thick
- 2 lbs. shrimp, peeled & deveined
- 3 green onions, chopped
- Hot sauce to taste

Directions:

1. Add the oil to the cooking pot and set to sauté on medium heat. Whisk in the flour until smooth. Cook, stirring until roux is a golden brown. Reduce heat to med-low and cook 20-30 minutes until roux is a deep brown.
2. Add the bell pepper, onion, and celery and increase heat to med-high. Cook, stirring frequently about 5 minutes. Add the garlic and cook 2 minutes more. Stir in Cajun seasoning.
3. Stirring constantly, slowly add the broth and water. Bring to a simmer and add the Worcestershire, pepper, and salt. Reduce heat to medium and simmer 30 minutes.
4. Add the sausage and cook until heated through, about 5 minutes. Add the shrimp and cook until they turn pink, about 5 minutes. Serve garnished with green onions and hot sauce to taste over cooked rice.

Nutrition:

- InfoCalories 111,Total Fat 7g,Total Carbs 4g,Protein 8g,Sodium 207mg.

Coconut Curried Mussels

Servings: 4
Cooking Time: 20 Minutes

Ingredients:

- 2 tbsp. water
- ½ cup onion, chopped fine
- ½ cup red bell pepper, seeded & chopped fine
- 3 cloves garlic, chopped fine
- ½ tsp pepper
- 2 tbsp. curry powder
- 1 cup coconut milk, unsweetened
- ½ cup vegetable broth
- 2 lbs. mussels, washed & cleaned
- ¼ cup cilantro, chopped

Directions:

1. Add the water, onion, bell pepper, and garlic to the cooking pot. Set to sauté on medium heat and cook, stirring occasionally until onions are soft, about 5-8 minutes, add more water if needed to prevent vegetables from sticking.
2. Stir in pepper, curry powder, coconut milk, and broth, stir well until smooth. Bring up to a simmer and add the mussels.
3. Add the lid and cook 5-6 minutes, or until all the mussels have opened. Discard any that do not open. Ladle into bowls and garnish with cilantro. Serve.

Nutrition:

- InfoCalories 331,Total Fat 18g,Total Carbs 15g,Protein 29g,Sodium 664mg.

Crab Cake Casserole

Servings:8
Cooking Time: 17 Minutes

Ingredients:

- 2 tablespoons canola oil
- 1 large onion, chopped
- 2 celery stalks, chopped
- 1 red bell pepper, chopped
- 1½ cups basmati rice, rinsed
- 2 cups chicken stock
- ¼ cup mayonnaise
- ¼ cup Dijon mustard
- 3 cans lump crab meat
- 1 cup shredded Cheddar cheese, divided
- 1 sleeve butter crackers, crumbled

Directions:

1. Select SEAR/SAUTÉ and set to HI. Select START/STOP to begin. Let preheat for 5 minutes.
2. Add the oil. Once hot, add the onion, celery, and bell pepper and stir. Cook for 5 minutes, stirring occasionally.
3. Stir in the rice and chicken stock. Assemble pressure lid, making sure the pressure release valve is in the SEAL position.
4. Select PRESSURE and set to HI. Set time to 2 minutes. Select START/STOP to begin.
5. When pressure cooking is complete, allow pressure to naturally release for 10 minutes. After 10 minutes, quick release any remaining pressure by moving the pressure release valve to the VENT position. Carefully remove lid when unit has finished releasing pressure.
6. Stir in the mayonnaise, mustard, crab, and ½ cup of Cheddar cheese. Top evenly with the crackers, then top with remaining ½ cup of cheese. Close crisping lid.
7. Select BAKE/ROAST, set temperature to 350°F or 175°C, and set time to 10 minutes. Select START/STOP to begin.
8. When cooking is complete, open lid and serve immediately.

Nutrition:

- InfoCalories: 448,Total Fat: 25g,Sodium: 819mg,Carbohydrates: 46g,Protein: 22g.

Basil Lemon Shrimp & Asparagus

Servings: 4
Cooking Time: 10 Minutes

Ingredients:

- 3 tbsp. water, divided
- 2 cloves garlic, chopped fine
- 2 tbsp. onion, chopped fine
- ½ tsp fresh ginger, grated
- ½ tsp salt
- ¼ tsp pepper
- ¼ tsp red pepper flakes
- 1 tbsp. fresh lemon juice
- 1 lb. asparagus, trimmed & cut in 1-inch pieces
- 1 lb. medium shrimp, peeled, deveined, tails removed
- 1 tsp lemon zest
- 3 tbsp. fresh basil, chopped

Directions:

1. Add 2 tablespoons water, garlic, and onion to the cooking pot and set to sauté on medium heat. Cook 1 minute, stirring.
2. Add remaining water, ginger, salt, pepper, red pepper flakes, lemon juice, and asparagus, stir to combine. Add the lid and cook 2-3 minutes until asparagus starts to turn bright green.
3. Add the shrimp and stir. Recover and cook another 3-5 minutes or until shrimp are pink and asparagus is fork-tender.
4. Stir in the lemon zest and basil and serve.

Nutrition:
- InfoCalories 110,Total Fat 1g,Total Carbs 7g,Protein 18g,Sodium 645mg.

Spicy Grilled Shrimp

Servings: 4
Cooking Time: 6 Minutes
Ingredients:
- 1 teaspoon garlic salt
- 1/2 teaspoon black pepper
- 1 tablespoon paprika
- 1 tablespoon garlic powder
- 2 tablespoons olive oil
- 1-pound jumbo shrimps, peeled and deveined
- 2 tablespoons brown erythritol

Directions:
1. Take a mixing bowl and stir in the listed ingredients to mix well.
2. Let it chill and marinate for 30-60 minutes.
3. Preheat Ninja Foodi by pressing the "GRILL" option and setting it to "MED" and timer to 6 minutes.
4. Let it preheat until you hear a beep.
5. Set prepared shrimps over grill grate, Lock and secure the Ninja Foodi's lid and cook for 3 minutes, flip and cook for 3 minutes more.
6. Serve and enjoy.

Nutrition:
- InfoCalories: 370; Fat: 27g; Carbohydrates: 23g; Protein: 6g

Salmon With Dill Chutney

Servings: 2
Cooking Time: 15 Min
Ingredients:
- 2 salmon fillets
- Juice from ½ lemon
- 2 cups water /500ml
- ¼ tsp paprika /1.25g
- salt and freshly ground pepper to taste
- For Chutney:
- ¼ cup extra virgin olive oil /62.5ml
- ¼ cup fresh dill /32.5g
- Juice from ½ lemon
- Sea salt to taste

Directions:
1. In a food processor, blend all the chutney Ingredients until creamy. Set aside. To your Foodi, add the water and place a reversible rack.
2. Arrange salmon fillets skin-side down on the steamer basket. Drizzle lemon juice over salmon and apply a seasoning of paprika.
3. Seal the pressure lid, choose Pressure, set to High, and set the timer to 3 minutes; press Start. When ready, release the pressure quickly. Season the fillets with pepper and salt, transfer to a serving plate and top with the dill chutney.

Clam & Corn Chowder

Servings: 4
Cooking Time: 5 Hours
Ingredients:
- 1 cup chicken broth, fat free
- 2 cups potatoes, peeled & cubed
- 1 cup corn
- 1 onion, peeled & chopped
- 1 bay leaf
- ½ tsp marjoram
- ½ tsp salt
- ¼ tsp pepper
- 1 cup skim milk
- 10½ oz. minced clams, undrained
- 2 tsp cornstarch

Directions:
1. Add the chicken broth, potatoes, corn, onion, bay leaf, marjoram, salt and pepper to the cooking pot, stir to mix.
2. Add the lid and set to slow cooking on high. Cook 4-5 hours or until potatoes are tender. Discard the bay leaf.
3. Transfer the mixture to a food processor and pulse until smooth. Return to the cooking pot.
4. Stir in ¾ cup milk and clams. Cover and cook another 15 minutes.
5. In a glass measuring cup, whisk together remaining milk and cornstarch until smooth. Stir into chowder and cook, stirring 2-3 minutes or until thickened. Serve.

Nutrition:
- InfoCalories 267,Total Fat 4g,Total Carbs 34g,Protein 23g,Sodium 348mg.

Shrimp And Sausage Paella

Servings: 4
Cooking Time: 70 Min
Ingredients:
- 1 pound andouille sausage; sliced /450g
- 1 pound baby squid, cut into ¼-inch rings /450g
- 1 pound jumbo shrimp, peeled and deveined /450g
- 1 white onion; chopped
- 4 garlic cloves, minced
- 1 red bell pepper; diced
- 2 cups Spanish rice /260g
- 4 cups chicken stock /1000ml
- ½ cup dry white wine /125ml
- 1 tbsp melted butter /15ml
- 1 tsp turmeric powder /5g
- 1½ tsp s sweet paprika /7.5g
- ½ tsp freshly ground black pepper /5g
- ½ tsp salt /5g

Directions:
1. Choose Sear/Sauté on the pot and set to Medium High. Choose Start/Stop to preheat the pot. Melt the butter and add the sausage. Cook until browned on both sides, about 3 minutes while stirring frequently. Remove the sausage to a plate and set aside.
2. Sauté the onion and garlic in the same fat for 3 minutes until fragrant and pour in the wine. Use a wooden spoon to scrape the bottom of the pot of any brown bits and cook for 2 minutes or until the wine reduces by half.
3. Stir in the rice and water. Season with the paprika, turmeric, black pepper, and salt. Seal the pressure lid, choose Pressure and set to High. Set the time to 5 minutes,

then Choose Start/Stop. When done cooking, do a quick pressure release and carefully open the lid.

4.   Choose Sear/Sauté, set to Medium High, and choose Start/Stop. Add the squid and shrimp to the pot and stir gently without mashing the rice.

5.   Seal the pressure lid again and cook for 6 minutes, until the shrimp are pink and opaque. Return the sausage to the pot and mix in the bell pepper. Warm through for 2 minutes. Dish the paella and serve immediately.

Buttery Scallops

Servings: 4
Cooking Time: 6 Minutes

Ingredients:
- 2 pounds sea scallops
- 12 cup butter
- 4 garlic cloves, minced
- 4 tablespoons rosemary, chopped
- Black pepper and salt to taste

Directions:
1.   Select "Sauté" mode on your Ninja Foodi.
2.   Add rosemary, garlic and butter, Sauté for 1 minute.
3.   Stir in scallops, Black pepper and salt, Sauté for 2 minutes.
4.   Close the crisping lid.
5.   Cook for 3 minutes to 350°F or 175°C.
6.   Serve and enjoy.

Nutrition:
- InfoCalories: 278g; Fat: 15g; Carbohydrates: 5g; Protein: 25g

Salmon Chowder

Servings: 8
Cooking Time: 30 Minutes

Ingredients:
- 3 tbsp. butter
- ½ cup celery, chopped
- ½ cup onion, chopped
- ½ cup green bell pepper, chopped
- 1 clove garlic, chopped fine
- 14 ½ oz. chicken broth, low sodium
- 1 cup potatoes, peeled & cubed
- 1 cup carrots, chopped
- 1 tsp salt
- ½ tsp pepper
- 1 tsp fresh dill, chopped
- 1 can cream-style corn
- 2 cups half and half
- 2 cups salmon, cut in 1-inch pieces

Directions:
1.   Add the butter to the cooking pot and set to sauté on med-high heat.
2.   Add the celery, onion, green pepper, and garlic and cook, stirring frequently, until vegetables start to soften.
3.   Add the broth, potatoes, carrots, salt, pepper and dill and stir to mix.
4.   Add the lid and set to pressure cook on high. Set the timer for 10 minutes. When the timer goes off, release the pressure with quick release.
5.   Set back to sauté on medium and add the corn, cream, and salmon. Bring to a simmer and cook 15 minutes, or until salmon is cooked through. Serve.

Nutrition:
- InfoCalories 244,Total Fat 10g,Total Carbs 21g,Protein 18g,Sodium 905mg.

Herb Salmon With Barley Haricot Verts

Servings: 4
Cooking Time: 50 Min

Ingredients:
- 4 salmon fillets
- 8 ounces green beans haricot verts, trimmed /240g
- 2 garlic cloves, minced
- 1 cup pearl barley /130g
- 2 cups water /500ml
- ½ tbsp brown sugar /65g
- ½ tbsp freshly squeezed lemon juice /7.5ml
- 1 tbsp olive oil /15ml
- 4 tbsps melted butter/60ml
- ½ tsp dried thyme /2.5g
- ½ tsp dried rosemary /2.5g
- 1 tsp salt; divided /5g
- 1 tsp freshly ground black pepper; divided /5g

Directions:
1.   Pour the barley and water in the pot and mix to combine. Place the reversible rack in the pot. Lay the salmon fillets on the rack. Seal the pressure lid, choose Pressure, set to High and set the time to 2 minutes. Press Start.
2.   In a bowl, toss the green beans with olive oil, ½ tsp or 5g of black pepper, and ½ tsp or 2.5g of salt.
3.   Then, in another bowl, mix the remaining black pepper and salt, the butter, brown sugar, lemon juice, rosemary, garlic, and rosemary.
4.   When done cooking the rice and salmon, perform a quick pressure release. Gently pat the salmon dry with a paper towel, then coat with the buttery herb sauce.
5.   Position the haricots vert around the salmon. Close the crisping lid; choose Broil and set the time to 7 minutes; press Start/Stop. When ready, remove the salmon from the rack, and serve with the barley and haricots vert.

Swordfish With Caper Sauce

Servings: 4
Cooking Time: 8 Minutes

Ingredients:
- 4 swordfish steaks, about 1-inch thick
- 4 tablespoons unsalted butter
- 1 lemon, sliced into 8 slices
- 1 tablespoon lemon juice
- 1 tablespoon olive oil
- 2 tablespoons capers, drained
- Sea salt, to taste
- Black pepper, to taste

Directions:
1.   Take a large shallow bowl and whisk together the lemon juice and oil.
2.   Season with swordfish steaks with black pepper and salt on each side, place in the oil mixture.
3.   Turn to coat both sides and refrigerate for 15 minutes.
4.   Preheat Ninja Foodi by pressing the "GRILL" option and setting it to "MAX" and timer to 8 minutes.
5.   Let it preheat until you hear a beep.
6.   Set the swordfish over the grill grate, Lock and secure the Ninja Foodi's lid and cook for 9 minutes.
7.   Then turn off the heat.
8.   Enjoy.

Nutrition:

- InfoCalories: 472; Fat: 31g; Carbohydrates: 2g; Protein: 48g

Tuscan Cod

Servings:4
Cooking Time: 32 Minutes
Ingredients:

- 2 tablespoons canola oil, divided
- 1½ pounds baby red potatoes, cut into ½-inch pieces
- 2½ teaspoons kosher salt, divided
- 1 teaspoon freshly ground black pepper, divided
- 1 cup panko bread crumbs
- 6 tablespoons unsalted butter, divided
- 2 teaspoons poultry seasoning
- Juice of 1 lemon
- 1 medium onion, thinly sliced
- 1½ cups cherry tomatoes, halved
- 4 garlic cloves, quartered lengthwise
- ⅓ cup Kalamata olives, roughly chopped
- 4 fresh cod fillets
- 1 teaspoon fresh mint, finely chopped
- 1 lemon, cut into wedges

Directions:

1. Select SEAR/SAUTÉ and set to HI. Select START/STOP to begin. Let preheat for 5 minutes.
2. Add 1 tablespoon of oil and the potatoes. Season with 1½ teaspoons of salt and ½ teaspoon of pepper. Sauté for about 15 minutes, stirring occasionally, until the potatoes are golden brown.
3. While potatoes are cooking, combine the bread crumbs, 4 tablespoons of butter, poultry seasoning, the remaining 1 teaspoon of salt and ½ teaspoon of pepper, and lemon juice in a medium bowl. Stir well.
4. Once the potatoes are browned, carefully remove them from the pot and set aside. Add the remaining 1 tablespoon of oil, then the onion. Sauté for 2 to 3 minutes, until the onions are lightly browned. Add the tomatoes, garlic, and olives and cook for about 2 minutes more, stirring occasionally. Return the potatoes to the pot, stir. Select START/STOP to pause cooking. Close crisping lid to retain heat.
5. Coat the cod on both sides with the remaining 2 tablespoons of butter. Evenly distribute the breadcrumb mixture on top of the cod, pressing the crumbs down firmly.
6. Open lid and place the Reversible Rack in the pot over the potato mixture, making sure it is the higher position. Place the cod fillets on the rack, bread-side up. Close crisping lid.
7. Select BAKE/ROAST, set temperature to 375°F or 190°C, and set time to 12 minutes. Select START/STOP to begin.
8. When cooking is complete, leave the cod in the pot with the crisping lid closed for 5 minutes to rest before serving. After resting, the internal temperature of the cod should be at least 145°F or 65°C and the bread crumbs should be golden brown. Serve with potato mixture and garnish with chopped mint and lemon wedges.

Nutrition:

- InfoCalories: 583,Total Fat: 28g,Sodium: 815mg,Carbohydrates: 48g,Protein: 37g.

Shrimp & Zoodles

Servings: 6
Cooking Time:x
Ingredients:

- 2 tbsp. olive oil, divided
- 1 lb. shrimp, peel & devein
- 2 cloves garlic, chopped fine
- 3 zucchini, peel & spiralize
- ½ tsp salt

- ¼ tsp pepper
- ½ tsp red pepper flakes
- 1 tbsp. fresh lemon juice
- 1 cup cherry tomatoes, halved

Directions:

1. Add 1 tablespoon oil to the cooking pot and set to sauté on medium heat. Add shrimp and cook until pink 2-3 minutes. Transfer to a plate and cover.
2. Add remaining oil to the pot with the garlic. Cook 1 minute, stirring.
3. Add the zucchini, salt, pepper, red pepper flakes, lemon juice, and tomatoes and toss to combine. Cook until zucchini is tender, about 5-7 minutes, stirring occasionally.
4. Place shrimp on top of the zucchini mixture, cover, and turn off heat. Let sit for 1 minute. Serve immediately.

Nutrition:

- InfoCalories 153,Total Fat 7g,Total Carbs 5g,Protein 19g,Sodium 283mg.

Potato Chowder With Peppery Prawns

Servings: 4
Cooking Time: 80 Min
Ingredients:

- 4 slices serrano ham; chopped
- 16 ounces frozen corn /500g
- 16 prawns, peeled and deveined
- 1 onion; chopped
- 2 Yukon Gold potatoes; chopped
- ¾ cup heavy cream /188ml
- 2 cups vegetable broth /500ml
- 2 tbsps olive oil /30ml
- 4 tbsps minced garlic; divided /60g
- 1 tsp dried rosemary /5g
- 1 tsp salt; divided /5g
- 1 tsp freshly ground black pepper; divided /5g
- ½ tsp red chili flakes /2.5g

Directions:

1. Choose Sear/Sauté on the pot and set to Medium High. Choose Start/Stop to preheat the pot. Add 1 tbsp or 15ml of the olive oil and cook the serrano ham, 2 tbsps of garlic, and onion, stirring occasionally; for 5 minutes. Fetch out one-third of the serrano ham into a bowl for garnishing.
2. Add the potatoes, corn, vegetable broth, rosemary, half of the salt, and half of the black pepper to the pot.
3. Seal the pressure lid, hit Pressure and set to High. Set the time to 10 minutes, and press Start.
4. In a bowl, toss the prawns in the remaining garlic, salt, black pepper, the remaining olive oil, and the red chili flakes. When done cooking, do a quick pressure release and carefully open the pressure lid.
5. Stir in the heavy cream and fix the reversible rack in the pot over the chowder.
6. Spread the prawn in the rack. Close the crisping lid. Choose Broil and set the time to 8 minutes. Choose Start/Stop. When the timer has ended, remove the rack from the pot.
7. Ladle the corn chowder into serving bowls and top with the prawns. Garnish with the reserved ham and serve immediately.

Chorizo And Shrimp Boil

Servings: 4
Cooking Time: 30 Min

Ingredients:

- 4 chorizo sausages; sliced
- 1 pound shrimp, peeled and deveined /450g
- 1 lemon, cut into wedges
- 3 red potatoes
- 3 ears corn, cut into 1½-inch rounds
- ¼ cup butter, melted /62.5ml
- 1 cup white wine /250ml
- 2 cups water /500ml
- 2 tbsp of seafood seasoning /30g
- salt to taste

Directions:

1. To your Foodi add all Ingredients except butter and lemon wedges. Do not stir. Seal the pressure lid, choose Pressure, set to High, and set the timer to 2 minutes; press Start. When ready, release the pressure quickly.
2. Drain the mixture through a colander. Transfer to a serving platter. Serve with melted butter and lemon wedges.

Asian Inspired Halibut

Servings: 4

Cooking Time: 15 Minutes

Ingredients:

- Nonstick cooking spray
- 4 halibut fillets
- 2 tbsp. soy sauce, low sodium
- 1/3 cup dry sherry
- 1 tbsp. brown sugar
- ¾ tsp ginger
- 6 oz. snow peas, thawed
- 15 oz. whole baby corn, drained

Directions:

1. Spray the cooking pot with cooking spray. Set to sauté on med-high heat.
2. Add the fish and cook 3-4 minutes per side until it flakes with a fork. Transfer to a plate and keep warm.
3. In a small bowl, whisk together soy sauce, sherry, sugar, and ginger. Add to the pot and cook, stirring to loosen brown bits from the bottom of the pot for 2 minutes.
4. Add the peas and corn and cook until heated through, stirring frequently. Add the fish back to the pot and coat with sauce.
5. Transfer the fish to serving plates and top with vegetable and sauce. Serve immediately.

Nutrition:

- InfoCalories 491,Total Fat 7g,Total Carbs 24g,Protein 80g,Sodium 852mg.

Crab Bisque

Servings: 6

Cooking Time: 15 Minutes

Ingredients:

- 3 tbsp. butter
- 1 carrot, chopped fine
- 2 stalks celery, chopped fine
- 2 tbsp. flour
- 1 clove garlic, chopped fine
- 1 tbsp. fresh parsley, chopped

- 2 cups chicken broth, low sodium
- ½ cup sherry
- ¼ tsp pepper
- 18 oz. lump crab meat
- 2 cups half and half

Directions:

1. Add the butter to the cooking pot and set to sauté on medium heat.
2. Once the butter has melted, add the carrots and celery and cook 5-7 minutes until vegetables start to soften.
3. Sprinkle in the flour and cook, stirring, one minute. Add remaining ingredients, except crab and cream, and stir to combine.
4. Bring to a boil and cook one minute. Reduce heat to low and stir in crab and cream. Cook, stirring until bisque is heated through. Serve immediately.

Nutrition:

- InfoCalories 200,Total Fat 8g,Total Carbs 12g,Protein 18g,Sodium 770mg.

Arroz Con Cod

Servings: 4

Cooking Time: 30 Minutes

Ingredients:

- ¼ cup olive oil
- 2 tbsp. garlic, chopped
- ½ cup red onion, chopped
- ½ cup red bell pepper, chopped
- ½ cup green bell pepper, chopped
- 2 cups long grain rice
- 3 tbsp. tomato paste
- 2 tsp turmeric
- 2 tbsp. cumin
- ½ tsp salt
- ¼ tsp pepper
- 4 cups chicken broth
- 1 bay leaf
- 1 lb. cod, cut in bite-size pieces
- ½ cup peas, cooked
- 4 tbsp. pimento, chopped
- 4 tsp cilantro, chopped

Directions:

1. Add the oil to the cooking pot and set to sauté on med-high.
2. Add the garlic, onion, and peppers, and cook, stirring frequently for 2 minutes.
3. Stir in rice, tomato paste, and seasonings, and cook another 2 minutes.
4. Add the broth and bay leaf and bring to a boil. Reduce heat, cover, and let simmer 5 minutes.
5. Add the fish, recover the pot and cook 15-20 minutes until all the liquid is absorbed. Turn off the cooker and let sit for 5 minutes.
6. To serve: spoon onto plates and top with cooked peas, pimento and cilantro.

Nutrition:

- InfoCalories 282,Total Fat 15g,Total Carbs 35g,Protein 4g,Sodium 1249mg.

Poultry

Ham-stuffed Turkey Rolls

Servings: 8
Cooking Time: 20 Minutes
Ingredients:
- 4 tablespoons fresh sage leaves
- 8 ham slices
- 8 6 ounces each turkey cutlets
- Black pepper and salt to taste
- 2 tablespoons butter, melted

Directions:
1. Season turkey cutlets with black pepper and salt.
2. Roll turkey cutlets and wrap each of them with ham slices tightly.
3. Coat each roll with butter and gently place sage leaves evenly over each cutlet.
4. Transfer them to your Ninja Foodi.
5. Lock and secure the Ninja Foodi's lid and select the "Bake/Roast" mode, bake for 10 minutes a 360 °F or 180°C.
6. Open the Ninja Foodi's lid and gently give it a flip, Lock and secure the Ninja Foodi's lid again and bake for 10 minutes more.
7. Once done, serve and enjoy.

Nutrition:
- InfoCalories: 467; Fat: 24g; Carbohydrates: 1.7g; Protein: 56g

Chicken Cacciatore

Servings: 4
Cooking Time: 40 Min
Ingredients:
- 1 pound chicken drumsticks, boneless, skinless /450g
- ½ cup dry red wine /125ml
- ¾ cup chicken stock /188ml
- 1 cup black olives, pitted and sliced /130g
- 2 bay leaves
- 1 pinch red pepper flakes
- 1 can diced tomatoes /840g
- 1carrot; chopped
- 1 red bell pepper; chopped
- 1 yellow bell pepper; chopped
- 1 onion; chopped
- 4 garlic cloves, thinly sliced
- 2 tsp olive oil /10ml
- 1 tsp dried basil /5g
- 1 tsp dried parsley /5g
- 2 tsp dried oregano /10g
- 1½ tsp freshly ground black pepper /7.5g
- 2 tsp salt /10g

Directions:
1. Warm oil on Sear/Sauté. Add pepper and salt to the chicken drumsticks. In batches, sear the chicken for 5-6 minutes until golden-brown. Set aside on a plate. Drain the cooker and remain with 1 tbsp of fat.
2. In the hot oil, sauté onion, garlic, and bell peppers for 4 minutes until softened; add red pepper flakes, basil, parsley, and oregano, and cook for 30 more seconds. Season with salt and pepper.
3. Stir in tomatoes, olives, chicken stock, red wine and bay leaves.
4. Return chicken to the pot. Seal the pressure lid, choose Pressure, set to High, and set the timer to 15 minutes. Press Start.

5. When ready, release the pressure quickly. Divide chicken between four serving bowls; top with tomato mixture before serving.

Honey Garlic Chicken And Okra

Servings: 4
Cooking Time: 25 Min
Ingredients:
- 4 boneless; skinless chicken breasts; sliced
- 4 spring onions, thinly sliced
- 6 garlic cloves, grated
- ⅓ cup honey /84ml
- 1 cup rice, rinsed /130g
- ¼ cup tomato puree /62.5ml
- ½ cup soy sauce /125ml
- 2 cups water /500ml
- 2 cups frozen okra /260g
- 1 tbsp cornstarch /15g
- 2 tbsp rice vinegar /30ml
- 1 tbsp olive oil /15ml
- 1 tbsp water /15ml
- 2 tsp toasted sesame seeds /10g
- ½ tsp salt /2.5g

Directions:
1. In the inner pot of the Foodi, mix garlic, tomato puree, vinegar, soy sauce, ginger, honey, and oil; toss in chicken to coat. In an ovenproof bowl, mix water, salt and rice. Set the reversible rack on top of chicken. Lower the bowl onto the reversible rack.
2. Seal the pressure lid, choose Pressure, set to High, and set the timer to 10 minutes; press Start. Release pressure naturally for 5 minutes, release the remaining pressure quickly.
3. Use a fork to fluff the rice. Lay okra onto the rice. Allow the okra steam in the residual heat for 3 minutes. Take the trivet and bowl from the pot. Set the chicken to a plate.
4. Press Sear/Sauté. In a small bowl, mix 1 tbsp of water and cornstarch until smooth; stir into the sauce and cook for 3 to 4 minutes until thickened.
5. Divide the rice, chicken, and okra between 4 bowls. Drizzle sauce over each portion; garnish with spring onions and sesame seeds.

Chicken Gumbo

Servings: 6
Cooking Time: 30 Minutes
Ingredients:
- 3 chicken breasts, boneless & skinless
- 8 oz. turkey sausage rope, sliced ¼-inch thick
- 1 onion, chopped
- 1 green bell pepper, chopped
- 2 stalks celery, chopped
- 3 cloves garlic, chopped fine
- 4 cups chicken broth, low sodium
- 1 ½ cups okra, sliced
- 2 tsp pepper
- 1 tsp cayenne pepper

- 1 tsp thyme
- ½ tsp salt
- ½ cup green onion, chopped
- 3 cups brown rice, cooked

Directions:

1. Place all the ingredients, except the green onions and rice, in the cooking pot and stir to mix.
2. Add the lid and set to pressure cook on high. Set the timer for 30 minutes. When the timer goes off use natural release to remove the lid.
3. Transfer the chicken to a cutting board and shred. Return chicken to the pot and stir to combine.
4. Divide rice evenly among 6 bowls. With a slotted spoon, ladle gumbo over rice and top with green onion. Serve.

Nutrition:

- InfoCalories 416,Total Fat 10g,Total Carbs 35g,Protein 45g,Sodium 686mg.

Thyme Chicken With Veggies

Servings: 4

Cooking Time: 40 Min

Ingredients:

- 4 skin-on, bone-in chicken legs
- ½ cup dry white wine /125ml
- 1¼ cups chicken stock /312.5ml
- 1 cup carrots, thinly sliced /130g
- 1 cup parsnip, thinly sliced /130g
- 4 slices lemon
- 4 cloves garlic; minced
- 3 tomatoes, thinly sliced
- 2 tbsp olive oil /30ml
- 1 tbsp honey /15ml
- 1 tsp fresh chopped thyme /5g
- salt and freshly ground black pepper to taste
- Fresh thyme; chopped for garnish

Directions:

1. Season the chicken with pepper and salt. Warm oil on Sear/Sauté. Arrange chicken legs into the hot oil; cook for 3 to 5 minutes each side until browned. Place in a bowl and set aside. Cook thyme and garlic in the chicken fat for 1 minute until soft and lightly golden.
2. Add wine into the pot to deglaze, scrape the pot's bottom to get rid of any brown bits of food. Simmer the wine for 2 to 3 minutes until slightly reduced in volume.
3. Add stock, carrots, parsnips, tomatoes, pepper and salt into the pot.
4. Lay reversible rack onto veggies. Into the Foodi's steamer basket, arrange chicken legs. Set the steamer basket onto the reversible rack. Drizzle the chicken with honey then top with lemon slices.
5. Seal the pressure lid, choose Pressure, set to High, and set the timer to 12 minutes. Press Start. Release pressure naturally for 10 minutes. Place the chicken onto a bowl. Drain the veggies and place them around the chicken. Garnish with fresh thyme leaves before serving.

Salsa Verde Chicken With Salsa Verde

Servings: 4

Cooking Time: 50 Min

Ingredients:

- Salsa Verde:
- 1 jalapeño pepper, deveined and sliced
- ¼ cup extra virgin olive oil /62.5ml
- ¼ cup parsley /32.5g
- ½ cup capers /65g
- 1 lime, juiced
- 1 tsp salt /5g
- Chicken:
- 4 boneless skinless chicken breasts
- 1 cup quinoa, rinsed /130g
- 2 cups water /500ml

Directions:

1. In a blender, mix olive oil, salt, lime juice, jalapeño pepper, capers, and parsley and blend until smooth. Arrange chicken breasts in the bottom of the Foodi pot. Over the chicken, add salsa verde mixture.
2. In a bowl that can fit in the cooker, mix quinoa and water. Set a reversible rack onto chicken and sauce. Set the bowl onto the reversible rack. Seal the pressure lid, choose Pressure, set to High, and set the timer to 20 minutes. Press Start.
3. When ready, release the pressure quickly. Remove the quinoa bowl and reversible rack. Using two forks, shred chicken into the sauce; stir to coat. Divide the quinoa, between plates. Top with chicken and salsa verde before serving.

Chicken With Prunes

Servings: 6

Cooking Time: 55 Min

Ingredients:

- 1 whole chicken, 3 lb /1350g
- ¼ cup packed brown sugar /32.5g
- ½ cup pitted prunes /65g
- 2 bay leaves
- 3 minced cloves of garlic
- 2 tbsp olive oil /30ml
- 2 tbsp capers /30g
- 1 tbsp dried oregano /15g
- 1 tbsp chopped fresh parsley /15g
- 2 tbsp red wine vinegar /30ml
- Salt and black pepper to taste

Directions:

1. In a big and deep bowl, mix the prunes, olives, capers, garlic, olive oil, bay leaves, oregano, vinegar, salt, and pepper.
2. Spread the mixture on the bottom of a baking tray, and place the chicken.
3. Preheat the Foodi to 360° °F or 180°C. Sprinkle a little bit of brown sugar on top of the chicken, close the crisping lid and cook for 45-55 minutes on Air Crisp mode. When ready, garnish with fresh parsley.

Turkey Meatballs

Servings: 4

Cooking Time: 4 Minutes

Ingredients:

- 1-pound ground turkey
- 1 cup onion, shredded
- 1/4 cup heavy whip cream
- 2 teaspoon salt

- 1 cup carrots, shredded
- 1/2 teaspoon ground caraway seeds
- 1 and 1/2 teaspoons black pepper
- 1/4 teaspoon ground allspice
- 1 cup almond meal
- 1/2 cup almond milk
- 2 tablespoons unsalted butter

Directions:

1. Transfer meat to a suitable.
2. Add cream, almond meal, onion, carrot, 1 teaspoon salt, caraway, 1/2 teaspoon pepper, allspice, and mix well.
3. Refrigerate the mixture for 30 minutes.
4. Once the mixture is cooled, use your hands to scoop the mixture into meatballs.
5. Place the turkey balls in your Ninja Foodi pot.
6. Add milk, pats of butter and sprinkle 1 teaspoon salt, 1 teaspoon black pepper.
7. Lock and secure the Ninja Foodi's lid, then cook on "HIGH" pressure for 4 minutes.
8. Quick-release pressure.
9. Unlock and secure the Ninja Foodi's lid and serve.
10. Enjoy.

Nutrition:

- InfoCalories: 338; Fat: 23g; Carbohydrates: 7g; Protein: 23g

Chicken With Roasted Red Pepper Sauce

Servings: 4
Cooking Time: 23 Min

Ingredients:

- 4 chicken breasts; skinless and boneless
- ¼ cup roasted red peppers; chopped /32.5g
- ½ cup chicken broth /125ml
- ½ cup heavy cream /125ml
- 1 tbsp basil pesto /15g
- 1 tbsp cornstarch /15g
- ⅓ tsp Italian Seasoning /1.67g
- ⅓ tsp minced garlic /1.67g
- Salt and black pepper to taste

Directions:

1. In the inner pot of the Foodi, add the chicken at the bottom. Pour the chicken broth and add Italian seasoning, garlic, salt, and pepper.
2. Close the pressure lid, secure the pressure valve, and select Pressure mode on High for 15 minutes. Press Start/Stop.
3. Once the timer has ended, do a natural pressure release for 5 minutes and open the lid. Use a spoon to remove the chicken onto a plate. Scoop out any fat or unwanted chunks from the sauce.
4. In a small bowl, add the cream, cornstarch, red peppers, and pesto. Mix them with a spoon. Pour the creamy mixture into the pot and close the crisping lid.
5. Select Broil mode and cook for 4 minutes. Serve the chicken with sauce over on a bed of cooked quinoa.

Tangy Chicken & Rice

Servings: 6
Cooking Time: 30 Minutes

Ingredients:

- 3 tsp chili powder
- 1 tsp paprika
- 1 tsp garlic powder
- 1 tsp onion powder

- ¼ tsp cayenne pepper
- 1 tsp salt
- ¼ tsp pepper
- 6 chicken thighs, boneless & skinless
- 2 tbsp. olive oil
- 1 cup rice, uncooked
- 2 ¼ cups chicken broth, low sodium
- 1 tbsp. + 2 tsp fresh lime juice
- 2 tbsp. cilantro, chopped

Directions:

1. In a small bowl, combine the spices and seasonings, mix well. Use half the mixture to season the chicken on both sides.
2. Add the oil to the pot and set to sauté on medium heat. Cook chicken until browned, about 3-4 minutes per side. Transfer to a plate.
3. Add rice, the remaining seasoning mixture, broth, and 1 tablespoon lime juice to the pot, mix well. Place the chicken on top of the rice.
4. Add the lid and cook 20-25 minutes until chicken is cooked through and the liquid is absorbed.
5. Transfer chicken to serving plates. Fluff the rice with a fork, top with cilantro and remaining lime juice. Serve immediately.

Nutrition:

- InfoCalories 327,Total Fat 13g,Total Carbs 29g,Protein 23g,Sodium 1168mg.

Chicken Meatballs Primavera

Servings: 4
Cooking Time: 30 Min

Ingredients:

- 1 lb. ground chicken /450g
- ½ lb. chopped asparagus /225g
- 1 cup chopped tomatoes /130g
- 1 cup chicken broth /250ml
- 1 red bell pepper, seeded and sliced
- 2 cups chopped green beans /260g
- 1 egg, cracked into a bowl
- 2 tbsp chopped basil + extra to garnish /30g
- 1 tbsp olive oil + ½ tbsp olive oil /22.5ml
- 6 tsp flour /30g
- 1 ½ tsp Italian Seasoning /7.5g
- Salt and black pepper to taste

Directions:

1. In a mixing bowl, add the chicken, egg, flour, salt, pepper, 2 tbsps of basil, 1 tbsp of olive oil, and Italian seasoning. Mix them well with hands and make 16 large balls out of the mixture. Set the meatballs aside.
2. Select Sear/Sauté mode. Heat half tsp of olive oil, and add peppers, green beans, and asparagus. Cook for 3 minutes, stirring frequently.
3. After 3 minutes, use a spoon the veggies onto a plate and set aside. Pour the remaining oil in the pot to heat and then fry the meatballs in it in batches. Fry them for 2 minutes on each side to brown them lightly.
4. After, put all the meatballs back into the pot as well as the vegetables. Also, pour the chicken broth over it.
5. Close the lid, secure the pressure valve, and select Pressure mode on High pressure for 10 minutes. Press Start/Stop. Do a quick pressure release. Close the crisping

lid and select Air Crisp. Cook for 5 minutes at 400 °F or 205°C, until nice and crispy.

6.   Dish the meatballs with sauce into a serving bowl and garnish it with basil. Serve with over cooked pasta.

Cheesy Chicken And Broccoli Casserole

Servings:6
Cooking Time: 30 Minutes
Ingredients:

- 4 boneless, skinless chicken breasts
- 2 cups chicken stock
- 1 cup whole milk
- 1 cans condensed Cheddar cheese soup
- 1 teaspoon paprika
- 2 cups shredded Cheddar cheese
- Kosher salt
- Freshly ground black pepper
- 2 cups crushed buttered crackers

Directions:

1.   Place the chicken and stock in the pot. Assemble pressure lid, making sure the pressure release valve is in the SEAL position.
2.   Select PRESSURE and set to HI. Set timer to 20 minutes. Select START/STOP to begin.
3.   When pressure cooking is complete, quick release the pressure by turning the pressure release valve to the VENT position. Carefully remove lid when unit has finished releasing pressure.
4.   Using silicone-tipped utensils, shred the chicken inside the pot.
5.   Add the milk, condensed soup, paprika, and cheese. Stir to combine with the chicken. Season with salt and pepper. Top with the crushed crackers. Close crisping lid.
6.   Select AIR CRISP, set temperature to 360°F or 180°C, and set time to 10 minutes. Select START/STOP to begin.
7.   When cooking is complete, open lid and let cool before serving.

Nutrition:

- InfoCalories: 449,Total Fat: 23g,Sodium: 925mg,Carbohydrates: 18g,Protein: 42g.

Cashew Chicken

Servings:4
Cooking Time: 13 Minutes
Ingredients:

- 1 pound chicken breast, cut into ½-inch pieces
- 4 tablespoons stir-fry sauce, divided
- 3 tablespoons canola oil
- 12 arbol chiles
- 1 teaspoon Sichuan peppercorns
- 2 teaspoons grated fresh ginger
- 2 garlic cloves, minced
- ¾ cup cashews
- 6 scallions, cut into 1-inch pieces
- 2 teaspoons dark soy sauce
- ½ teaspoon sesame oil

Directions:

1.   Place the chicken in a zip-top bag and add 2 tablespoons of stir-fry sauce. Let marinate for 4 hours, or overnight.
2.   Select SEAR/SAUTÉ and set to HI. Select START/STOP to begin. Let preheat for 5 minutes.
3.   Add the oil, chiles, peppercorns, ginger, and garlic and cook for 1 minute.
4.   Add half the chicken and cook for 2 minutes, stirring occasionally. Transfer the chicken to a plate and set aside. Add the

remaining chicken and cook for 2 minutes, stirring occasionally. Return the first batch of chicken to the pot and add the cashews. Cook for 2 minutes, stirring occasionally.
5.   Add the scallions, soy sauce, sesame oil, and remaining 2 tablespoons of stir-fry sauce to pot and cook for 1 minute, stirring frequently.
6.   When cooking is complete, serve immediately over steamed rice, if desired.

Nutrition:

- InfoCalories: 431,Total Fat: 26g,Sodium: 809mg,Carbohydrates: 19g,Protein: 29g.

Hula Chicken

Servings: 4
Cooking Time: 10 Minutes
Ingredients:

- 2 tbsp. soy sauce, low sodium
- 1 tbsp. brown sugar
- 1 tsp fresh ginger, grated fine
- 3 cloves garlic, chopped fine
- ¼ tsp pepper
- 4 chicken breasts, boneless & skinless
- Nonstick cooking spray
- 1 green onion, sliced

Directions:

1.   Add the soy sauce, brown sugar, ginger, garlic, and pepper to a large Ziploc bag. Seal and turn to mix.
2.   Add the chicken, reseal and refrigerate at least 4 hours or overnight.
3.   Spray the cooking rack with cooking spray and place in the cooking pot.
4.   Place the chicken on the rack and add the tender-crisp lid. Set to roast on 325°F or 165°C. Cook 5-6 minutes per side until chicken is no longer pink. Transfer to plates and garnish with green onions. Serve immediately.

Nutrition:

- InfoCalories 146,Total Fat 2g,Total Carbs 5g,Protein 26g,Sodium 315mg.

Chicken With Mushroom Sauce

Servings: 10
Cooking Time: 6 Hours
Ingredients:

- 8 oz. tomato sauce
- 1 cup mushrooms, sliced
- ½ cup dry white wine
- 1 onion, chopped
- 1 clove garlic, chopped fine
- ¼ tsp salt
- ¼ tsp pepper
- 3 lbs. chicken pieces, skinless
- 2 tbsp. water
- 1 tbsp. flour

Directions:

1.   Add the tomato sauce, mushrooms, wine, onion, garlic, salt and pepper to the cooking pot, stir to mix.
2.   Add the chicken and turn to coat well
3.   Add the lid and set to slow cook on low heat. Cook 6 hours or until chicken is cooked through and tender. Transfer chicken to a serving plate.

4. In a small bowl, whisk together water and flour until smooth. Stir into the sauce and cook 10-15 minutes, stirring frequently, until sauce thickens. Serve chicken topped with sauce.

Nutrition:
- InfoCalories 176,Total Fat 4g,Total Carbs 4g,Protein 28g,Sodium 164mg.

Chicken Burrito Bowl

Servings:4
Cooking Time: 10 Minutes

Ingredients:
- 1 pound boneless, skinless chicken breasts, cut into 1-inch chunks
- 1 tablespoon chili powder
- 1½ teaspoons cumin
- 1 teaspoon sea salt
- 1 teaspoon freshly ground black pepper
- ½ teaspoon paprika
- ¼ teaspoon garlic powder
- ¼ teaspoon onion powder
- ¼ teaspoon cayenne pepper
- ¼ teaspoon dried oregano
- 1 cup chicken stock
- ¼ cup water
- 1¼ cups of your favorite salsa
- 1 can corn kernels, drained
- 1 can black beans, rinsed and drained
- 1 cup rice
- ¾ cup shredded Cheddar cheese

Directions:
1. Add the chicken, chili powder, cumin, salt, black pepper, paprika, garlic powder, onion powder, cayenne pepper, oregano, chicken stock, water, salsa, corn, and beans and stir well.
2. Add the rice to the top of the ingredients in the pot. Assemble pressure lid, making sure the pressure release valve is in the SEAL position.
3. Select PRESSURE and set to HI. Set time to 10 minutes. Select START/STOP to begin.
4. When pressure cooking is complete, quick release the pressure by moving the pressure release valve to the VENT position. Carefully remove lid when the unit has finished releasing pressure.
5. Add the cheese and stir. Serve immediately.

Nutrition:
- InfoCalories: 570,Total Fat: 11g,Sodium: 1344mg,Carbohydrates: 77g,Protein: 45g.

Chicken Chickpea Chili

Servings: 4
Cooking Time: 25 Min

Ingredients:
- 1 pound boneless; skinless chicken breast; cubed /450g
- 2 cans chickpeas, drained and rinsed /435g
- 1 jalapeño pepper; diced
- 1 lime; cut into six wedges
- 3 large serrano peppers; diced
- 1 onion; diced
- ½ cup chopped fresh cilantro /65g
- ½ cup shredded Monterey Jack cheese /65g
- 2 ½ cups water; divided /675ml
- 1 tbsp olive oil /15ml

- 2 tbsp chili powder /30g
- 1 tsp ground cumin /5g
- 1 tsp minced fresh garlic /5g
- 1 tsp salt /5g

Directions:
1. Warm oil on Sear/Sauté. Add in onion, serrano peppers, and jalapeno pepper and cook for 5 minutes until tender; add salt, cumin and garlic for seasoning.
2. Stir chicken with vegetable mixture; cook for 3 to 6 minutes until no longer pink; add 2 cups or 500ml water and chickpeas.
3. Seal the pressure lid, choose Pressure, set to High, and set the timer to 5 minutes. Press Start. Release pressure naturally for 5 minutes. Press Start. Stir chili powder with remaining ½ cup or 125ml water; mix in chili.
4. Press Sear/Sauté. Boil the chili as you stir and cook until slightly thickened. Divide chili into plates; garnish with cheese and cilantro. Over the chili, squeeze a lime wedge.

Moo Shu Chicken

Servings: 4
Cooking Time: 20 Minutes

Ingredients:
- 1 tbsp. sesame oil
- 1 cup mushrooms, sliced
- 2 cups cabbage, shredded
- ½ cup green onion, sliced thin
- 3 cups chicken, cooked & shredded
- 2 eggs, lightly beaten
- ¼ cup hoisin sauce
- 2 tbsp. tamari
- 2 tsp sriracha sauce

Directions:
1. Add the oil to the cooking pot and set to sauté on med-high heat.
2. Add the mushrooms and cook 5-6 minutes, stirring frequently, until mushrooms have browned and liquid has evaporated.
3. Add cabbage and green onion, cook, stirring, 2 minutes.
4. Stir in chicken and cook 3-5 minutes until heated through.
5. Add the eggs and cook, stirring to scramble, until eggs are cooked.
6. Stir in remaining ingredients. Reduce heat and simmer until heated through. Serve immediately.

Nutrition:
- InfoCalories 378,Total Fat 25g,Total Carbs 15g,Protein 23g,Sodium 1067mg.

Chicken Meatballs In Tomato Sauce

Servings: 5
Cooking Time: 35 Min

Ingredients:
- 1 pound ground chicken /450g
- 1 egg
- 15 ounces canned tomato sauce /450g
- ¼ cup bread crumbs /32.5g
- ¼ cup Pecorino cheese /32.5g
- 1 cup chicken broth /250ml

- ⅓ cup crumbled blue cheese /44g
- 3 tbsp red hot sauce /45ml
- 1 tbsp ranch dressing /15g
- 2 tbsp olive oil /30ml
- 1 tsp dried basil /5g
- A handful of parsley; chopped
- salt and ground black pepper to taste

Directions:

1. In a bowl, mix ground chicken, egg, pecorino, basil, pepper, salt, ranch dressing, blue cheese, 3 tbsp or 45ml hot sauce, and bread crumbs; shape the mixture into meatballs.
2. Warm oil on Sear/Sauté. Add in the meatballs and cook for 2 to 3 minutes until browned on all sides. Add in tomato sauce and broth. Seal the pressure lid, choose Pressure, set to High, and set the timer to 7 minutes. Press Start.
3. When ready, release the pressure quickly. Remove meatballs carefully and place to a serving plate; top with parsley and serve.

Chicken And Broccoli Stir-fry

Servings:4

Cooking Time: 20 Minutes

Ingredients:

- 1 cup long-grain white rice
- 1 cup chicken stock
- 2 tablespoons canola oil
- 3 boneless, skinless chicken breasts, cut into 1-inch cubes
- 1 medium head broccoli, cut into 1-inch florets
- 2 teaspoons kosher salt
- ½ teaspoon freshly ground black pepper
- 1 tablespoon ground ginger
- ¼ cup teriyaki sauce
- Sesame seeds, for garnish

Directions:

1. Place the rice and chicken stock into the pot. Assemble pressure lid, making sure the pressure release valve is in the SEAL position.
2. Select PRESSURE and set to HI. Set time to 2 minutes. Select START/STOP to begin.
3. When pressure cooking is complete, allow pressure to naturally release for 10 minutes. After 10 minutes, quick release remaining pressure by turning the pressure release valve to the VENT position. Carefully remove lid when unit has finished releasing pressure.
4. Transfer the rice to a bowl and cover to keep warm. Clean the cooking pot and return to unit.
5. Select SEAR/SAUTÉ and set to HI. Select START/STOP to begin. Let preheat for 5 minutes.
6. Add the oil and heat for 1 minute. Add the chicken and cook, stirring frequently, for about 6 minutes.
7. Stir in the broccoli, salt, pepper, and ginger. Cook for 5 minutes, stirring frequently. Stir in the teriyaki sauce and cook, stirring frequently, until the chicken has reached internal temperature of 165°F or 75°C on a food thermometer.
8. Serve the chicken and broccoli mixture over the rice. Garnish with sesame seeds if desired.

Nutrition:

- InfoCalories: 425,Total Fat: 10g,Sodium: 1176mg,Carbohydrates: 49g,Protein: 35g.

Chicken Wings With Lemon

Servings: 4

Cooking Time: 40 Min

Ingredients:

- 8 chicken wings
- ½ cup chicken broth /125ml
- 2 lemons, juiced
- ½ dried oregano
- 2 tbsp olive oil /30ml
- ½ tsp cayenne pepper /2.5g
- ½ tsp chili powder /2.5g
- ½ tsp garlic powder /2.5g
- ½ tsp onion powder /2.5g
- Sea salt and ground black pepper to taste

Directions:

1. Coat the chicken wings with olive oil; season with chili powder, onion powder, salt, oregano, garlic powder, cayenne, and pepper.
2. In the steel pot of the Foodi, add your wings and chicken broth. Seal the pressure lid, choose Pressure, set to High, and set the timer to 4 minutes. Press Start. When ready, do a quick pressure release. Preheat an oven to high.
3. Onto a greased baking sheet, place the wings in a single layer and drizzle over the lemon juice. Bake for 5 minutes until skin is crispy.

Chicken With Sun Dried Pesto

Servings: 4

Cooking Time: 20 Minutes

Ingredients:

- 4 chicken breasts, boneless & skinless
- 5 sun-dried tomatoes
- ¼ cup fresh basil
- 2 tbsp. walnuts
- 1 ½ tbsp. olive oil
- 1 clove garlic
- 1/8 tsp salt
- 1/8 tsp pepper
- 1 tbsp. parmesan cheese

Directions:

1. Place the rack in the cooking pot. Spray a small baking sheet with cooking spray.
2. Place remaining ingredients, except parmesan, in a food processor or blender and pulse until thoroughly mixed.
3. Place chicken on prepared pan and spread pesto evenly over the top. Place on the rack and add the tender-crisp lid. Set to roast on 350°F or 175°C. Cook chicken 20-25 minutes until cooked through. Sprinkle with parmesan cheese and serve.

Nutrition:

- InfoCalories 235,Total Fat 12g,Total Carbs 2g,Protein 30g,Sodium 352mg.

Ground Turkey And Potato Chili

Servings: 6

Cooking Time: 55 Min

Ingredients:

- 1 pound ground turkey /450g
- 2 bell peppers; chopped
- 6 potatoes, peeled and sliced
- 1 small onion; diced
- 2 garlic cloves; minced
- 1 cups tomato puree /250ml
- 1 cups diced tomatoes /130g
- 1 cup chicken broth /250ml

- 1 cup carrots; chopped /130g
- 1 cups fresh or frozen corn kernels, roasted /130g
- 1 tbsp olive oil /15ml
- 1 tbsp ground cumin /15g
- 1 tbsp chili powder /15g
- salt and fresh ground black pepper

Directions:

1. Warm the olive on Sear/Sauté and stir-fry onions and garlic until soft, for about 3 minutes. Press Start. Stir in turkey and cook until thoroughly browned, about 5-6 minutes. Add the remaining ingredients, and stir to combine.

2. Seal the pressure lid, choose Pressure, set to High, and set the timer to 25 minutes; press Start. Once ready, do a quick release. Set on Sear/Sauté. Cook uncovered for 15 more minutes. Serve warm.

Chicken And Sweet Potato Corn Chowder

Servings: 8

Cooking Time: 40 Min

Ingredients:

- 4 boneless; skinless chicken breast; diced
- 19 ounces corn kernels, frozen /570g
- 1 sweet potato, peeled and cubed
- 4 ounces canned diced green chiles, drained /120g
- 3 garlic cloves; minced
- 2 cups cheddar cheese, shredded /260g
- 2 cups creme fraiche /500ml
- 1 cup chicken stock /250ml
- Cilantro leaves; chopped
- 2 tsp chili powder /10g
- 1 tsp ground cumin /5g
- Salt and black pepper to taste

Directions:

1. Mix chicken, corn, chili powder, cumin, chicken stock, sweet potato, green chiles, and garlic in the pot of the Foodi. Seal the pressure lid, choose Pressure, set to High, and set the timer to 10 minutes. Press Start.

2. When ready, release the pressure quickly. Set the chicken to a cutting board and use two forks to shred it. Return to pot and stir well into the liquid.

3. Stir in cheese and creme fraiche; season with pepper and salt. Cook for 2 to 3 minutes until cheese is melted. Place chowder into plates and top with cilantro.

Pulled Chicken And Peach Salsa

Servings: 4

Cooking Time: 40 Min

Ingredients:

- 4 boneless; skinless chicken thighs
- 15 ounces canned peach chunks /450g
- 2 cloves garlic; minced
- 14 ounces canned diced tomatoes /420g
- ½ tsp cumin /2.5g
- ½ tsp salt /2.5g
- Cheddar shredded cheese
- Fresh chopped mint leaves

Directions:

1. Strain canned peach chunks. Reserve the juice and set aside. In your Foodi, add chicken, tomatoes, cumin, garlic, peach juice, and salt.

2. Seal the pressure lid, choose Pressure, set to High, and set the timer to 15 minutes. Press Start. When ready, do a quick pressure release.

3. Shred chicken with the use of two forks. Transfer to a serving plate. Add peach chunks to the cooking juices and mix until well combined.

4. Pour the peach salsa over the chicken, top with chopped mint leaves and shredded cheese. Serve immediately.

Turkey & Squash Casserole

Servings: 8

Cooking Time: 55 Minutes

Ingredients:

- 2 tsp olive oil
- 1 onion, chopped
- 1 lb. zucchini, sliced ¼-inch thick
- 1 lb. yellow squash, sliced ¼-inch thick
- 14 ½ oz. tomatoes, diced
- ¼ cup fresh basil, chopped
- 1 tsp garlic powder
- 10 ¾ oz. cream of chicken soup, low sodium
- 1 cup sour cream, fat free
- 1 cup sharp cheddar cheese, reduced fat, grated
- 4 cups turkey, cooked & chopped
- ½ tsp black pepper
- 2 tbsp. whole wheat bread crumbs

Directions:

1. Add the oil to the cooking pot and set to sauté on med-high heat.

2. Add the onion, zucchini, and yellow squash and cook until soft, about 10 minutes.

3. Transfer to a large bowl and stir in tomatoes, basil, and garlic powder.

4. In a medium bowl, combine soup, sour cream, cheese, turkey, and pepper, mix well.

5. Spread half the vegetable mixture on the bottom of the pot. Top with half the chicken mixture. Repeat. Sprinkle the bread crumbs over the top.

6. Add the tender-crisp lid and set to bake on 350°F or 175°C. Bake 45 minutes or until hot and bubbly. Serve.

Nutrition:

- InfoCalories 219,Total Fat 5g,Total Carbs 18g,Protein 25g,Sodium 469mg.

Turkey Croquettes

Servings: 10

Cooking Time: 20 Minutes

Ingredients:

- Nonstick cooking spray
- 2 ½ cups turkey, cooked
- 1 stalk celery, chopped
- 2 green onions, chopped
- ½ cup cauliflower, cooked
- ½ cup broccoli, cooked
- 1 cup stuffing, cooked
- 1 cup cracker crumbs
- 1 egg, lightly beaten
- 1/8 tsp salt
- 1/8 tsp pepper
- 1 cup French fried onions, crushed

Directions:
1. Spray the fryer basket with cooking spray.
2. Add the turkey, celery, onion, cauliflower, and broccoli to a food processor and pulse until finely chopped. Transfer to a large bowl.
3. Stir in stuffing and 1 cup of the cracker crumbs until combined.
4. Add the egg, salt and pepper and stir to combine. Form into 10 patties.
5. Place the crushed fried onions in a shallow dish. Coat patties on both sides in the onions and place in the basket. Lightly spray the tops with cooking spray.
6. Add the tender-crisp lid and set to air fry on 375°F or 190°C. Cook 5-7 minutes until golden brown. Flip over and spray with cooking spray again, cook another 5-7 minutes. Serve immediately.

Nutrition:
- InfoCalories 133, Total Fat 4g, Total Carbs 16g, Protein 9g, Sodium 449mg.

Sticky Orange Chicken

Servings: 4
Cooking Time: 30 Min

Ingredients:
- 2 chicken breasts; cubed
- 1 cup diced orange /130g
- ⅓ cup soy sauce /188ml
- ⅓ cup chicken stock /188ml
- ⅓ cup hoisin sauce /188ml
- 3 cups hot cooked quinoa /390g
- ½ cup honey /125ml
- ½ cup orange juice /125ml
- 1 garlic clove; minced
- 2 tsp cornstarch /10g
- 2 tsp water /10ml

Directions:
1. Arrange the chicken to the bottom of the Foodi's pot. In a bowl, mix honey, soy sauce, garlic, hoisin sauce, chicken stock, and orange juice, until the honey is dissolved; pour the mixture over the chicken.
2. Seal the pressure lid, choose Pressure, set to High, and set the timer to 7 minutes. Press Start. When ready, release the pressure quickly. Take the chicken from the pot and set to a bowl. Press Sear/Sauté.
3. In a small bowl, mix water with cornstarch; pour into the liquid within the pot and cook for 3 minutes until thick. Stir diced orange and chicken into the sauce until well coated. Serve with quinoa.

Honey Garlic Chicken

Servings: 4
Cooking Time: 30 Min

Ingredients:
- 4 boneless; skinless chicken breast; cut into chunks
- 4 garlic cloves, smashed
- 1 onion; diced
- ½ cup honey /125ml
- 1 tbsp cornstarch /15g
- 1 tbsp water /15ml
- 2 tbsp lime juice /30ml
- 3 tbsp soy sauce /45ml
- 2 tsp sesame oil /10ml
- 1 tsp rice vinegar /5ml
- Salt and black pepper to taste

Directions:
1. Mix garlic, onion and chicken in your Foodi. In a bowl, combine honey, sesame oil, lime juice, soy sauce, and rice vinegar; pour over the chicken mixture.
2. Seal the pressure lid, choose Pressure, set to High, and set the timer to 15 minutes. Press Start. When ready, release the pressure quickly.
3. Mix water and cornstarch until well dissolved; stir into the sauce. Press Sear/Sauté. Simmer the sauce and cook for 2 to 3 minutes as you stir until thickened.

Cheesy Chicken & Zucchini Rolls

Servings: 4
Cooking Time: 15 Minutes

Ingredients:
- Nonstick cooking spray
- 2 chicken breasts, boneless & skinless
- ½ tsp salt
- ¼ tsp pepper
- 2 zucchini, sliced very thin
- 4 slices provolone cheese, fat free
- ½ cup bread crumbs

Directions:
1. Spray the fryer basket with cooking spray.
2. Cut the chicken in half horizontally. Place pieces between 2 sheets of plastic wrap and pound out to ¼-inch thick.
3. Lay the chicken pieces, one at a time, on a plate and season with salt and pepper.
4. Place slices of zucchini and cheese on the chicken. Roll up and secure with a toothpick.
5. Place the bread crumbs in a shallow dish. Coat chicken rolls with bread crumbs and place in the basket.
6. Add the tender-crisp lid and set to air fry on 375°F or 190°C. Cook 15 minutes until golden brown on the outsides and cooked through on the inside, turning over halfway through cooking time. Serve immediately.

Nutrition:
- InfoCalories 166, Total Fat 2g, Total Carbs 12g, Protein 23g, Sodium 472mg.

Chicken In Thai Peanut Sauce

Servings: 8
Cooking Time: 10 Minutes

Ingredients:
- 2 tbsp. oil
- 2 lbs. chicken thighs, boneless & skinless
- ½ cup chicken broth, low sodium
- ¼ cup soy sauce, low sodium
- 3 tbsp. cilantro, chopped
- 2 tbsp. lime juice
- ¼ tsp red pepper flakes
- 1 tsp ginger
- ¼ cup peanut butter
- 1 tbsp. corn starch
- 2 tbsp. water
- ¼ cup peanuts, chopped
- 2 green onions, sliced

Directions:
1. Add the oil to the cooking pot and set to sauté on med-high heat.

2. Add the chicken, in batches, and cook to brown all sides. Transfer to a plate.

3. Add the broth, soy sauce, cilantro, lime juice, pepper flakes, and ginger to the pot, stir to scrape up any brown bits on the bottom of the pot.

4. Stir in the peanut butter until melted. Return the chicken back to the pot and stir to coat with sauce.

5. Add the lid and set to pressure cook on high. Set the timer for 10 minutes. Once the timer goes off, use quick release to remove the pressure. Transfer chicken back to a plate.

6. In a small bowl, whisk together cornstarch and water until smooth. Stir mixture into the sauce and set the cooker back to sauté on medium heat.

7. Bring sauce to a boil, stirring constantly, and cook until sauce thickens, about 2-3 minutes. Add chicken and stir to coat wall. Serve garnished with peanuts and green onions.

Nutrition:

- InfoCalories 679,Total Fat 40g,Total Carbs 8g,Protein 72g,Sodium 2421mg.

Whole Chicken With Lemon And Onion Stuffing

Servings: 6

Cooking Time: 55 Min

Ingredients:

- 4 lb. whole chicken /1800g
- 1 yellow onion, peeled and quartered
- 1 lemon, quartered
- 2 cloves garlic, peeled
- 1 ¼ cups chicken broth /312.5ml
- 1 tbsp herbes de Provence Seasoning /15g
- 1 tbsp olive oil /15ml
- 1 tsp garlic powder /5g
- Salt and black pepper to season

Directions:

1. Put the chicken on a clean flat surface and pat dry using paper towels. Sprinkle the top and cavity of the chicken with salt, black pepper, Herbes de Provence, and garlic powder.

2. Stuff the onion, lemon quarters, and garlic cloves into the cavity. In the Foodi, fit the reversible rack. Pour the broth in and place the chicken on the rack. Seal the lid, and select Pressure mode on High for 25 minutes.

3. Press Start/Stop to start cooking. Once ready, do a natural pressure release for about 10 minutes, then a quick pressure release to let the remaining steam out, and press Stop.

4. Close the crisping lid and broil the chicken for 5 minutes on Broil mode, to ensure that it attains a golden brown color on each side.

5. Dish the chicken on a bed of steamed mixed veggies. Right here, the choice is yours to whip up some good veggies together as your appetite tells you.

Crispy Chicken With Carrots And Potatoes

Servings: 4

Cooking Time: 35 Min

Ingredients:

- 4 bone-in skin-on chicken thighs
- 1 pound potatoes, quartered /450g
- 2 carrots; sliced into rounds
- 2 dashes hot sauce

- ¼ cup chicken stock /62.5ml
- 2 tbsp melted butter /30ml
- 1 tbsp olive oil /15ml
- 1 tsp dried oregano /5g
- ½ tsp dry mustard /2.5g
- ½ tsp garlic powder /2.5g
- ¼ tsp sweet paprika /1.25g
- ½ tsp salt /2.5g
- 2 tsp Worcestershire sauce /10ml
- 2 tsp turmeric powder /10g

Directions:

1. Season the chicken on both sides with salt. In a small bowl, mix the melted butter, Worcestershire sauce, turmeric, oregano, dry mustard, garlic powder, sweet paprika, and hot sauce to be properly combined and stir in the chicken stock.

2. On your Foodi, choose Sear/Sauté and adjust to Medium-High. Press Start to preheat the inner pot. Heat olive oil and add the chicken thighs and fry for 4 to 5 minutes or until browned. Turn and briefly sear the other side, about 1 minute. Remove from the pot.

3. Add the potatoes and carrots to the pot and stir to coat with the fat. Pour in about half of the spicy sauce and mix to coat. Put the chicken thighs on top and drizzle with the remaining sauce.

4. Seal the pressure lid, choose pressure; adjust the pressure to High and the cook time to 3 minutes; press Start. After cooking, do a quick pressure release, and carefully open the lid.

5. Transfer the chicken to the reversible rack. Use a spoon to gently move the potatoes and carrots aside and fetch some of the sauce over the chicken. Mix the potatoes and carrots back into the sauce and carefully set the rack in the pot.

6. Close the crisping lid and Choose Bake/Roast; adjust the temperature to 375°F or 190°C and the cook time to 16 minutes. Press Start to begin crisping the chicken. When done cooking, open the lid and transfer the potatoes, carrots and chicken to a serving platter, drizzling with any remaining sauce.

Country Chicken Casserole

Servings: 6

Cooking Time: 50 Minutes

Ingredients:

- 1 tbsp. olive oil
- ½ cup onion, chopped
- 1 cup mushrooms, sliced
- 1 ½ cups brown rice, cooked
- 2 cups broccoli, steamed & chopped
- 10 ½ oz. cream of chicken soup, low fat
- ½ cup sour cream, fat free
- 1 ¼ cup cheddar cheese, reduced fat, grated & divided
- 2 tbsp. Dijon mustard
- 1 tsp garlic powder
- ½ tsp pepper
- 2 cups chicken, cooked & chopped

Directions:

1. Add oil to the cooking pot and set to sauté on medium heat.

2. Add the onion and mushrooms and cook 3-5 minutes until they start to soften.

10. When done cooking, open the lid and transfer the chicken to a serving platter. Spoon the sauce with mushrooms and pearl onions all around the chicken and crumble the reserved ham on top.

Italian Chicken Muffins

Servings: 4

Cooking Time: 25 Minutes

Ingredients:

- Nonstick cooking spray
- 4 chicken breast halves, boneless & skinless
- ½ tsp salt, divided
- ½ tsp pepper, divided
- 1/3 cup part-skim ricotta cheese
- ¼ cup mozzarella cheese, grated
- 2 tbsp. parmesan cheese
- ½ tsp Italian seasoning
- ½ tsp garlic powder
- 2 tbsp. whole-wheat panko bread crumbs
- 1 tbsp. light butter, melted
- Paprika for sprinkling

Directions:

1. Place the rack in the cooking pot. Spray 4 cups of a 6- cup muffin tin.
2. Lay chicken between 2 sheets of plastic wrap and pound to ¼-inch thick. Season with ¼ teaspoon of salt and pepper.
3. In a medium bowl, combine ricotta, mozzarella, parmesan, Italian seasoning, garlic powder, and remaining salt and pepper, mix well. Spoon evenly onto centers of chicken. Wrap chicken around filling and place, seam side down, in prepared muffin cups.
4. In a small bowl, stir together bread crumbs and butter, sprinkle over the chicken then top with paprika.
5. Place muffin tin on rack and add the tender-crisp lid. Set to bake on 350°F or 175°C. Cook chicken 25-30 minutes or until chicken is cooked through. Serve immediately.

Nutrition:

- InfoCalories 224,Total Fat 8g,Total Carbs 4g,Protein 31g,Sodium 485mg.

Turkey & Cabbage Enchiladas

Servings: 4

Cooking Time: 30 Minutes

Ingredients:

- Nonstick cooking spray
- 8 large cabbage leaves
- 1 tbsp. olive oil
- ½ cup onion, chopped
- ½ red bell pepper, chopped
- 3 cloves garlic, chopped fine
- 2 tsp cumin
- 1 tbsp. chili powder
- 1 tsp salt
- ¼ tsp crushed red pepper flakes
- 2 cups turkey, cooked & shredded
- 1 cup enchilada sauce, sugar free
- ½ cup cheddar cheese, fat free, grated

Directions:

1. Spray a small baking dish with cooking spray.
2. Bring a large pot of water to boil. Add cabbage leaves and cook 30 seconds. Transfer leaves to paper towel lined surface and pat dry.
3. Add the oil to the cooking pot and set to sauté on medium heat.

4. Add the onion, bell pepper, and garlic and cook, stirring occasionally, until onions are translucent, about 5 minutes.
5. Stir in cumin, chili powder, salt, red pepper flakes, and turkey. Cook just until heat through. Transfer mixture to a bowl.
6. Add the rack to the cooking pot.
7. Lay cabbage leaves on work surface. Divide turkey mixture evenly between leaves. Fold in the sides and roll up. Place in the prepared dish, seam side down. Pour the enchilada sauce over the top and sprinkle with cheese.
8. Place dish on the rack and add the tender-crisp lid. Set to bake on 400°F or 205°C. Cook enchiladas 15-20 minutes until cheese is melted and bubbly. Let rest 5 minutes before serving.

Nutrition:

- InfoCalories 289,Total Fat 12g,Total Carbs 4g,Protein 32g,Sodium 735mg.

Chicken With Cilantro Rice

Servings: 4

Cooking Time: 70 Min

Ingredients:

- 1 pound bone-in, skin-on chicken thighs /450g
- 1 cup basmati rice /130g
- ¾ cup chicken broth /188ml
- ½ cup tomato sauce /125ml
- 1 red onion; diced
- 1 yellow bell pepper; diced
- 2 tbsp ghee divided /30g
- 1 tbsp cayenne powder /15g
- 1 tsp ground cumin /5g
- 1 tsp Italian herb mix /5g
- ½ tsp salt /2.5g
- Chopped fresh cilantro, for garnish
- Lime wedges; for serving

Directions:

1. Choose Sear/Sauté on the pot and set to Medium High. Choose Start/Stop to preheat the pot. Melt half of the ghee in the pot, and cook the onion for 3 minutes, stirring occasionally, until softened.
2. Include the yellow bell pepper, cayenne pepper, cumin, herb mix, and salt, and cook for 2 minutes more with frequent stirring.
3. Pour the rice, broth, and tomato sauce into the pot. Place the reversible rack in the higher position of the pot, which is over the rice. Put the chicken on the rack.
4. Seal the pressure lid, choose pressure, set to High, and set the time to 30 minutes. Choose Start/Stop to begin cooking the rice. When the time is over, perform a quick pressure release and carefully open the lid.
5. Brush the chicken thighs with the remaining 1 tbsp or 15g of ghee. Close the crisping lid. Choose Broil and set the time to 5 minutes. Press Start/Stop.
6. When ready, check for your desired crispiness and remove the rack from the pot. Plate the chicken, garnish with cilantro, and serve with lime wedges.

Chicken And Zucchini Pilaf

Servings: 4

Cooking Time: 40 Min

Ingredients:

- 1 pound boneless and skinless chicken legs /450g
- 1 zucchini; chopped
- 2 cups chicken stock /500ml
- 1 cup leeks; chopped /130g
- 1 cup rice, rinsed /130g
- 2 garlic cloves; minced
- 1 tbsp chopped fresh rosemary/15g
- 2 tsp chopped fresh thyme leaves /10g
- 2 tsp olive oil /10ml
- salt and ground black pepper to taste

Directions:

1. Set your Foodi to Sear/Sauté, set to Medium High, and choose Start/Stop to preheat the pot. Warm oil. Add in zucchini and cook for 5 minutes until tender.
2. Stir in thyme, leeks, rosemary, pepper, salt and garlic. Cook the mixture for 3-4 minutes. Add ½ cup or 125ml chicken stock into the pot to deglaze, scrape the bottom to get rid of any browned bits of food.
3. When liquid stops simmering, add in the remaining stock, rice, and chicken with more pepper and salt.
4. Seal the pressure lid, choose Pressure, set to High, and set the timer to 5 minutes. Press Start. Once ready, do a quick release.

Paprika Chicken

Servings: 4

Cooking Time: 5 Minutes

Ingredients:

- 4 chicken breasts, skin on
- Black pepper and salt, to taste
- 1 tablespoon olive oil
- ½ cup sweet onion, chopped
- ½ cup heavy whip cream
- 2 teaspoons smoked paprika
- ½ cup sour cream
- 2 tablespoons fresh parsley, chopped

Directions:

1. Season the four chicken breasts with black pepper and salt.
2. Select "Sauté" mode on your Ninja Foodi and add oil; let the oil heat up.
3. Add chicken and sear both sides until properly browned, should take about 15 minutes.
4. Remove chicken and transfer them to a plate.
5. Take a suitable skillet and place it over medium heat; stir in onion.
6. Sauté for 4 minutes until tender.
7. Stir in cream, paprika and bring the liquid to a simmer.
8. Return chicken to the skillet and alongside any juices.
9. Transfer the whole mixture to your Ninja Foodi and lock lid, cook on "HIGH" pressure for 5 minutes.
10. Release pressure naturally over 10 minutes.
11. Stir in sour cream, serve and enjoy.

Nutrition:

- InfoCalories: 389; Fat: 30g; Carbohydrates: 4g; Protein: 25g

Turkey Green Chili

Servings: 8

Cooking Time: 4 Hours

Ingredients:

- Nonstick cooking spray
- 2 poblano chilies
- 1 ½ lbs. fresh green tomatillos

- 5 cloves garlic, peel on
- 3 cloves garlic, chopped fine
- 1 jalapeno, seeded & chopped
- 1 bunch of cilantro, chopped
- 2 tsp salt, divided
- 2 tbsp. lime juice
- 1/8 tsp sugar
- 3 lbs. turkey thighs
- 2 tbsp. extra virgin olive oil
- 3 cups onion, chopped
- 1 teaspoon cumin
- 2 ½ cups chicken broth, low sodium
- 1 tsp chipotle powder
- 2 tbsp. fresh oregano, chopped
- 2 bay leaves
- 1/8 tsp ground cloves

Directions:

1. Lightly spray the fryer basket with cooking spray.
2. Place the poblano's in the basket. Add the tender-crisp lid and set to broil. Cook chilies until they have charred on all sides, turning every couple of minutes. Transfer to a paper bag, close and let the chilies sit for 5 minutes.
3. After 5 minutes, remove the charred skin, stems and seeds from the chilies.
4. Place the tomatillos, cut side down, in the fryer basket along with the garlic cloves. Add the tender-crisp lid and broil 5-7 minutes until nicely browned. Let cool to the touch then remove the garlic peel.
5. Place the tomatillos, garlic, jalapeno, poblanos, cilantro, 1 teaspoon salt, lime juice, and sugar in a blender. Process on low to start, then increase the speed until mixture is smooth.
6. Season the turkey with salt and pepper.
7. Add the oil to the cooking pot and set to sear on med-high. Add the turkey, in batches, and sear until lightly browned on all sides. Transfer to a plate.
8. Add the onions and cumin and cook, stirring to scrape up any brown bits on the bottom of the pot, until onions are translucent. Add the chopped garlic and cook 30 seconds more.
9. Add the tomatillo sauce, broth, chipotle powder, oregano, bay leaves, 1 teaspoon salt, ½ teaspoon pepper, and clove to the pot and stir to mix. Add the turkey and turn to coat well.
10. Add the lid and set to slow cook on high. Cook 3-4 hours or until turkey starts to fall off the bone. Transfer turkey to a work surface and remove the skin and bones. Chop the meat and return it to the pot. Serve, this is delicious on its own or makes a great filling for burritos.

Nutrition:

- InfoCalories 97,Total Fat 5g,Total Carbs 3g,Protein 9g,Sodium 337mg.

Chicken Piccata

Servings: 4

Cooking Time: 4 Hours

Ingredients:

- Nonstick cooking spray
- ¼ cup flour
- 1 tsp garlic powder
- ½ tsp salt
- ¼ tsp pepper

- 2 chicken breasts, boneless, skinless & halved horizontally
- 2 cups chicken broth, low sodium
- 1 tbsp. fresh lemon juice
- ½ cup heavy cream

Directions:

1. Spray the cooking pot with cooking spray.
2. In a small bowl, combine flour, garlic powder, salt, and pepper, mix well.
3. Coat chicken in flour mixture on all sides. Set the cooker to sear and add the chicken, brown on both sides. Pour in broth.
4. Add the lid and set to slow cook on low. Cook 4 hours or until chicken is cooked through.
5. Stir in lemon juice and cream. Season with salt and pepper and increase temperature to high. Cook another 10 minutes until sauce has thickened slightly.
6. Transfer chicken to serving plates and top with sauce. Serve.

Nutrition:

- InfoCalories 248,Total Fat 10g,Total Carbs 8g,Protein 31g,Sodium 1071mg.

Cran-apple Turkey Cutlets

Servings: 4

Cooking Time: 10 Minutes

Ingredients:

- Nonstick cooking spray
- 4 turkey breast cutlets
- 1 Granny Smith apple, chopped fine
- 2 tbsp. cranberries, dried
- 2 tsp orange peel, grated fine
- 2 tbsp. orange juice

Directions:

1. Spray the cooking pot with cooking spray. Set to sauté on medium heat.
2. Add the turkey cutlets and cook 3-4 minutes per side or until no longer pink. Transfer to serving plate and keep warm.
3. Add remaining ingredients to the pot and stir to mix. Cook, stirring occasionally, about 4 minutes or until apples are tender. Spoon over turkey and serve.

Nutrition:

- InfoCalories 175,Total Fat 2g,Total Carbs 12g,Protein 27g,Sodium 129mg.

Quesadilla Casserole

Servings: 8

Cooking Time: 30 Minutes

Ingredients:

- Nonstick cooking spray
- 2 cups chicken, cooked & shredded
- ½ cup sour cream, fat free
- 1 cup cheddar cheese, reduced fat, grated, divided
- 2 tsp cumin, divided
- 1 tbsp. chili powder, divided
- 1 tsp salt
- ¼ tsp pepper, divided
- 1 cup corn
- 15 oz. black beans, drained & rinsed
- 4 large whole grain tortillas

Directions:

1. Spray the cooking pot with cooking spray.

2. In a large bowl, combine chicken, sour cream, half the cheese, half the cumin, half the chili powder, salt, and half the pepper and mix well.
3. In a separate bowl, combine the corn, beans, and remaining spices, mix well.
4. Lay 2 of the tortillas in the bottom of the cooking pot. Spread half the chicken mixture over the tortillas and top with half the bean mixture. Repeat. Sprinkle the remaining cheese over the top.
5. Add the tender-crisp lid and set to bake on 400°F or 205°C. Bake 25-30 minutes until cheese is melted and casserole is hot. Serve immediately.

Nutrition:

- InfoCalories 354,Total Fat 13g,Total Carbs 35g,Protein 23g,Sodium 533mg.

Shredded Buffalo Chicken

Servings: 4

Cooking Time: 5 Minutes

Ingredients:

- 2 lbs. chicken breasts, boneless, skinless & cut in 3-inch pieces
- ¾ cup hot pepper sauce
- ½ cup butter
- 1 tbsp. Stevia brown sugar
- 1 tbsp. Worcestershire sauce

Directions:

1. Add all the ingredients to the cooking pot and stir to mix.
2. Add the lid and set to pressure cook on high. Set the timer for 3 minutes. Once the timer goes off, use manual release to remove the pressure.
3. Use an immersion blender to shred the chicken, or transfer mixture to a food processor and pulse until chicken is shredded. Serve.

Nutrition:

- InfoCalories 402,Total Fat 27g,Total Carbs 4g,Protein 35g,Sodium 458mg.

Red Chili Chicken

Servings: 6

Cooking Time: 1 Hour

Ingredients:

- 1 tbsp. olive oil
- 1 ¼ cup Mexican red chili sauce
- 2 tbsp. cider vinegar
- ½ tsp cloves
- ½ tsp allspice
- 1 tsp cinnamon
- ¼ tsp cumin
- ¼ tsp pepper
- ¼ tsp oregano
- 1 tsp garlic, chopped fine
- 3 lbs. chicken thighs
- 1 tsp salt

Directions:

1. Add oil to the cooking pot and set to sauté on medium heat.
2. Add the chili sauce, vinegar, cloves, allspice, cinnamon, cumin, pepper, oregano, and garlic. Bring to a simmer and cook 5 minutes. Turn off heat and let cool.

3. Sprinkle chicken with salt and place in a large Ziploc bag. Add the sauce and turn to coat. Refrigerate at least 1 hour or overnight is best.

4. Place the chicken, skin side up, in the cooking pot. Add the tender-crisp lid and set to roast on 350°F or 175°C. Cook 34-50 minutes or until cooked through and juices run clear. Serve garnished with cilantro.

Nutrition:

- InfoCalories 179,Total Fat 13g,Total Carbs 2g,Protein 14g,Sodium 83mg.

Tuscany Turkey Soup

Servings: 4
Cooking Time: 40 Min

Ingredients:

- 1 pound hot turkey sausage /450g
- 4 Italian bread slices
- 3 celery stalks; chopped
- 3 garlic cloves; chopped
- 1 can cannellini beans, rinsed /450g
- 9 ounces refrigerated tortellini /270g
- 1 Parmesan cheese rind
- 1 red onion; chopped
- ½ cup dry white wine /125ml
- 4 cups chicken broth /1000ml
- 2 cups chopped spinach /260g
- ½ cup grated Parmesan cheese /130g
- 2 tbsp melted butter /30ml
- 2 tbsp olive oil /30ml
- ½ tsp fennel seeds /2.5g
- 1 tsp salt /5g
- Cooking spray

Directions:

1. On the Foodi, choose Sear/Sauté and adjust to Medium. Press Start to preheat the inner pot. Heat olive oil and cook the sausage for 4 minutes, while stirring occasionally until golden brown.

2. Stir in the celery, garlic, and onion, season with the salt and cook for 2 to 3 minutes, stirring occasionally. Pour in the wine and bring the mixture to a boil until the wine reduces by half. Scrape the bottom of the pot to let off any browned bits. Add the chicken stock, fennel seeds, tortellini, Parmesan rind, cannellini beans, and spinach.

3. Lock the pressure lid into place and to seal. Select Pressure; adjust the pressure to High and the cook time to 5 minutes; press Start. Brush the butter on the bread slices, and sprinkle with half of the cheese. Once the timer is over, perform a natural pressure release for 5 minutes.

4. Grease the reversible rack with cooking spray and fix in the upper position of the pot. Lay the bread slices on the rack.

5. Close the crisping lid and Choose Broil. Adjust the cook time to 5 minutes; press Start.

6. When the bread has browned and crisp, transfer from the rack to a cutting board and let cool for a couple of minutes. Cut the slices into cubes.

7. Ladle the soup into bowls and sprinkle with the remaining cheese. Share the croutons among the bowls and serve.

Buffalo Chicken And Navy Bean Chili

Servings: 6
Cooking Time: 45 Min

Ingredients:

- 1 ½ pounds chicken sausage; sliced /675g
- 1 can diced tomatoes with green chilies /420g
- 2 cans navy beans, drained and rinsed /420g
- 1 can crushed tomatoes /840g
- ¾ cup Buffalo wing sauce /188ml
- 1 shallot; diced
- ½ cup fennel; chopped /65g
- ¼ cup minced garlic /32.5g
- 1 tbsp olive oil /15ml
- 1 tbsp smoked paprika /15ml
- 2 tsp chili powder /10g
- 2 tsp ground cumin /10g
- ½ tsp salt /2.5g
- ½ tsp ground white pepper /2.5g

Directions:

1. Warm oil on Sear/Sauté. Add the sausages and brown for 5 minutes, turning frequently. Set aside on a plate.

2. In the same fat, sauté onion, roasted red peppers, fennel, and garlic for 4 minutes until soft; season with paprika, cumin, pepper, salt, and chili powder.

3. Stir in crushed tomatoes; diced tomatoes with green chilies, buffalo sauce, and navy beans. Return the sausages to the pot.

4. Seal the pressure lid, choose Pressure, set to High, and set the timer to 30 minutes. Press Start. When ready, do a quick pressure release. Spoon chili into bowls and serve warm.

Bacon Ranch Chicken Bake

Servings:6
Cooking Time: 30 Minutes

Ingredients:

- 1 pound chicken breast, cut in 1-inch cubes
- 2 tablespoons extra-virgin olive oil
- 3 tablespoons ranch seasoning mix, divided
- 4 strips bacon, chopped
- 1 small onion, chopped
- 2 garlic cloves, minced
- 1 cup long-grain white rice
- 2 cups chicken broth
- ½ cup half-and-half
- 2 cups shredded Cheddar cheese, divided
- 2 tablespoons chopped fresh parsley

Directions:

1. Select SEAR/SAUTÉ and set to HI. Select START/STOP to begin. Let preheat for 5 minutes.

2. In a large bowl, toss the chicken with the olive oil and 2 tablespoons of ranch seasoning mix.

3. Add the bacon to the pot and cook, stirring frequently, for about 6 minutes, or until crispy. Using a slotted spoon, transfer the bacon to a paper towel-lined plate to drain.

4. Add the onion and cook for about 5 minutes. Add the garlic and cook for 1 minute more. Add the chicken and stir, cooking until chicken is cooked through, about 3 minutes.

5. Add the rice, chicken broth, and remaining ranch mix. Assemble pressure lid, making sure the pressure release valve is in the SEAL position.

6. Select PRESSURE and set to HI. Set time to 7 minutes. Select START/STOP to begin.

7. When complete, quick release the pressure by turning the valve to the VENT position. Carefully remove lid when unit has finished releasing pressure.

8. Stir in half-and-half and 1 cup of Cheddar cheese. Top with the remaining 1 cup of cheese. Close crisping lid.
9. Select BROIL and set time to 8 minutes. Select START/STOP to begin. When cooking is complete, serve garnished with fresh parsley.

Nutrition:
- InfoCalories: 512,Total Fat: 27g,Sodium: 999mg,Carbohydrates: 28g,Protein: 35g.

Turkey Rellenos

Servings: 4
Cooking Time: 20 Minutes
Ingredients:
- Nonstick cooking spray
- 4 poblano chilies
- ½ lb. hot Italian turkey sausage, casings removed
- 1 cup cottage cheese, reduced fat, drained
- ½ cup mozzarella cheese, grated

Directions:
1. Lightly spray fryer basket with cooking spray and place in the cooking pot.
2. Split the chilies with a knife and remove the seeds, do not remove the stems. Place in the basket.
3. Add the tender-crisp lid and set to broil. Cook chilies until skin chars on all sides. Transfer to a large Ziploc bag and seal. When the chilies have cooled, carefully remove the skin.
4. Remove the fryer basket and set to cooker to sauté on med-high heat. Cook sausage until no longer pink. Transfer to a medium bowl.
5. Add the cottage cheese to the sausage and mix well.
6. Spoon the sausage mixture into the chilies and lay them in the basket, spit side up. Sprinkle the mozzarella cheese over.
7. Add the basket back to the pot and set to bake on 350°F or 175°C. Bake 15 minutes until the cheese is melted and bubbly. Serve immediately.

Nutrition:
- InfoCalories 179,Total Fat 7g,Total Carbs 9g,Protein 20g,Sodium 977mg.

Creamy Slow Cooked Chicken

Servings: 8
Cooking Time: 4 Hours
Ingredients:
- 4-5 lb. chicken, whole
- 1 tsp salt
- ½ tsp pepper
- 1 tbsp. butter, unsalted
- 1 tbsp. olive oil
- 8 cloves garlic, peeled
- 2 cinnamon sticks
- 2 cups skim milk
- 1 tsp thyme
- Zest of two large oranges

Directions:
1. Season the chicken with salt and pepper.
2. Add the butter and oil to the cooking pot and set to sear on med-high.
3. Add the chicken and brown on all sides, about 4 minutes per side. Transfer to a plate.
4. Add the garlic and cinnamon to the ppot and cook about 2 minutes, stirring frequently.

5. Add the remaining ingredients to the pot and stir to mix. Return the chicken to the pot and turn to coat.
6. Add the lid and set to slow cook on high. Cook 4 hours or until chicken is cooked through and tender. Let sit 5 minutes before serving.

Nutrition:
- InfoCalories 176,Total Fat 10g,Total Carbs 4g,Protein 17g,Sodium 208mg.

Salsa Chicken With Feta

Servings: 6
Cooking Time: 30 Min
Ingredients:
- 2 pounds boneless skinless chicken drumsticks /900g
- 1 cup feta cheese, crumbled /130g
- 1 ½ cups hot tomato salsa /375ml
- 1 onion; chopped
- ¼ tsp salt /1.25g

Directions:
1. Sprinkle salt over the chicken; set in the inner steel pot of Foodi. Stir in salsa to coat the chicken. Seal the pressure lid, choose Pressure, set to High, and set the timer to 15 minutes. Press Start. When ready, do a quick pressure release.
2. Press Sear/Sauté and cook for 5 to 10 minutes as you stir until excess liquid has evaporated. Top with feta cheese and serve.

Rosemary Lemon Chicken

Servings: 2
Cooking Time: 60 Min
Ingredients:
- 2 chicken breasts
- 2 rosemary sprigs
- ½ lemon; cut into wedges
- 1 tbsp oyster sauce /15ml
- 3 tbsp brown sugar /45g
- 1 tbsp soy sauce /15ml
- ½ tbsp olive oil /7.5ml
- 1 tsp minced ginger /5g

Directions:
1. Place the ginger, soy sauce, and olive oil, in a bowl. Add the chicken and coat well. Cover the bowl and refrigerate for 30 minutes. Transfer the marinated chicken to the Foodi basket.
2. Close the crisping lid and cook for about 6 minutes on Air Crisp mode at 370 F. or 188°C
3. Mix the oyster sauce, rosemary and brown sugar in a small bowl. Pour the sauce over the chicken. Arrange the lemon wedges in the dish. Return to the Foodi and cook for 13 more minutes on Air Crisp mode.

Chicken And Quinoa Soup

Servings: 6
Cooking Time: 30 Min
Ingredients:
- 2 large boneless; skinless chicken breasts; cubed
- 6 ounces quinoa, rinsed /180g
- 4 ounces mascarpone cheese, at room temperature /120g

- 1 cup milk /250ml
- 1 cup heavy cream /250ml
- 1 cup red onion; chopped /130g
- 1 cup carrots; chopped /130g
- 1 cup celery; chopped /130g
- 4 cups chicken broth 1000ml
- 2 tbsp butter /30g
- 1 tbsp fresh parsley; chopped /15g
- Salt and freshly ground black pepper to taste

Directions:

1. Melt butter on Sear/Sauté. Add carrot, onion, and celery and cook for 5 minutes until tender. Add chicken broth to the pot; mix in parsley, quinoa and chicken. Add pepper and salt for seasoning.
2. Seal the pressure lid, choose Pressure, set to High, and set the timer to 5 minutes. Press Start. When ready, release the pressure quickly. Press Sear/Sauté.
3. Add mascarpone cheese to the soup and stir well to melt completely; mix in heavy cream and milk. Simmer the soup for 3 to 4 minutes until thickened and creamy.

Indian Butter Chicken

Servings: 8
Cooking Time: 15 Minutes
Ingredients:

- 2 14 oz. cans tomatoes, diced & undrained
- 2 jalapeño peppers, seeded & chopped
- 2 tbsp. fresh ginger, peeled & chopped
- 1 tbsp. paprika
- 2 tsp cumin
- 2 tsp garam masala
- 2 tsp salt
- ½ cup butter, unsalted
- 10 chicken thighs, boneless & skinless
- 2 tbsp. cornstarch
- 2 tbsp. water
- ¾ cup heavy cream
- ¾ cup plain Greek yogurt
- ¼ cup cilantro, chopped & packed

Directions:

1. Add the tomatoes, jalapenos, ginger, paprika, cumin, garam masala, and salt to a food processor or blender, pulse until pureed.
2. Add the butter to the cooking pot and set to sauté on medium heat.
3. Once butter has melted, add chicken, a few at a time, and cook until nicely browned on all sides. Transfer chicken to a cutting board.
4. Add tomato mixture and cook, stirring up all the brown bits on the bottom of the pot. Turn off the heat.
5. Slice the chicken into bite-size pieces and return to the pot with the cooking juices, stir to mix.
6. Add the lid and set to pressure cook on high. Set the timer for 5 minutes. Once the timer goes off use quick release to remove the pressure.
7. In a small bowl, whisk together cornstarch and water until smooth. Add to the cooking pot and set to sauté on med-high heat. Bring to a boil and cook until sauce has thickened, about 1-2 minutes.
8. Turn off the heat and stir in sour cream, yogurt, and cilantro. Serve.

Nutrition:

- InfoCalories 376,Total Fat 26g,Total Carbs 8g,Protein 27g,Sodium 1296mg.

Chicken Tenders With Broccoli

Servings: 2
Cooking Time: 70 Min
Ingredients:

- 4 boneless; skinless chicken tenders
- 1 head broccoli; cut into florets
- ¼ cup barbecue sauce /62.5ml
- ¼ cup lemon marmalade /32.5g
- 1 cup basmati rice /130g
- 1 cup + 2 tbsp water/280ml
- ½ tbsp soy sauce /7.5ml
- 1 tbsp sesame seeds, for garnish /15g
- 2 tbsp sliced green onions, for garnish /30g
- 2 tbsp melted butter; divided /30ml
- ¼ tsp salt /1.25g
- ¼ tsp freshly ground black pepper /1.25g
- Cooking spray

Directions:

1. Pour the rice and water in the pot and stir to combine. Seal the pressure lid, choose Pressure, set to High, and the timer to 2 minutes. Press Start/Stop to boil the rice.
2. Meanwhile, in a medium bowl, toss the broccoli with 1 tbsp of melted butter, and season with the salt and black pepper. When done cooking, perform a quick pressure release, and carefully open the lid.
3. Place the reversible rack in the higher position inside the pot, which will be over the rice. Then, spray the rack with cooking spray. Lay the chicken tenders on the rack and brush with the remaining 1 tbsp of melted butter. Arrange the broccoli around the chicken tenders.
4. Close the crisping lid. Choose Air Crisp, set the temperature to 400°F or 205°C, and set the time to 10 minutes. Press Start/Stop to begin. In a bowl, mix the barbecue sauce, lemon marmalade, and soy sauce until well combined. When done crisping, coat the chicken with the lemon sauce.
5. Use tongs to turn the chicken over and apply the lemon sauce in the other side. Close the crisping lid, select Broil and set the time to 5 minutes; press Start/Stop.
6. After cooking is complete, check for your desired crispiness and remove the rack from the pot. Spoon the rice into serving plates with the chicken and broccoli. Garnish with the sesame seeds and green onions and serve.

Chicken With Bacon And Beans

Servings: 4
Cooking Time: 45 Min
Ingredients:

- 4 boneless; skinless chicken thighs
- 4 garlic cloves; minced
- 15 ounces red kidney beans, drained and rinsed /450g
- 4 slices bacon, crumbled
- 1 can whole tomatoes /435g
- 1 red bell pepper; chopped
- 1 onion; diced
- 1 cup shredded Monterey Jack cheese /130g
- 1 cup sliced red onion /130g
- ¼ cup chopped cilantro /32.5g
- 1 cup chicken broth /250ml
- 1 tbsp tomato paste /15ml

- 1 tbsp olive oil /15ml
- 1 tbsp oregano /15g
- 1 tbsp ground cumin/15g
- 1 tsp chili powder /5g
- ½ tsp cayenne pepper /2.5g
- 1 tsp salt /5g
- 1 cup cooked corn /130g

Directions:

1. Warm oil on Sear/Sauté. Sear the chicken for 3 minutes for each side until browned. Set the chicken on a plate. In the same oil, fry bacon until crispy, about 5 minutes and set aside.
2. Add in onions and cook for 2 to 3 minutes until fragrant. Stir in garlic, oregano, cayenne pepper, cumin, tomato paste, bell pepper, and chili powder and cook for 30 more seconds. Pour the chicken broth, salt, and tomatoes and bring to a boil. Press Start/Stop.
3. Take back the chicken and bacon to the pot and ensure it is submerged in the braising liquid. Seal the pressure lid, choose Pressure, set to High, and set the timer to 15 minutes. Press Start. When ready, release the pressure quickly.
4. Pour the kidney beans in the cooker, press Sear/Sauté and bring the liquid to a boil; cook for 10 minutes. Serve topped with shredded cheese and chopped cilantro.

Spanish Chicken & Rice

Servings: 4
Cooking Time: 25 Minutes

Ingredients:

- 1 tbsp. olive oil
- 4 chicken breasts, boneless & skinless
- 1 onion, chopped fine
- 1 bell pepper, chopped fine
- 1 cup brown rice, instant
- ¾ cup chicken broth, low sodium
- 14 ½ oz. tomatoes, diced, undrained
- 1 tsp thyme
- ¼ tsp crushed red pepper flakes
- ¼ tsp salt
- ½ tsp pepper

Directions:

1. Add the oil to the cooking pot and set to sauté on medium heat.
2. Add chicken and cook until browned on both sides, about 5 minutes per side. Transfer to a plate.
3. Add onion and bell pepper and cook 5-6 minutes or until tender.
4. Place the chicken back in the pot and add rice, broth, tomatoes, and seasonings, stir to combine. Reduce heat to low, cover, and simmer 10 minutes or until chicken is cooked through.
5. Turn off the cooker and let sit, covered, 5 minutes. Fluff rice with a fork and serve.

Nutrition:

- InfoCalories 376,Total Fat 8g,Total Carbs 44g,Protein 31g,Sodium 379mg.

Chicken With Bbq Sauce

Servings: 6
Cooking Time: 20 Min

Ingredients:

- 2 pounds boneless skinless chicken breasts /900g
- 1 small onion; minced
- 4 garlic cloves
- 1 cup carrots, thinly sliced /130g

- 1½ cups barbecue sauce /375ml
- 1 tsp salt /5g

Directions:

1. Apply a seasoning of salt to the chicken and place in the inner pot of the Foodi; add onion, carrots, garlic and barbeque sauce. Toss the chicken to coat.
2. Seal the pressure lid, choose Pressure, set to High, and set the timer to 15 minutes. Press Start. Once ready, do a quick release. Use two forks to shred chicken and stir into the sauce.

Greek Style Turkey Meatballs

Servings: 6
Cooking Time: 30 Min

Ingredients:

- 1 pound ground turkey /450g
- 1 carrot; minced
- ½ celery stalk; minced
- 1 onion; minced and divided
- 1 egg, lightly beaten
- 3 cups tomato puree /750ml
- 2 cups water /500ml
- ½ cup plain bread crumbs /65g
- ⅓ cup feta cheese, crumbled /44g
- 1 tbsp olive oil /15ml
- 2 tsp salt; divided /10g
- ½ tsp dried oregano /2.5g
- ¼ tsp ground black pepper /1.25g

Directions:

1. In a mixing bowl, thoroughly combine half the onion, oregano, ground turkey, salt, bread crumbs, pepper, and egg and stir until everything is well incorporated.
2. Heat oil on Sear/Sauté, and cook celery, remaining onion, and carrot for 5 minutes until soft. Pour in water, and tomato puree. Adjust the seasonings as necessary.
3. Roll the mixture into meatballs, and drop into the sauce. Seal the pressure lid, choose Pressure, set to High, and set the timer to 5 minutes. Press Start. Allow the cooker to cool and release pressure naturally for 20 minutes. Serve topped with feta cheese.

Chicken With Rice And Peas

Servings: 4
Cooking Time: 30 Min

Ingredients:

- 4 boneless; skinless chicken breasts; sliced
- 1 onion; chopped
- 1 celery stalk; diced
- 1 garlic clove; minced
- 2 cups chicken broth; divided /500ml
- 1 cup long grain rice /130g
- 1 cup frozen green peas /130g
- 1 tbsp oil olive /15ml
- 1 tbsp tomato puree /15ml
- ½ tsp paprika /2.5g
- ¼ tsp dried oregano/1.25g
- ¼ tsp dried thyme /1.25g
- ⅛ tsp cayenne pepper /0.625g
- ⅛ tsp ground white pepper /0.625g
- Salt to taste

Directions:

1. Season chicken with garlic powder, oregano, white pepper, thyme, paprika, cayenne pepper, and salt. Warm the oil on Sear/Sauté. Add in onion and cook for 4 minutes until fragrant. Mix in tomato puree to coat.
2. Add ¼ cup or 65ml chicken stock into the Foodi to deglaze the pan, scrape the pan's bottom to get rid of browned bits of food. Mix in celery, rice, and the seasoned chicken. Add in the remaining broth to the chicken mixture.
3. Seal the pressure lid, choose Pressure, set to High, and set the timer to 8 minutes. Press Start. Once ready, do a quick release. Mix in green peas, cover with the lid and let sit for 5 minutes. Serve warm.

Crunchy Chicken & Almond Casserole

Servings: 6
Cooking Time: 30 Minutes
Ingredients:
- Nonstick cooking spray
- 3 cups chicken breast, cooked & chopped
- ¾ cup mozzarella cheese, grated
- 10 ¾ oz. condensed cream of chicken soup, low fat
- ¼ cup skim milk
- 1 cup red bell pepper, chopped
- ¼ cup celery, chopped
- ¼ cup green onions, sliced
- ¼ tsp pepper
- ¼ cup cornflakes, crushed
- ¼ cup almonds, sliced

Directions:
1. Spray the cooking pot with cooking spray.
2. In a large bowl, combine chicken, cheese, soup, milk, bell pepper, celery, green onions, and pepper. Pour into the pot.
3. In a small bowl, combine cornflakes and almonds, sprinkle over the top of the chicken mixture.
4. Add the tender-crisp lid and set to bake on 400°F or 205°C. Bake 30 minutes until casserole is hot and bubbly. Turn off the heat and let sit 10 minutes before serving.

Nutrition:
- InfoCalories 266, Total Fat 13g, Total Carbs 7g, Protein 28g, Sodium 526mg.

Beef, Pork & Lamb

Adobo Steak

Servings: 4
Cooking Time: 25 Minutes
Ingredients:
- 2 cups of water
- 8 steaks, cubed, 28 ounces pack
- Pepper to taste
- 1 and 3/4 teaspoons adobo seasoning
- 1 can 8 ounces tomato sauce
- 1/3 cup green pitted olives
- 2 tablespoons brine
- 1 small red pepper
- 1/2 a medium onion, sliced

Directions:
1. Chop peppers, onions into ¼ inch strips.
2. Prepare beef by seasoning with adobo and pepper.
3. Add into Ninja Foodi.
4. Stir in remaining ingredients and Lock lid, cook on "HIGH" pressure for 25 minutes.
5. Release pressure naturally.
6. Serve and enjoy.

Nutrition:
- InfoCalories: 154; Fat: 5g; Carbohydrates: 3g; Protein: 23g

Layered Taco Casserole

Servings: 8
Cooking Time: 35 Minutes
Ingredients:
- 2 lbs. lean ground beef
- 1 tsp garlic, chopped fine
- 2 tbsp. chili powder
- 1 tsp onion powder
- ½ cup salsa
- ¼ cup water
- 16 oz. re-fried beans, low fat
- ½ cup sour cream, low fat
- 1 cup cheddar cheese, low fat, grated
- ¼ cup green onion, chopped

Directions:
1. Add the beef to the cooking pot and set to sauté on med-high heat. Cook, breaking up with spatula, until no longer pink. Stir in garlic, chili powder, and onion powder and cook 1 minute more.
2. Stir in salsa and water and cook, stirring occasionally, until liquid has reduced.
3. Spread beans on top of the meat. Top with sour cream then sprinkle the cheese evenly over the top.
4. Add the tender-crisp lid and set to bake on 350°F or 175°C. Bake 25-30 minutes or until hot and bubbly.
5. Let cool slightly then serve garnished with green onions.

Nutrition:
- InfoCalories 360, Total Fat 22g, Total Carbs 11g, Protein 28g, Sodium 513mg.

Greek Beef Gyros

Servings: 4
Cooking Time: 55 Min
Ingredients:
- 1 pound beef sirloin; cut into thin strips /450g
- 1 onion, thinly sliced
- 4 slices pita bread
- 1 clove garlic; minced
- 1 cup Greek yogurt /130g
- ⅓ cup beef broth /88ml
- 2 tbsp fresh dill; chopped /30g
- 2 tbsp fresh lemon juice /30ml
- 2 tbsp olive oil /30ml
- 2 tsp dry oregano /10g
- salt and ground black pepper to taste

Directions:
1. In the Foodi, mix beef, beef broth, oregano, garlic, lemon juice, pepper, onion, olive oil, and salt.
2. Seal the pressure lid, choose Pressure, set to High, and set the timer to 30 minutes. Press Start. Release pressure naturally for 15 minutes, then turn steam vent valve to Venting to release the remaining pressure quickly. Divide the beef mixture between the pita bread slices, top with yogurt and dill, and roll up to serve.

Bacon & Sauerkraut With Apples

Servings: 6
Cooking Time: 30 Minutes
Ingredients:
- ¼ lb. apple-wood smoked bacon
- 1 onion, chopped fine
- 2 Granny Smith apples, peeled, cored, & grated
- 2 cloves garlic, chopped fine
- 1 tsp caraway seeds, ground
- 3 cups apple juice, unsweetened
- ¼ cup white wine vinegar
- 2 lbs. refrigerated sauerkraut, drained

Directions:
1. Add the bacon to the cooking pot and set to sauté on medium heat. Cook until bacon has browned and fat is rendered. Transfer to paper towel lined plat. Drain all but 1 tablespoon of the fat.
2. Add the onions and apples to the pot and cook 6-7 minutes, until onions are translucent. Add the garlic and caraway and cook 1 minute more.
3. Stir in apple juice and vinegar, increase heat to med-high and bring to a boil. Let boil about 5 minutes until liquid is reduced to a syrup.
4. Chop the bacon and add it and the sauerkraut to the pot, stir to mix. Reduce heat to low and cook 10 minutes until heated through and sauerkraut is tender. Salt and pepper to taste and serve.

Nutrition:
- InfoCalories 58,Total Fat 2g,Total Carbs 9g,Protein 1g,Sodium 170mg.

Garlicky Pork Chops

Servings: 2
Cooking Time: 10 Minutes
Ingredients:
- 1 tablespoon coconut butter
- 1 tablespoon coconut oil
- 2 teaspoons cloves garlic, grated

- 2 teaspoons parsley, chopped
- Black pepper and salt to taste
- 4 pork chops, sliced into strips

Directions:
1. Combine all the ingredients except the pork strips. Mix well.
2. Marinate the pork in the mixture for 1 hour. Put the pork on the Ninja Foodi basket.
3. Set it inside the pot. Seal with the crisping lid. Choose air crisp function.
4. Cook at 400 °F or 205°C or 10 minutes.

Nutrition:
- InfoCalories: 388; Fat: 23.3g; Carbohydrate: 0.5g; Protein: 18.1g

Ham, Bean & Butternut Soup

Servings: 6
Cooking Time: 4 ½ Hours
Ingredients:
- 2 tbsp. extra virgin olive oil
- 2 cups onion, chopped
- 3 bay leaves
- 2 stalks celery, chopped
- 4 cloves garlic, chopped fine
- 3 ½ cups sugar pumpkin, cut in 1-inch pieces
- ½ lb. ham hock
- 8 cups chicken broth, low sodium
- 1 tomato, chopped
- ½ tsp thyme
- 30 oz. cannellini beans, drained & rinsed
- ¼ tsp pepper
- 4 Swiss chard leaves, rib removed & chopped

Directions:
1. Add the oil to the cooking pot and set to sauté on med-high heat.
2. Add the onion and bay leaves and cook, stirring frequently, until onion starts to soften, about 2-3 minutes.
3. Add celery and cook 3 minutes. Add garlic and cook 1 minute more.
4. Add pumpkin, broth, tomatoes, thyme, and ham hock, stir to mix. Add the lid and set to slow cook on high. Cook 4 hours or until ham if falling off the bone.
5. Transfer ham hock to a plate to cool slightly. Stir the beans, pepper, and chard into the soup. Recover and let cook until chard is wilted.
6. Remove the ham from the bone and chop it. Return it to the pot and continue cooking until heated through. Discard bay leaves before serving.

Nutrition:
- InfoCalories 51,Total Fat 2g,Total Carbs 7g,Protein 3g,Sodium 224mg.

Chipotle Burgers

Servings: 6
Cooking Time: 20 Minutes
Ingredients:
- Nonstick cooking spray
- 2 poblano chilies
- 1 tsp. olive oil
- 1 ¼ tsp salt, divided
- 1 ½ lbs. lean ground beef

- 1/3 cup onion, grated
- 3 chipotle peppers in adobo sauce, chopped fine
- 1 tbsp. adobo sauce
- 1 tsp cumin
- 1 tsp pepper
- 6 slices jack cheese
- 6 hamburger buns
- 2 avocados, sliced
- 1/3 cup cilantro, chopped
- Hot sauce, to taste

Directions:

1. Spray the fryer basket with cooking spray and add to the cooking pot.
2. Place the whole poblano chilies in the basket. Add the tender-crisp lid and set to air fry on 400°F or 205°C. Cook chilies until charred on all sides. Transfer chilies to Ziploc bag, seal, and let rest 15 minutes.
3. Remove the skins and seeds from the chilies. Slice them into ribbons and place in a medium bowl. Drizzle with oil and season with ¼ teaspoon salt, toss to coat. Cover until ready to use.
4. In a large bowl, combine ground beef, onion, chipotles, adobo sauce, remaining salt, cumin, and pepper. Mix until everything is combined. Form into 6 patties.
5. Spray the rack with cooking spray and place it in the cooking pot. Place the patties on the rack.
6. Add the tender-crisp lid and set to broil. Cook patties 6-7 minutes per side, or until patties reach desired doneness. Top each patty with cheese and broil until cheese is melted.
7. To serve, place patty on bottom bun, top with avocado and some of the roasted chilies, cilantro and hot sauce. Serve immediately.

Nutrition:

- InfoCalories 168,Total Fat 8g,Total Carbs 11g,Protein 13g,Sodium 498mg.

Spiced Lamb Shoulder

Servings: 6
Cooking Time: 1 Hours

Ingredients:

- 1 tbsp. olive oil
- 3 ½ lb. lamb shoulder, bone-in, rolled & tied
- 1 cinnamon stick
- 2 red chilies, dried, broken in pieces
- 1 tbsp. fresh ginger, grated
- 1 tbsp. garlic paste
- ½ cup water
- 1 tsp cumin
- 2 tsp coriander
- 1 tsp salt
- 3 peppercorns, lightly crushed

Directions:

1. Add the oil to the cooking pot and set to sauté on med-high.
2. Add the lamb and sear on all sides. Add the tender-crisp lid and set to roast on 350°F or 175°C. Roast the lamb for 20 minutes. Transfer the lamb to a plate.
3. Set the cooker back to sauté on medium heat. Add the cinnamon stick and red chilies to the pot. Cook 1-2 minutes until aromatic.
4. Stir in ginger, garlic paste, and water and bring to a boil. Stir in the cumin, coriander, salt, and peppercorns. Let the sauce simmer 5-10 minutes.

5. Add the lamb back to the sauce. Add the lid and set to pressure cook on high. Set the timer for 20 minutes. When the timer goes off, use manual release to remove the pressure.
6. Transfer the lamb to a cutting board, tent with foil and let it rest 10 minutes.
7. Discard the cinnamon stick and pour the sauce in a blender, process until smooth.
8. To serve, slice the meat and top with the sauce.

Nutrition:

- InfoCalories 379,Total Fat 21g,Total Carbs 2g,Protein 45g,Sodium 580mg.

Chunky Pork Meatloaf With Mashed Potatoes

Servings: 4
Cooking Time: 55 Min

Ingredients:

- 2 pounds potatoes; cut into large chunks /900g
- 12 ounces pork meatloaf /360g
- 2 garlic cloves; minced
- 2 large eggs
- 12 individual saltine crackers, crushed
- 1¾ cups full cream milk; divided /438ml
- 1 cup chopped white onion /130g
- ½ cup heavy cream /125ml
- ¼ cup barbecue sauce /62.5ml
- 1 tbsp olive oil /15ml
- 3 tbsp chopped fresh cilantro /45g
- 3 tbsp unsalted butter /45g
- ¼ tsp dried rosemary /1.25g
- 1 tsp yellow mustard /5g
- 1 tsp Worcestershire sauce /5ml
- 2 tsp salt /10g
- ½ tsp black pepper /2.5g

Directions:

1. Select Sear/Sauté and adjust to Medium. Press Start to preheat the pot for 5 minutes. Heat the olive oil until shimmering and sauté the onion and garlic in the oil. Cook for about 2 minutes until the onion softens. Transfer the onion and garlic to a plate and set aside.
2. In a bowl, crumble the meatloaf mix into small pieces. Sprinkle with 1 tsp of salt, the pepper, cilantro, and thyme. Add the sautéed onion and garlic. Sprinkle the crushed saltine crackers over the meat and seasonings.
3. In a small bowl, beat ¼ cup of milk, the eggs, mustard, and Worcestershire sauce. Pour the mixture on the layered cracker crumbs and gently mix the ingredients in the bowl with your hands. Shape the meat mixture into an 8-inch round.
4. Cover the reversible rack with aluminum foil and carefully lift the meatloaf into the rack. Pour the remaining 1½ cups of milk and the heavy cream into the inner pot. Add the potatoes, butter, and remaining salt. Place the rack with meatloaf over the potatoes in the upper position in the pot.
5. Seal the pressure lid, choose Pressure; adjust the pressure to High and the cook time to 25 minutes; press Start. After cooking, perform a quick pressure release, and carefully open the pressure lid. Brush the meatloaf with the barbecue sauce.

6. Close the crisping lid; choose Broil and adjust the cook time to 7 minutes. Press Start to begin grilling. When the top has browned, remove the rack, and transfer the meatloaf to a serving platter. Mash the potatoes in the pot. Slice the meatloaf and serve with the mashed potatoes.

Beef And Bacon Chili

Servings: 6
Cooking Time: 1 Hr
Ingredients:
- 2 pounds stewing beef, trimmed /900g
- 29 ounces canned whole tomatoes /870g
- 15 ounces canned kidney beans, drained and rinsed /450g
- 4 ounces smoked bacon; cut into strips /120g
- 1 chipotle in adobo sauce, finely chopped
- 1 onion; diced
- 2 bell peppers; diced
- 3 garlic cloves; minced
- 2 cups beef broth /500ml
- 1 tbsp ground cumin/15g
- 2 tsp olive oil; divided /10ml
- 1 tsp chili powder /5g
- ½ tsp cayenne pepper /2.5g
- 4 tsp salt; divided /20g
- 1 tsp freshly ground black pepper; divided /5g

Directions:
1. Set on Sear/Sauté, set to Medium High, and choose Start/Stop to preheat the pot and fry the bacon until crispy, about 5 minutes. Set aside.
2. Rub the beef with ½ tsp or 5g black pepper and 1 tsp or 5g salt. In the bacon fat, brown beef for 5-6 minutes; transfer to a plate.
3. Warm the oil. Add in garlic, peppers and onion and cook for 3 to 4 minutes until soft. Stir in cumin, cayenne pepper, the extra pepper and salt; chopped chipotle, and chili powder and cook for 30 seconds until soft.
4. Return beef and bacon to the pot with vegetables and spices; add in tomatoes and broth.
5. Seal the pressure lid, choose Pressure, set to High, and set the timer to 45 minutes. Press Start. When ready, release the pressure quickly. Stir in beans. Let simmer on Keep Warm for 10 minutes until flavors combine.

Beef Brisket

Servings:4
Cooking Time: 1 Hour, 10 Minutes
Ingredients:
- 3 pounds beef brisket, quartered
- 1 onion, cut into quarters
- 2 cups beef broth
- Splash Worcestershire sauce
- 1 teaspoon kosher salt

Directions:
1. Select SEAR/SAUTÉ and set temperature to MD:HI. Select START/STOP to begin and allow to preheat for 5 minutes.
2. Add the brisket (fat side down) into the cooking pot and sear for 5 minutes. Using tongs, carefully flip the brisket over and sear on the other side for an additional 5 minutes.
3. In the cooking pot, combine the onion, beef broth, Worcestershire sauce, and salt.
4. Assemble the pressure lid, making sure the pressure release valve is in the SEAL position.

5. Select PRESSURE and set to HI. Set the time to 60 minutes. Select START/STOP to begin.
6. When pressure cooking is complete, allow the pressure to naturally release for 20 minutes. After 20 minutes, quick release any remaining pressure by moving the pressure release valve to the VENT position. Carefully remove lid when unit has finished releasing pressure.
7. Shred or slice the meat, as desired for serving.
Nutrition:
- InfoCalories: 486,Total Fat: 20g,Sodium: 782mg,Carbohydrates: 3g,Protein: 72g.

Braised Lamb Shanks

Servings:4
Cooking Time: 4 Hours 15 Minutes
Ingredients:
- 2 bone-in lamb shanks, 2 to 2½ pounds each
- Kosher salt
- Freshly ground black pepper
- 2 tablespoons canola oil
- 2 Yukon gold potatoes, cut into 1-inch pieces
- 2 carrots, cut into 2-inch pieces
- 2 parsnips, peeled and cut into 2-inch pieces
- 1 bag frozen pearl onions
- 1 bottle red wine
- 1 cup chicken stock
- 1 tablespoon chopped fresh rosemary

Directions:
1. Select SEAR/SAUTÉ and set to HI. Select START/STOP to begin. Let preheat for 5 minutes.
2. Season the lamb shanks with salt and pepper.
3. Add the oil and lamb. Cook for 5 minutes on one side, then turn and cook for an additional 5 minutes. Remove the lamb and set aside.
4. Add the potatoes, carrots, parsnips, and pearl onions. Cook for 5 minutes, stirring occasionally.
5. Stir in the red wine, chicken stock, and rosemary. Add the lamb back to the pot and press down on the shanks to ensure they are mostly submerged in liquid. Assemble pressure lid, making sure the pressure release valve is in the VENT position.
6. Select SLOW COOK and set to HI. Set time to 4 hours. Select START/STOP to begin.
7. When cooking is complete, remove lid and serve.
Nutrition:
- InfoCalories: 791,Total Fat: 34g,Sodium: 591mg,Carbohydrates: 47g,Protein: 51g.

Beef Pho With Swiss Chard

Servings: 6
Cooking Time: 1 Hr 10 Min
Ingredients:
- 2 pounds Beef Neck Bones /900g
- 10 ounces sirloin steak /300g
- 8 ounces rice noodles /240g
- 1 yellow onion, quartered
- A handful of fresh cilantro; chopped
- 2 scallions; chopped
- 2 jalapeño peppers; sliced
- ¼ cup minced fresh ginger /32.5g
- 9 cups water /2250ml

- 2 cups Swiss chard; chopped /260g
- 2 tsp coriander seeds /10g
- 2 tsp ground cinnamon /10g
- 2 tsp ground cloves /10g
- 2 tbsp coconut oil /30ml
- 3 tbsp sugar /45g
- 2 tbsp fish sauce /30ml
- 2 ½ tsp kosher salt /12.5g
- Freshly ground black pepper to taste

Directions:

1. Melt the oil on Sear/Sauté. Add ginger and onions and cook for 4 minutes until the onions are softened. Stir in cloves, cinnamon and coriander seeds and cook for 1 minute until soft. Add in water, salt, beef meat and bones.
2. Seal the pressure lid, choose Pressure, set to High, and set the timer to 30 minutes. Press Start. Release pressure naturally for 10 minutes.
3. Transfer the meat to a large bowl; cover with it enough water and soak for 10 minutes. Drain the water and slice the beef. In hot water, soak rice noodles for 8 minutes until softened and pliable; drain and rinse with cold water. Drain liquid from cooker into a separate pot through a fine-mesh strainer; get rid of any solids.
4. Add fish sauce and sugar to the broth; transfer into the Foodi and simmer on Sear/Sauté. Place the noodles in four separate soup bowls. Top with steak slices, scallions, swiss chard; sliced jalapeño pepper, cilantro, red onion, and pepper. Spoon the broth over each bowl to serve.

Peppercorn Meatloaf

Servings: 8
Cooking Time: 35 Min

Ingredients:

- 4 lb. ground beef /1800g
- 10 whole peppercorns, for garnishing
- 1 onion; diced
- 1 cup breadcrumbs /130g
- 1 tbsp parsley /15g
- 1 tbsp Worcestershire sauce /15ml
- 3 tbsp ketchup /45ml
- 1 tbsp basil /15g
- 1 tbsp oregano /15g
- ½ tsp salt /2.5g
- 1 tsp ground peppercorns /5g

Directions:

1. Place the beef in a large bowl. Add all of the ingredients except the whole peppercorns and the breadcrumbs. Mix with your hand until well combined. Stir in the breadcrumbs.
2. Put the meatloaf on a lined baking dish. Insert in the Foodi, close the crisping lid and cook for 25 minutes on Air Crisp mode at 350 °F or 175°C.
3. Garnish the meatloaf with the whole peppercorns and let cool slightly before serving.

Maple Glazed Pork Chops

Servings: 4
Cooking Time: 12 Minutes

Ingredients:

- 2 tablespoons choc zero maple syrup
- 4 tablespoons mustard
- 2 tablespoons garlic, minced
- Black pepper and salt to taste

- 4 pork chops
- Cooking spray

Directions:

1. Mix the choc zero maple syrup, mustard, garlic, black pepper and salt in a suitable.
2. Marinate the choc zero maple syruped pork chops in the mixture for 20 minutes.
3. Place the pork chops on the Ninja Foodi basket.
4. Put the basket inside the pot. Seal with the crisping lid.
5. Set it to air crisp. Cook at 350 °F or 175°C for about 12 minutes, flipping halfway through.

Nutrition:

- InfoCalories: 348; Fat: 23.3g; Carbohydrate: 14g; Protein: 21.1g

Beef Stew

Servings: 4
Cooking Time: 40 Minutes

Ingredients:

- 1 tablespoon olive oil
- 1-1/2 lb. beef stew meat, sliced into cubes
- 1 teaspoon Italian seasoning
- Black pepper and salt to taste
- 2 tablespoons Worcestershire sauce
- 1 onion, chopped
- 3 cloves garlic, minced
- 1 lb. cauliflower, chopped
- 16 oz. baby carrots, sliced into cubes
- 10 oz. tomato sauce
- 2-1/2 cups beef broth
- 2 tablespoons corn starch
- 2 tablespoons water

Directions:

1. Set the Ninja Foodi to sauté. Pour in the oil. Add the beef.
2. Season with Italian seasoning, black pepper and salt. Cook until brown.
3. Stir in the rest of the ingredients. Cover the pot.
4. Set it to pressure. Cook at "HIGH" pressure for 35 minutes.
5. Release the pressure naturally. Mix cornstarch with water in a suitable bowl and pour into the pot.
6. Switch to sauté and simmer for 3 minutes or until the sauce has thickened.

Nutrition:

- InfoCalories: 508; Fat: 15.6g; Carbohydrate: 3.7g; Protein: 57.9g

Lone Star Chili

Servings: 8
Cooking Time: 8 Hours

Ingredients:

- 2 tbsp. flour
- 2 lbs. lean beef chuck, cubed
- 1 tbsp. olive oil
- 1 onion, chopped fine
- 2 jalapeño peppers, chopped
- 4 cloves garlic, chopped fine
- 1 tbsp. cumin
- 4 oz. green chilies, drained & chopped

- 3 tbsp. Ancho chili powder
- 1 tsp crushed red pepper flakes
- 1 tsp oregano
- 3 cups beef broth, fat-free & low-sodium
- 28 oz. tomatoes, diced, undrained
- ¼ cup Greek yogurt, fat free
- 3 tbsp. green onions, chopped

Directions:

1. Place the flour in a large Ziploc bag. Add the beef and toss to coat.
2. Add the oil to the cooking pot and set to sauté on med-high.
3. Add the beef and cook, stirring occasionally, until browned on all sides. Add the onions and jalapenos and cook until soft. Stir in the garlic and cook 1 minute more.
4. Stir in remaining ingredients, except yogurt and green onions, mix well. Add the lid and set to slow cook on low. Cook 7-8 hours until chili is thick and beef is tender.
5. Ladle into bowls and top with a dollop of yogurt and green onions. Serve.

Nutrition:

- InfoCalories 267,Total Fat 9g,Total Carbs 8g,Protein 36g,Sodium 317mg.

Corned Cabbage Beef

Servings: 4

Cooking Time: 100 Minutes

Ingredients:

- 1 corned beef brisket
- 4 cups of water
- 1 small onion, peeled and quartered
- 3 garlic cloves, smashed and peeled
- 2 bay leaves
- 3 whole black peppercorns
- 1/2 teaspoon allspice berries
- 1 teaspoon dried thyme
- 5 medium carrots
- 1 cabbage, cut into wedges

Directions:

1. Stir in corned beef, onion, garlic cloves, water, allspice, peppercorn, thymes to the Ninja Foodi.
2. Lock up the lid and cook for about 90 minutes at "HIGH" pressure.
3. Allow the pressure to release naturally once done.
4. Open up and transfer the meat to your serving plate.
5. Cover it with tin foil and allow it to cool for 15 minutes.
6. Stir in carrots and cabbage to the lid and let them cook for 10 minutes at "HIGH" pressure.
7. Once done, do a quick release. Take out the prepped veggies and serve with your corned beef.

Nutrition:

- InfoCalories: 297; Fats: 17g; Carbohydrates:1g; Protein: 14g

Spiced Lamb Meatballs

Servings:8

Cooking Time: 29 Minutes

Ingredients:

- 2 pounds ground lamb
- ¼ cup bread crumbs
- 2 large eggs, beaten
- 3 garlic cloves, minced

- 2 teaspoons ground cumin
- 1 teaspoon smoked paprika
- ½ teaspoon cinnamon
- ½ teaspoon chili flakes
- ¼ cup minced onion
- ¼ cup chopped parsley
- Kosher salt
- Freshly ground black pepper
- Cooking spray

Directions:

1. In a large bowl, add the lamb, bread crumbs, eggs, garlic, cumin, paprika, cinnamon, chili flakes, onion, parsley, salt, and pepper. Using your hands, mix together until combined and sticky.
2. Using a ¼ cup measuring cup, measure out the mixture and roll into meatballs by hand.
3. Insert Cook & Crisp Basket into pot. Close crisping lid. Select AIR CRISP, set temperature to 390°F or 200°C, and set time to 29 minutes. Select START/STOP to begin. Let preheat for 5 minutes.
4. Open lid and place half the meatballs into the basket. Spray them with the cooking spray. Close lid and cook for 12 minutes.
5. Open lid and place the cooked meatballs in a bowl. Add the remaining meatballs to the basket and coat them with the cooking spray. Close lid and cook for the remaining 12 minutes.
6. When cooking is complete, open lid and serve.

Nutrition:

- InfoCalories: 329,Total Fat: 16g,Sodium: 129mg,Carbohydrates: 4g,Protein: 21g.

Char Siew Pork Ribs

Servings: 6

Cooking Time: 4 Hours 55 Min

Ingredients:

- 2 lb. pork ribs /900g
- 2 tbsp char siew sauce /30ml
- 2 tbsp minced ginger /30g
- 2 tbsp hoisin sauce /30ml
- 2 tbsp sesame oil /30ml
- 1 tbsp honey /15ml
- 4 garlic cloves; minced
- 1 tbsp soy sauce /15ml

Directions:

1. Whisk together all marinade ingredients, in a small bowl. Coat the ribs well with the mixture. Place in a container with a lid, and refrigerate for 4 hours.
2. Place the ribs in the basket but do not throw away the liquid from the container. Close the crisping lid and cook for 40 minutes on Air Crisp at 350 °F or 175°C. Stir in the liquid, increase the temperature to 350 °F or 175°C, and cook for 10 minutes.

Beef, Barley & Mushroom Stew

Servings: 8

Cooking Time: 1 Hour 15 Minutes

Ingredients:

- 2 tbsp. butter, unsalted
- 2 lbs. beef chuck, cubed
- 1 tsp salt

- 3 cups onions, chopped
- 1 lb. mushrooms, sliced
- 1 quart beef broth, low sodium
- 3 cups water
- 2 tsp marjoram
- 1 cup pearl barley
- 1 cup carrot, chopped
- 3 cups turnips, peeled & chopped
- ½ tsp pepper
- ½ cup sour cream
- 8 small sprigs fresh dill

Directions:

1. Add the butter to the cooking pot and set to sauté on medium heat.
2. Working in batches, cook the beef until brown on all sides, seasoning with salt as it cooks. Transfer browned beef to a bowl.
3. Add the onions and cook, stirring up brown bits from the bottom of the pot, about 5-6 minutes or until they begin to brown.
4. Add the mushrooms and increase heat to med-high. Cook 2-3 minutes.
5. Add the beef back to the pot and stir in marjoram, broth, and water, stir to mix.
6. Add the lid and set to pressure cook on high. Set timer for 30 minutes. When timer goes off use quick release to remove the pressure.
7. Stir in barley, turnips, and carrots. Add the lid and pressure cook on high another 30 minutes. When the timer goes off, use quick release to remove the pressure.
8. Ladle into bowls and garnish sour cream and dill. Serve immediately.

Nutrition:

- InfoCalories 67,Total Fat 2g,Total Carbs 5g,Protein 7g,Sodium 162mg.

Sticky Baby Back Ribs

Servings: 8
Cooking Time: 30 Minutes
Ingredients:

- 1 tsp onion powder
- 1 tsp garlic powder
- 1 tbsp. chili powder
- 1 tbsp. brown sugar
- 1 tsp pepper
- 1 tsp smoked paprika
- 1 tsp salt
- 1 cup water
- 4 lbs. baby back ribs, bone-in
- 1 cup barbecue sauce, no sugar added

Directions:

1. In a small bowl, combine the onion powder, garlic powder, chili powder, brown sugar, paprika, pepper, and salt. Mix well. Coat all sides of the ribs with the seasoning mixture, lightly rubbing the mixture into the ribs. Wrap the ribs in plastic wrap and refrigerate for 2 hours or overnight.
2. Add the trivet to the cooking pot. Pour in the water. Place the ribs in the cooking pot in a circle, standing up.
3. Add the lid and set to pressure cook on high. Set the timer for 23 minutes. When the timer goes off let sit for 5 minutes. Then use manual release to remove the pressure.
4. Transfer ribs to serving plates, brush with barbecue sauce and serve.

Nutrition:

- InfoCalories 587,Total Fat 26g,Total Carbs 17g,Protein 67g,Sodium 894mg.

Gingery Beef And Broccoli

Servings: 4
Cooking Time: 70 Min
Ingredients:

- 2 pounds skirt steak; cut into strips /900g
- 1 head broccoli, trimmed into florets
- 3 scallions, thinly sliced
- 4 garlic cloves; minced
- ½ cup coconut aminos /65g
- ½ cup water, plus 3 tbsp. /170ml
- ⅔ cup dark brown sugar /88g
- 1 tbsp olive oil /15ml
- 2 tbsp cornstarch /30g
- ½ tsp ginger puree /2.5ml

Directions:

1. Choose Sear/Sauté on the pot and set to Medium High; hit Start/Stop to preheat the pot. Pour the oil and beef in the preheated pot and brown the beef strips on both sides, about 5 minutes in total. Remove the beef from the pot and set aside.
2. Add the garlic to the oil and Sear/Sauté for 1 minute or until fragrant. Stir in the coconut aminos, ½ cup or 125ml of water, brown sugar, and ginger to the pot. Mix evenly and add the beef. Seal the pressure lid, choose Pressure, set to High, and set the time to 10 minutes. Choose Start/Stop to begin cooking.
3. Meanwhile, in a small bowl whisk combine the cornstarch and the remaining water.
4. When done cooking, perform a quick pressure release. Choose Sear/Sauté and set to Medium Low. Choose Start/Stop. Pour in the cornstarch mixture and stir continuously until the sauce becomes syrupy. Add the broccoli, stir to coat in the sauce, and cook for another 5 minutes. Once ready, garnish with scallions, and serve.

Beef Tips & Mushrooms

Servings: 8
Cooking Time: 5 Hours
Ingredients:

- 2 tbsp. olive oil
- 3 lbs. beef stew meat
- Salt & pepper, to taste
- 3 cups beef broth, low sodium
- 1 pkg. dry onion soup mix
- 1 tbsp. Worcestershire sauce
- 1 onion chopped
- 2 cups mushrooms, sliced
- 3 cloves garlic, chopped fine
- ¼ cup water
- 3 tbsp. cornstarch

Directions:

1. Add the oil to the cooking pot and set to sauté on med-high heat.
2. Season the beef with salt and pepper. Add to the pot, in batches, and cook until browned on all sides. Transfer to a bowl until all the beef has been seared.

3. Return all the beef to the pot and add broth, soup mix, onions, mushrooms, and garlic, stir to combine.
4. Add the lid and set to slow cook on low. Cook 5-6 hours until beef is tender.
5. 30 minutes before the beef tips are done, whisk together the water and cornstarch until smooth and stir into the beef mixture. Stir well before serving over noodles, mashed potatoes or mashed cauliflower to keep it low carb.

Nutrition:

- InfoCalories 285,Total Fat 11g,Total Carbs 9g,Protein 40g,Sodium 1178mg.

Thai Roasted Beef

Servings: 2
Cooking Time: 4 Hours 20 Min
Ingredients:

- 1 lb. ground beef /450g
- Thumb-sized piece of ginger; chopped
- 3 chilies, deseeded and chopped
- 4 garlic cloves; chopped
- Juice of 1 lime
- 2 tbsp oil /30ml
- 2 tbsp fish sauce/30ml
- 2 tbsp soy sauce /30ml
- 2 tbsp mirin /30ml
- 2 tbsp coriander; chopped /30g
- 2 tbsp basil; chopped /30g
- ½ tsp salt /2.5g
- ½ tsp pepper /2.5g
- 1 tsp brown sugar

Directions:

1. Place all ingredients, except beef, salt, and pepper, in a blender; pulse until smooth. Season the beef with salt and pepper. Place the meat and Thai mixture in a zipper bag. Shake well to combine and let marinate in the fridge for about 4 hours.
2. Place the beef in the Foodi basket and cook for about 12 minutes, or a little more for well done, on Air Crisp mode at 350 °F or 175°C. Let sit for 5 minutes before serving.

Pot Roast With Biscuits

Servings: 6
Cooking Time: 75 Min
Ingredients:

- 1 chuck roast /1350g
- 1 pound small butternut squash; diced /450g
- 1 small red onion, peeled and quartered
- 2 carrots, peeled and cut into 1-inch pieces
- 6 refrigerated biscuits
- 1 bay leaf
- ⅔ cup dry red wine /176ml
- ⅔ cup beef broth /176ml
- ¾ cup frozen pearl onions /98g
- 2 tbsp olive oil /30ml
- 1½ tsp salt /7.5g
- 1 tsp dried oregano leaves /5g
- ¼ tsp black pepper /1.25g

Directions:

1. On the Foodi, choose Sear/Sauté and adjust to Medium-High. Press Start to preheat the pot. Heat the olive oil until shimmering. Season the beef on both sides with salt and add to the pot. Cook, undisturbed, for 3 minutes or until deeply browned. Flip the roast

over and brown the other side for 3 minutes. Transfer the beef to a wire rack.
2. Pour the oil out of the pot and add the wine to the pot. Stir with a wooden spoon, scraping the bottom of the pot to let off any browned bits. Bring to a boil and cook for 1 to 2 minutes or until the wine has reduced by half.
3. Mix in the beef broth, oregano, bay leaf, black pepper, and red onion. Stir to combine and add the beef with its juices. Seal the pressure lid and choose Pressure; adjust the pressure to High and the cook time to 35 minutes. Press Start to begin cooking.
4. After cooking, perform a quick pressure release. Carefully open the pressure lid.
5. Add the butternut squash, carrots, and pearl onions to the pot. Lock the pressure lid into place, set to Seal position and Choose Pressure; adjust the pressure to High and the cook time to 2 minutes. Press Start to cook the vegetables.
6. After cooking, perform a quick pressure release, and open the lid. Transfer the beef to a cutting board and cover with aluminum foil.
7. Put the reversible rack in the upper position of the pot and cover with a circular piece of aluminum foil. Put the biscuits on the rack and put the rack in the pot.
8. Close the crisping lid and Choose Bake/Roast; adjust the temperature to 300°F or 150°C and the cook time to 15 minutes. Press Start. After 8 minutes, open the lid and carefully flip the biscuits over. After baking, remove the rack and biscuits. Allow the biscuits to cool for a few minutes before serving.
9. While the biscuits cook, remove the foil from the beef and cut it against the grain into slices. Remove and discard the bay leaf and transfer the beef to a serving platter. Spoon the vegetables and the sauce over the beef. Serve with the biscuits.

Taco Meatballs

Servings: 4
Cooking Time: 11 Minutes
Ingredients:

- 2 cups ground beef
- 1 egg, beaten
- 1 teaspoon taco seasoning
- 1 tablespoon sugar-free marinara sauce
- 1 teaspoon garlic, minced
- 1/2 teaspoon salt

Directions:

1. Take a suitable mixing bowl and place all the ingredients into the bowl.
2. Stir in all the ingredients into the bowl. Mix together all the ingredients by using a spoon or fingertips. Then make the small size meatballs and put them in a layer in the air fryer rack.
3. Lower the air fryer lid.
4. Cook the meatballs for 11 minutes at 350 °F or 175°C.
5. Serve immediately and enjoy.

Nutrition:

- InfoCalories: 205; Fat: 12.2g; Carbohydrates: 2.2g; Protein: 19.4g

Korean-style Barbecue Meatloaf

Servings:4
Cooking Time: 30 Minutes

Ingredients:

- 1 pound beef, pork, and veal meatloaf mix
- 1 large egg
- 1 cup panko bread crumbs
- ½ cup whole milk
- ⅓ cup minced onion
- ¼ cup chopped cilantro
- 1 garlic clove, grated
- 1 tablespoon grated fresh ginger
- ½ tablespoon fish sauce
- 1½ teaspoons sesame oil
- 1 tablespoon, plus 1 teaspoon
- soy sauce
- ¼ cup, plus 1 tablespoon
- gochujang
- 1 cup water
- 1 tablespoon honey

Directions:

1. In a large bowl, stir together the beef, egg, bread crumbs, milk, onion, cilantro, garlic, ginger, fish sauce, sesame oil, 1 teaspoon of soy sauce, and 1 tablespoon of gochujang.
2. Place the meat mixture in the Ninja Loaf Pan or an 8½-inch loaf pan and cover tightly with aluminum foil.
3. Pour the water into the pot. Place the loaf pan on the Reversible Rack, making sure the rack is in the lower position. Place the rack with pan in the pot. Assemble pressure lid, making sure the pressure release valve is in the SEAL position.
4. Select PRESSURE and set to HI. Set time to 15 minutes. Select START/STOP to begin.
5. When pressure cooking is complete, quick release the pressure by moving the pressure release valve to the VENT position. Carefully remove lid when unit has finished releasing pressure.
6. Carefully remove the foil from the pan. Close crisping lid.
7. Select BAKE/ROAST, set temperature to 360°F or 180°C, and set time to 15 minutes. Select START/STOP to begin.
8. In a small bowl stir together the remaining ¼ cup of gochujang, 1 tablespoon of soy sauce, and honey.
9. After 7 minutes, open lid and top the meatloaf with the gochujang barbecue mixture. Close lid and continue cooking.
10. When cooking is complete, open lid and remove meatloaf from the pot. Let cool for 10 minutes before serving.

Nutrition:

- InfoCalories: 389,Total Fat: 22g,Sodium: 887mg,Carbohydrates: 24g,Protein: 31g.

Cuban Flank Steak

Servings: 6
Cooking Time: 8 Hours
Ingredients:

- 15 oz. tomatoes, crushed
- 1 tbsp. apple cider vinegar
- 2 cloves garlic, chopped fine
- 1 tbsp. cumin
- 1 jalapeño, chopped fine
- 2 lbs. flank steak
- 2 red bell peppers, chopped
- 1 onion, chopped
- ½ tsp salt
- ¼ cup black olives, pitted & chopped
- 3 tbsp. green onions, sliced

Directions:

1. Add all ingredients, except the olives, to the cooking pot. Stir to coat.
2. Add the lid and set to slow cook on low. Cook 8 hours or until beef is tender.
3. Transfer beef to a large bowl and shred, using 2 forks. Return the beef to the pot.
4. Add the olives and stir to combine. Serve as is garnished with green onions, or over hot, cooked rice.

Nutrition:

- InfoCalories 348,Total Fat 13g,Total Carbs 11g,Protein 45g,Sodium 380mg.

Sticky Barbeque Baby Back Ribs

Servings: 4
Cooking Time: 35 Min
Ingredients:

- 1 rack baby back ribs; cut into quarters /1350g
- 1 cup beer /250ml
- 1 cup barbecue sauce /250ml
- 3 tbsp brown sugar /45g
- 1½ tbsp smoked paprika /22.5g
- 1 tbsp salt /15g
- 1 tbsp black pepper /15g
- 2 tsp garlic powder /10g

Directions:

1. In a bowl, mix the paprika, brown sugar, garlic, salt, and black pepper. Season all sides of the ribs with the rub. Pour the beer into the pot, put the ribs in the Crisping Basket, and place the basket in the pot. Seal the pressure lid, choose Pressure, set to High, and set the time to 10 minutes. Choose Start/Stop.
2. When done cooking, perform a quick pressure release, and carefully the open the lid. Close the crisping lid. Choose Air Crisp, set the temperature to 400°F or 205°C, and the time to 15 minutes. Choose Start/Stop to begin crisping.
3. After 10 minutes, open the lid, and brush the ribs with the barbecue sauce. Close the lid to cook further for 5 minutes.

Polish Sausage & Sauerkraut

Servings: 6
Cooking Time: 7 Hours
Ingredients:

- 2 tbsp. olive oil
- 1 onion, chopped
- ½ lb. bacon, chopped
- ½ lb. smoked Polish sausage, cut in 1-inch pieces
- 1 head cabbage, chopped
- 1 lb. sauerkraut, rinsed & drained
- 1 cup beef broth, low sodium
- 2 bay leaves
- 1 cup dry red wine

Directions:

1. Add the oil to the cooking pot and set to sauté on medium heat.
2. Add the onions and cook, stirring occasionally, until onions are golden. Use a slotted spoon to transfer onions to a bowl.
3. Add bacon to the pot and cook 2-3 minutes. Add sausage and cook until nicely browned, about 5 minutes.

Use a slotted spoon to transfer meat to the bowl with onions. Drain off any remaining fat.

4. Add the cabbage, sauerkraut, and broth to the pot and mix well. Add the lid and set to slow cook on low. Cook 4 hours.

5. Stir in the onion mixture, bay leaves, and wine. Recover and cook another 2-3 hours until vegetables are tender. Discard bay leaves, stir and serve.

Nutrition:

- InfoCalories 390,Total Fat 27g,Total Carbs 16g,Protein 15g,Sodium 1607mg.

Beef Mole

Servings: 8

Cooking Time: 8 Hours

Ingredients:

- 2 lbs. beef stew meat, cut in 1-inch cubes
- 3 tsp salt, divided
- 2 tbsp. olive oil
- 2 onions, chopped fine
- 4 cloves garlic, chopped fine
- 1 chili, seeded & chopped fine
- 3 tsp chili powder
- 1 tsp ancho chili powder
- 2 tsp oregano
- 2 tsp cumin
- 1 tsp paprika
- 1 lb. dried red beans, soaked in water overnight, drained
- 5 cups water
- 2 cups beer
- 2 15 oz. tomatoes, crushed
- 1 tbsp. brown sugar
- 2 oz. unsweetened chocolate, chopped
- 1 bay leaf
- 3 tbsp. lime juice

Directions:

1. Place the beef in a large Ziploc bag with 1 ½ teaspoons salt, seal and rub gently to massage the salt into the meat. Refrigerate overnight.

2. Add the oil to the cooking pot and set to sauté on med-high heat.

3. Working in batches, add the beef and cook until deep brown on all sides. Transfer to a bowl.

4. Add the onions to the pot and cook about 5 minutes or until softened. Stir in garlic, chilies, remaining salt, chili powders, oregano, cumin, and paprika and cook 1 minute more.

5. Stir in beans, water, beer, tomatoes, brown sugar, and chocolate and mix well. Stir in the beef and add the bay leaf.

6. Add the lid and set to slow cook on low. Cook 8 hours or until beef is tender. Stir in lime juice and serve.

Nutrition:

- InfoCalories 127,Total Fat 8g,Total Carbs 7g,Protein 7g,Sodium 310mg.

Chinese Bbq Ribs

Servings: 6

Cooking Time: 8 Hours

Ingredients:

- 4 tbsp. hoisin sauce
- 4 tbsp. oyster sauce
- 2 tbsp. soy sauce, low sodium
- 2 tbsp. rice wine
- 2 lbs. pork ribs, cut in 6 pieces

- Nonstick cooking spray
- 2-inch piece fresh ginger, grated
- 3 green onions, sliced
- 2 tbsp. honey

Directions:

1. In a large bowl, whisk together hoisin sauce, oyster sauce, soy sauce, and rice wine. Add the ribs and turn to coat. Cover and refrigerate overnight.

2. Spray the cooking pot with cooking spray.

3. Add the ribs and marinade. Top with ginger and green onions. Add the lid and set to slow cook on low. Cook 6-8 hours or until ribs are tender.

4. Transfer ribs to a serving plate. Spray the rack with the cooking spray and place in the pot. Lay the ribs, in a single layer, on the rack and brush with honey.

5. Add the tender-crisp lid and set to broil. Cook 3-4 minutes to caramelize the ribs. Serve.

Nutrition:

- InfoCalories 135,Total Fat 4g,Total Carbs 6g,Protein 17g,Sodium 419mg.

Cheesy Ham & Potato Casserole

Servings: 6

Cooking Time: 35 Minutes

Ingredients:

- 1 tbsp. butter
- 1 sweet potato, peeled & chopped
- 1 cup onion, chopped
- 2 cloves garlic, chopped fine
- 8 oz. cream cheese, low fat
- 14 ½ oz. chicken broth, low sodium
- ½ cup sour cream, low fat
- ½ tsp thyme, crushed
- ¼ tsp pepper
- 32 oz. hash brown potatoes, thawed
- 1 ½ cups white cheddar cheese, low fat, grated
- 1 cup ham, chopped
- 1 cup grape tomatoes, sliced
- 2 green onions, sliced

Directions:

1. Add butter to the cooking pot and set to sauté on medium heat. Once the butter has melted, add sweet potato, onion, and garlic and cook 5-8 minutes or until potato is tender.

2. Stir in cream cheese until melted. Add broth, sour cream, thyme, and pepper and mix well.

3. Add hash browns, cheese, and ham and mix until combined. Lay the sliced tomatoes evenly over the top.

4. Add the tender-crisp lid and set to bake on 375°F or 190°C. Bake 30-35 minutes until hot and bubbly and top is lightly browned. Let rest 5 minutes, then serve garnished with green onions.

Nutrition:

- InfoCalories 369,Total Fat 13g,Total Carbs 41g,Protein 21g,Sodium 1541mg.

Barbecue Juicy Pork Chops

Servings: 4

Cooking Time: 100 Min

Ingredients:

- 4 bone-in pork chops

- 1½ cups chicken broth /375ml
- 1 tbsp freshly ground black pepper /15g
- 1 tbsp olive oil /15ml
- 4 tbsp barbecue sauce /60ml
- 3 tbsp brown sugar /45g
- 1 tbsp salt /15g
- 1½ tbsp smoked paprika /22.5g
- 2 tsp garlic powder /10g

Directions:

1. Choose Sear/Sauté and set to High. Choose Start/Stop to preheat the pot. In a small bowl, mix the brown sugar, salt, paprika, garlic powder, and black pepper. Season both sides of the pork with the rub. Heat the oil in the preheated pot and sear the pork chops, one at a time, on both sides, about 5 minutes per chop. Set aside.
2. Pour the chicken broth into the pot and with a wooden spoon, scrape the bottom of the pot of any browned bits. Place the Crisping Basket in the upper position of the pot. Put the pork chops in the basket and brush with 2 tbsps of barbecue sauce.
3. Seal the pressure lid, choose Pressure and set to High. Set the time to 5 minutes, then Choose Start/Stop to begin cooking. When the timer is done, perform a natural pressure release for 10 minutes, then a quick pressure release, and carefully open the lid.
4. Apply the remaining barbecue sauce on both sides of the pork and close the crisping lid. Choose Broil and set the time to 3 minutes. Press Start/Stop to begin. When ready, check for your desired crispiness and remove the pork from the basket.

Italian Sausage And Cannellini Stew

Servings: 6
Cooking Time: 45 Min

Ingredients:

- 1 pound Italian sausages, halved /450g
- 2 cups vegetable stock /500ml
- 3 cups fresh spinach /390g
- 1 cup Cannellini Beans; soaked and rinsed /130g
- 1 carrot; chopped
- 1 onion; chopped
- 1 celery stalk; chopped
- 1 sprig fresh rosemary
- 1 bay leaf
- 1 sprig fresh sage
- 1 tbsp olive oil /15ml
- 1 tsp salt /5g

Directions:

1. Warm oil on Sear/Sauté. Add in sausage pieces and sear for 5 minutes until browned; set aside on a plate. To the pot, add celery, onion, bay leaf, sage, carrot, and rosemary; cook for 3 minutes to soften slightly.
2. Stir in vegetable stock and beans. Arrange seared sausage pieces on top of the beans. Seal the pressure lid, choose Pressure, set to High, and set the timer to 10 minutes. Press Start. Release pressure naturally for 20 minutes,
3. Once ready, do a quick release. Get rid of bay leaf, rosemary and sage. Mix spinach into the mixture to serve.

Butter Pork Chops

Servings: 4
Cooking Time: 10 Minutes

Ingredients:

- 4 pork chops
- Black pepper and salt, to taste

- 2 tablespoons butter
- 2 teaspoons garlic, minced
- 1/2 cup herbed chicken stock
- 1/2 cup heavy whip cream
- 1/2 a lemon, juiced

Directions:

1. Season the four pork chops with black pepper and salt.
2. Select "Sauté" mode on Ninja Foodi and add oil to heat up.
3. Add pork chops and sauté both sides until the golden, total for 6 minutes.
4. Remove thighs to a platter and keep it on the side.
5. Add garlic and cook for 2 minutes.
6. Whisk in chicken stock, heavy cream, lemon juice and bring the sauce to simmer and reintroduce the pork chops.
7. Lock and secure the Ninja Foodi's lid and cook for 10 minutes on "HIGH" pressure.
8. Release pressure naturally over 10 minutes.
9. Serve warm and enjoy.

Nutrition:

- InfoCalories: 294; Fat: 26g; Carbohydrates: 4g; Protein: 12g

Asian-glazed Pork Shoulder

Servings:4
Cooking Time: 1 Hour, 5 Minutes

Ingredients:

- 1 boneless pork shoulder, between 2½ and 3 pounds
- 2½ cups garlic-hoisin sauce, divided, plus additional for glazing
- ¾ cups water
- 1 head broccoli, cut into 2-inch florets
- 1 tablespoon canola oil
- Kosher salt
- Freshly ground black pepper

Directions:

1. Place the pork shoulder and 1½ cups of hoisin sauce in large, resealable plastic bag. Move contents to ensure that all pork has been coated with the sauce and seal bag. Refrigerate and let marinate for at least 10 minutes and up to 4 hours.
2. Place Cook & Crisp Basket in pot. Place the water in the pot. Place the pork in the basket. Assemble pressure lid, making sure the pressure release valve is in the SEAL position.
3. Select PRESSURE and set to HI. Set time to 45 minutes. Select START/STOP to begin.
4. Combine the broccoli, oil, ½ cup of hoisin sauce, and salt and pepper in a large bowl. Mix well to coat broccoli with sauce and seasonings.
5. When pressure cooking is complete, quick release the pressure by moving the pressure release valve to the VENT position. Carefully remove lid when unit has finished releasing pressure.
6. Move the pork to one side of the basket and place broccoli in the other side. Brush the remaining ½ cup of hoisin sauce over the pork. Close crisping lid.
7. Select AIR CRISP, set temperature to 390°F or 200°C, and set time to 20 minutes. Select START/STOP to begin.
8. Every 5 minutes or so, open lid and glaze pork with additional hoisin sauce. Close lid and continue cooking.

Begin checking pork for desired crispiness after 15 minutes, cooking for up to an additional 5 minutes if desired.
9.   When cooking is complete, remove pork and broccoli and serve in a family-style dish. If desired, pour some of the cooking liquid over the top of pork and broccoli for even more flavor.

Nutrition:

- InfoCalories: 1139,Total Fat: 67g,Sodium: 2802mg,Carbohydrates: 77g,Protein: 55g.

Red Pork And Chickpea Stew

Servings: 6

Cooking Time: 40 Min

Ingredients:

- 1 boneless pork shoulder, trimmed and cubed /1350g
- 15 ounces canned chickpeas, drained and rinsed /435g
- 1½ cups water /375ml
- ½ cup sweet paprika /65g
- 1 bay leaf
- 2 red bell peppers; chopped
- 6 cloves garlic; minced
- 1 white onion; chopped
- 1 tbsp cornstarch /15g
- 1 tbsp olive oil /15ml
- 1 tbsp chilli powder/15g
- 1 tbsp water/ 15ml
- 2 tsp salt /10g

Directions:

1.   Set on Sear/Sauté, set to Medium High, and choose Start/Stop to preheat the pot; add pork and oil and allow cooking for 5 minutes until browned.
2.   Add in the onion, paprika, bay leaf, salt, water, chickpeas, and chili powder. Seal the pressure lid, choose Pressure, set to High, and set the timer to 8 minutes. Press Start.
3.   Do a quick release and discard bay leaf. Remove 1 cup of cooking liquid from the Foodi; add to a blender alongside garlic, water, cornstarch, and red bell peppers; blend well until smooth. Add the blended mixture into the stew and mix well.

Beef Stroganoff

Servings:6

Cooking Time: 55 Minutes

Ingredients:

- 2 tablespoons unsalted butter
- 1 yellow onion, diced
- 4 cups cremini mushrooms, sliced
- 2 pounds beef stew meat, cut in 1- to 2-inch cubes
- 2 teaspoons freshly ground black pepper
- 2 sprigs fresh thyme
- 2 tablespoons soy sauce
- 2 cups chicken stock
- 1 package egg noodles
- 2 tablespoons cornstarch
- 2 tablespoons water
- ½ cup sour cream

Directions:

1.   Select SEAR/SAUTÉ and set to MED. Select START/STOP to begin. Let preheat for 3 minutes.
2.   Add the butter, onion, and mushrooms and sauté for 5 minutes.
3.   Add the beef, black pepper, thyme, soy sauce, and chicken stock. Simmer for 2 to 3 minutes. Assemble pressure lid, making sure the pressure release valve is in the SEAL position.

4.   Select PRESSURE and set to HI. Set time to 10 minutes. Select START/STOP to begin.
5.   When pressure cooking is complete, quick release the pressure by turning the pressure release valve to the VENT position. Carefully remove lid when unit has finished releasing pressure.
6.   Add the egg noodles. Stir well. Assemble pressure lid, making sure the pressure release valve is in the SEAL position.
7.   Select PRESSURE and set to HI. Set time to 5 minutes. Select START/STOP to begin.
8.   In a small bowl, mix the cornstarch and water until smooth.
9.   When pressure cooking is complete, quick release the pressure by turning the pressure release valve to the VENT position. Carefully remove lid when unit has finished releasing pressure.
10. Stir in cornstarch until incorporated. Stir in the sour cream. Serve immediately.

Nutrition:

- InfoCalories: 448,Total Fat: 16g,Sodium: 605mg,Carbohydrates: 35g,Protein: 41g.

Mississippi Pot Roast With Potatoes

Servings: 6

Cooking Time: 1 Hr 40 Min

Ingredients:

- 2 pounds chuck roast /900g
- 5 potatoes, peeled and sliced
- 10 pepperoncini
- 2 bay leaves
- 1 onion, finely chopped
- ½ cup pepperoncini juice /125ml
- 6 cups beef broth /1500ml
- ¼ cup butter /32.5g
- 1 tbsp canola oil /15ml
- ½ tsp dried thyme /2.5g
- ½ tsp dried parsley /2.5g
- 1 tsp onion powder /5g
- 1 tsp garlic powder /5g
- 2 tsp salt /10g
- ½ tsp black pepper /2.5g

Directions:

1.   Warm oil on Sear/Sauté. Season chuck roast with pepper and salt, then sear in the hot oil for 2 to 4 minutes for each side until browned. Set aside.
2.   Melt butter and cook onion for 3 minutes until fragrant. Sprinkle with dried parsley, onion powder, dried thyme, and garlic powder and stir for 30 seconds.
3.   Into the pot, stir bay leaves, beef broth, pepperoncini juice, and pepperoncini. Nestle chuck roast down into the liquid. Seal the pressure lid, choose Pressure, set to High, and set the timer to 60 minutes. Press Start.
4.   Release pressure naturally for about 10 minutes. Set the chuck roast to a cutting board and use two forks to shred. Serve immediately.

Hot Dogs With Peppers

Servings: 6

Cooking Time: 15 Min

Ingredients:

- 6 sausages pork sausage links

- 1 green bell pepper; sliced into strips
- 1 red bell pepper; sliced into strips
- 1 yellow bell pepper; sliced into strips
- 2 spring onions; sliced
- 1 ½ cups beer /375ml
- 6 hot dog rolls
- 1 tbsp olive oil /15ml

Directions:

1. Warm oil on Sear/Sauté. Add in sausage links and sear for 5 minutes until browned; set aside on a plate. Into the Foodi, pile peppers. Lay the sausages on top. Add beer into the pot.
2. Seal the pressure lid, choose Pressure, set to High, and set the timer to 5 minutes. Press Start. When ready, release the pressure quickly. Serve sausages in buns topped with onions and peppers.

Zucchini & Beef Lasagna

Servings: 4

Cooking Time: 1 Hour

Ingredients:

- 2 zucchini, cut lengthwise in ½-thick slices
- ½ tsp salt
- Nonstick cooking spray
- 3 tomatoes
- 1 cup onion, chopped
- 2 cloves garlic, chopped fine
- 1 serrano chili, chopped fine
- 1 ½ cups mushrooms, chopped
- 1 lb. lean ground beef
- ½ cube chicken bouillon
- 1 tsp paprika
- 1 tsp thyme
- 1 tsp basil
- ½ tsp salt
- ¼ tsp pepper
- ½ cup mozzarella cheese, grated

Directions:

1. Place zucchini in a large bowl, sprinkle with salt and let sit 10 minutes.
2. Spray the rack with cooking spray and add it to the cooking pot. Pat zucchini dry with paper towels and lay them on the rack, these will need to be done in batches. Add the tender-crisp lid and set to broil, cook zucchini 3 minutes. Transfer to a paper-towel lined baking sheet.
3. Bring a pot of water to a boil. Cut the ends off the tomatoes and make an X insertion on the top. Place in boiling water for 2-3 minutes. Transfer to bowl of ice water and remove the skin. Chop the tomatoes.
4. Spray the cooking pot with cooking spray and set to sauté on med-high heat. Add onion, garlic, and chili and cook 1 minute. Add the tomatoes and mushrooms and cook 3-4 minutes or until almost tender. Transfer to a bowl.
5. Add the beef to the cooking pot and cook, breaking up with a spatula, until no longer pink.
6. Add the vegetables to the beef along with the bouillon and remaining spices. Reduce heat to low and simmer 25 minutes, stirring occasionally.
7. Spray an 8x8-inch baking dish with cooking spray. Lay 1/3 of the zucchini across the bottom. Top with 1/3 of the meat mixture. Repeat layers two more times. Sprinkle cheese evenly over the top.
8. Add the rack back to the cooking pot and place lasagna on it. Add the tender-crisp lid and set to bake on 375°F or 190°C. Bake 35

minutes. Transfer to cutting board and let rest 10 minutes before serving.

Nutrition:

- InfoCalories 309,Total Fat 18g,Total Carbs 9g,Protein 28g,Sodium 775mg.

Beef Bourguignon(2)

Servings: 4

Cooking Time: 45 Min

Ingredients:

- 2 lb. stewing beef; cut in large chunks /900g
- ½ lb. mushrooms; sliced /225g
- 2 carrots, peeled and chopped
- 1 onion; sliced
- 2 cloves garlic, crushed
- 1 cup red wine /250ml
- ½ cup cognac /65g
- 2 cups beef broth /500ml
- 1 bunch thyme
- ¼ cup pearl onion /3.5g
- 2 ½ tbsp olive oil/37.5ml
- 2 tbsp flour /30g
- 3 tsp tomato paste /15g
- ¼ tsp red wine vinegar /1.25ml
- Salt and pepper, to taste

Directions:

1. Select Sear/Sauté mode. Season the beef with salt, pepper, and a light sprinkle of flour. Heat the oil in the pot, and brown the meat on all sides. Pour the cognac into the pot and stir the mixture with a spoon to deglaze the bottom. Stir in thyme, red wine, broth, paste, garlic, mushrooms, onion, and pearl onions.
2. Close the lid, secure the pressure valve, and select Pressure mode on High for 25 minutes. Press Start/Stop.
3. Once the timer is off, do a natural pressure release for 10 minutes, then a quick pressure release to let out the remaining steam. Close the crisping lid and cook for 10 minutes on Broil mode. When ready, open the lid.
4. Use the spoon to remove the thyme, adjust the taste with salt and pepper, and add the vinegar. Stir the sauce and serve hot, with a side of rice.

Fresh Kielbasa And Braised Sweet And Sour Cabbage

Servings:6

Cooking Time: 1 Hour

Ingredients:

- 1½ pounds fresh kielbasa sausage links
- ½ stick (¼ cup) unsalted butter
- ½ medium onion, thinly sliced
- 2 garlic cloves, minced
- 1 large head red cabbage, cut into ¼-inch slices
- ¼ cup granulated sugar
- ⅓ cup apple cider vinegar
- ½ cup water
- 2 teaspoons caraway seeds
- Kosher salt
- Freshly ground black pepper

Directions:

6. Add the tender-crisp lid and set to air fry on 375°F or 190°C. Cook fritters 4-5 minutes per side until golden brown and cooked through. Serve immediately.

Nutrition:

- InfoCalories 180,Total Fat 10g,Total Carbs 15g,Protein 7g,Sodium 451mg.

Beef And Garbanzo Bean Chili

Servings: 10

Cooking Time: 45 Min

Ingredients:

- 1 pound garbanzo beans; soaked overnight, rinsed /900g
- 2 ½ pounds ground beef /1150g
- 1 can tomato puree /180ml
- 1 small jalapeño with seeds; minced
- 6 garlic cloves; minced
- 2 onions, finely chopped
- 2 ½ cups beef broth /625ml
- ¼ cup chili powder /32.5g
- 2 tbsp ground cumin /30g
- 1 tbsp olive oil /15ml
- 1 tsp garlic powder /5g
- ¼ tsp cayenne pepper /1.25g
- 1 tsp dried oregano /5g
- 2 tsp salt /10g
- 1 tsp smoked paprika /5g

Directions:

1. Add the garbanzo beans to the Foodi and pour in cold water to cover 1 inch. Seal the pressure lid, choose Pressure, set to High, and set the timer to 20 minutes. Press Start. When ready, release the pressure quickly.
2. Drain beans and rinse with cold water. Set aside. Wipe clean the Foodi and set to Sear/Sauté, set to Medium High, and choose Start/Stop to preheat the pot. Press Start. Warm olive oil, add in onion, and cook for 3 minutes until soft.
3. Add jalapeño, ground beef, and minced garlic, and stir-fry for 5 minutes until everything is cooked through. Stir in chili powder, kosher salt, garlic powder, paprika, cumin, oregano, and cayenne pepper, and cook until soft, about 30 seconds. Pour beef broth, garbanzo beans, and tomato paste into the pot.
4. Seal the pressure lid, choose Pressure, set to High, and set the timer to 20 minutes; press Start. When ready, release pressure naturally for about 10 minutes. Open the lid, press Sear/Sauté, and cook as you stir until desired consistency is attained. Spoon chili into bowls and serve.

Chorizo Stuffed Yellow Bell Peppers

Servings: 4

Cooking Time: 40 Min

Ingredients:

- ¾ pound chorizo /337.5g
- 1 small onion; diced
- ⅔ cup diced fresh tomatoes /88g
- 1½ cups cooked rice /195g
- 1 cup shredded Mexican blend cheese; divided /130g
- 4 large yellow bell peppers
- 2 tsp olive oil /10ml

Directions:

1. Cut about ¼ to ⅓ inch off the top of each pepper. Cut through the ribs inside the peppers and pull out the core and remove as much of the ribs as possible.

2. On the Foodi, choose Sear/Sauté and adjust to Medium. Press Start to preheat the inner pot for 5 minutes. Heat the oil in the pot until shimmering and cook in the chorizo while breaking the meat with a spatula. Cook until just starting to brown, about 2 minutes.
3. Add the onion and sauté until the vegetables soften and the chorizo has now browned, about 3 minutes.
4. Turn the Foodi off and scoop the chorizo and vegetables into a medium bowl. Add the tomatoes, rice, and ½ cup or 65g of cheese to the bowl. Mix to combine well.
5. Spoon the filling mixture into the bell peppers to the brim. Clean the inner pot with a paper towel and return the pot to the base. Pour 1 cup or 250ml of water into the pot and fix the rack in the pot in the lower position. Put the peppers on the rack and cover the tops loosely with a piece of foil.
6. Lock the pressure lid into place and set to Seal. Choose Pressure; adjust the pressure to High and the time to 12 minutes. Press Start.
7. After cooking, perform a quick pressure release and carefully open the lid. Remove the foil from the top of the peppers and sprinkle the remaining ½ cup or 65g of cheese on the peppers.
8. Close the crisping lid; choose Broil, adjust the time to 5 minutes, and press Start to broil the cheese. After 4 minutes, open the lid and check the peppers. The cheese should have melted and browned a bit. If not, close the lid and continue cooking. Let the peppers cool for several minutes before serving.

Pork Sandwiches With Slaw

Servings: 8

Cooking Time: 20 Min

Ingredients:

- 2 lb. chuck roast /900g
- 1 white onion; sliced
- 2 cups beef broth /500ml
- ¼ cup sugar /32.5g
- 1 tsp Spanish paprika /5g
- 1 tsp garlic powder /5g
- 2 tbsp apple cider vinegar /30ml
- Salt to taste
- Assembling:
- 4 Buns, halved
- 1 cup red cabbage, shredded /130g
- 1 cup white cabbage, shredded /130g
- 1 cup white Cheddar cheese, grated /130g
- 4 tbsp mayonnaise /60ml

Directions:

1. Place the pork roast on a clean flat surface and sprinkle with paprika, garlic powder, sugar, and salt. Use your hands to rub the seasoning on the meat.
2. Open the Foodi, add beef broth, onions, pork, and apple cider vinegar. Close the lid, secure the pressure valve, and select Pressure mode on High pressure for 12 minutes. Press Start/Stop.
3. Once the timer has ended, do a quick pressure release. Remove the roast to a cutting board, and use two forks to shred them. Return to the pot, close the crisping lid, and cook for 3 minutes on Air Crisp at 300 °F or 150°C.

4. In the buns, spread the mayo, add the shredded pork, some cooked onions from the pot, and shredded red and white cabbage. Top with the cheese.

Baked Rigatoni With Beef Tomato Sauce

Servings: 4
Cooking Time: 75 Min
Ingredients:
- 2 pounds ground beef /900g
- 2 cans tomato sauce /720ml
- 16-ounce dry rigatoni /480g
- 1 cup cottage cheese /130g
- 1 cup shredded mozzarella cheese /130g
- ½ cup chopped fresh parsley /65g
- 1 cup water /250ml
- 1 cup dry red wine /250ml
- 1 tbsp butter /15g
- ½ tsp garlic powder /2.5g
- ½ tsp salt /2.5g

Directions:
1. Choose Sear/Sauté and set to High. Choose Start/Stop to preheat the pot. Melt the butter, add the beef and cook for 5 minutes, or until browned and cooked well. Stir in the tomato sauce, water, wine, and rigatoni; season with the garlic powder and salt.
2. Put the pressure lid together and lock in the Seal position. Choose Pressure, set to Low, and set the time to 2 minutes. Choose Start/Stop to begin cooking.
3. When the timer is done, perform a natural pressure release for 10 minutes, then a quick pressure release and carefully open the lid. Stir in the cottage cheese and evenly sprinkle the top of the pasta with the mozzarella cheese. Close the crisping lid.
4. Choose Broil, and set the time to 3 minutes. Choose Start/Stop to begin. Cook for 3 minutes, or until the cheese has melted, slightly browned, and bubbly. Garnish with the parsley and serve immediately.

Pork Pie

Servings:8
Cooking Time: 45 Minutes
Ingredients:
- 2 tablespoons extra-virgin olive oil
- 1 pound ground pork
- 1 yellow onion, diced
- 1 can black beans, drained
- 1 cup frozen corn kernels
- 1 can green chiles
- 2 tablespoons chili powder
- 1 box cornbread mix
- 1½ cups milk
- 1 cup shredded Cheddar cheese

Directions:
1. Select SEAR/SAUTÉ and set temperature to MED. Select START/STOP to begin. Let preheat for 3 minutes.
2. Add the olive oil, pork, and onion. Brown the pork, stirring frequently to break the meat into smaller pieces, until cooked through, about 5 minutes.
3. Add the beans, corn, chiles, and chili powder and stir. Simmer, stirring frequently, about 10 minutes.
4. In a medium bowl, combine the cornbread mix, milk, and cheese. Pour it over simmering mixture in an even layer. Close crisping lid.

5. Select BAKE/ROAST, set temperature to 360°F or 180°C, and set time for 25 minutes. Select START/STOP to begin.
6. After 20 minutes, use wooden toothpick to check if cornbread is done. If the toothpick inserted into the cornbread does not come out clean, close lid and cook for the remaining 5 minutes.
7. When cooking is complete, open lid. Let cool for 10 minutes before slicing and serving.
Nutrition:
- InfoCalories: 491,Total Fat: 24g,Sodium: 667mg,Carbohydrates: 47g,Protein: 24g.

Pork Italiana

Servings: 8
Cooking Time:x
Ingredients:
- 2 tbsp. olive oil, divided
- 1 ½ lb. pork loin, cut in 3/4-inch cubes
- 1 green bell pepper, chopped
- 2 onions, chopped
- 2 cloves garlic, chopped fine
- 1 ½ tsp salt
- 1 bay leaf
- 8 oz. tomatoes, undrained
- ¼ tsp pepper
- 2 cups brown rice
- 4 cups water
- 2 chicken bouillon cube
- ½ cup sherry
- 1/8 tsp saffron
- ½ tsp water
- 1 cup green peas
- 4 oz. pimentos, drained
- 12 green olives

Directions:
1. Add 1 tablespoon oil to the cooking pot and set to sauté on med-high heat.
2. Add the pork and cook until browned on all sides, stirring occasionally. Transfer to a bowl.
3. Add remaining oil, bell pepper, onion, and garlic. Cook until pepper is tender, about 5 minutes.
4. Return pork to the pot and stir in salt, bay leaf, tomatoes, and pepper, mix well.
5. Add rice, water, bouillon, and sherry. Place the saffron in a small bowl and add ½ teaspoon water, stir until saffron dissolves. Stir into pork mixture.
6. Bring pork mixture to a boil. Reduce heat to low, cover, and simmer 15-20 minutes until pork is tender and rice is cooked.
7. Serve garnished with peas, olives, and pimientos.
Nutrition:
- InfoCalories 369,Total Fat 9g,Total Carbs 45g,Protein 25g,Sodium 741mg.

Speedy Pork Stir Fry

Servings: 4
Cooking Time: 5 Minutes
Ingredients:
- 2 tbsp. soy sauce, low sodium
- 1 tsp sugar

- 1 tsp cornstarch
- 1 lb. pork loin, cut in ¼-inch strips
- 4 tbsp. peanut oil
- 5 cloves garlic, sliced thin
- 1 tsp. red pepper flakes
- 10 green onions, sliced
- ½ tsp sesame oil

Directions:

1. In a large bowl, whisk together soy sauce, sugar, and cornstarch until smooth.
2. Add the pork to the bowl and toss to coat. Let sit for 10 minutes.
3. Add the oil to the cooking pot and set to sauté on med-high heat.
4. Add the garlic and pepper flakes and cook, stirring, about 30 seconds or until garlic starts to brown.
5. Add the pork mixture and cook until meat is no longer pink, stirring constantly.
6. Add the green onions and cook 1 minute more. Turn off the heat and stir in the sesame oil. Serve as is or over hot, cooked rice.

Nutrition:

- InfoCalories 182,Total Fat 12g,Total Carbs 3g,Protein 15g,Sodium 279mg.

Moroccan Beef

Servings: 10
Cooking Time: 7 Hours 40 Minutes

Ingredients:

- 2 lbs. beef chuck roast, cubed
- 1 tbsp. salt
- 1 tbsp. butter, unsalted
- 2 tomatoes, sliced
- 2 tbsp. honey
- 1 tbsp. harissa paste
- 1 tbsp. tablespoon ras el hanout
- ½ tsp cinnamon
- ½ lb. dried apricots, sliced
- 1 yellow bell pepper, seeded & sliced
- 1 cup onion, sliced thin
- 3 cloves garlic, chopped
- ¼ cup dates, chopped
- 2 cups rice, cooked
- ¼ cup cilantro, chopped
- ¼ cup sesame seeds, toasted

Directions:

1. Season meat with salt and mix well.
2. Add the butter to the cooking pot and set to sauté on med-high heat.
3. Once butter has melted, add meat and cook, stirring occasionally, until browned on all sides.
4. In a large bowl, combine tomatoes, honey, harissa, ras el hanout seasoning, and cinnamon, mix well. Stir in apricots, bell pepper, onion, garlic, and dates. Pour over the beef.
5. Add the lid and set to slow cook on low. Cook 7-9 hours until beef and vegetables are tender.
6. Divide rice evenly among serving plates. Top with beef mixture and garnish with cilantro and sesame seeds. Serve.

Nutrition:

- InfoCalories 456,Total Fat 12g,Total Carbs 61g,Protein 29g,Sodium 992mg.

Cheese And Pepperoni Calzones

Servings:4
Cooking Time: 18 Minutes

Ingredients:

- All-purpose flour, for dusting
- 16 ounces store-bought pizza dough
- 1 egg, beaten
- 2 cups shredded mozzarella cheese
- 1 cup ricotta cheese
- ½ cup grated Parmesan cheese
- ½ cup sliced pepperoni
- Cooking spray
- Pizza sauce, for dipping

Directions:

1. Dust a clean work surface with the flour. Divide the pizza dough into four equal pieces. Place the dough on the floured surface and roll each piece into an 8-inch round of even thickness. Dust your rolling pin and work surface with additional flour, as needed, to ensure the dough does not stick. Brush egg wash around the edges of each round.
2. Place Cook & Crisp Basket in pot. Close crisping lid. Select AIR CRISP, set temperature to 390°F or 200°C, and set time to 5 minutes. Select START/STOP to begin preheating.
3. In a medium bowl, combine the mozzarella, ricotta, and Parmesan cheese. Fold in the pepperoni.
4. Spoon one-quarter of the cheese mixture onto one side of each dough round. Fold the other half over the filling and press firmly to seal the edges together. Brush each calzone all over with the egg wash.
5. Once unit is preheated, open lid and coat the basket with cooking spray. Place two calzones in the basket in a single layer. Close crisping lid.
6. Select AIR CRISP, set temperature to 390°F or 200°C, and set time to 9 minutes. Select START/STOP to begin.
7. After 7 minutes, open lid to check for doneness. If desired, cook for up to 2 minutes more, until golden brown.
8. When cooking is complete, remove calzone from basket. Repeat steps 5 and 6 with the remaining calzones. Serve warm.

Nutrition:

- InfoCalories: 593,Total Fat: 29g,Sodium: 1253mg,Carbohydrates: 51g,Protein: 37g.

Simple Beef & Shallot Curry

Servings: 4
Cooking Time: 40 Minutes

Ingredients:

- 1 lb. beef stew meat
- ¼ tsp salt
- 1/8 tsp turmeric
- 2 tbsp. olive oil
- 2 tbsp. shallots, sliced
- 1 tbsp. fresh ginger, grated
- 1 tbsp. garlic, chopped fine
- 3 cups water
- 2 tsp fish sauce
- 8 shallots, peeled & left whole
- ½ tsp chili powder

Directions:

1. In a large bowl, combine beef, salt, and turmeric, use your fingers to massage the seasonings into the meat. Cover and refrigerate 1 hour.
2. Add the oil to the cooking pot and set to sauté on med-high.
3. Add the sliced shallot and cook until golden brown, 6-8 minutes. Transfer to a bowl.
4. Add the garlic and ginger to the pot and cook 1 minute or until fragrant.
5. Add the beef and cook until no pink shows, about 5-6 minutes. Stir in the water and fish sauce until combined.
6. Add the lid and set to pressure cook on high. Set the timer for 20 minutes. When the timer goes off, use manual release to remove the pressure.
7. Set back to sauté on med-high and add the fried shallots, whole shallots, and chili powder. Cook, stirring frequently, until shallots are soft and sauce has thickened, about 10 minutes. Serve.

Nutrition:

- InfoCalories 70,Total Fat 9g,Total Carbs 4g,Protein 7g,Sodium 130mg.

Pork Chops With Green Beans And Scalloped Potatoes

Servings:2
Cooking Time: 45 Minutes

Ingredients:

- 1½ cups chicken broth
- 2 cups half-and-half
- ¼ cup cornstarch
- 2 teaspoons garlic powder
- Kosher salt
- Freshly ground black pepper
- 4 Russet potatoes, sliced ¼-inch thick
- 4 cups shredded Cheddar cheese, divided
- 2 bone-in pork chops
- ½ pound green beans, ends trimmed
- 1 teaspoon minced garlic
- 1 teaspoon extra-virgin olive oil

Directions:

1. In a medium bowl, whisk together the chicken broth, half-and-half, cornstarch, garlic powder, salt, and pepper. Pour just enough broth mixture to cover the bottom of the pot.
2. Layer half of the sliced potatoes in the bottom of the pot. Cover the potatoes with 1 cup of cheese, then layer the remaining potatoes over the cheese. Cover the second layer of potatoes with 1 cup of cheese, then pour in the remaining broth mixture to cover potatoes. Assemble pressure lid, making sure the pressure release valve is in the SEAL position.
3. Select PRESSURE and set to HI. Set time to 25 minutes. Select START/STOP to begin.
4. When pressure cooking is complete, allow pressure to release naturally for 25 minutes. After 25 minutes, quick release remaining pressure by moving the pressure release valve to the VENT position. Carefully remove lid when unit has finished releasing pressure.
5. Cover the potatoes with remaining 2 cups of cheese. Place the Reversible Rack in the broil position in the pot. Close crisping lid.
6. Select BROIL and set time to 20 minutes. Select START/STOP to begin.
7. Season the pork chops with salt and pepper.
8. After 4 minutes, open lid. Place the pork chops on the rack. Close the lid and continue cooking for another 12 minutes.
9. In a large bowl, toss the green beans with the garlic and oil, and season with salt and pepper.

10. After 12 minutes, open lid and add the green beans to the rack with the pork chops. Close lid and continue cooking for the remaining 4 minutes.
11. When cooking is complete, open lid and serve.

Nutrition:

- InfoCalories: 1916,Total Fat: 118g,Sodium: 3116mg,Carbohydrates: 107g,Protein: 105g.

Rosemary Crusted Lamb Chops

Servings: 3
Cooking Time: 10 Minutes

Ingredients:

- 2 tbsp. fresh rosemary, chopped fine
- 2 tsp salt
- 1 tsp pepper
- 1 clove garlic, chopped fine
- 4 tbsp. olive oil, divided
- 1 lb. lamb chops

Directions:

1. In a small bowl, combine rosemary, salt, pepper, garlic, and 2 tablespoon oil, mix well. Coat lamb on both sides. Cover and let sit 30 minutes.
2. Add the remaining oil to the cooking pot and set to seat on medium heat.
3. If you are using double rib chops, sear on all sides, about 2-3 minutes per side for medium rare chops. If you are using single rib chops cook about 1 minute on each side for medium rare. For a medium chop, turn off the heat and cover the pot, let lamb sit for 5 minutes.
4. Transfer chops to a plate and tent with foil, let rest 5 minutes before serving.

Nutrition:

- InfoCalories 272,Total Fat 23g,Total Carbs 1g,Protein 16g,Sodium 938mg.

Beef Bulgogi

Servings: 4
Cooking Time: 10 Minutes

Ingredients:

- 1 lb. lean ground beef
- 10 cloves garlic, chopped
- 1 onion, chopped fine
- 4 tbsp. soy sauce, low sodium
- 2 tbsp. mirin
- 2 tbsp. sugar
- 1 tbsp. apricot jam
- ½ tsp pepper
- 1 tbsp. olive oil
- 5 green onions, chopped
- 1 tsp sesame seeds
- 1 tsp sesame oil

Directions:

1. In a large bowl, combine beef, garlic, onion, soy sauce, mirin, sugar, jam, and pepper, mix well.
2. Add oil to the cooking pot and set to sauté on med-high heat.
3. Add the beef mixture and cook, breaking up the beef with a spatula, 8-10 minutes until meat is fully cooked and all liquid has evaporated.

4. Stir in the green onions. Turn off the heat and add sesame seeds and sesame oil, toss to distribute and serve immediately.

Nutrition:
- InfoCalories 419,Total Fat 28g,Total Carbs 19g,Protein 23g,Sodium 602mg.

Beef Stew With Beer

Servings: 4
Cooking Time: 60 Min

Ingredients:
- 2 lb. beef stewed meat; cut into bite-size pieces /900g
- 1 packet dry onion soup mix
- 2 cloves garlic; minced
- 2 cups beef broth /500ml
- ¼ cup flour /32.5g
- 1 medium bottle beer
- 3 tbsp butter/45g
- 2 tbsp Worcestershire sauce /30ml
- 1 tbsp tomato paste /15g
- Salt and black pepper to taste

Directions:
1. In a zipper bag, add beef, salt, all-purpose flour, and pepper. Close the bag up and shake it to coat the meat well with the mixture. Select Sear/Sauté mode on the Foodi. Melt the butter, and brown the beef on both sides, for 5 minutes.
2. Pour the broth to deglaze the bottom of the pot. Stir in tomato paste, beer, Worcestershire sauce, and the onion soup mix.
3. Close the lid, secure the pressure valve, and select Pressure mode on High pressure for 25 minutes. Press Start/Stop to start cooking.
4. Once the timer is done, do a natural pressure release for 10 minutes, and then a quick pressure release to let out any remaining steam.
5. Open the pressure lid and close the crisping lid. Cook on Broil mode for 10 minutes. Spoon the beef stew into serving bowls and serve with over a bed of vegetable mash with steamed greens.

Traditional Beef Stroganoff

Servings: 6
Cooking Time: 1 Hr 15 Min

Ingredients:
- 2 pounds beef stew meat /900g
- 8 ounces sour cream /240g
- 2 garlic cloves; minced
- 1 onion; chopped
- 3 cups fresh mushrooms; chopped /390g
- 1 cup long-grain rice, cooked /130g
- 1 cup beef broth /250ml
- ¼ cup flour /32.5g
- 2 tbsp olive oil /30ml
- 1 tbsp chopped fresh parsley /15g
- salt and ground black pepper to taste

Directions:
1. In a large bowl, combine salt, pepper and flour. Add beef and massage to coat beef in flour mixture. Warm oil on Sear/Sauté. Brown the beef for 4 to 5 minutes. Add garlic and onion and cook for 3 minutes until fragrant. Add beef broth to the pot.
2. Seal the pressure lid, choose Pressure, set to High, and set the timer to 35 minutes. Press Start. When ready, release the pressure quickly.

3. Open the lid and stir mushrooms and sour cream into the beef mixture. Seal the pressure lid again, choose Pressure, set to High, and set the timer to 2 minutes. Press Start.
4. When ready, release the pressure quickly. Season the stroganoff with pepper and salt; scoop over cooked rice before serving.

Mexican Pot Roast

Servings: 8
Cooking Time: 8 Hours

Ingredients:
- 3 lb. beef chuck roast
- 4 cups lemon-lime soda
- 1 tsp chili powder
- 1 tsp salt
- 3 cloves garlic, chopped
- 2 limes juiced

Directions:
1. Place the roast in the cooking pot and pour the soda over the top. Sprinkle with chili powder, salt, and garlic.
2. Add the lid and set to slow cook on low. Cook 8 hours or until roast is tender.
3. Transfer roast to a large bowl and use 2 forks to shred. Pour the lime juice over the meat and serve hot.

Nutrition:
- InfoCalories 367,Total Fat 14g,Total Carbs 14g,Protein 46g,Sodium 449mg.

Beef & Broccoli Casserole

Servings: 4
Cooking Time: 40 Minutes

Ingredients:
- 12 oz. broccoli florets
- 1 lb. extra lean ground beef
- 14 oz. tomato sauce
- 1 stalk celery, chopped fine
- 1 tsp salt
- 1 tsp garlic powder
- ¼ tsp cayenne pepper
- 1 ¾ cup cheddar cheese, grated, divided
- ¼ cup parmesan cheese

Directions:
1. Add the broccoli to large microwave safe bowl, cover and microwave about 5 minutes until tender. Dump onto paper towel lined baking sheet to drain.
2. Add the beef to the cooking pot and set to sauté on med-high heat. Cook, breaking meat up with a spatula, about 5 minutes or until no longer pink.
3. Add tomato sauce, celery, salt, garlic powder, and cayenne stir well. Simmer 10 minutes or until sauce thickens.
4. Add the broccoli and half the cheddar cheese and stir to combine. Sprinkle remaining cheddar and parmesan over the top.
5. Add the tender-crisp lid and set to bake on 375°F or 190°C. Bake 20 minutes until hot and bubbling. Let rest 10 minutes before serving.

Nutrition:
- InfoCalories 432,Total Fat 25g,Total Carbs 13g,Protein 42g,Sodium 1590mg.

Beef And Broccoli Sauce

Servings: 4

Cooking Time: 35 Min

Ingredients:

- 2 lb. chuck roast, boneless and cut into thin strips /900g
- 4 cloves garlic; minced
- 1 cup beef broth /250ml
- ¾ cup soy sauce /188ml
- 7 cups broccoli florets /910g
- 1 tbsp cornstarch /15g
- 1 tbsp olive oil /15ml
- Salt to taste

Directions:

1. Open the lid of Foodi, and select Sear/Sauté mode. Add the olive oil, and once heated, add the beef and minced garlic. Cook the meat until brown. Stir in soy sauce and beef broth.
2. Close the lid, secure the pressure valve, and select Pressure mode on High pressure for 10 minutes. Press Start/Stop to start cooking.
3. Once the timer has ended, do a quick pressure release and remove the meat and set aside.
4. Use a soup spoon to fetch out a quarter of the liquid into a bowl, add the cornstarch, and mix it until it is well dissolved.
5. Pour the starch mixture into the pot and place the reversible rack. Place the broccoli florets on it and seal the pressure lid. Select Steam mode on LOW for 5 minutes.
6. When ready, do a quick pressure release and open the lid. Remove the rack, stir the sauce, add the meat and close the crisping lid.
7. Cook for 5 minutes on Broil mode. The sauce should be thick enough when you finish cooking. Dish the beef broccoli sauce into a serving bowl and serve with a side of cooked pasta.

Stuffed Cabbage Rolls

Servings: 6

Cooking Time: 5 Hours

Ingredients:

- 12 cabbage leaves
- 3 ¼ tsp salt, divided
- 15 oz. tomato sauce
- 2 tbsp. honey
- 1 tsp paprika
- ½ tsp thyme
- 2 tbsp. lemon juice
- 2 tbsp. ketchup
- 1 tsp Worcestershire sauce
- 1 ¼ tsp pepper
- 1 cup long grain brown rice, cooked
- 1 egg, beaten
- ¼ cup milk
- ¼ cup onion, chopped fine
- 1 clove garlic, chopped fine
- 1 lb. lean ground beef

Directions:

1. Fill a large pot with water and add 2 teaspoons salt. Bring to a boil on high heat. Add cabbage leaves and boil 2 minutes. Transfer leaves to a plate and let cool.
2. In a medium bowl, whisk together tomato sauce, honey, spices, lemon juice, ketchup, Worcestershire, remaining salt, and pepper until smooth.

3. In a separate bowl, combine rice, egg, milk, onion, garlic, and beef. Stir in ¼ of the sauce and mix well.
4. Spoon ¼ cup of beef mixture into the center of each cabbage leaf. Roll up, tucking in the ends. Place in the cooking pot. Pour remaining sauce over the rolls.
5. Add the lid and set to slow cook in high. Cook 4-5 hours until cabbage is tender and filling is cooked through. Serve.

Nutrition:

- InfoCalories 282, Total Fat 10g, Total Carbs 25g, Protein 24g, Sodium 1732mg.

Beef And Cherry Tagine

Servings: 4

Cooking Time: 1 Hr 20 Min

Ingredients:

- 1 ½ pounds stewing beef, trimmed /675g
- 1 onion; chopped
- 1-star anise
- ¼ cup toasted almonds, slivered /32.5g
- 1 cup dried cherries, halved /130g
- 1 cup water /250ml
- 1 tbsp honey /15ml
- 2 tbsp olive oil /30ml
- ¼ tsp ground allspice /1.25g
- 1 tsp ground cinnamon /5g
- ½ tsp paprika /2.5g
- ½ tsp turmeric /2.5g
- ½ tsp salt /2.5g
- ¼ tsp ground ginger /1.25g

Directions:

1. Set your Foodi to Sear/Sauté, set to Medium High, and choose Start/Stop to preheat the pot. Warm olive oil. Add in onions and cook for 3 minutes until fragrant. Mix in beef and cook for 2 minutes each side until browned.
2. Stir in anise, cinnamon, turmeric, allspice, salt, paprika, and ginger; cook for 2 minutes until aromatic.
3. Add in honey and water. Seal the pressure lid, choose Pressure, set to High, and set the timer to 50 minutes. Press Start.
4. Meanwhile, in a bowl, soak dried cherries in hot water until softened. Once ready, release pressure naturally for 15 minutes. Drain cherries and stir into the tagine. Top with toasted almonds before serving.

Steak And Chips

Servings: 4

Cooking Time: 50 Min

Ingredients:

- 4 potatoes; cut into wedges
- 4 rib eye steaks
- 1 tbsp olive oil /15ml
- 1 tsp sweet paprika /5g
- 1 tsp salt; divided /5g
- 1 tsp ground black pepper /5g
- Cooking spray

Directions:

1. Put the Crisping Basket in the pot. Close the crisping lid. Choose Air Crisp, set the temperature to 390°F or 200°C, and set the time to 5 minutes. Press Start. Meanwhile, rub all over with olive oil. Put the potatoes in

the preheated Crisping Basket and season with ½ tsp or 2.5g of salt and ½ tsp or 2.5g of black pepper and sweet paprika.
2.   Close the crisping lid. Choose Air Crisp, set the temperature to 400°F or 205°C, and set the time to 35 minutes. Choose Start/Stop to begin baking.
3.   Season the steak on both sides with the remaining salt and black pepper. When done cooking, remove potatoes to a plate.
4.   Grease the Crisping Basket with cooking spray and put the steaks in the basket.
5.   Close the crisping lid. Choose Air Crisp, set the temperature to 400°F or 205°C, and set the time to 8 minutes. Choose Start/Stop to begin grilling.
6.   When ready, check the steaks for your preferred doneness and cook for a few more minutes if needed. Take out the steaks from the basket and rest for 5 minutes. Serve the steaks with the potato wedges and the steak sauce.

Italian Pasta Potpie

Servings:8
Cooking Time: 55 Minutes
Ingredients:
*   5 cups, plus 1 teaspoon water, divided
*   1 box rigatoni pasta
*   4 fresh Italian sausage links
*   1 bag frozen cooked meatballs
*   16 ounces whole milk ricotta
*   1 jar marinara sauce
*   2 cups shredded mozzarella cheese
*   1 refrigerated store-bought pie crust, room temperature
*   1 large egg
Directions:
1.   Pour 5 cups of water and the rigatoni in the pot. Assemble pressure lid, making sure the pressure release valve is in the SEAL position.
2.   Select PRESSURE and set to LO. Set time to 0 minutes. Select START/STOP to begin.
3.   When pressure cooking is complete, quick release the pressure by turning the pressure release valve to the VENT position. Carefully remove lid when unit has finished releasing pressure.
4.   Drain the pasta and set it aside, keeping warm. Wipe out pot and return it to base. Insert Cook & Crisp Basket into pot. Close crisping lid.
5.   Select AIR CRISP, set temperature to 390°F or 200°C, and set time to 15 minutes. Select START/STOP to begin. Let preheat for 5 minutes.
6.   Open lid and place the sausages in the basket. Close lid and cook for 10 minutes.
7.   When cooking is complete, remove sausages to a cutting board. Add the meatballs to the basket. Close crisping lid.
8.   Select AIR CRISP, set temperature to 390°F or 200°C, and set time to 10 minutes. Select START/STOP to begin.
9.   Slice sausages into very thin rounds.
10. When cooking is complete, transfer the meatballs to the cutting board and slice them in half.
11. In the pot, in this order, add a layer of ricotta, marinara sauce, sausage, mozzarella cheese, pasta, marinara sauce, meatballs, mozzarella cheese, pasta, ricotta, and marinara sauce. Place the pie crust on top of the filling.
12. In a small bowl, whisk together the egg and remaining 1 teaspoon of water. Brush this on top of the pie crust. With a knife, slice a couple of small holes in the middle of crust to vent it. Close crisping lid.

13. Select BAKE/ROAST, set temperature to 350°F or 175°C, and set time to 30 minutes. Select START/STOP to begin.
14. When cooking is complete, open lid. Let sit for 10 minutes before serving.
Nutrition:
*   InfoCalories: 821,Total Fat: 41g,Sodium: 1414mg,Carbohydrates: 67g,Protein: 40g.

Mongolian Beef

Servings: 2
Cooking Time: 11 Minutes
Ingredients:
*   1 lb. flank steak, sliced
*   1/4 cup corn starch
*   Sauce:
*   2 teaspoon vegetable oil
*   1/2 teaspoon ginger, minced
*   1 tablespoon garlic, minced
*   1/2 cup soy sauce
*   1/2 cup water
*   3/4 cup brown erythritol
Directions:
1.   Coat the beef with corn starch. Put in the Ninja Foodi basket.
2.   Seal the crisping lid. Set it to air crisp.
3.   Cook at 390 °F or 200°C for about 10 minutes per side.
4.   Remove and set aside. Set the pot to sauté. Stir in the vegetable oil.
5.   Sauté the ginger and garlic for 1 minute. Stir in the soy sauce, water and brown erythritol.
6.   Pour the prepared sauce on top of the beef.
Nutrition:
*   InfoCalories: 399; Fat: 11.7g; Carbohydrate: 39g; Protein: 33.7g

Easy Ham Stromboli

Servings: 8
Cooking Time: 20 Minute
Ingredients:
*   11 oz. crusty French loaf, refrigerated, unbaked
*   6 oz. deli ham, sliced thin
*   3 green onions, sliced
*   8 slices bacon, cooked & crumbled
*   1 ½ cups Swiss cheese, grated
Directions:
1.   Unroll dough on a sheet of parchment paper. Lay ham over dough, leaving ½-inch border. Sprinkle evenly with onions, bacon, and cheese.
2.   Roll up, starting with a long side. Pinch seam to seal and tuck ends under.
3.   Add the rack to the cooking pot and place Stromboli, on the parchment paper, on the rack. Us a sharp knife to cut several ¼-inch deep slices on top of the loaf.
4.   Add the tender-crisp lid and set to bake on 350°F or 175°C. Bake 2-30 minutes until golden brown. Use the parchment paper to transfer to a wire rack. Let cool slightly before slicing and serving.
Nutrition:
*   InfoCalories 329,Total Fat 19g,Total Carbs 24g,Protein 16g,Sodium 605mg.

Lime Glazed Pork Tenderloin

Servings: 8

Cooking Time: 45 Minutes

Ingredients:

- ¼ cup honey
- 1/3 cup lime juice
- 1 tsp lime zest, grated
- 2 cloves garlic, chopped fine
- 2 tbsp. yellow mustard
- ½ tsp salt
- ½ tsp pepper
- 2 pork tenderloins, 1 lb. each, fat trimmed
- Nonstick cooking spray

Directions:

1. In a large Ziploc bag combine, honey, lime juice, zest, garlic, mustard, salt, and pepper. Seal the bag and shake to mix.
2. Add the tenderloins and turn to coat. Refrigerate overnight.
3. Spray the rack with cooking spray and add it to the cooking pot.
4. Place the tenderloins on the rack, discard marinade. Add the tender-crisp lid and set to roast on 400°F or 205°C. Cook tenderloins 40-45 minutes or until they reach desired doneness. Transfer to serving plate and let rest 10 minutes before slicing and serving.

Nutrition:

- InfoCalories 162,Total Fat 3g,Total Carbs 10g,Protein 24g,Sodium 249mg.

Pork Chops With Squash Purée And Mushroom Gravy

Servings: 4

Cooking Time: 45 Min

Ingredients:

- 4 pork chops
- 1 pound butternut squash; cubed /450g
- 2 sprigs rosemary, leaves removed and chopped
- 2 sprigs thyme, leaves removed and chopped
- 4 cloves garlic; minced
- 1 cup mushrooms; chopped /130g
- 1 cup chicken broth /250ml
- 1 tbsp olive oil /15ml
- 2 tbsp olive oil /30ml
- 1 tbsp soy sauce /15ml
- 1 tsp cornstarch 5g

Directions:

1. Set on Sear/Sauté, set to Medium High, and choose Start/Stop to preheat the pot and heat rosemary, thyme and 1 tbsp or 15ml of olive oil. Add the pork chops and sear for 1 minute for each side until lightly browned.
2. Sauté garlic and mushrooms in the pressure cooker for 5-6 minutes until mushrooms are tender. Add soy sauce and chicken broth. Transfer pork chops to a wire trivet and place it into the pressure cooker. Over the chops, place a cake pan. Add butternut squash in the pot and drizzle with 1 tbsp olive oil.
3. Seal the pressure lid, choose Pressure, set to High, and set the timer to 10 minutes. Press Start. When ready, release the pressure quickly. Remove the pan and trivet from the pot. Stir cornstarch into the mushroom mixture for 2 to 3 minutes until the sauce thickens.
4. Transfer the mushroom sauce to an immersion blender and blend until you attain the desired consistency. Scoop sauce into a cup with a pour spout. Smash the squash into a purée. Set pork chops on a plate and ladle squash puree next to them. Top the pork chops with gravy.

Caribbean Ropa Vieja

Servings: 6

Cooking Time: 1 Hr 10 Min

Ingredients:

- 2 pounds beef skirt steak /900g
- ¼ cup cheddar cheese, shredded /32.5g
- 1 cup tomato sauce /250ml
- 3½ cups beef stock /875ml
- 1 cup dry red wine /250ml
- ¼ cup minced garlic /32.5g
- ¼ cup olive oil /62.5ml
- 1 green bell pepper, thinly sliced
- 1 red bell pepper, thinly sliced
- 2 bay leaves
- 1 red onion, halved and thinly sliced
- 1 tbsp vinegar /15ml
- 1 tsp dried oregano /5g
- 1 tsp ground cumin 5g
- Salt and ground black pepper to taste

Directions:

1. Season the skirt steak with pepper and salt. Add water into Foodi; mix in bay leaves and flank steak. Seal the pressure lid, choose Pressure, set to High, and set the timer to 35 minutes. Press Start. When ready, release the pressure quickly.
2. Remove skirt steak to a cutting board and allow to sit for about 5 minutes. Press Start. When cooled, shred the beef using two forks. Drain the pressure cooker, and reserve the bay leaves and 1 cup liquid.
3. Warm the oil on Sear/Sauté. Add onion, red bell pepper, cumin, garlic, green bell pepper, and oregano and continue cooking for 5 minutes until vegetables are softened.
4. Stir in reserved liquid, tomato sauce, bay leaves and red wine. Return shredded beef to the pot with vinegar; season with pepper and salt.
5. Seal the pressure lid, choose Pressure, set to High, and set the timer to 15 minutes. Press Start. Release pressure naturally for 10 minutes, then turn steam vent valve to Venting to release the remaining pressure quickly. Serve with shredded cheese.

Sausage With Celeriac And Potato Mash

Servings: 4

Cooking Time: 45 Min

Ingredients:

- 4 potatoes, peeled and diced
- 4 pork sausages
- 1 onion
- 2 cups vegetable broth /500ml
- 1 cup celeriac; chopped /130g
- ¼ cup milk /62.5ml
- ½ cup water /125ml
- 1 tbsp heavy cream /15ml
- 1 tbsp olive oil /15ml
- 2 tbsp butter /30g
- 1 tsp Dijon mustard /5g

- ½ tsp dry mustard powder /2.5g
- Fresh flat-leaf parsley; chopped
- salt and ground black pepper to taste

Directions:

1. Warm oil on Sear/Sauté. Add in sausages and cook for 1 to 2 minutes for each side until browned. Set the sausages to a plate. To the same pot, add onion and cook for 3 minutes until fragrant.
2. Add sausages on top of onions and pour water and broth over them. Place a trivet over onions and sausages. Put potatoes and celeriac in the steamer basket and transfer it to the trivet.
3. Seal the pressure lid, choose Pressure, set to High, and set the timer to 11 minutes. Press Start. When ready, release the pressure quickly.
4. Transfer potatoes and celeriac to a bowl and set sausages on a plate and cover them with aluminum foil. Using a potato masher, mash potatoes and celeriac together with black pepper, milk, salt and butter until mash becomes creamy and fluffy. Adjust the seasonings.
5. Set your Foodi to Sear/Sauté. Add the onion mixture and bring to a boil. Cook for 5 to 10 minutes until the mixture is reduced and thickened. Into the gravy, stir in dry mustard, salt, pepper, mustard and cream. Place the mash in 4 bowls in equal parts, top with a sausage or two, and gravy. Add parsley for garnishing.

Chipotle Beef Brisket

Servings: 4

Cooking Time: 1 Hr 10 Min

Ingredients:

- 2 pounds, beef brisket /900g
- 1 cup beef broth/250ml
- ¼ cup red wine /62.5ml
- 2 tbsp olive oil /30ml
- 1 tbsp Worcestershire sauce /15ml
- ½ tsp ground cumin /2.5g
- ½ tsp garlic powder /2.5g
- 1 tsp chipotle powder /5g
- ¼ tsp cayenne pepper/1.25g
- 2 tsp smoked paprika /10g
- ½ tsp dried oregano /2.5g
- ½ tsp salt /2.5g
- ½ tsp ground black pepper /2.5g
- A handful of parsley; chopped

Directions:

1. In a bowl, combine oregano, cumin, cayenne pepper, garlic powder, salt, paprika, pepper, Worcestershire sauce and chipotle powder; rub the seasoning mixture on the beef to coat. Warm olive oil on Sear/Sauté. Add in beef and cook for 3 to 4 minutes each side until browned completely. Pour in beef broth and red wine.
2. Seal the pressure lid, choose Pressure, set to High, and set the timer to 50 minutes. Press Start. Release the pressure naturally, for about 10 minutes.
3. Place the beef on a cutting board and Allow cooling for 10 minutes before slicing. Arrange the beef slices on a serving platter, pour the cooking sauce over and scatter with parsley to serve.

Pork Tenderloin With Warm Balsamic And Apple Chutney

Servings:4

Cooking Time: 23 Minutes

Ingredients:

- 1 pound pork tenderloin

- 2½ tablespoons minced rosemary, divided
- 2½ tablespoons minced thyme, divided
- Kosher salt
- Freshly ground black pepper
- 2 tablespoons extra-virgin olive oil
- 1 small white onion
- 1 tablespoon minced garlic
- ¾ cup apple juice
- 2 apples, cut into ½-inch cubes
- 2½ tablespoons balsamic vinegar
- 1 tablespoon honey
- 2½ teaspoons cornstarch
- 3 tablespoons unsalted butter, cubed

Directions:

1. Select SEAR/SAUTÉ and set to HI. Select START/STOP to begin. Let preheat for 5 minutes.
2. Season the pork with 1 tablespoon of rosemary, 1 tablespoon of thyme, salt, and pepper.
3. Once unit is preheated, add the olive oil. Once hot, add the pork and sear for 3 minutes on each side. Once seared, place the pork on a plate and set aside.
4. Add the onion, garlic, and apple juice. Stir, scraping the bottom of the pot to remove any brown bits. Add apples and vinegar and stir. Return the pork to the pot, nestling it in the apple mixture. Assemble pressure lid, making sure the pressure release valve is in the SEAL position.
5. Select PRESSURE and set to HI. Set time to 7 minutes. Select START/STOP to begin.
6. When pressure cooking is complete, allow pressure to naturally release for 14 minutes. After 14 minutes, quick release the pressure by turning the pressure release valve to the VENT position. Carefully remove lid when unit has finished releasing pressure.
7. Remove the pork from the pot, place it on a plate, and cover with aluminum foil.
8. Slightly mash the apples with a potato masher. Stir the honey into the mixture.
9. Remove ¼ cup of cooking liquid from the pot and mix it with the cornstarch until smooth. Pour this mixture into the pot and stir until thickened. Add the butter, 1 tablespoon of rosemary, and 1 tablespoon of thyme and stir until the butter is melted.
10. Slice the pork and serve it with the chutney. Garish with the remaining ½ tablespoon of rosemary and ½ tablespoon of thyme.

Nutrition:

- InfoCalories: 406,Total Fat: 20g,Sodium: 107mg,Carbohydrates: 33g,Protein: 24g.

Spicy Pork Grain Bowl

Servings:4

Cooking Time: 17 Minutes

Ingredients:

- ¼ cup smoked paprika
- 2 tablespoons ground cumin
- ½ teaspoon cayenne pepper
- 2 tablespoons dark brown sugar
- 3 tablespoons kosher salt, divided
- 2 teaspoons freshly ground black pepper
- 2 boneless pork chops
- 2 cups quinoa

- 3 cups chicken stock

Directions:

1. In a small bowl, mix together the paprika, cumin, cayenne pepper, sugar, salt, and pepper.
2. Pat the pork chops dry with a paper towel, then rub the spice mixture over the meat ensuring that it's fully covered.
3. Place the quinoa, chicken stock, and salt into the pot. Assemble pressure lid, making sure the pressure release valve is in the SEAL position.
4. Select PRESSURE and set to HI. Set time to 2 minutes. Select START/STOP to begin.
5. When pressure cooking is complete, allow pressure to naturally release for 10 minutes. After 10 minutes, quick release remaining pressure by turning the pressure release valve to the VENT position. Carefully remove lid when unit has finished releasing pressure.
6. Place Reversible Rack in pot in the higher position. Place the pork on the rack. Close crisping lid.
7. Select AIR CRISP, set temperature to 375°F or 190°C, and set time to 15 minutes. Select START/STOP to begin.
8. After 8 minutes, open lid, and using tongs, flip the pork chops. Close lid and continue cooking until the pork chops have reached an internal temperature of 165°F or 75°C.
9. When cooking is complete, remove the pork and rice from the pot. Slice the pork and serve in bowls over the rice with desired toppings, such as mint, avocado, mango, blueberries, sprouts, or grape tomatoes.

Nutrition:

- InfoCalories: 499,Total Fat: 14g,Sodium: 1255mg,Carbohydrates: 65g,Protein: 31g.

Korean Pork Chops

Servings: 4

Cooking Time: 10 Minutes

Ingredients:

- ½ cup soy sauce, low sodium
- 4 tbsp. honey
- 12 cloves garlic, chopped
- 4 tsp ginger
- 2 tsp sesame oil
- 2 tbsp. sweet chili sauce
- 4 top loin pork chops
- 2 tsp olive oil

Directions:

1. In a medium bowl, whisk together soy sauce, honey, garlic, ginger, sesame oil, and chili sauce until smooth. Reserve ½ the marinade for later.
2. Add the pork chops to the bowl and turn to coat. Let sit 10 minutes.
3. Add the olive oil to the cooking pot and set to sauté on med-high heat.
4. Add the pork chops and cook 5 minutes until browned. Turn the chops over and add the reserved marinade to the pot. Cook another 5 minutes or until chops are cooked through. Let rest 3 minutes before serving.

Nutrition:

- InfoCalories 364,Total Fat 8g,Total Carbs 24g,Protein 46g,Sodium 2218mg.

African Pork Stew

Servings: 6

Cooking Time: 8 Hours

Ingredients:

- 14½ oz. yellow hominy, drained
- 3 cups red beans, drained & rinsed
- 1 onion, chopped
- 2 tbsp. garlic, chopped fine
- 2 bay leaves
- 1 tsp Adobo powder
- 2 lbs. pork loin, cubed
- 2 potatoes, peeled & cubed
- 1 lb. smoked sausage, sliced
- 1 can diced tomatoes
- 2 tbsp. olive oil
- 3 slices bacon, chopped

Directions:

1. Add all the ingredients to the cooking pot and stir to combine.
2. Add the lid and set to slow cook on low. Cook 6-8 hours or until meat and vegetables are tender.
3. Discard the bay leaves, stir well and serve.

Nutrition:

- InfoCalories 784,Total Fat 37g,Total Carbs 55g,Protein 55g,Sodium 1185mg.

Corned Beef

Servings: 4

Cooking Time: 60 Minutes

Ingredients:

- 4 pounds beef brisket
- 2 garlic cloves, peeled and minced
- 2 yellow onions, peeled and sliced
- 11 ounces celery, sliced
- 1 tablespoon dried dill
- 3 bay leaves
- 4 cinnamon sticks, cut into halves
- Black pepper and salt to taste
- 17 ounces of water

Directions:

1. Take a suitable and stir in beef, add water and cover, let it soak for 2-3 hours.
2. Drain and transfer to the Ninja Foodi.
3. Stir in celery, onions, garlic, bay leaves, dill, cinnamon, dill, salt, pepper and the rest of the water to the Ninja Foodi.
4. Stir and combine it well.
5. Lock and secure the Ninja Foodi's lid, then cook on "HIGH" pressure for 50 minutes.
6. Release pressure naturally over 10 minutes.
7. Transfer meat to cutting board and slice, divide amongst plates and pour the cooking liquid alongside veggies over the servings.
8. Enjoy.

Nutrition:

- InfoCalories: 289; Fat: 21g; Carbohydrates: 14g; Protein: 9g

Short Ribs With Egg Noodles

Servings: 4

Cooking Time: 65 Min

Ingredients:

- 4 pounds bone-in short ribs /1800g
- 1 garlic clove; minced

- 1½ cups panko bread crumbs /195g
- Low-sodium beef broth
- 6 ounces egg noodles /180g
- 3 tbsp melted unsalted butter /45ml
- 2 tbsp prepared horseradish /30g
- 6 tbsp Dijon mustard /90g
- 2½ tsp salt /12.5g
- ½ tsp freshly ground black pepper /2.5g

Directions:

1. Season the short ribs on all sides with 1½ tsp s or 7.5g of salt. Pour 1 cup 250ml of broth into the inner pot. Put the reversible rack in the lower position in the pot, and place the short ribs on top. Seal the pressure lid, choose Pressure; adjust the pressure to High and the time to 25 minutes; press Start. After cooking, perform a natural pressure release for 5 minutes, then a quick pressure release, and carefully open the lid. Remove the rack and short ribs.

2. Pour the cooking liquid into a measuring cup to get 2 cups. If lesser than 2 cups, add more broth and season with salt and pepper.

3. Add the egg noodles and the remaining salt. Stir and submerge the noodles as much as possible. Seal the pressure lid, choose Pressure; adjust the pressure to High and the cook time to 4 minutes; press Start.

4. In a bowl, combine the horseradish, Dijon mustard, garlic, and black pepper. Brush the sauce on all sides of the short ribs and reserve any extra sauce.

5. In a bowl, mix the butter and breadcrumbs. Coat the ribs with the crumbs. Put the ribs back on the rack. After cooking, do a quick pressure release, and carefully open the lid. Stir the noodles, which may not be quite done but will continue cooking.

6. Return the rack and beef to the pot in the upper position.

7. Close the crisping lid and Choose Bake/Roast; adjust the temperature to 400°F or 205°C and the cook time to 15 minutes. Press Start. After 8 minutes, open the lid and turn the ribs over. Close the lid and continue cooking. Serve the beef and noodles, with the extra sauce on the side, if desired.

Pulled Pork Tacos

Servings: 5
Cooking Time: 1 Hr 25 Min

Ingredients:

- 2 pounds pork shoulder, trimmed; cut into chunks /900g
- 3 cups shredded cabbage /390g
- 5 taco tortillas
- 1 cup beer /250ml
- 1 cup vegetable broth /250ml
- 1/4 cup plus 2 tbsp lemon juice /92.5ml
- 1/4 cup mayonnaise /62.5ml
- 3 tbsp sugar /45g
- 2 tbsp honey /30ml
- 3 tsp taco seasoning /15g
- 1 tsp ground black pepper /5g
- 2 tsp mustard /10g

Directions:

1. In a bowl, combine sugar, taco seasoning, and black pepper; rub the mixture onto pork pieces to coat well. Allow to settling for 30 minutes. Into the Foodi, add 1/4 cup or 62.5ml lemon juice, broth, pork and beer.

2. Seal the pressure lid, choose Pressure, set to High, and set the timer to 50 minutes. Press Start. Meanwhile in a large bowl, mix mayonnaise, mustard, 2 tbsp lemon juice, cabbage and honey until well coated.

3. Release pressure naturally for 15 minutes before doing a quick release. Transfer the pork to a cutting board and Allow cooling before using two forks to shred. Skim and get rid of fat from liquid in the pressure cooker. Return pork to the pot and mix with the liquid. Top the pork with slaw on taco tortillas before serving.

Ropa Vieja

Servings:6
Cooking Time: 1 Hour, 25 Minutes

Ingredients:

- 2 tablespoons canola oil, divided
- 1 red bell pepper, thinly sliced
- 1 yellow bell pepper, thinly sliced
- 1 green bell pepper, thinly sliced
- 1 large onion, thinly sliced
- 4 garlic cloves, minced
- Kosher salt
- Freshly ground black pepper
- 2½ pounds chuck roast, cut in half
- 1 cup beef stock
- 2 bay leaves
- ½ cup dry white wine
- 1 tablespoon white vinegar
- 1 can crushed tomatoes
- 1 can tomato paste
- 2 teaspoons dried oregano
- 1½ teaspoons ground cumin
- 1 teaspoon paprika
- ⅛ teaspoon ground allspice
- 1 cup green olives with pimentos
- Cilantro, for garnish
- Lime wedges, for garnish

Directions:

1. Select SEAR/SAUTÉ and set to HI. Select START/STOP to begin. Let preheat for 5 minutes.

2. Add 1 tablespoon of oil, the bell peppers, onions, and garlic, and season with salt and pepper. Cook, stirring occasionally, for about 5 minutes, or until vegetables have softened and are fragrant.

3. Liberally season the chuck with salt and pepper.

4. When the vegetables are cooked, remove and set aside.

5. Add the remaining 1 tablespoon of oil and meat. Sear the roast on both sides so that a dark crust forms, about 5 minutes per side.

6. Add the beef stock and bay leaves. Scrape the bottom of the pot with a rubber or wooden spoon to release any browned bits stuck to it. Assemble pressure lid, making sure the pressure release valve is in the SEAL position.

7. Select PRESSURE and set to HI. Set time to 40 minutes. Select START/STOP to begin.

8. When pressure cooking is complete, quick release the pressure by turning the pressure release valve to the VENT position. Carefully remove lid when unit has finished releasing pressure.

9. Carefully shred the beef in the pot using two forks.

10. Select SEAR/SAUTÉ and set to MED. Select START/STOP to begin. Add the vegetables, wine, vinegar, crushed tomatoes, tomato paste, oregano, cumin, paprika, and allspice and stir with a rubber or wooden spoon, being

sure to scrape the bottom of the pot. Simmer, stirring occasionally, for about 25 minutes or until sauce has reduced and thickened.
11. Add the olives and continue cooking for 2 minutes. Serve, garnished with cilantro and lime wedges.

Nutrition:

- InfoCalories: 479,Total Fat: 23g,Sodium: 624mg,Carbohydrates: 21g,Protein: 44g.

Tender Beef & Onion Rings

Servings: 6
Cooking Time: 25 Minutes

Ingredients:

- 2 lb. chuck roast, cubed
- ¼ cup soy sauce, low sodium
- 1 tbsp. lemon juice
- ½ tsp pepper
- 1 cup water
- 3 tbsp. olive oil
- 3 cloves garlic, chopped fine
- 1 onion, sliced & separated in rings

Directions:

1. In a large bowl, combine beef, soy sauce, lemon juice, and pepper, mix well. Cover and let sit 1 hour.
2. Add the beef mixture to the cooking pot. Stir in water. Add the lid and set to pressure cook on high. Set timer for 20 minutes. When the timer goes off, use natural release to remove the pressure.
3. Use a slotted spoon to transfer beef to a bowl.
4. Set cooker to sauté on medium heat. Cook until sauce reduces and thickens, about 3-4 minutes.
5. Stir in oil and garlic. Add the beef back to the pot and cook until sauce turns a light brown, about 4-5 minutes. Add the onion rings and cook 2 minutes, or until onions are almost soft. Serve.

Nutrition:

- InfoCalories 529,Total Fat 29g,Total Carbs 4g,Protein 62g,Sodium 1059mg.

Carne Guisada

Servings: 4
Cooking Time: 45 Minutes

Ingredients:

- 3 pounds beef stew
- 3 tablespoon seasoned salt
- 1 tablespoon oregano chilli powder
- 1 tablespoon cumin
- 1 pinch crushed red pepper
- 2 tablespoons olive oil
- 1/2 medium lime, juiced
- 1 cup beef bone broth
- 3 ounces tomato paste
- 1 large onion, sliced

Directions:

1. Trim the beef stew to taste into small bite-sized portions.
2. Toss the beef stew pieces with dry seasoning.
3. Select "Sauté" mode on your Ninja Foodi and stir in oil; allow the oil to heat up.
4. Add seasoned beef pieces and brown them.
5. Combine the browned beef pieces with the rest of the ingredients.
6. Lock the Ninja foodi's lid and cook on "HIGH" pressure for 3 minutes.
7. Release the pressure naturally.

8. Enjoy.

Nutrition:

- InfoProtein: 33g; Carbohydrates: 11g; Fats: 12g; Calories: 274

Balsamic Braised Lamb Shanks

Servings: 4
Cooking Time: 1 Hour

Ingredients:

- 3 lbs. lamb shanks
- 1 tsp salt, divided
- ½ tsp pepper, divided
- 1 tbsp. coconut oil
- 3 carrots, peeled & chopped
- 3 stalks celery, chopped
- 4 cloves garlic, chopped fine
- 1 onion, chopped
- 1 tbsp. tomato paste
- 14 oz. fire roasted tomatoes
- 1 cup beef broth, low sodium
- ½ tsp crushed red pepper flakes
- 1 tbsp. balsamic vinegar
- 2 tbsp. fresh Italian parsley, chopped

Directions:

1. Season lamb with salt and pepper.
2. Add oil to the cooking pot and set to sauté on med-high.
3. Add the lamb and brown on all sides. Transfer to a large serving plate.
4. Add the carrots, celery, garlic, and onion and season with salt and pepper. Cook, stirring frequently, until onion is translucent.
5. Add tomato paste, and roasted tomatoes, stir to mix. Return the lamb to the pot along with broth, pepper flakes, and vinegar.
6. Add the lid and set to pressure cook on high. Set the timer for 45 minutes. When the timer goes off, use natural release to remove the pressure.
7. Transfer lamb to a serving plate and spoon sauce over them Garnish with parsley and serve.

Nutrition:

- InfoCalories 525,Total Fat 17g,Total Carbs 17g,Protein 78g,Sodium 1025mg.

Beef Prime Roast

Servings: 4
Cooking Time: 45 Minutes

Ingredients:

- 2 pounds chuck roast
- 1 tablespoon olive oil
- 1 teaspoon salt
- 1 teaspoon black pepper
- 1 teaspoon onion powder
- 1 teaspoon garlic powder
- 4 cups beef stock

Directions:

1. Place roast in Ninja Food pot and season it well with black pepper and salt.
2. Stir in oil and set the pot to Sauté mode, sear each side of the roast for 3 minutes until slightly browned.
3. Add beef broth, onion powder, garlic powder, and stir.

4. Lock and secure the Ninja Foodi's lid, then cook on "HIGH" pressure for 40 minutes.
5. Once done, naturally release the pressure over 10 minutes.
6. Open the Ninja Foodi's lid and serve hot. Enjoy.

Nutrition:
- InfoCalories: 308; Fat: 22g; Carbohydrates: 2g; Protein: 24g

Beef Sirloin Steak

Servings: 4

Cooking Time: 17 Minutes

Ingredients:
- 3 tablespoons butter
- 1/2 teaspoon garlic powder
- 1-2 pounds beef sirloin steaks
- Black pepper and salt to taste
- 1 garlic clove, minced

Directions:
1. Select "Sauté" mode on your Ninja Foodi and add butter; let the butter melt.
2. Stir in beef sirloin steaks.
3. Sauté for 2 minutes on each side.
4. Add garlic powder, garlic clove, salt, and pepper.
5. Lock and secure the Ninja Foodi's lid and cook on "Medium-High" pressure for 15 minutes.
6. Release pressure naturally over 10 minutes.
7. Transfer prepare Steaks to a serving platter, enjoy.

Nutrition:
- InfoCalories: 246; Fat: 13g; Carbohydrates: 2g; Protein: 31g

Taco Stuffed Shells

Servings: 6

Cooking Time: 25 Minutes

Ingredients:
- 1 lb. lean ground beef
- 1 pkt. taco seasoning
- 2/3 cup water
- 1 ½ cups salsa
- 1 cup cheddar cheese, grated
- 12 oz. jumbo pasta shells, cooked & drained

Directions:
1. Add ground beef to the cooking pot and set to sauté on med-high heat. Cook, breaking up with a spatula, until no longer pink. Drain the fat.
2. Stir in the taco seasoning and water and cook, stirring occasionally, until water has evaporated.

3. Stir in 1 cup salsa and ¾ cup cheese, mix well. Turn off the heat. Spoon into shells and place, in a single layer, in the cooking pot. Top with remaining salsa and cheese.
4. Add the tender-crisp lid and set to bake on 350°F or 175°C. Bake 15-20 minutes until hot and bubbly and cheese has melted. Serve.

Nutrition:
- InfoCalories 347,Total Fat 16g,Total Carbs 21g,Protein 29g,Sodium 971mg.

Beef Bourguignon

Servings: 6

Cooking Time: 9 Hours

Ingredients:
- 5 slices bacon, chopped fine
- 3 lbs. beef chuck, cut in 1-inch cubes
- 1 cup red cooking wine
- 2 cups beef broth, low sodium
- ½ cup tomato sauce
- ¼ cup soy sauce
- ¼ cup flour
- 3 cloves garlic, chopped fine
- 2 tbsp. thyme, chopped fine
- 5 carrots, sliced
- 1 lb. baby potatoes
- 8 oz. mushrooms, sliced
- 2 tbsp. fresh parsley, chopped

Directions:
1. Add the bacon to the cooking pot and set to sauté on med high. Cook until crisp. Transfer to a bowl.
2. Season the beef with salt and pepper. Add to the pot and brown on all sides. Add to the bacon.
3. Add the wine to the pot and stir to scrape up the brown bits from the bottom of the pot. Simmer 2-3 minutes to reduce.
4. Stir in broth, tomato sauce, and soy sauce. Slowly whisk in flour.
5. Add the beef and bacon back to the pot along with remaining ingredients, except parsley, and stir to mix. Add the lid and set to slow cook on low. Cook 8-10 hours or until beef is tender. Stir and serve garnished with parsley.

Nutrition:
- InfoCalories 649,Total Fat 28g,Total Carbs 28g,Protein 69g,Sodium 1344mg.

Vegan & Vegetable

Stir Fried Veggies

Servings: 6
Cooking Time: 5 Minutes

Ingredients:

- 1 tbsp. olive oil
- 2 bell peppers, cut in strips
- 1 cup sugar snap peas
- 1 cup carrots, sliced thin
- 1 cup mushrooms, sliced thin
- 2 cups broccoli, separate into small florets
- 1 cup baby corn
- ½ cup water chestnuts
- ¼ cup soy sauce
- 3 cloves garlic, chopped fine
- 3 tbsp. brown sugar
- 1 tsp sesame oil
- ½ cup vegetable broth
- 1 tbsp. cornstarch
- ¼ cup green onions, sliced

Directions:

1. Add oil to the cooking pot and set to saute on med-high heat.
2. Add bell pepper, peas, carrots, mushrooms, broccoli, corn, and water chestnuts. Cook, stirring frequently, 2-3 minutes until almost tender.
3. In a small bowl, whisk together soy sauce, garlic, brown sugar, sesame oil, broth, and cornstarch until combined.
4. Pour over vegetables and cook, stirring, until sauce has thickened. Spoon onto serving plates and garnish with green onions.

Nutrition:

- InfoCalories 150,Total Fat 5g,Total Carbs 26g,Protein 5g,Sodium 738mg.

Balsamic Cabbage With Endives

Servings: 4
Cooking Time: 15 Minutes

Ingredients:

- 1 green cabbage head, shredded
- 2 endives, trimmed and sliced lengthwise
- Black pepper and salt to the taste
- 1 tablespoon olive oil
- 2 shallots, chopped
- ½ cup chicken stock
- 1 tablespoon sweet paprika
- 1 tablespoon balsamic vinegar

Directions:

1. Set the Foodi on Sauté mode, stir in the oil, heat it up, add the shallots and sauté for 2 minutes.
2. Add the cabbage, the endives and the other ingredients.
3. Put the Ninja Foodi's lid on and cook on High for 13 minutes.
4. Release the pressure quickly for 5 minutes, divide the mix between plates and serve.

Nutrition:

- InfoCalories: 120; Fat: 2g; Carbohydrates: 3.3g; Protein: 4

Mushroom Risotto With Swiss Chard

Servings: 4

Cooking Time: 60 Min

Ingredients:

- 1 small bunch Swiss chard; chopped
- ½ cup sautéed mushrooms /65g
- ½ cup caramelized onions /65g
- ⅓ cup white wine /88ml
- 2 cups vegetable stock /500ml
- ⅓ cup grated Pecorino Romano cheese /44g
- 1 cup short grain rice /130g
- 3 tbsps ghee; divided /45g
- ½ tsp salt /2.5g

Directions:

1. Press Sear/Sauté and adjust to Medium. Press Start to preheat the inner pot. Melt 2 tbsps of ghee and sauté the Swiss chard for 5 minutes until wilted. Spoon into a bowl and set aside.
2. Use a paper towel to wipe out any remaining liquid in the pot and melt the remaining ghee. Stir in the rice and cook for about 1 minute.
3. Add the white wine and cook for 2 to 3 minutes, with occasional stirring until the wine has evaporated. Add in stock and salt; stir to combine.
4. Seal the pressure lid, choose Pressure; adjust the pressure to High and the cook time to 8 minutes; press Start. When the timer is done reading, perform a quick pressure release and carefully open the lid.
5. Stir in the mushrooms, swiss chard, and onions and let the risotto heat for 1 minute. Mix the cheese into the rice to melt, and adjust the taste with salt.Spoon the risotto into serving bowls and serve immediately.

Green Minestrone

Servings: 4
Cooking Time: 30 Min

Ingredients:

- 1 head broccoli, cut into florets
- 1 zucchini; chopped
- 2 cups chopped kale /260g
- 1 cup green beans /130g
- 2 cups vegetable broth /260g
- 4 celery stalks; sliced thinly
- 1 leek; sliced thinly
- 3 whole black peppercorns
- 2 tbsp olive oil /30ml
- water to cover
- salt to taste

Directions:

1. Into the pressure cooker, add broccoli, leek, green beans, salt, peppercorns, zucchini, and celery. Mix in vegetable broth, oil, and water.
2. Seal the pressure lid, choose Pressure, set to High, and set the timer to 4 minutes. Press Start.
3. Release pressure naturally for 5 minutes, then release the remaining pressure quickly. Add kale into the soup and stir; set to Keep Warm and cook until tender.

Minty Radishes

Servings: 4

Cooking Time: 15 Minutes

Ingredients:

- 1-pound radishes, halved
- black pepper and salt
- 2 tablespoons balsamic vinegar
- 2 tablespoon mint, chopped
- 2 tablespoons olive oil

Directions:

1. In your Ninja Foodi's basket, combine the radishes with the vinegar and the other ingredients.
2. Cook on Air Crisp at 380 °F or 195°C for 15 minutes.
3. Divide the radishes between plates and serve.

Nutrition:

- InfoCalories: 170; Fat: 4.5g; Carbohydrates: 7.4g; Protein: 4.6g

Broccoli Cauliflower

Servings: 4

Cooking Time: 15 Minutes

Ingredients:

- 2 cups broccoli florets
- 1 cup cauliflower florets
- 2 tablespoons lime juice
- 1 tablespoon avocado oil
- 1/3 cup tomato sauce
- 2 teaspoons ginger, grated
- 2 teaspoons garlic, minced
- 1 tablespoon chives, chopped

Directions:

1. Set the Foodi on Sauté mode, stir in the oil, heat it up, add the garlic and the ginger and sauté for 2 minutes.
2. Stir in the broccoli, cauliflower and the rest of the ingredients.
3. Put the Ninja Foodi's lid on and cook on High for 13 minutes.
4. naturally Release the pressure for 10 minutes, divide everything between plates and serve.

Nutrition:

- InfoCalories: 118; Fat: 1.5g; Carbohydrates: 4.3g; Protein: 6g

Veggie Loaded Pasta

Servings:8

Cooking Time: 2 Minutes

Ingredients:

- 1 box dry pasta, such as rigatoni or penne
- 4 cups water
- 2 tablespoons extra-virgin olive oil, divided
- 2 teaspoons kosher salt, divided
- 3 avocados
- Juice of 2 limes
- 2 tablespoons minced cilantro
- 1 red onion, chopped
- 1 cup cherry tomatoes, halved
- 4 heaping cups spinach, half an 11-ounce container
- ¼ cup shredded Parmesan cheese, divided
- Freshly ground black pepper, for serving

Directions:

1. Place the pasta, water, 1 tablespoon of olive oil, and 1 teaspoon of salt in the pot. Stir to incorporate. Assemble pressure lid, making sure the pressure release valve is in the SEAL position.

2. Select PRESSURE and set to LO. Set time to 2 minutes. Select START/STOP to begin.
3. While pasta is cooking, place the avocados in a medium-sized mixing bowl and mash well with a wooden spatula until a thick paste forms. Add all remaining ingredients to the bowl and mix well to combine.
4. When pressure cooking is complete, allow pressure to naturally release for 10 minutes. After 10 minutes, quick release remaining pressure by moving the pressure release valve to the VENT position. Carefully remove lid when unit has finished releasing pressure.
5. If necessary, strain pasta to remove any residual water and return pasta to pot. Add avocado mixture to pot and stir.
6. Garnish pasta with Parmesan cheese and black pepper, as desired, then serve.

Nutrition:

- InfoCalories: 372,Total Fat: 16g,Sodium: 149mg,Carbohydrates: 49g,Protein: 11g.

Grilled Tofu Sandwich

Servings: 1

Cooking Time: 20 Min

Ingredients:

- 2 slices of bread
- ¼ cup red cabbage, shredded /32.5g
- 1-inch thick Tofu slice
- 2 tsp olive oil divided /10ml
- ¼ tsp vinegar /1.25ml
- Salt and pepper, to taste

Directions:

1. Place the bread slices and toast for 3 minutes on Roast mode at 350 F; set aside. Brush the tofu with 1 tsp of oil, and place in the basket of the Ninja Foodi. Bake for 5 minutes on each side on Roast mode at 350 °F or 175°C.
2. Combine the cabbage, remaining oil, and vinegar, and season with salt and pepper.
3. Place the tofu on top of one bread slice, place the cabbage over, and top with the other bread slice.

Veggie Mash With Parmesan

Servings: 6

Cooking Time: 15 Min

Ingredients:

- 3 pounds Yukon Gold potatoes, cut into 1-inch pieces /1350g
- 1 garlic clove, minced
- 1 cup Parmesan cheese, shredded /130g
- ¼ cup butter, melted /32.5ml
- 1 ½ cups cauliflower, broken into florets /195g
- 1 carrot; chopped
- ¼ cup milk /62.5ml
- 1 tsp salt /5g
- Fresh parsley for garnish

Directions:

1. Into your pot, add veggies, salt and cover with enough water. Seal the pressure lid, choose Pressure, set to High, and set the timer to 10 minutes. Press Start. When ready, release the pressure quickly.
2. Drain the vegetables and mash them with a potato masher; add garlic, butter and milk, and whisk until

everything is well incorporated. Serve topped with parmesan cheese and chopped parsley.

Turkey Stuffed Potatoes

Servings: 4

Cooking Time: 30 Min

Ingredients:

- 1 pound turkey breasts /450g
- 4 potatoes
- 1 Fresno chili pepper; chopped
- 2 cups vegetable broth /500ml
- 2 tbsp fresh cilantro; chopped /30g
- 1 tsp ground cumin /5g
- ½ tsp onion powder /2.5g
- 1 tsp chili powder /5g
- ½ tsp garlic powder/2.5g

Directions:

1. In the pot, combine chicken broth, cumin, garlic powder, onion powder, and chili powder; toss in turkey to coat.
2. Place a reversible rack over the turkey. Use a fork to pierce the potatoes and set them into the reversible rack.
3. Seal the pressure lid, choose Pressure, set to High, and set the timer to 20 minutes. Press Start. When ready, release the pressure quickly. Remove reversible rack from the cooker. Place the potatoes on a plate.
4. Place turkey in a mixing bowl and use two forks to shred. Half each potato lengthwise. Stuff with shredded turkey; top with cilantro, onion, and fresno pepper and serve.

Quinoa Stuffed Butternut Squash

Servings:4

Cooking Time: 13 Minutes

Ingredients:

- 2 tablespoons extra-virgin olive oil
- 1 tablespoon minced garlic
- 1 small shallot, minced
- Kosher salt
- Freshly ground black pepper
- ½ cup dried cranberries
- 1 cup tri-colored quinoa
- 2¾ cups water, divided
- 2 cups roughly chopped kale
- 1 small butternut squash, top trimmed, halved lengthwise
- 1 tablespoon freshly squeezed orange juice
- Zest of 1 orange
- 1 jar pine nuts
- 1 can chickpeas, rinsed and drained

Directions:

1. Select SEAR/SAUTÉ and set to HI. Select START/STOP to begin. Let preheat for 5 minutes.
2. Add the olive oil, garlic, shallot, salt, and pepper. Cook until garlic and shallot have softened and turned golden brown, about 2 minutes.
3. Stir in the cranberries, quinoa, and 1¼ cups of water. Assemble pressure lid, making sure the pressure release valve is in the SEAL position.
4. Select PRESSURE and set to HI. Set time to 2 minutes. Select START/STOP to begin.
5. When pressure cooking is complete, allow pressure to naturally release for 10 minutes. After 10 minutes, quick release remaining

pressure by turning the pressure release valve to the VENT position. Carefully remove lid when the unit has finished releasing pressure.
6. Place the quinoa in a large bowl. Stir in the kale. Cover the bowl with aluminum foil and set aside.
7. Pour the remaining 1½ cups of water into the pot. Place the butternut squash cut-side up on the Reversible Rack, then lower it into the pot. Assemble pressure lid, making sure the pressure release valve is in the SEAL position.
8. Select PRESSURE and set to HI. Set the time to 8 minutes. Select START/STOP to begin.
9. Mix the orange juice, orange zest, pine nuts, and chickpeas into the quinoa mixture.
10. When pressure cooking is complete, quick release the pressure by turning the pressure release valve to the VENT position. Carefully remove lid when unit has finished releasing pressure.
11. Carefully remove rack from pot. Using a spoon slightly hollow out the squash. Spoon the quinoa mixture into the squash. Cut in half and serve.

Nutrition:

- InfoCalories: 563,Total Fat: 21g,Sodium: 66mg,Carbohydrates: 83g,Protein: 16g.

Baked Linguine

Servings: 8

Cooking Time: 30 Minutes

Ingredients:

- 1 tbsp. olive oil
- 1 zucchini, cut in 1-inch pieces
- 1 red bell pepper, cut in 1-inch pieces
- 1 eggplant, cut in 1-inch pieces
- 26 oz. light spaghetti sauce
- 1 cup salsa
- 1 lb. linguine, cooked & drained
- ¾ cup mozzarella cheese, grated

Directions:

1. Add the oil to the cooking pot and set to sauté on med-high heat.
2. Add the zucchini, pepper, and eggplant and cook, stirring occasionally, until tender, about 6-8 minutes.
3. Stir in spaghetti sauce and salsa until combined. Add linguine and mix well. Sprinkle cheese over the top.
4. Add the tender-crisp lid and set to bake on 350°F or 175°C. Bake 25-30 minutes until cheese is melted and linguine is heated through. Serve.

Nutrition:

- InfoCalories 200,Total Fat 4g,Total Carbs 33g,Protein 9g,Sodium 698mg.

Veggie Lasagna

Servings: 4

Cooking Time: 35 Minutes

Ingredients:

- Nonstick cooking spray
- 2 Portobello mushrooms, sliced ¼-inch thick
- 1 eggplant, cut lengthwise in 6 slices
- 1 yellow squash, cut lengthwise in 4 slices
- 1 red bell pepper, cut in ½-inch strips
- ½ tsp garlic powder

- ½ tsp salt
- ½ tsp black pepper
- ½ cup ricotta cheese, fat free, divided
- 2 tbsp. fresh basil, chopped, divided
- ¾ cup mozzarella cheese, grated fine, divided
- ¼ cup tomato sauce

Directions:

1. Spray the cooking pot and rack with cooking spray.
2. Place a single layer of vegetables in the cooking pot. Add the rack and place remaining vegetables on it. Season vegetables with garlic powder, salt, and pepper.
3. Add the tender-crisp lid and set to roast on 425°F or 220°C. Cook vegetables 15-20 minutes until tender, stirring halfway through cooking time. Transfer to a large plate.
4. Spray an 8x8-inch baking pan with cooking spray.
5. Line the bottom of the pan with 3 slices of eggplant. Spread ¼ cup ricotta cheese, 1 tablespoon basil, and ¼ cup mozzarella over eggplant.
6. Layer with remaining vegetables, then remaining ricotta, basil and ¼ cup mozzarella on top. End with 3 slices of eggplant and pour tomato sauce over then sprinkle remaining cheese over the top.
7. Add the rack back to the cooking pot and place the lasagna on it. Add the tender-crisp lid and set to bake on 350°F or 175°C. Bake 15-20 minutes until cheese is melted and lasagna is heated through, serve.

Nutrition:

- InfoCalories 145,Total Fat 3g,Total Carbs 18g,Protein 14g,Sodium 490mg.

Zucchini Rice Gratin

Servings: 6

Cooking Time: 1 Hour

Ingredients:

- Nonstick cooking spray
- 5 tbsp. olive oil, divided
- 1 onion, chopped fine
- 2 cloves garlic, chopped fine
- ½ cup rice
- ½ tsp salt
- ¼ tsp pepper
- 2 ½ lbs. zucchini, trimmed & grated
- ½ cup vegetable broth, low sodium
- 2/3 cup parmesan cheese, divided

Directions:

1. Spray a 2-qt. baking dish with cooking spray.
2. Add 3 tablespoons of the oil to the cooking pot and set to sauté on medium heat.
3. Add the onions and cook until translucent, about 8-10 minutes. Increase heat to med-high and cook until lightly browned, stirring. Stir in garlic and cook 1 minute more.
4. Add the rice and cook, stirring for 2 minutes. Season with salt and pepper. Add to zucchini in a large bowl and mix well.
5. Stir in broth and all but 2 tablespoons of the cheese. Transfer to prepared dish and cover with foil.
6. Place the rack in the pot and place the dish on it. Add the tender-crisp lid and set to bake on 325°F or 165°C. Bake 50-60 minutes or until rice is tender.
7. Remove foil and drizzle top with remaining oil and cheese. Set to broil, broil 2-3 minutes until top is golden brown and cheese is melted. Serve.

Nutrition:

- InfoCalories 113,Total Fat 8g,Total Carbs 8g,Protein 3g,Sodium 187mg.

Pesto With Cheesy Bread

Servings: 4

Cooking Time: 60 Min

Ingredients:

- 1 medium red onion; diced
- 1 celery stalk; diced
- 1 large carrot, peeled and diced
- 1 small yellow squash; diced
- 1 can chopped tomatoes /420g
- 1 can cannellini beans, rinsed and drained /810g
- 1 bay leaf
- 1 cup chopped zucchini /130g
- ¼ cup shredded Pecorino Romano cheese /32.5g
- ⅓ cup olive oil based pesto /88ml
- 3 cups water /750ml
- 1 Pecorino Romano rind
- 1 garlic clove, minced
- 4 slices white bread
- 3 tbsps butter; at room temperature /45g
- 3 tbsps ghee /45g
- 1 tsp mixed herbs /5g
- ¼ tsp cayenne pepper/1.25g
- ½ tsp salt /2.5g

Directions:

1. On your Foodi, choose Sear/Sauté, and adjust to Medium to preheat the inner pot. Press Start. Add the ghee to the pot to melt and sauté the onion, celery, and carrot for 3 minutes or until the vegetables start to soften.
2. Stir in the yellow squash, tomatoes, beans, water, zucchini, bay leaf, mixed herbs, cayenne pepper, salt, and Pecorino Romano rind.
3. Seal the pressure lid, choose Pressure, adjust to High, and set the time to 4 minutes. Press Start. In a bowl, mix the butter, shredded cheese, and garlic. Spread the mixture on the bread slices.
4. After cooking the soup, perform a natural pressure release for 2 minutes, then a quick pressure release and carefully open the lid.
5. Adjust the taste of the soup with salt and black pepper, and remove the bay leaf. Put the reversible rack in the upper position of the pot and lay the bread slices in the rack with the buttered-side up.
6. Close the crisping lid. Choose Broil; adjust the cook time to 5 minutes, and Press Start/Stop to begin broiling.
7. When the bread is crispy, carefully remove the rack, and set aside. Ladle the soup into serving bowls and drizzle the pesto over. Serve with the garlic toasts.

Radish Apples Salad

Servings: 4

Cooking Time: 15 Minutes

Ingredients:

- 1-pound radishes, roughly cubed
- 2 apples, cored and cut into wedges
- ¼ cup chicken stock
- 2 spring onions, chopped
- 3 tablespoons tomato paste
- Juice of 1 lime

- Cooking spray
- 1 tablespoon cilantro, chopped

Directions:

1. In your Ninja Foodi, combine the radishes with the apples and the other ingredients.
2. Put the Ninja Foodi's lid on and cook on High for 15 minutes.
3. Release the pressure quickly for 5 minutes, divide everything between plates and serve.

Nutrition:

- InfoCalories: 122; Fat: 5g; Carbohydrates: 4.5g; Protein: 3g

Garlic Potatoes

Servings: 4
Cooking Time: 30 Min

Ingredients:

- 1½ pounds potatoes /675g
- ½ cup vegetable broth /125ml
- 3 cloves garlic, thinly sliced
- 3 tbsp butter /45g
- 2 tbsp fresh rosemary; chopped /30g
- ½ tsp fresh parsley; chopped /2.5g
- ½ tsp fresh thyme; chopped /2.5g
- 1/4 tsp ground black pepper 1.25g

Directions:

1. Use a small knife to pierce each potato to ensure there are no blowouts when placed under pressure. Melt butter on Sear/Sauté. Add in potatoes, rosemary, parsley, pepper, thyme, and garlic, and cook for 10 minutes until potatoes are browned and the mixture is aromatic.
2. In a bowl, mix miso paste and vegetable stock; stir into the mixture in the pressure cooker.
3. Seal the pressure lid, choose Pressure, set to High, and set the timer to 5 minutes. Press Start. Do a pressure quickly.

Cauliflower Chunks With Lemon Sauce

Servings: 4
Cooking Time: 15 Minutes

Ingredients:

- 1-pound cauliflower, cut into chunks
- 1 tablespoon dill, chopped
- 1 tablespoon lemon zest, grated
- Juice of ½ lemon
- 2 tablespoons butter, melted
- Black pepper and salt to the taste

Directions:

1. Set the Foodi on Sauté mode, stir in the butter, melt it, add the cauliflower chunks and brown for 5 minutes.
2. Add the lemon zest and the other ingredients set the machine on Air Crisp and cook at 390 °F or 200°C for 10 minutes.
3. Divide everything between plates and serve.

Nutrition:

- InfoCalories: 122; Fat: 3.3g; Carbohydrates: 3g; Protein: 2g

Italian Spinach & Tomato Soup

Servings: 6
Cooking Time: 4 Hours

Ingredients:

- 1 tsp olive oil
- 1 onion, chopped
- 3 cloves garlic, chopped fine

- 3 large tomatoes, chopped
- 2 tsp Italian seasoning
- 28 oz. vegetable broth, low sodium
- 10 oz. fresh spinach, trimmed
- ½ tsp pepper
- 2 tbsp. parmesan cheese

Directions:

1. Add the oil to the cooking pot and set to sauté on med-high.
2. Add the onion and garlic and cook, stirring occasionally, 5 minutes or until onion starts to brown.
3. Stir in remaining ingredients, except spinach and parmesan, and mix well. Add the lid and set to slow cook on high. Cook 3-4 hours until tomatoes are tender. Stir occasionally.
4. Add the spinach and cook until it wilts. Ladle into bowls and sprinkle with parmesan. Serve.

Nutrition:

- InfoCalories 60,Total Fat 2g,Total Carbs 10g,Protein 3g,Sodium 602mg.

Asparagus With Feta

Servings: 4
Cooking Time: 15 Min

Ingredients:

- 1-pound asparagus spears, ends trimmed /450g
- 1 lemon, cut into wedges
- 1 cup feta cheese; cubed /130g
- 1 cup water /250ml
- 1 tbsp olive oil /15ml
- salt and freshly ground black pepper to taste

Directions:

1. Into the pot, add water and set trivet over the water. Place steamer basket on the trivet. Place the asparagus into the steamer basket. Seal the pressure lid, choose Pressure, set to High, and set the timer to 1 minute. Press Start.
2. When ready, release the pressure quickly. Add olive oil in a bowl and toss in asparagus until well coated; season with pepper and salt. Serve alongside feta cheese and lemon wedges.

Artichoke With Mayo

Servings: 4
Cooking Time: 20 Min

Ingredients:

- 2 large artichokes
- 2 garlic cloves, smashed
- ½ cup mayonnaise /125ml
- 2 cups water /500ml
- Juice of 1 lime
- Salt and black pepper to taste

Directions:

1. Using a serrated knife, trim about 1 inch from the artichokes' top. Into the pot, add water and set trivet over. Lay the artichokes on the trivet. Seal lid and cook for 14 minutes. Press Start.
2. When ready, release the pressure quickly. Mix the mayonnaise with garlic and lime juice; season with salt and pepper. Serve artichokes in a platter with garlic mayo on the side.

Cabbage With Carrots

Servings: 4
Cooking Time: 20 Minutes
Ingredients:

- 1 Napa cabbage, shredded
- 2 carrots, sliced
- 2 tablespoons olive oil
- 1 red onion, chopped
- Black pepper and salt to the taste
- 2 tablespoons sweet paprika
- ½ cup tomato sauce

Directions:

1. Set the Foodi on Sauté mode, stir in the oil, heat it up, add the onion and sauté for 5 minutes.
2. Add the carrots, the cabbage and the other ingredients, toss.
3. Put the Ninja Foodi's lid on and cook on High for 15 minutes.
4. Release the pressure quickly for 5 minutes, divide everything between plates and serve.

Nutrition:

- InfoCalories: 140; Fat: 3.4g; Carbohydrates: 1.2g; Protein: 3.5 g

Tahini Sweet Potato Mash

Servings: 4
Cooking Time: 25 Min
Ingredients:

- 2 pounds sweet potatoes, peeled and cubed /900g
- 1 cup water /250ml
- 2 tbsp tahini /30g
- 1 tbsp sugar /15g
- ¼ tsp ground nutmeg /1.25g
- sea salt to taste
- Chopped fresh chives; for garnish

Directions:

1. In the Foodi, add 1 cup or 250ml cold water and set a steamer basket into the pot. Add sweet potato cubes into the steamer basket. Seal the pressure lid, choose Pressure, set to High, and set the timer to 8 minutes. Press Start. When ready, release the pressure quickly.
2. In a large mixing bowl, add cooked sweet potatoes and slightly mash. Using a hand mixer, whip in nutmeg, sugar, and tahini until the sweet potatoes attain the consistency you desire; add salt for seasoning. Top with chives and serve.

Cheesy Corn Pudding

Servings: 6
Cooking Time: 3 Hours
Ingredients:

- 10 oz. corn, thawed & divided
- 1 cup milk
- 2 tbsp. flour
- ½ tsp cumin
- 1 tsp salt
- ¼ tsp pepper
- 3 eggs, lightly beaten
- 2 cups Monterey Jack cheese, grated
- 1 jalapeno pepper, seeded & chopped fine

Directions:

1. Add ¾ cup corn, milk, flour, cumin, salt, and pepper to a food processor or blender. Pulse until smooth.
2. Spray the cooking pot with cooking spray.

3. Pour the corn mixture into the pot then stir in remaining ingredients until combined.
4. Add the lid and set to slow cook on low. Cook 3 hours or until pudding is set. Serve hot.

Nutrition:

- InfoCalories 298,Total Fat 18g,Total Carbs 17g,Protein 17g,Sodium 707mg.

Tomato And Poblano Stuffed Squash

Servings: 3
Cooking Time: 50 Min
Ingredients:

- ½ butternut squash
- 6 grape tomatoes, halved
- ¼ cup grated mozzarella, optional /32.5g
- 1 poblano pepper, cut into strips
- 2 tsp olive oil divided /10ml
- Salt and pepper, to taste

Directions:

1. Meanwhile, cut trim the ends and cut the squash lengthwise. You will only need one half for this recipe. Scoop the flash out, so you make room for the filling. Brush 1 tsp oil over the squash. Place in the Ninja Foodi and roast for 30 minutes.
2. Combine the other tsp of olive oil with the tomatoes and poblanos. Season with salt and pepper, to taste. Place the peppers and tomatoes into the squash. Close the crisping lid and cook for 15 more minutes on Air Crisp mode at 350 °F or 175°C. If using mozzarella, add it on top of the squash, two minutes before the end.

Mushroom Goulash

Servings: 6
Cooking Time: 40 Minutes
Ingredients:

- 2 tbsp. olive oil, divided
- ½ onion, sliced thin
- 1 red bell pepper, chopped
- 2 lbs. mushrooms, chopped
- ½ tsp salt
- ¼ tsp pepper
- 14 oz. tomatoes, diced
- 2 cups vegetable broth, low sodium
- 1 tsp garlic powder
- 1 ½ tbsp. paprika
- 5 -6 sprigs fresh thyme

Directions:

1. Add half the oil to the cooking pot and set to sauté on med-high.
2. Add the onion and cook until they start to get soft, about 4 minutes. Add the red pepper and cook 3-5 minutes or until onions start to caramelize. Transfer to a plate.
3. Add the remaining oil to the pot and let it get hot. Add the mushrooms and cook until liquid is almost evaporated, stirring occasionally. Season with salt and pepper.
4. Add the peppers and onions back to the pot along with tomatoes, broth, garlic powder, paprika, and thyme, stir to mix well. Bring to a boil, cover, reduce heat to med-low and let simmer 20 minutes. Serve.

Nutrition:

- InfoCalories 115,Total Fat 5g,Total Carbs 14g,Protein 6g,Sodium 544mg.

Burrito Bowls

Servings: 4

Cooking Time: 30 Min

Ingredients:

- 1 can diced tomatoes /435g
- 1 can black beans, drained and rinsed /435g
- 1 ½ cups vegetable stock /375ml
- 1 cup frozen corn kernels /130g
- 1 cup quinoa, rinsed /130g
- 1 avocado; sliced
- 1 onion
- 2 garlic cloves, minced
- 2 tbsp chopped cilantro /30g
- 1 tbsp roughly chopped fresh coriander /15g
- 2 tbsp olive oil /30ml
- 1 tbsp chili powder /15g
- 2 tsp ground cumin /10g
- 2 tsp paprika /10g
- 1 tsp salt /5g
- ½ tsp black pepper /2.5g
- ¼ tsp cayenne pepper /1.25g
- Cheddar cheese, grated for garnish

Directions:

1. Warm oil on Sear/Sauté. Add in onion and cook for 3 to 5 minutes until fragrant. Add garlic and cook for 2 more minutes until soft and golden brown. Add in chili powder, paprika, cayenne pepper, salt, cumin, and black pepper and cook for 1 minute until spices are soft.
2. Pour quinoa into onion and spice mixture and stir to coat quinoa completely in spices. Add diced tomatoes, black beans, vegetable stock, and corn; stir to combine.
3. Seal the pressure lid, choose Pressure, set to High, and set the timer to 7 minutes. Press Start. When ready, release the pressure quickly. Open the lid and let sit for 6 minutes until flavors combine. Use a fork to fluff quinoa and season with pepper and salt if desired.
4. Into quinoa and beans mixture, stir in cilantro and divide among plates. Top with cheese and avocado slices.

Stuffed Summer Squash

Servings: 4

Cooking Time: 25 Minutes

Ingredients:

- 2 yellow squash, halved lengthwise & seeded
- 1 cup brown rice, cooked
- 2 tbsp. liquid egg substitute
- 2 tbsp. parmesan cheese, divided
- ½ tsp onion powder
- 2 tsp fresh parsley, chopped
- ¼ tsp pepper
- Nonstick cooking spray

Directions:

1. Add enough water to cover ½ inch up the sides of the cooking pot. Add the squash.
2. Add the lid and set to pressure cook on high. Set timer for 5 minutes. When timer goes off, use manual release to remove the pressure. Drain.
3. In a small bowl, combine rice, egg substitute, 1 tablespoon parmesan, parsley, onion powder, and pepper and mix well.
4. Place squash, cut side up, in the cooking pot. Divide the rice mixture evenly between the squash halves. Sprinkle remaining cheese over the top. Spray lightly with cooking spray.

5. Add the tender-crisp lid and set to bake on 350°F or 175°C. Bake 15-20 minutes until cheese is melted and starting to brown. Serve.

Nutrition:

- InfoCalories 84,Total Fat 1g,Total Carbs 15g,Protein 3g,Sodium 66mg.

Curried Vegetables

Servings: 6

Cooking Time: 10 Minutes

Ingredients:

- 1 ½ tbsp. olive oil
- 1 ½ cups onion, chopped
- 1 ½ tbsp. fresh ginger, grated
- 1 ½ tbsp. garlic, chopped fine
- 4 ½ carrots, peeled & chopped
- 1 ½ red bell peppers, sliced in thin strips
- 1 ½ orange bell peppers, sliced in thin strips
- 4 cups coconut milk, unsweetened
- 1 ½ cups kale, ribs removed & chopped
- ¾ cup water
- 3 tbsp. curry powder

Directions:

1. Add oil to the cooking pot and set to sauté on med-high heat.
2. Add the onion and cook until translucent, about 3-4 minutes. Add ginger and garlic and cook 1 minute more.
3. Stir in carrots and bell peppers and cook until peppers are tender, about 3-4 minutes.
4. Stir in coconut milk, kale, water and curry paste until combined.
5. Add the lid and set to pressure cook on high. Set timer for 2 minutes. Once timer goes off, use quick release to remove the pressure. Stir well and serve.

Nutrition:

- InfoCalories 323,Total Fat 27g,Total Carbs 20g,Protein 4g,Sodium 57mg.

Eggplant Casserole

Servings: 8

Cooking Time: 1 Hour

Ingredients:

- Nonstick cooking spray
- 1 lb. eggplant, peeled, cubed
- ½ cup seasoned bread crumbs, divided
- 2 eggs
- ¼ tsp Italian seasoning
- ½ tsp garlic powder
- 1/8 tsp salt
- 1/8 tsp pepper
- 2 tomatoes, sliced

Directions:

1. Spray an 8x8-inch baking dish with cooking spray.
2. Add enough water to the cooking pot to come 2 inches up the sides. Set to sauté on high heat and bring to a boil.
3. Add the eggplant, reduce heat to medium, cover and cook 20-30 minutes until soft. Drain.
4. Add the eggplant to a large bowl and mash with a fork. Stir in ¼ cup bread crumbs, eggs, Italian seasoning, garlic, salt, and pepper and mix well.

5. Add the rack to the cooking pot. Spread the eggplant mixture in the prepared dish. Top with sliced tomatoes. Sprinkle tomatoes with remaining bread crumbs and spray with cooking spray. Place the dish on the rack.

6. Add the tender-crisp lid and set to bake on 350°F or 175°C. Bake 25-30 minutes or until tomatoes are tender and starting to brown around the edges. Serve.

Nutrition:

- InfoCalories 67, Total Fat 2g, Total Carbs 10g, Protein 3g, Sodium 181mg.

Crème De La Broc

Servings: 6

Cooking Time: 25 Min

Ingredients:

- 1 ½ cups grated yellow and white Cheddar cheese + extra for topping /195g
- 1 ½ oz. cream cheese /195g
- 1 medium Red onion; chopped
- 3 cloves garlic, minced
- 4 cups chopped broccoli florets, only the bushy tops/520g
- 3 cups heavy cream /750ml
- 3 cups vegetable broth /750ml
- 4 tbsp butter /60g
- 4 tbsp flour /60g
- 1 tsp Italian Seasoning /5g
- Salt and black pepper to taste

Directions:

1. Select Sear/Sauté mode, adjust to High and melt the butter once the pot is ready. Add the flour and use a spoon to stir until it clumps up. Gradually pour in the heavy cream while stirring until white sauce forms. Fetch out the butter sauce into a bowl and set aside.

2. Press Stop and add the onions, garlic, broth, broccoli, Italian seasoning, and cream cheese. Use a wooden spoon to stir the mixture.

3. Seal the lid, and select Pressure mode on High pressure for 12 minutes. Press Start/Stop. Once the timer has ended, do a quick pressure release.

4. Add in butter sauce and cheddar cheese, salt, and pepper. Close the crisping lid and cook on Broil mode for 3 minutes. Dish the soup into serving bowls, top it with extra cheese, to serve.

Spanish Rice

Servings: 4

Cooking Time: 50 Min

Ingredients:

- 1 small onion; chopped
- 1 can pinto beans, drained and rinsed /480g
- 2 garlic cloves, minced
- 1 banana pepper, seeded and chopped
- ¼ cup stewed tomatoes /32.5g
- ½ cup vegetable stock /125ml
- 1 cup jasmine rice /130g
- ⅓ cup red salsa /88g
- 3 tbsps ghee /45g
- 1 tbsp chopped fresh parsley /15g
- 1 tsp Mexican Seasoning Mix /5g
- 1 tsp salt /5g

Directions:

1. On your Foodi, choose Sear/Sauté and adjust to Medium. Press Start to preheat the inner pot. Add the ghee to melt until no longer foaming and cook the onion, garlic, and banana pepper in the ghee. Cook for 2 minutes or until fragrant.

2. Stir in the rice, salsa, tomato sauce, vegetable stock, Mexican seasoning, pinto beans, and salt. Seal the pressure lid, choose Pressure and adjust the pressure to High and the cook time to 6 minutes; press Start.

3. After cooking, do a natural pressure release for 10 minutes. Stir in the parsley, dish the rice, and serve.

Spicy Kimchi And Tofu Fried Rice

Servings: 6

Cooking Time: 30 Minutes

Ingredients:

- 1 cup Texmati brown rice
- 1¼ cups water
- 2 tablespoons canola oil
- 2 garlic cloves, minced
- 1 tablespoon minced fresh ginger
- 8 ounces extra-firm tofu, cut into ½-inch squares
- ½ cup frozen peas and carrots
- 1 large egg, beaten
- ½ cup kimchi, chopped
- 2 scallions, sliced thin
- ¼ cup basil, coarsely chopped
- 1 tablespoon soy sauce
- Kosher salt
- Freshly ground black pepper

Directions:

1. Rinse the rice under cold running water in a fine-mesh strainer.

2. Place the rice and water in the pot. Assemble pressure lid, making sure the pressure release valve is in the SEAL position.

3. Select PRESSURE and set to HI. Set time to 2 minutes. Select START/STOP to begin.

4. When pressure cooking is complete, allow pressure to naturally release for 10 minutes. After 10 minutes, quick release remaining pressure by moving the pressure release valve to the VENT position. Carefully remove lid when unit has finished releasing pressure.

5. Evenly layer the rice on a sheet pan and refrigerate until cool, preferably overnight.

6. Select SEAR/SAUTÉ and set to HI. Select START/STOP to begin. Add the canola oil and let heat for 5 minutes.

7. Add the garlic and ginger and cook for 1 minute. Add the tofu, rice, and peas and carrots, and cook for 5 minutes, stirring occasionally.

8. Move the rice to one side and add the egg to empty side of pot. Cook 30 seconds, stirring occasionally to scramble it. Add the kimchi, scallions, basil, and soy sauce, and stir. Cook for 5 minutes, stirring frequently.

9. Season with salt, pepper, and more soy sauce, if needed. Serve.

Nutrition:

- InfoCalories: 229, Total Fat: 9g, Sodium: 928mg, Carbohydrates: 30g, Protein: 8g.

Veggie And Quinoa Stuffed Peppers

Servings: 1
Cooking Time: 16 Min
Ingredients:

- ¼ cup cooked quinoa /32.5g
- ½ diced tomato, plus one tomato slice
- 1 bell pepper
- ½ tbsp diced onion /7.5g
- 1 tsp olive oil /5ml
- ¼ tsp smoked paprika/1.25g
- ¼ tsp dried basil /1.25g
- Salt and pepper, to taste

Directions:

1. Core and clean the bell pepper to prepare it for stuffing. Brush the pepper with half of the olive oil on the outside.
2. In a small bowl, combine all of the other Ingredients, except the tomato slice and reserved half-tsp olive oil. Stuff the pepper with the filling. Top with the tomato slice.
3. Brush the tomato slice with the remaining half-tsp of oil and sprinkle with basil. Close the crisping lid and cook for 10 minutes on Air Crisp mode at 350 °F or 175°C.

Simple Spanakopita

Servings: 8
Cooking Time: 1 Hour
Ingredients:

- Nonstick cooking spray
- 10 oz. refrigerated pizza dough
- 1 onion, chopped
- 1 clove garlic, chopped fine
- ½ tsp basil
- ¾ cup cottage cheese, low fat
- 3 oz. feta cheese, low fat, crumbled
- ¾ cup evaporated skim milk
- 8 egg whites
- 20 oz. spinach, chopped, thawed

Directions:

1. Spray an 8-inch pie dish with cooking spray.
2. On a lightly floured surface, roll the pizza dough out to a 12-inch circle. Place in prepared pie dish.
3. Spray the cooking pot with cooking spray and set to sauté on med-high heat.
4. Add the onion, garlic, and basil and cook until onions are tender, about 3-4 minutes stirring frequently.
5. In a large bowl, beat together cottage cheese and feta until smooth and creamy.
6. Beat in milk and egg whites until combined. Stir in onion mixture and spinach. Pour into the pie crust.
7. Add the rack to the cooking pot and place the pie dish on it. Add the tender-crisp lid and set to bake on 350°F or 175°C. Bake 55-60 minutes or until a knife inserted in center comes out clean. Remove from cooking pot and cool 15 minutes before serving.

Nutrition:

- InfoCalories 292,Total Fat 16g,Total Carbs 25g,Protein 14g,Sodium 500mg.

Tasty Acorn Squash

Servings: 4
Cooking Time: 30 Min
Ingredients:

- 1 lb. acorn squash, peeled and cut into chunks /450g
- ½ cup water /125ml
- 2 tbsp butter /30g
- 1 tbsp dark brown sugar /15g
- 1 tbsp cinnamon /15g
- 3 tbsp honey; divided 45ml
- salt and ground black pepper to taste

Directions:

1. In a small bowl, mix 1 tbsp honey and water; pour into the pressure cooker's pot. Add in squash. Seal the and cook on High pressure for 4 minutes. Press Start. When ready, release the pressure quickly.
2. Transfer the squash to a serving dish. Turn Foodi to Sear/Sauté.
3. Mix brown sugar, cinnamon, the remaining 2 tbsp honey and the liquid in the pot; cook as you stir for 4 minutes to obtain a thick consistency and starts to turn caramelized and golden. Spread honey glaze over squash; add pepper and salt for seasoning.

Tofu & Carrot Toss

Servings: 4
Cooking Time: 20 Minutes
Ingredients:

- 1 tbsp. coconut oil
- 1 lb. carrots, grated
- 1 lb. extra firm tofu, drained, pressed & crumbled
- 1/3 cup soy sauce
- 1/3 cup sesame seeds
- 1 tsp dark sesame oil
- 1/4 cup cilantro, chopped

Directions:

1. Add oil to the cooking pot and set to sauté on med-high heat.
2. Add carrots and cook 15 minutes, stirring occasionally.
3. Add tofu and cook until carrots are tender, about 5 minutes. Stir in soy sauce and sesame seeds and cook 1 minute more, stirring constantly.
4. Turn the heat off and stir in sesame oil and cilantro. Serve over rice.

Nutrition:

- InfoCalories 279,Total Fat 20g,Total Carbs 16g,Protein 17g,Sodium 851mg.

Bbq Lentils

Servings: 4
Cooking Time: 35 Minutes
Ingredients:

- 1 tbsp. extra virgin olive oil
- 1 onion, chopped fine
- 1 carrot, chopped fine
- 2 cloves garlic, chopped fine
- 1 cup dry brown lentils
- 2 ½ cups water
- 1 6 oz. tomato paste
- 3 tbsp. apple cider vinegar
- 2 tbsp. blackstrap molasses
- 2 tbsp. applesauce, unsweetened
- 1 ½ tsp garlic powder
- 1 ½ tsp onion powder
- 1 tsp mustard

- 1 tsp salt
- ½ tsp pepper
- ½ tsp paprika
- 1/8 tsp cayenne pepper
- 4 whole wheat hamburger buns

Directions:
1. Add the oil to the cooking pot and set to sauté on med-high heat.
2. Add the onion and cook 5 minutes, stirring frequently.
3. Add the carrot and cook another 8 minutes, until tender. Add garlic and cook 1 minute more.
4. Add remaining ingredients to the pot and stir to mix well. Add the lid and set to pressure cook on high. Set the timer for 20 minutes. Once the timer goes off, use quick release to remove the pressure.
5. Stir well and serve on whole wheat buns.

Nutrition:
- InfoCalories 123,Total Fat 4g,Total Carbs 21g,Protein 3g,Sodium 619mg.

Cauliflower Steaks & Veggies

Servings: 6
Cooking Time: 45 Minutes
Ingredients:
- ¼ cup butter, melted
- 1 tbsp. olive oil
- 3 tbsp. lemon juice
- 2 tsp fresh parsley, chopped
- ¾ tsp onion powder
- ¾ tsp garlic powder
- ½ tsp salt
- ¼ tsp pepper
- 1 head cauliflower, cut in ½-inch thick slices
- 12 baby carrots
- 6 small potatoes, halved
- 1 zucchini, cut in 1-inch pieces

Directions:
1. In a large bowl, whisk together butter, oil, lemon juice, parsley, onion powder, garlic powder, salt, and pepper.
2. Line a baking sheet with foil. Brush both sides of cauliflower steaks with butter mixture and place on baking sheet.
3. Add remaining vegetables to the butter mixture and toss to coat. Place in the cooking pot. Add the rack and place the cauliflower on the rack.
4. Add the tender-crisp lid and set to roast on 400°F or 205°C. Bake 40-45 minutes until vegetables are tender and starting to brown, turning over halfway through cooking time. Serve.

Nutrition:
- InfoCalories 260,Total Fat 11g,Total Carbs 38g,Protein 6g,Sodium 313mg.

Quick Indian-style Curry

Servings:8
Cooking Time: 35 Minutes
Ingredients:
- 1 tablespoon vegetable oil
- 1 small onion, diced
- 1 small bell pepper, diced
- 1 large potato, cut into 1-inch cubes
- 1 teaspoon ground turmeric
- 1 teaspoon cumin seeds
- 1 teaspoon ground cumin

- 1 teaspoon garam masala (optional)
- 1 teaspoon curry powder
- 1 jar curry sauce, plus 1 jar water
- 1 can diced tomatoes
- 1 cup dried red lentils
- 8 ounces paneer, cubed (optional)
- 1 cup fresh cilantro, roughly chopped (optional)
- Salt
- Freshly ground black pepper

Directions:
1. Select SEAR/SAUTÉ and set temperature to HI. Select START/STOP to begin and allow to preheat for 5 minutes.
2. Add the oil to the pot and allow to heat for 1 minute. Add the onion and bell pepper and sauté for 3 to 4 minutes.
3. Add the potato, turmeric, cumin seeds, cumin, garam masala, and curry powder. Stir and cook for 5 minutes.
4. Stir in the curry sauce, water, tomatoes, and lentils.
5. Assemble the pressure lid, making sure the pressure release valve is in the SEAL position.
6. Select PRESSURE and set to HI. Set the time to 15 minutes. Select START/STOP to begin.
7. When pressure cooking is complete, allow the pressure to naturally release for 10 minutes. After 10 minutes, quick release any remaining pressure by moving the pressure release valve to the VENT position. Carefully remove the lid when the unit has finished releasing pressure.
8. Stir in the paneer (if using) and cilantro. Taste and season with salt and pepper, as needed.

Nutrition:
- InfoCalories: 217,Total Fat: 6g,Sodium: 27mg,Carbohydrates: 33g,Protein: 8g.

Cheese And Mushroom Tarts

Servings: 4
Cooking Time: 75 Min
Ingredients:
- 1 small white onion; sliced
- 1 sheet puff pastry, thawed
- 5 ounces oyster mushrooms; sliced /150g
- 1 cup shredded Swiss cheese /130g
- ¼ cup dry white wine /62.5ml
- 1 tbsp thinly sliced fresh green onions /15ml
- 2 tbsps melted butter; divided /30ml
- ¼ tsp salt /1.25g
- ¼ tsp freshly ground black pepper /1.25g

Directions:
1. Choose Sear/Sauté, set to High, and set the time to 5 minutes. Choose Start/Stop to preheat the pot. Add 1 tbsp of butter, the onion, and mushrooms to the pot. Sauté for 5 minutes or until the vegetables are tender and browned.
2. Season with salt and black pepper, pour in the white wine, and cook until evaporated, about 2 minutes. Spoon the vegetables into a bowl and set aside.
3. Unwrap the puff pastry and cut into 4 squares. Pierce the dough with a fork and brush both sides with the remaining oil. Share half of the cheese evenly over the puff pastry squares, leaving a ½- inch border around the edges. Also, share the mushroom mixture over the pastry squares and top with the remaining cheese.

4. Put the Crisping Basket in the pot. Close the crisping lid, choose Air Crisp, set the temperature to 400°F or 205°C, and the time to 5 minutes.
5. Once the pot has preheated, put 1 tart in the Crisping Basket. Close the crisping lid, choose Air Crisp, set the temperature to 360°F or 180°C, and set the time to 6 minutes; press Start.
6. After 6 minutes, check the tart for your preferred brownness. Take the tart out of the basket and transfer to a plate. Repeat the process with the remaining tarts. Garnish with the green onions and serve.

Tomato Galette

Servings:4
Cooking Time: 40 Minutes
Ingredients:
- ½ pound mixed tomatoes, cut into ¼-inch slices
- 3 inches of leek, thinly sliced
- 2 garlic cloves, diced
- Kosher salt
- 1 store-bought refrigerated pie crust
- 2 tablespoons bread crumbs
- 4 tablespoons shredded Parmesan cheese, divided
- 4 tablespoons shredded mozzarella, divided
- 1 egg, beaten
- Freshly ground black pepper

Directions:
1. Place the tomatoes, leeks, and garlic into large bowl. Sprinkle with salt and set aside for at least 5 minutes to draw out the juices from the vegetables.
2. Strain the excess juice off the tomato mixture and pat down the vegetables with paper towels.
3. Unroll the pie crust and place it in the Ninja Multi-Purpose Pan or a 1½-quart round ceramic baking dish and form it to the bottom of the pan. Lay the extra dough loosely on the sides of the pan.
4. Sprinkle the bread crumbs in a thin layer on the pie crust bottom, then scatter 3 tablespoons each of Parmesan and mozzarella cheese on top. Place the tomato mixture in a heap in the middle of the dough and top with the remaining 1 tablespoon each of Parmesan and mozzarella cheese.
5. Fold the edges of the crust over the tomatoes and brush with the egg.
6. Close crisping lid. Select BAKE/ROAST, set temperature to 350°F or 175°C, and set time to 45 minutes. Select START/STOP to begin. Let preheat for 5 minutes.
7. Place pan on the Reversible Rack, making sure the rack is in the lower position. Cover galette loosely with aluminum foil (do not seal the pan).
8. Once unit has preheated, open lid and carefully place the rack with pan in the pot. Close crisping lid.
9. After 20 minutes, open lid and remove the foil. Close lid and continue cooking.
10. When cooking is complete, remove rack with pan and set aside to let cool. Cut into slices, season with pepper, and serve.

Nutrition:
- InfoCalories: 288,Total Fat: 15g,Sodium: 409mg,Carbohydrates: 31g,Protein: 9g.

Veggie Primavera

Servings: 6
Cooking Time: 25 Minutes
Ingredients:
- 2 tbsp. olive oil

- 1 tsp Italian seasoning
- 1 tsp garlic powder
- ½ tsp salt
- ½ tsp pepper
- 12 oz. baby red potatoes, quartered
- 2 ears corn, husked & cut into 1-inch rounds
- 4 oz. baby carrots
- ½ red onion, cut in wedges
- 4 oz. fresh sugar snap peas

Directions:
1. In a large bowl, combine oil, Italian seasoning, garlic powder, salt, and pepper, mix well.
2. Add remaining ingredients, except peas, and toss to coat the vegetables.
3. Spray the cooking pot with cooking spray and add the vegetable mixture.
4. Add the tender-crisp lid and set to roast on 425°F or 220°C. Roast vegetables 15 minutes, turning halfway through cooking time.
5. Add the peas and stir to mix. Roast another 10-15 minutes until vegetables are lightly browned and tender. Serve immediately.

Nutrition:
- InfoCalories 142,Total Fat 5g,Total Carbs 23g,Protein 3g,Sodium 222mg.

Zucchini Quinoa Stuffed Red Peppers

Servings: 4
Cooking Time: 40 Min
Ingredients:
- 1 small zucchini; chopped
- 4 red bell peppers
- 2 large tomatoes; chopped
- 1 small onion; chopped
- 2 cloves garlic, minced
- 1 cup quinoa, rinsed /130g
- 1 cup grated Gouda cheese /130g
- ½ cup chopped mushrooms /65g
- 1 ½ cup water /375ml
- 2 cups chicken broth /500ml
- 1 tbsp olive oil /15ml
- ½ tsp smoked paprika /2.5g
- Salt and black pepper to taste

Directions:
1. Select Sear/Sauté mode on High. Once it is ready, add the olive oil to heat and then add the onion and garlic. Sauté for 3 minutes to soften, stirring occasionally.
2. Include the tomatoes, cook for 3 minutes and then add the quinoa, zucchinis, and mushrooms. Season with paprika, salt, and black pepper and stir with a spoon. Cook for 5 to 7 minutes, then, turn the pot off.
3. Use a knife to cut the bell peppers in halves (lengthwise) and remove their seeds and stems.
4. Spoon the quinoa mixture into the bell peppers. Put the peppers in a greased baking dish and pour the broth over.
5. Wipe the pot clean with some paper towels, and pour the water into it. After, fit the steamer rack at the bottom of the pot.

6. Place the baking dish on top of the reversible rack, cover with aluminum foil, close the lid, secure the pressure valve, and select Pressure mode on High pressure for 15 minutes. Press Start/Stop.

7. Once the timer has ended, do a quick pressure release and open the lid. Remove the aluminum foil and sprinkle with the gouda cheese.

8. Close the crisping lid, select Bake/Roast mode and cook for 10 minutes on 375 °F or 190°C. Arrange the stuffed peppers on a serving platter and serve right away or as a side to a meat dish.

Italian Baked Zucchini

Servings: 6

Cooking Time: 45 Minutes

Ingredients:
- Nonstick cooking spray
- 2 tsp olive oil
- 2 lbs. zucchini, sliced ¼-inch thick
- ¼ cup onion, chopped
- 3 plum tomatoes, cut in ½- inch pieces
- 1 tbsp. parmesan cheese
- ½ cup Italian blend cheese, grated
- 1 tsp garlic powder
- 1 tsp Italian seasoning
- ¼ tsp pepper
- 1 tbsp. Italian bread crumbs

Directions:
1. Spray the cooking pot with cooking spray.
2. Add the oil to the cooking pot and set to sauté on med-high heat.
3. Add the zucchini and onion and cook, stirring occasionally, 5 minutes, until softened.
4. Stir in tomatoes, parmesan, Italian blend cheese, garlic powder, Italian seasonings, and pepper. Cook 3 minutes, stirring occasionally. Sprinkle bread crumbs over the top.
5. Add the tender-crisp lid and set to bake on 375°F or 190°C. Bake 25-30 minutes until golden brown. Serve.

Nutrition:
- InfoCalories 91,Total Fat 4g,Total Carbs 8g,Protein 7g,Sodium 146mg.

Mashed Broccoli With Cream Cheese

Servings: 4

Cooking Time: 12 Min

Ingredients:
- 3 heads broccoli; chopped
- 2 cloves garlic, crushed
- 6 oz. cream cheese /180g
- 2 cups water /500ml
- 2 tbsp butter, unsalted /30g
- Salt and black pepper to taste

Directions:
1. Turn on the Ninja Foodi and select Sear/Sauté mode, adjust to High. Drop in the butter, once it melts add the garlic and cook for 30 seconds while stirring frequently to prevent the garlic from burning.
2. Then, add the broccoli, water, salt, and pepper. Close the lid, secure the pressure valve, and select Pressure mode on High pressure for 5 minutes. Press Start/Stop.
3. Once the timer has ended, do a quick pressure release and use a stick blender to mash the Ingredients until smooth to your desired consistency and well combined.

4. Stir in Cream cheese. Adjust the taste with salt and pepper. Close the crisping lid and cook for 2 minutes on Broil mode. Serve warm.

Rosemary Sweet Potato Medallions

Servings: 4

Cooking Time: 25 Min

Ingredients:
- 4 sweet potatoes, scrubbed clean and dried
- 1 cup water /250ml
- 2 tbsp butter /30g
- 1 tbsp fresh rosemary /15g
- 1 tsp garlic powder /5g
- salt to taste

Directions:
1. Into the pot, add water and place the reversible rack over the water. Use a fork to prick sweet potatoes all over and set onto the reversible rack.
2. Seal the pressure lid, choose Pressure, set to High, and set the timer to 12 minutes. Press Start. When ready, release the pressure quickly. Transfer sweet potatoes to a cutting board and slice into 1/2-inch medallions and ensure they are peeled.
3. Melt butter in the pressure cooker on Sear/Sauté. Add in the medallions and cook each side for 2 to 3 minutes until browned. Apply salt and garlic powder to season. Serve topped with fresh rosemary.

Sour Cream & Onion Frittata

Servings: 6

Cooking Time: 15 Minutes

Ingredients:
- 1 lb. new potatoes, boiled peeled & sliced ¼-inch thick
- 1 ½ tbsp. olive oil
- 1 ½ tbsp. butter
- 1 onion, sliced thin
- 10 eggs
- ¾ cup cheddar cheese
- ½ tsp salt
- ¼ tsp pepper
- ½ cup sour cream

Directions:
1. Add oil and butter to the cooking pot and set to sauté on med-high heat.
2. Add the onions and cook 3-5 minutes until soft. Add the potatoes and cook until golden brown, about 5 minutes, stirring occasionally.
3. In a large bowl, beat eggs. Stir in cheese, salt and pepper. Pour over the onion mixture. Spoon sour cream over the eggs and swirl it evenly around the frittata. Reduce heat to medium and cook 2-4 minutes until edges are set, do not stir.
4. Add the tender-crisp lid and set to bake on 400°F or 205°C. Bake frittata 10-12 minutes until eggs are completely set.
5. Use a knife to loosen the edges and invert onto a cutting board. Let cool slightly before serving.

Nutrition:
- InfoCalories 330,Total Fat 23g,Total Carbs 16g,Protein 15g,Sodium 248mg.

Chorizo Mac And Cheese

Servings: 6
Cooking Time: 30 Min
Ingredients:

- 1 pound macaroni /450g
- 3 ounces chorizo; chopped /90g
- 2 cups milk /500ml
- 2 cups Cheddar cheese, shredded /260g
- 3 cups water /750ml
- 2 tbsp minced garlic /30g
- 1 tbsp garlic powder /15g
- salt to taste

Directions:
1. Put chorizo in the pot of your Foodi, select Sear/Sauté and stir-fry until crisp, about 5 minutes. Press Start. Set aside. Wipe the pot with kitchen paper. Add in water, macaroni, and salt to taste. Seal lid and cook on for 5 minutes High Pressure. Press Start.
2. When ready, release the pressure quickly. Stir in cheese and milk until the cheese melts. Divide the mac and cheese between serving bowls. Top with chorizo and serve.

Veggie Lover's Pizza

Servings:1
Cooking Time: 8 Minutes
Ingredients:

- 1 store-bought pizza dough, rolled into an 8-inch circle
- ¼ cup traditional pizza sauce
- 1 teaspoon minced garlic
- ⅔ cup shredded mozzarella cheese
- ¼ cup chopped green bell pepper
- ¼ cup sliced mushrooms
- Crushed red pepper flakes, for garnish

Directions:
1. Select BAKE/ROAST, set the temperature to 400°F or 205°C, and set time to 5 minutes to preheat. Select START/STOP to begin.
2. Place the rolled dough in the Ninja Cook & Crisp Basket. Spread the pizza sauce over the crust, leaving about a 1-inch border uncovered. Sprinkle on the garlic, top with the mozzarella cheese, and evenly distribute the green bell pepper and mushrooms over the pizza.
3. Place the Cook & Crisp Basket into the pot and close the crisping lid.
4. Select BAKE/ROAST, set the temperature to 400°F or 205°C, and set the time to 8 minutes. Select START/STOP to begin.
5. When cooking is complete, carefully open the lid and remove the pizza. Serve, garnished with red pepper flakes, if using.

Nutrition:

- InfoCalories: 636,Total Fat: 20g,Sodium: 1150mg,Carbohydrates: 95g,Protein: 33g.

Palak Paneer

Servings: 4
Cooking Time: 20 Min
Ingredients:

- 1 pound spinach; chopped /450g
- 1 tomato; chopped
- 2 cups paneer; cubed /260g
- 1 cup water /250ml
- ¼ cup milk /62.5ml
- 2 tbsp butter /30g

- 1 tsp minced fresh ginger /5g
- 1 tsp minced fresh garlic /5g
- 1 red onion; chopped
- 1 tsp cumin seeds /5g
- 1 tsp coriander seeds /5g
- 1 tsp salt, or to taste /5g
- 1 tsp chilli powder/5g

Directions:
1. Warm butter on Sear/Sauté, set to Medium High, and choose Start/Stop to preheat the pot. Press Start.
2. Add in garlic, cumin seeds, coriander seeds, chilli powder, ginger, and garlic and fry for 1 minute until fragrant; add onion and cook for 2 more minutes until crispy. Add in salt, water and chopped spinach.
3. Seal the pressure lid, choose Pressure, set to High, and set the timer to 1 minute. Press Start.
4. When ready, release the pressure quickly. Add spinach mixture to a blender and blend to obtain a smooth paste. Mix paneer and tomato with spinach mixture.

Artichoke Lasagna Rolls

Servings: 10
Cooking Time: 55 Minutes
Ingredients:

- 2 tsp olive oil
- ½ cup onion, chopped fine
- 24 oz. tomato and basil pasta sauce
- 1 cup ricotta cheese, low fat
- 1 egg
- 3 cloves garlic, chopped fine
- 14 oz. artichoke hearts, drained, quartered
- 2 tbsp. fresh basil, chopped
- 2 tbsp. parmesan cheese
- 10 lasagna noodles, cooked & drained

Directions:
1. Add oil to the cooking pot and set to sauté on med-high heat.
2. Add the onion and cook 5 minutes until soft. Stir in tomato sauce and cook another 5 minutes. Transfer all but 1 cup of the sauce to a bowl.
3. In a large bowl, combine ricotta cheese, egg, garlic, artichokes, basil, and parmesan cheese, mix well.
4. Lay lasagna noodles on a work surface and spoon cheese mixture over noodles. Roll up tightly and stand up in the cooking pot.
5. Pour remaining sauce over the top. Add the tender-crisp lid and set to bake on 350°F or 175°C. Bake 40-45 minutes. Serve.

Nutrition:

- InfoCalories 172,Total Fat 6g,Total Carbs 23g,Protein 8g,Sodium 330mg.

Okra Stew

Servings: 4
Cooking Time: 12 Minutes
Ingredients:

- 1-pound okra, trimmed
- 2 leeks, sliced
- Black pepper and salt to the taste
- 1 cup tomato sauce
- ¼ cup pine nuts, toasted

- 1 tablespoon cilantro, chopped

Directions:

1. In your Ninja Foodi, mix the okra with the leeks and the other ingredients except the cilantro.
2. Put the Ninja Foodi's lid on and cook on High for 12 minutes.
3. Release the pressure quickly for 5 minutes, divide the okra mix into bowls and serve with the cilantro sprinkled on top.

Nutrition:

- InfoCalories: 146; Fat: 3g; Carbohydrates: 4g; Protein: 3g

Vegan Stuffed Peppers

Servings: 4

Cooking Time: 35 Minutes

Ingredients:

- Nonstick cooking spray
- 2 bell peppers, halved lengthwise & cleaned
- 2 tbsp. olive oil
- ½ cup onion, chopped
- 4 cloves garlic, chopped fine
- 2 tomatoes, chopped fine
- ¼ tsp salt
- ¼ cup fresh parsley, chopped
- 1/3 cup dry bread crumbs
- 2 tbsp. dry white wine
- ¼ tsp pepper
- 2 tbsp. parmesan cheese

Directions:

1. Spray an 8x8-inch baking dish with cooking spray.
2. Fill the cooking pot halfway full with water. Set to sauté on high heat and bring to a boil.
3. Add the pepper halves and boil 4-5 minutes or until they start to soften. Drain and place peppers in cold water. Drain again.
4. Add oil to the cooking pot and set to medium heat. Add onion and garlic and cook just until onion has softened. Turn off heat and stir in remaining ingredients, except pepper and parmesan cheese, mix well.
5. Spoon the onion mixture into the peppers and place them in prepared dish. Sprinkle with parmesan cheese.
6. Place the rack in the cooking pot and add the peppers. Add the tender-crisp lid and set to bake on 350°F or 175°C. Bake 35-40 minutes until filling is hot and peppers are tender. Serve immediately.

Nutrition:

- InfoCalories 152,Total Fat 8g,Total Carbs 17g,Protein 4g,Sodium 285mg.

Cauliflower Cakes

Servings: 6

Cooking Time: 15 Minutes

Ingredients:

- 1 cup water
- 1 head cauliflower, cut in florets
- ¼ cup onion, chopped
- ½ cup cheddar cheese, low fat, grated
- ½ cup panko bread crumbs
- 2 eggs, lightly beaten
- ½ tsp salt
- ¼ tsp cayenne pepper
- Nonstick cooking spray

Directions:

1. Add water, cauliflower and onion to the cooking pot. Add the lid and set to pressure cook on high. Set the timer for 6 minutes. When the timer goes off, use quick release to remove the pressure. Drain and add the vegetables to a large bowl.
2. Mash the cauliflower with an electric mixer beating until smooth.
3. Stir in remaining ingredients. Form into 12 patties.
4. Spray the fryer basket with cooking spray. Place the patties in a single layer in the basket. Add the tender-crisp lid and set to air fry on 375°F or 190°C. Cook cauliflower 4-5 minutes per side until golden brown. Serve immediately.

Nutrition:

- InfoCalories 102,Total Fat 3g,Total Carbs 12g,Protein 8g,Sodium 395mg.

Stir Fried Cabbage

Servings: 6

Cooking Time: 10 Minutes

Ingredients:

- 1 tbsp. olive oil
- 1 onion, halved & sliced
- 2 carrots, sliced thin
- 3 cloves garlic, chopped fine
- ½ head green cabbage, shredded
- 2 tbsp. soy sauce, low sodium
- ½ tsp ginger
- 1 tbsp. water

Directions:

1. Add oil to the cooking pot and set to sauté on med-high heat.
2. Add the onion, carrots, garlic, and cabbage and cook, stirring frequently, until tender, about 6-8 minutes.
3. Stir in remaining ingredients and cook another 5 minutes until heated through. Serve immediately.

Nutrition:

- InfoCalories 44,Total Fat 2g,Total Carbs 5g,Protein 1g,Sodium 185mg.

Spicy Salmon With Wild Rice

Servings: 4

Cooking Time: 50 Min

Ingredients:

- 1 cup wild rice /130g
- 1 cup vegetable stock /250ml
- 2 limes, juiced
- 2 jalapeño peppers, seeded and diced
- 4 garlic cloves, minced
- 4 skinless salmon fillets
- A bunch of asparagus, trimmed and cut diagonally
- 2 tbsps chopped fresh parsley /30g
- 3 tbsps olive oil; divided /45ml
- 2 tbsps honey /30ml
- 1 tsp sweet paprika /5g
- 1 tsp salt /5g
- 1 tsp freshly ground black pepper /5g

Directions:

1. Pour the brown rice and vegetable stock in the pot; stir to combine. Put the reversible rack in the pot in the higher position and lay the salmon fillets on the rack.

2. Seal the pressure lid, choose Pressure, set to High, and set the time to 2 minutes; press Start. In a bowl, toss the broccoli with 1 tbsp of olive oil and season with the salt and black pepper. In another bowl, evenly combine the remaining oil, the lime juice, honey, paprika, jalapeño, garlic, and parsley.

3. When done cooking, do a quick pressure release, and carefully open the pressure lid.

4. Pat the salmon dry with a paper towel and coat the fish with the honey sauce while reserving a little for garnishing.

5. Arrange the asparagus around the salmon. Close the crisping lid; choose Broil and set the time to 7 minutes. Choose Start/Stop.

6. When ready, remove the salmon from the rack. Dish the salmon with asparagus and rice. Garnish with parsley and remaining sauce. Serve immediately.

Creamy Spinach Soup

Servings: 6

Cooking Time: 20 Minutes

Ingredients:

- Nonstick cooking spray
- 1 tsp garlic, chopped fine
- ½ cup green onions, sliced thin
- 3 ½ cups vegetable broth, low sodium
- 20 oz. fresh spinach, chopped
- 3 tbsp. cornstarch
- 3 cups skim milk
- ½ tsp nutmeg
- 1/8 tsp salt
- ½ tsp pepper

Directions:

1. Spray the cooking pot with cooking spray. Set to sauté on med-high heat.

2. Add the garlic and green onions and cook 3-4 minutes, stirring frequently, until soft. Stir in broth and spinach.

3. Add the lid and set to pressure cook on high. Set the timer for 8 minutes. When the timer goes off, use natural release to remove the pressure.

4. Set back to sauté on medium heat.

5. In a small bowl, whisk together cornstarch and milk until smooth. Stir into soup until combined. Add remaining ingredients and cook, stirring constantly, 6-8 minutes until soup has thickened. Serve immediately.

Nutrition:

- InfoCalories 95,Total Fat 1g,Total Carbs 16g,Protein 7g,Sodium 559mg.

Tex Mex Black Bean Soup

Servings: 8

Cooking Time: 15 Minutes

Ingredients:

- Nonstick cooking spray
- ½ cup onion, chopped
- 3 15 oz. cans black beans, no added salt
- 3 ½ cups vegetable broth, low sodium
- 2 cups water
- 16 oz. salsa
- 1 tsp cumin
- 1 tsp garlic powder
- ½ tsp pepper

Directions:

1. Spray the cooking pot with cooking spray. Set to sauté on med-high heat.

2. Add the onion and cook 3-4 minutes until soft. Stir in the broth and water.

3. Drain and rinse 2 cans of beans and add to the cooking pot. Place the other can, undrained, in a food processor or blender and process until smooth. Stir into mixture in the pot.

4. Add the remaining ingredients and mix well. Add the lid and set to pressure cook on high. Set the timer for 8 minutes.

5. Once the timer goes off, use natural release to remove the pressure. Stir well and ladle into bowls and serve.

Nutrition:

- InfoCalories 172,Total Fat 1g,Total Carbs 33g,Protein 11g,Sodium 1255mg.

Roasted Squash And Rice With Crispy Tofu

Servings: 4

Cooking Time: 70 Min

Ingredients:

- 1 small butternut squash, peeled and diced
- 1 block extra-firm tofu, drained and cubed /450g
- 1 cup jasmine rice, cooked /130g
- ¾ cup water /188ml
- 1 tbsp coconut aminos /15g
- 2 tbsps melted butter; divided /30ml
- 2 tsp s arrowroot starch /10g
- 1 tsp salt /5g
- 1 tsp freshly ground black pepper /5g

Directions:

1. Pour the rice and water into the pot and mix with a spoon. Seal the pressure lid, choose Pressure, set to High and set the time to 2 minutes. Choose Start/Stop to boil the rice.

2. in a bowl, toss the butternut squash with 1 tbsp of melted butter and season with the salt and black pepper. Set aside.

3. In another bowl, mix the remaining butter with the coconut aminos, and toss the tofu in the mixture. Pour the arrowroot starch over the tofu and toss again to combine well.

4. When done cooking the rice, perform a quick pressure release, and carefully open the pressure lid. Put the reversible rack in the pot in the higher position and line with aluminum foil. Arrange the tofu and butternut squash on the rack.

5. Close the crisping lid. Choose Air Crisp, set the temperature to 400°F or 205°C, and set the time to 20 minutes. Choose Start/Stop to begin cooking.

6. After 10 minutes, use tongs to turn the butternut squash and tofu. When done cooking, check for your desired crispiness and serve the tofu and squash with the rice.

Potato Filled Bread Rolls

Servings: 4

Cooking Time: 25 Min

Ingredients:

- 8 slices of bread
- 2 green chilies, deseeded; chopped
- 5 large potatoes, boiled, mashed
- 2 sprigs curry leaf
- 1 medium onion; chopped
- 1 tbsp olive oil /15ml
- ½ tsp mustard seeds /2.5g
- ½ tsp turmeric /2.5g
- Salt, to taste

Directions:

1. Combine the olive oil, onion, curry leaves, and mustard seed, in the Ninja Foodi basket. Cook for 5 minutes. Mix the onion mixture with the mashed potatoes, chilies, turmeric, and some salt. Divide the dough into 8 equal pieces.
2. Trim the sides of the bread, and wet it with some water. Make sure to get rid of the excess water. Take one wet bread slice in your palm and place one of the potato pieces in the center.
3. Roll the bread over the filling, sealing the edges. Place the rolls onto a prepared baking dish, close the crisping lid and cook for 12 minutes on Air Crisp at 350 °F or 175°C.

Crispy Kale Chips

Servings: 2

Cooking Time: 9 Min

Ingredients:

- 4 cups kale, stemmed and packed /520g
- 1 tbsp of yeast flakes /15g
- 2 tbsp of olive oil /30ml
- 1 tsp of vegan seasoning /5g
- Salt to taste

Directions:

1. In a bowl, add the oil, the kale, the vegan seasoning, and the yeast and mix well. Dump the coated kale in the Ninja Foodi's basket.
2. Set the heat to 370°F or 185°C, close the crisping lid and fry for a total of 6 minutes on Air Crisp mode. Shake it from time to time.

Broccoli & Pesto Penne

Servings: 4

Cooking Time: 35 Minutes

Ingredients:

- 8 oz. whole wheat penne
- 2 cups baby broccoli
- 1 cup oven roasted tomatoes
- 1 tsp garlic, chopped fine
- ¼ cup pesto
- ¼ cup feta cheese, crumbled
- ½ tbsp. lemon juice
- 2 tbsp. fresh basil, chopped

Directions:

1. Add enough water to the cooking pot to cook the pasta. Set to sauté on high and bring to a boil.
2. Add the penne and cook according to package directions. Add the broccoli to the pot in the last 2 minutes of cooking time. Drain and return to the pot.
3. Reduce heat to med-high. Add tomatoes and garlic and cook 2 minutes, stirring frequently.

4. Stir in the pesto, half the feta, and lemon juice. Toss to combine. Spoon onto serving plates and top with remaining feta and basil before serving.

Nutrition:

- InfoCalories 338,Total Fat 12g,Total Carbs 52g,Protein 11g,Sodium 267mg.

Sweet Potato Noodles With Cashew Sauce

Servings: 4

Cooking Time: 10 Minutes

Ingredients:

- 1 cup cashews
- ¾ cup water
- ½ tsp salt
- 1 clove garlic
- 2 tbsp. olive oil, divided
- 4 large sweet potatoes, spiralized
- 2 cups baby spinach
- ½ cup fresh basil, chopped

Directions:

1. Add cashews to a small bowl and cover with water. Let soak 2 hours.
2. Drain off the water, rinse, and add to a food processor with ¾ cup water, salt, and garlic. Pulse until smooth.
3. Add half the oil to the cooking pot and set to sauté on med-high heat.
4. Add sweet potatoes and cook 6-7 minutes until tender-crisp.
5. Add spinach and toss until it wilts, 1-2 minutes.
6. Turn off the heat and stir in half the herbs and the cashew sauce.
7. Divide evenly among serving plates, drizzle with olive oil and garnish with remaining herbs. Serve.

Nutrition:

- InfoCalories 523,Total Fat 35g,Total Carbs 45g,Protein 13g,Sodium 528mg.

Aloo Gobi With Cilantro

Servings: 4

Cooking Time: 40 Min

Ingredients:

- 1 head cauliflower, cored and cut into florets
- 1 potato, peeled and diced
- 4 garlic cloves, minced
- 1 tomato, cored and chopped
- 1 jalapeño pepper, deseeded and minced
- 1 onion, minced
- 1 cup water /250ml
- 1 tbsp curry paste /15g
- 1 tbsp vegetable oil /15ml
- 1 tbsp ghee /15g
- 2 tsp cumin seeds /10g
- 1 tsp ground turmeric /5g
- ½ tsp chili pepper /2.5g
- salt to taste
- A handful of cilantro leaves; chopped

Directions:

1. Warm oil on Sear/Sauté. Add in potato and cauliflower and cook for 8 to 10 minutes until lightly

browned; add salt for seasoning. Set the vegetables to a bowl.
2.   Add ghee to the pot. Mix in cumin seeds and cook for 10 seconds until they start to pop; add onion and cook for 3 minutes until softened. Mix in garlic; cook for seconds.
3.   Add in tomato, curry paste, chili pepper, jalapeño pepper, curry paste, and turmeric; cook for 3 to 5 minutes until the tomato starts to break down.
4.   Return potato and cauliflower to the pot. Add water over the vegetables, add more salt if need be, and stir. Seal the pressure lid, choose Pressure, set to High, and set the timer to 4 minutes. Press Start. Release pressure naturally. Top with cilantro and serve.

Spinach, Tomatoes, And Butternut Squash Stew

Servings: 6
Cooking Time: 65 Min
Ingredients:

- 2 lb. butternut squash, peeled and cubed /900g
- 1 can sundried tomatoes, undrained /450g
- 2 cans chickpeas, drained /450g
- 1 white onion; diced
- 4 garlic cloves, minced
- 4 cups baby spinach /520g
- 4 cups vegetable broth /1000ml
- 1 tbsp butter /15g
- ½ tsp smoked paprika /2.5g
- 1 tsp coriander powder /5g
- 1½ tsp s cumin powder /7.5g
- ½ tsp salt /2.5g
- ½ tsp freshly ground black pepper /2.5g

Directions:
1.   Choose Sear/Sauté, set to Medium High, and the timer to 5 minutes; press Start/Stop to preheat the pot. Combine the butter, onion, and garlic in the pot. Cook, stirring occasionally; for 5 minutes or until soft and fragrant.
2.   Add the butternut squash, vegetable broth, tomatoes, chickpeas, cumin, paprika, coriander, salt, and black pepper to the pot. Put the pressure lid together and lock in the Seal position.
3.   Choose Pressure, set to High, and set the time to 8 minutes; press Start/Stop.
4.   When the timer is done reading, perform a quick pressure release. Stir in the spinach to wilt, adjust the taste with salt and black pepper, and serve warm.

Creamy Golden Casserole

Servings: 6
Cooking Time: 40 Minutes
Ingredients:

- Nonstick cooking spray
- 2 lbs. summer squash, cut in 1-inch pieces
- ¾ cup sharp cheddar cheese, reduced fat, grated & divided
- ¼ cup light mayonnaise
- 2 eggs
- ¼ tsp salt
- ¼ tsp pepper

Directions:
1.   Spray a 2-qt baking dish with cooking spray.
2.   Add the squash to the cooking pot along with just enough water to cover. Set to saute on high heat and bring to a boil.
3.   Reduce heat to medium and cook 8-10 minutes or until squash is tender. Drain.

4.   Place the squash in a large bowl and add ½ cup cheese, mayonnaise, eggs, salt, and pepper and mix well. Spoon into prepared dish and sprinkle with remaining cheese.
5.   Place the rack in the cooking pot and add the dish. Add the tender-crisp lid and set to bake on 375°F or 190°C. Bake 30 minutes until heated through and top is golden brown. Serve.
Nutrition:

- InfoCalories 120,Total Fat 8g,Total Carbs 6g,Protein 7g,Sodium 303mg.

Noodles With Tofu And Peanuts

Servings: 4
Cooking Time: 20 Min
Ingredients:

- 1 package tofu; cubed
- 8 ounces egg noodles /240g
- 2 bell peppers; sliced
- 3 scallions, thinly sliced
- ¼ cup roasted peanuts /32.5g
- ¼ cup soy sauce /62.5ml
- ¼ cup orange juice /62.5ml
- 1 tbsp fresh ginger, peeled and minced /15g
- 2 tbsp vinegar /30ml
- 1 tbsp sesame oil /15ml
- 1 tbsp sriracha /15ml

Directions:
1.   In the pressure cooker, mix tofu, bell peppers, orange juice, sesame oil, ginger, egg noodles, soy sauce, vinegar, and sriracha; cover with enough water.
2.   Seal the pressure lid, choose Pressure, set to High, and set the timer to 2 minutes. Press Start. When ready, release the pressure quickly. Place the mixture into four plates; apply a topping of scallions and peanuts before serving.

Caramelized Sweet Potatoes

Servings: 4
Cooking Time: 20 Minutes
Ingredients:

- 1 cup water
- 2 large sweet potatoes
- 2 tbsp. butter
- ½ tsp salt
- ¼ tsp pepper

Directions:
1.   Add the trivet and water to the cooking pot.
2.   Prick the potatoes with a fork and place on the trivet. Add the lid and set to pressure cook on high. Set timer for 15 minutes. Once timer goes off, use natural release to remove the pressure.
3.   Transfer potatoes to a cutting board and slice ½-inch thick.
4.   Remove the trivet and add butter to the pot. Set to sauté on med-high heat.
5.   Add the potatoes and cook, turning occasionally, until potatoes are nicely browned on both sides. Season with salt and pepper and serve.
Nutrition:

- InfoCalories 107,Total Fat 6g,Total Carbs 14g,Protein 1g,Sodium 227mg.

Vegetarian Stir Fry

Servings: 6
Cooking Time: 10 Minutes

Ingredients:
- 4 cloves garlic, chopped fine
- 2 tbsp. blue agave
- 1 tbsp. light soy sauce
- ¼ tsp ginger
- 1 tbsp. cornstarch
- 1 tsp sesame seeds
- 2 tsp olive oil
- 2 cups fresh broccoli florets
- ¼ lb. fresh snow peas, trimmed
- 1 red bell pepper, cut in ¼-inch strips
- 1 onion, cut in wedges

Directions:
1. In a small bowl, whisk together garlic, agave, soy sauce, ginger, and cornstarch until combined.
2. Set cooker to sauté on medium heat. Add sesame seeds and toast, stirring frequently, 2-3 minutes. Transfer to a plate.
3. Add the oil and increase the heat to med-high. Add broccoli, peas, bell pepper, and onion. Cook until tender-crisp, stirring occasionally, about 4-5 minutes.
4. Stir in the agave mixture and cook 2 minutes until sauce thicken. Serve immediately.

Nutrition:
- InfoCalories 58,Total Fat 2g,Total Carbs 8g,Protein 2g,Sodium 98mg.

Pomegranate Radish Mix

Servings: 4
Cooking Time: 8 Minutes

Ingredients:
- 1-pound radishes, roughly cubed
- Black pepper and salt to the taste
- 2 garlic cloves, minced
- ½ cup chicken stock
- 2 tablespoons pomegranate juice
- ¼ cup pomegranate seeds

Directions:
1. In your Ninja Foodi, combine the radishes with the stock and the other ingredients.
2. Put the Ninja Foodi's lid on and cook on High for 8 minutes.
3. Release the pressure quickly for 5 minutes, divide everything between plates and serve.

Nutrition:
- InfoCalories: 133; Fat: 2.3g; Carbohydrates: 2.4g; Protein: 2g

Veggie Taco Soup

Servings: 6
Cooking Time: 4 Hours

Ingredients:
- Nonstick cooking spray
- 6 corn tortillas, cut in strips
- 3 ½ cups vegetable broth, low sodium
- 14 ½ oz. tomatoes, diced, undrained
- 15 oz. spicy chili beans, undrained
- 4 oz. green chilies, diced & drained
- ¾ cup onions, chopped

- 1 clove garlic, chopped fine
- 2 tsp red wine vinegar
- ¼ tsp crushed red pepper flakes
- ¼ cup cilantro, chopped
- ½ tsp salt

Directions:
1. Spray fryer basket with cooking spray. Add the tortilla strips and spray with cooking spray.
2. Add the tender-crisp lid and set to air fry on 375°F or 190°C. Cook until crisp, about 5 minutes, turning every couple of minutes. Set aside.
3. Add all ingredients, except cilantro, salt, and tortillas, to the cooking pot, mix well.
4. Add the lid and set to slow cook on high. Cook 3-4 hours, stirring occasionally.
5. Add salt and cilantro and stir well. Ladle into bowls and top with tortilla strips. Serve.

Nutrition:
- InfoCalories 172,Total Fat 1g,Total Carbs 33g,Protein 8g,Sodium 617mg.

Baby Porcupine Meatballs

Servings: 4
Cooking Time: 30 Min

Ingredients:
- 1 lb. of ground beef /450g
- 1 onion; chopped
- 1 green bell pepper, finely chopped
- 1 garlic clove, minced
- 1 cup rice /130g
- 2 cups of tomato juice /500ml
- 2 tbsp Worcestershire sauce /30ml
- 1 tsp celery salt /5g
- 1 tsp oregano /5g

Directions:
1. Combine the rice, ground beef, onion, celery, salt, green peppers, and garlic. Shape into balls of 1 inch each. Arrange the balls in the basket of the Ninja Foodi. Close the crisping lid and cook for 15 minutes at 320°F or 160°C.
2. After 8 minutes, shape the balls. Heat the tomato juice, cloves, oregano, and Worcestershire sauce in a saucepan over medium heat.
3. Pour in the meatballs, bring to a boil, reduce the heat and simmer for 10 minutes, stirring often. Serve warm.

Crispy Cheese Lings

Servings: 4
Cooking Time: 15 Min

Ingredients:
- 4 cups grated cheddar cheese /520g
- 1 cup all-purpose flour /130g
- 1 tbsp baking powder /15g
- 1 tbsp butter /15g
- 1-2 tbsp water /30ml
- ¼ tsp chili powder /1.25g
- ¼ tsp salt, to taste /1.25g

Directions:
1. Mix the flour and the baking powder. Add the chili powder, salt, butter, cheese and 1-2 tbsp of water to the mixture.

2. Make a stiff dough. Knead the dough for a while. Sprinkle a tbsp or so of flour on the table. Take a rolling pin and roll the dough into ½ -inch thickness.

3. Cut the dough in any shape you want. Close the crisping lid and fry the cheese lings for 6 minutes at 370° °F or 185°C on Air Crisp mode.

Parsley Mashed Cauliflower

Servings: 4
Cooking Time: 15 Min
Ingredients:
- 1 head cauliflower
- 1/4 cup heavy cream /62.5g
- 2 cups water /500ml
- 1 tbsp fresh parsley, finely chopped /15g
- 1 tbsp butter /15g
- ¼ tsp celery salt /1.25g
- ⅛ tsp freshly ground black pepper /0.625g

Directions:
1. Into the pot, add water and set trivet on top and lay cauliflower head onto the trivet. Seal the pressure lid, choose Pressure, set to High, and set the timer to 8 minutes. Press Start.
2. When ready, release the pressure quickly. Remove the trivet and drain liquid from the pot before returning to the base.
3. Take back the cauliflower to the pot alongside the pepper, heavy cream, salt and butter; use an immersion blender to blend until smooth. Top with parsley and serve.

Soups & Stews

Lasagna Soup

Servings:8
Cooking Time: 16 Minutes
Ingredients:
- 1 tablespoon extra-virgin olive oil
- 16 ounces Italian sausage
- 1 small onion, diced
- 4 garlic cloves, minced
- 1 jar marinara sauce
- 2 cups water
- 1 cup vegetable broth
- 1 teaspoon dried basil
- 1 teaspoon dried oregano
- ½ teaspoon dried thyme
- Freshly ground black pepper
- 8 ounces lasagna noodles, broken up
- 1 cup ricotta cheese
- ½ cup grated Parmesan cheese
- 1 teaspoon dried parsley
- ½ cup heavy (whipping) cream
- 1 cup shredded mozzarella cheese

Directions:
1. Select SEAR/SAUTÉ and set to HI. Select START/STOP to begin. Let preheat for 5 minutes.
2. Add the oil and sausage and cook for about 5 minutes. Using a wooden spoon, break apart the sausage and stir.
3. Add the onions and cook, stirring occasionally, for 3 minutes. Add the garlic and cook for 2 minutes, or until the meat is no longer pink.
4. Add the marinara sauce, water, vegetable broth, basil, oregano, thyme, pepper, and lasagna noodles. Assemble pressure lid, making sure the pressure release valve is in the SEAL position.
5. Select PRESSURE and set to HI. Set time to 6 minutes. Select START/STOP to begin.
6. In a medium bowl, combine the ricotta cheese, Parmesan cheese, and parsley. Cover and refrigerate.

7. When pressure cooking is complete, quick release the pressure by turning the pressure release valve to the VENT position. Carefully remove lid when unit has finished releasing pressure.
8. Stir in the heavy cream. Add the cheese mixture and stir. Top the soup with the mozzarella. Close crisping lid.
9. Select BROIL and set time to 5 minutes. Select START/STOP to begin.
10. When cooking is complete, serve immediately.

Nutrition:
- InfoCalories: 398,Total Fat: 22g,Sodium: 892mg,Carbohydrates: 29g,Protein: 23g.

Chicken Potpie Soup

Servings:6
Cooking Time: 1 Hour
Ingredients:
- 4 chicken breasts
- 2 cups chicken stock
- 2 tablespoons unsalted butter
- 1 yellow onion, diced
- 16 ounces frozen mixed vegetables
- 1 cup heavy (whipping) cream
- 1 can condensed cream of chicken soup
- 2 tablespoons cornstarch
- 2 tablespoons water
- Salt
- Freshly ground black pepper
- 1 tube refrigerated biscuit dough

Directions:
1. Place the chicken and stock in the pot. Assemble pressure lid, making sure the pressure release valve is in the SEAL position.
2. Select PRESSURE and set to HI. Set time to 15 minutes. Select START/STOP to begin.
3. Once pressure cooking is complete, quick release the pressure by turning the pressure release valve to the VENT

position. Carefully remove lid when the unit has finished releasing pressure.

4. Using a silicone-tipped utensil, shred the chicken.

5. Select SEAR/SAUTÉ and set to MED. Add the butter, onion, mixed vegetables, cream, and condensed soup and stir. Select START/STOP to begin. Simmer for 10 minutes.

6. In a small bowl, whisk together the cornstarch and water. Slowly whisk the cornstarch mixture into the soup. Set temperature to LO and simmer for 10 minutes more. Season with salt and pepper.

7. Carefully arrange the biscuits on top of the simmering soup. Close crisping lid.

8. Select BAKE/ROAST, set temperature to 325°F or 165°C, and set time to 15 minutes. Select START/STOP to begin.

9. When cooking is complete, remove the biscuits. To serve, place a biscuit in a bowl and ladle soup over it.

Nutrition:

- InfoCalories: 731,Total Fat: 26g,Sodium: 1167mg,Carbohydrates: 56g,Protein: 45g.

Italian Sausage, Potato, And Kale Soup

Servings:8

Cooking Time: 18 Minutes

Ingredients:

- 1 tablespoon extra-virgin olive oil
- 1½ pounds hot Italian sausage, ground
- 1 pound sweet Italian sausage, ground
- 1 large yellow onion, diced
- 2 tablespoons minced garlic
- 4 large Russet potatoes, cut in ½-inch thick quarters
- 5 cups chicken stock
- 2 tablespoons Italian seasoning
- 2 teaspoons crushed red pepper flakes
- Salt
- Freshly ground black pepper
- 6 cups kale, chopped
- ½ cup heavy (whipping) cream

Directions:

1. Select SEAR/SAUTÉ. Set temperature to MD:HI. Select START/STOP to begin. Let preheat for 5 minutes.

2. Add the olive oil and hot and sweet Italian sausage. Cook, breaking up the sausage with a spatula, until the meat is cooked all the way through, about 5 minutes.

3. Add the onion, garlic, potatoes, chicken stock, Italian seasoning, and crushed red pepper flakes. Season with salt and pepper. Stir to combine. Assemble pressure lid, making sure the pressure release valve is in the SEAL position.

4. Select PRESSURE and set to HI. Set time to 10 minutes. Select START/STOP to begin.

5. When pressure cooking is complete, quick release the pressure by turning the pressure release valve to the VENT position. Carefully remove lid when the unit has finished releasing pressure.

6. Stir in the kale and heavy cream. Serve.

Nutrition:

- InfoCalories: 689,Total Fat: 45g,Sodium: 1185mg,Carbohydrates: 38g,Protein: 33g.

Jamaican Jerk Chicken Stew

Servings:6

Cooking Time: 28 Minutes

Ingredients:

- 2 tablespoons canola oil

- 6 boneless, skinless chicken thighs, cut in 2-inch
- pieces
- 2 tablespoons Jamaican jerk spice
- 1 white onion, peeled and chopped
- 2 red bell peppers, chopped
- ½ head green cabbage, core removed and cut into 2-inch pieces
- 1½ cups wild rice blend, rinsed
- 4 cups chicken stock
- ½ cup prepared Jamaican jerk sauce
- Kosher salt

Directions:

1. Select SEAR/SAUTÉ and set to HI. Select START/STOP to begin. Let preheat for 5 minutes.

2. Add the oil, chicken, and jerk spice and stir. Cook for 5 minutes, stirring occasionally.

3. Add the onions, bell pepper, and cabbage and stir. Cook for 5 minutes, stirring occasionally.

4. Add the wild rice and stock, stirring well to combine. Assemble pressure lid, making sure the pressure release valve is in the SEAL position.

5. Select PRESSURE and set to HI. Set time to 18 minutes. Select START/STOP to begin.

6. When pressure cooking is complete, allow pressure to naturally release for 10 minutes. After 10 minutes, quick release any remaining pressure by moving the pressure release valve to the VENT position. Carefully remove lid when unit has finished releasing pressure.

7. Add the jerk sauce to pot, stirring well to combine. Let the stew sit for 5 minutes, allowing it to thicken. Season with salt and serve.

Nutrition:

- InfoCalories: 404,Total Fat: 10g,Sodium: 373mg,Carbohydrates: 53g,Protein: 29g.

Fish Chowder And Biscuits

Servings:8

Cooking Time: 30 Minutes

Ingredients:

- 5 strips bacon, sliced
- 1 white onion, chopped
- 3 celery stalks, chopped
- 4 cups chicken stock
- 2 Russet potatoes, rinsed and cut in 1-inch pieces
- 4 frozen haddock fillets
- Kosher salt
- ½ cup clam juice
- ⅓ cup all-purpose flour
- 2 cans evaporated milk
- 1 tube refrigerated biscuit dough

Directions:

1. Select SEAR/SAUTÉ and set to HI. Select START/STOP to begin. Let preheat for 5 minutes.

2. Add the bacon and cook, stirring frequently, for 5 minutes. Add the onion and celery and cook for an additional 5 minutes, stirring occasionally.

3. Add the chicken stock, potatoes, and haddock filets. Season with salt. Assemble pressure lid, making sure the pressure release valve is in the SEAL position.

4. Select PRESSURE and set to HI. Set time to 5 minutes. Select START/STOP to begin.

5.   Whisk together the clam juice and flour in a small bowl, ensuring there are no flour clumps in the mixture.
6.   When pressure cooking is complete, quick release the pressure by moving the pressure release valve to the VENT position. Carefully remove lid when unit has finished releasing pressure.
7.   Select SEAR/SAUTÉ and set to MED. Select START/STOP to begin. Add the clam juice mixture, stirring well to combine. Add the evaporated milk and continue to stir frequently for 3 to 5 minutes, until chowder has thickened to your desired texture.
8.   Place the Reversible Rack in the pot in the higher position. Place the biscuits on the rack; it may be necessary to tear the last biscuit or two into smaller pieces in order to fit them all on the rack. Close crisping lid.
9.   Select BAKE/ROAST, set temperature to 350°F or 175°C, and set time to 12 minutes. Select START/STOP to begin.
10. After 10 minutes, check the biscuits for doneness. If desired, cook for up to an additional 2 minutes.
11. When cooking is complete, open lid and remove rack from pot. Serve the chowder and top each portion with biscuits.

Nutrition:
- InfoCalories: 518,Total Fat: 22g,Sodium: 1189mg,Carbohydrates: 49g,Protein: 33g.

Braised Pork And Black Bean Stew

Servings:8
Cooking Time: 30 Minutes
Ingredients:

- 2 pounds boneless pork shoulder, cut into 1-inch pieces
- ¼ cup all-purpose flour
- ¼ cup unsalted butter
- ½ small onion, diced
- 1 carrot, diced
- 1 celery stalk, diced
- 2 garlic cloves, minced
- 1 tablespoon tomato paste
- 1 tablespoon cumin
- 1 tablespoon smoked paprika
- 4 cups chicken stock
- 1 can diced tomatoes with chiles
- 1 can black beans, rinsed and drained
- 1 can hominy, rinsed and drained
- Sea salt
- Freshly ground black pepper

Directions:
1.   In a large bowl, coat the pork pieces with the flour.
2.   Select SEAR/SAUTÉ and set to HI. Select START/STOP to begin. Let preheat for 5 minutes.
3.   Add the butter. Once melted, add the pork and sear for 5 minutes, turning the pieces so they begin to brown on all sides.
4.   Add the onion, carrot, celery, garlic, tomato paste, cumin, and paprika and cook, stirring occasionally, for 3 minutes.
5.   Add the chicken stock and tomatoes. Assemble pressure lid, making sure the pressure release valve is in the SEAL position.
6.   Select PRESSURE and set to HI. Set time to 15 minutes. Select START/STOP to begin.
7.   When pressure cooking is complete, quick release the pressure by turning the pressure release valve to the VENT position. Carefully remove lid when the unit has finished releasing pressure.
8.   Select SEAR/SAUTÉ and set to HI. Select START/STOP to begin.
9.   Whisk in the beans and hominy. Season with salt and pepper and cook for 2 minutes. Serve.

Nutrition:
- InfoCalories: 342,Total Fat: 12g,Sodium: 638mg,Carbohydrates: 27g,Protein: 29g.

Chicken Noodle Soup

Servings:8
Cooking Time: 19 Minutes
Ingredients:

- 2 tablespoons unsalted butter
- 1 large onion, chopped
- 2 carrots, chopped
- 2 celery stalks, chopped
- 2 pounds boneless chicken breast
- 4 cups chicken broth
- 4 cups water
- 1 tablespoon chopped fresh parsley
- 1 teaspoon dried thyme
- 1 teaspoon dried oregano
- ½ teaspoon sea salt
- ½ teaspoon freshly ground black pepper
- 5 ounces egg noodles

Directions:
1.   Select SEAR/SAUTÉ and set to HI. Select START/STOP to begin. Let preheat for 5 minutes.
2.   Add the butter. Once melted, add the onion, carrots, and celery. Cook, stirring occasionally, for 5 minutes.
3.   Add the chicken, chicken broth, water, parsley, thyme, oregano, salt, and pepper. Assemble pressure lid, making sure the pressure release valve is in the SEAL position.
4.   Select PRESSURE and set to HI. Set time to 8 minutes. Select START/STOP to begin.
5.   When pressure cooking is complete, quick release the pressure by moving the pressure release valve to the VENT position. Carefully remove lid when unit has finished releasing pressure.
6.   Remove the chicken from the soup and shred it with two forks. Set aside.
7.   Add the egg noodles. Select SEAR/SAUTÉ and set to MED. Select START/STOP to begin.
8.   Cook for 6 minutes, uncovered, or until the noodles are tender. Stir the shredded chicken back into the pot. Serve.

Nutrition:
- InfoCalories: 237,Total Fat: 5g,Sodium: 413mg,Carbohydrates: 17g,Protein: 30g.

Chickpea, Spinach, And Sweet Potato Stew

Servings:6
Cooking Time: 23 Minutes
Ingredients:

- 1 tablespoon extra-virgin olive oil
- 1 yellow onion, diced
- 4 garlic cloves, minced
- 4 sweet potatoes, peeled and diced
- 4 cups vegetable broth
- 1 can fire-roasted diced tomatoes, undrained
- 2 cans chickpeas, drained
- 1½ teaspoons ground cumin
- 1 teaspoon ground coriander

- ½ teaspoon paprika
- ½ teaspoon sea salt
- ½ teaspoon freshly ground black pepper
- 4 cups baby spinach

Directions:

1. Select SEAR/SAUTÉ and set to MD:HI. Select START/STOP to begin. Allow the pot to preheat for 5 minutes.
2. Combine the oil, onion, and garlic in the pot. Cook, stirring occasionally, for 5 minutes.
3. Add the sweet potatoes, vegetable broth, tomatoes, chickpeas, cumin, coriander, paprika, salt, and black pepper to the pot. Assemble the pressure lid, making sure the pressure release valve is in the SEAL position.
4. Select PRESSURE and set to HI. Set the time to 8 minutes, then select START/STOP to begin.
5. When pressure cooking is complete, quick release the pressure by moving the pressure release valve to the VENT position. Carefully remove the lid when the unit has finished releasing pressure.
6. Add the spinach to the pot and stir until wilted. Serve.

Nutrition:

- InfoCalories: 220,Total Fat: 4g,Sodium: 593mg,Carbohydrates: 42g,Protein: 7g.

Goulash (hungarian Beef Soup)

Servings:6

Cooking Time: 55 Minutes

Ingredients:

- ½ cup all-purpose flour
- 1 tablespoon kosher salt
- ½ teaspoon freshly ground black pepper
- 2 pounds beef stew meat
- 2 tablespoons canola oil
- 1 medium red bell pepper, seeded and chopped
- 4 garlic cloves, minced
- 1 large yellow onion, diced
- 2 tablespoons smoked paprika
- 1½ pounds small Yukon Gold potatoes, halved
- 2 cups beef broth
- 2 tablespoons tomato paste
- ¼ cup sour cream
- Fresh parsley, for garnish

Directions:

1. Select SEAR/SAUTÉ and set to HI. Select START/STOP to begin. Let preheat for 5 minutes.
2. Mix together the flour, salt, and pepper in a small bowl. Dip the pieces of beef into the flour mixture, shaking off any extra flour.
3. Add the oil and let heat for 1 minute. Place the beef in the pot and brown it on all sides, about 10 minutes.
4. Add the bell pepper, garlic, onion, and smoked paprika. Sauté for about 8 minutes or until the onion is translucent.

5. Add the potatoes, beef broth, and tomato paste and stir. Assemble pressure lid, making sure the pressure release valve is in the SEAL position.
6. Select PRESSURE and set to LO. Set time to 30 minutes. Select START/STOP to begin.
7. When pressure cooking is complete, quick release the pressure by moving the pressure release valve to the VENT position. Carefully remove lid when unit has finished releasing pressure.
8. Add the sour cream and mix thoroughly. Garnish with parsley, if desired, and serve immediately.

Nutrition:

- InfoCalories: 413,Total Fat: 13g,Sodium: 432mg,Carbohydrates: 64g,Protein: 37g.

Creamy Pumpkin Soup

Servings:8

Cooking Time: 23 Minutes

Ingredients:

- ¼ cup unsalted butter
- ½ small onion, diced
- 1 celery stalk, diced
- 1 carrot, diced
- 2 garlic cloves, minced
- 1 can pumpkin purée
- 1½ teaspoons poultry spice blend
- 3 cups chicken stock
- 1 package cream cheese
- 1 cup heavy (whipping) cream
- ¼ cup maple syrup
- Sea salt
- Freshly ground black pepper

Directions:

1. Select SEAR/SAUTÉ and set to HI. Select START/STOP to begin. Let preheat for 5 minutes.
2. Add the butter. Once melted, add the onions, celery, carrot, and garlic. Cook, stirring occasionally, for 3 minutes
3. Add the pumpkin, poultry spice, and chicken stock. Assemble pressure lid, making sure the pressure release valve is in the SEAL position.
4. Select PRESSURE and set to HI. Set time to 15 minutes. Select START/STOP to begin.
5. When pressure cooking is complete, quick release the pressure by turning the pressure release valve to the VENT position. Carefully remove lid when the unit has finished releasing pressure.
6. Whisk in the cream cheese, heavy cream, and maple syrup. Season with salt and pepper. Using an immersion blender, purée the soup until smooth.

Nutrition:

- InfoCalories: 334,Total Fat: 28g,Sodium: 266mg,Carbohydrates: 17g,Protein: 6g.

Desserts

Pumpkin Crème Brulee

Servings: 4

Cooking Time: 3:00 Hours

Ingredients:

- 1 egg yolk
- 1 egg, lightly beaten
- ¾ cup heavy cream
- 4 tbsp. pumpkin puree
- 1 tsp vanilla
- 4 tbsp. sugar, divided
- ¾ tsp pumpkin pie spice

Directions:

1. In a medium bowl, whisk together egg yolk and beaten egg, mix well.
2. Whisk in cream, slowly until combined.
3. Stir in pumpkin and vanilla and mix until combined.
4. In a small bowl, stir together 2 tablespoons sugar and pie spice. Add to pumpkin mixture and stir to blend.
5. Fill 4 small ramekins with mixture and place in the cooking pot. Carefully pour water around the ramekins, it should reach halfway up the sides.
6. Add the lid and set to slow cooking on low. Cook 2-3 hours or until custard is set.
7. Sprinkle remaining 2 tablespoons over the top of the custards. Add the tender-crisp lid and set to broil on 450°F or 230°C. Cook another 2-3 minutes or until sugar caramelizes, be careful not to let it burn. Transfer ramekins to wire rack to cool before serving.

Nutrition:

- InfoCalories 334,Total Fat 21g,Total Carbs 30g,Protein 6g,Sodium 59mg.

Milk Dumplings In Sweet Sauce

Servings: 20

Cooking Time: 30 Min

Ingredients:

- 2 ½ cups Sugar /325g
- 6 cups Milk /1500ml
- 6 cups Water /1500ml
- 3 tbsp Lime Juice /45ml
- 1 tsp ground Cardamom /5g

Directions:

1. Bring to a boil the milk, on Sear/Sauté, and stir in the lime juice. The solids should start to separate. Pour milk through a cheesecloth-lined colander. Drain as much liquid as you can. Place the paneer on a smooth surface. Form a ball and divide into 20 equal pieces.
2. Pour water in the Foofi and bring to a boil on Sear/Sauté. Add in sugar and cardamom and cook until dissolved. Shape the dumplings into balls, and place them in the syrup.
3. Seal the pressure lid and choose Pressure, set to High, and set the time to 5 minutes. Press Start. Once done, do a quick pressure release. Let cool and refrigerate for at least 2 hours.

Classic Custard

Servings: 4

Cooking Time: 30 Minutes

Ingredients:

- Nonstick cooking spray
- 4 eggs
- ½ cup half and half
- 2 cups almond milk, unsweetened
- 1/3 cup Stevia
- 1 tsp vanilla
- ¼ tsp cinnamon

Directions:

1. Spray four ramekins with cooking spray.
2. In a large bowl, whisk all the ingredients together until combined. Pour into prepared ramekins
3. Place the ramekins in the cooking pot and pour enough water around them it comes ½ inch up the sides of the ramekins.
4. Add the tender-crisp lid and set to bake on 350°F or 175°C. Bake 30 minutes or until custard is set. Transfer to a wire rack and let cool before serving.

Nutrition:

- InfoCalories 135,Total Fat 5g,Total Carbs 23g,Protein 11g,Sodium 164mg.

Maply Soufflés

Servings: 4

Cooking Time: 10 Minutes

Ingredients:

- Butter flavored cooking spray
- 1/3 cup maple syrup
- 2 eggs, separated
- ½ tsp vanilla
- 2 tbsp. flour
- 1/8 tsp salt
- Powdered sugar for dusting

Directions:

1. Spray 4 ramekins with cooking spray.
2. In a medium bowl, beat syrup, egg yolks, and vanilla until thickened, about 1 minute.
3. Add flour and beat until combined.
4. In a large bowl, beat egg whites until stiff peaks form, about 2 minutes. Gently fold ¼ of the egg whites into syrup mixture just until combined. Fold the syrup mixture into the remaining egg whites just until combined. Divide evenly among ramekins.
5. Place ramekins in the cooking pot and add the tender-crisp lid. Set to bake on 375°F or 190°C. Bake 10-12 minutes, or until puffed and golden brown. Dust with powdered sugar and serve immediately.

Nutrition:

- InfoCalories 119,Total Fat 2g,Total Carbs 21g,Protein 3g,Sodium 116mg.

Raspberry Cobbler

Servings: 8

Cooking Time: 2 Hours

Ingredients:

- 1 cup almond flour
- ¼ cup coconut flour
- ¾ cup Erythritol

- 1 teaspoon baking soda
- ¼ teaspoon ground cinnamon
- 1/8 teaspoon salt
- ¼ cup unsweetened coconut milk
- 2 tablespoons coconut oil
- 1 large egg, beaten lightly
- 4 cups fresh raspberries

Directions:

1. Grease the Ninja Foodi's insert.
2. In a large bowl, mix together flours, Erythritol, baking soda, cinnamon and salt.
3. In another bowl, stir in the coconut milk, coconut oil and egg and beat until well combined.
4. Add the prepared egg mixture into the flour mixture and mix until just combined.
5. In the pot of the prepared Ninja Foodi, add the mixture evenly and top with raspberries.
6. Close the Ninja Foodi's lid with a crisping lid and select "Slow Cooker".
7. Set on "Low" for 2 hours.
8. Press the "Start/Stop" button to initiate cooking.
9. Place the pan onto a wire rack to cool slightly.
10. Serve warm.

Nutrition:

- InfoCalories: 164; Fats: 12.5g; Carbohydrates: 10.9g; Proteins: 4.7

Mini Chocolate Cheesecakes

Servings: 4

Cooking Time: 18 Minutes

Ingredients:

- 1 egg
- 8 ounces cream cheese, softened
- ¼ cup Erythritol
- 1 tablespoon powdered peanut butter
- ¾ tablespoon cacao powder

Directions:

1. Grease the Ninja Foodi's insert.
2. In a blender, stir in the eggs and cream cheese and pulse until smooth.
3. Add the rest of the ingredients and pulse until well combined.
4. Transfer the mixture into 2 8-ounce mason jars evenly.
5. In the Ninja Foodi's insert, place 1 cup of water.
6. Set a "Reversible Rack" in the Ninja Foodi's insert.
7. Place the mason jars over the "Reversible Rack".
8. Close the Ninja Foodi's lid with a pressure lid and place the pressure valve in the "Seal" position.
9. Select "Pressure" mode and set it to "High" for 18 minutes.
10. Press the "Start/Stop" button to initiate cooking.
11. Switch the pressure valve to "Vent" and do a "Natural" release.
12. Open the Ninja Foodi's lid and place the ramekins onto a wire rack to cool.
13. Refrigerate to chill for at least 6-8 hours before serving.

Nutrition:

- InfoCalories: 222; Fats: 28.4g; Carbohydrates: 2.9g; Proteins: 6.5g

Pecan Pie Bars

Servings: 16

Cooking Time: 25 Minutes

Ingredients:

- Butter flavored cooking spray
- 1/3 cup + 4 tbsp. butter soft
- ¾ cup Stevia brown sugar, packed, divided
- ¼ cup almond flour
- ¼ tsp salt
- ¼ cup maple syrup
- ¼ cup milk
- ¼ tsp vanilla
- 1 ½ cups pecans, chopped

Directions:

1. Place the rack in the cooking pot. Line an 8x8-inch baking pan with foil, leaving some overlap over the sides and spray with cooking spray.
2. In a medium bowl, beat 1/3 cup butter and ¼ cup Stevia until light and fluffy.
3. Add the flour and salt, beat until combined. Press evenly on the bottom of the prepared pan.
4. Place pan on the rack and add the tender-crisp lid. Set to bake on 350°F or 175°C. Bake 10-13 minutes.
5. In a medium saucepan over medium heat, combine butter, remaining Stevia, syrup, and milk. Bring to a simmer, stirring occasionally. Cook 1 minute.
6. Remove butter mixture from heat and stir in vanilla and pecans. Pour evenly over crust. Bake another 10-12 minutes or until bubbling, center will still be soft.
7. Transfer to wire rack and cool completely. Once the bars are room temperature, cover and refrigerate until ready to serve.

Nutrition:

- InfoCalories 177, Total Fat 17g, Total Carbs 17g, Protein 2g, Sodium 84mg.

Cheat Apple Pie

Servings: 9

Cooking Time: 30 Min

Ingredients:

- 4 apples; diced
- 1 egg, beaten
- 3 large puff pastry sheets
- 2 oz. sugar /60g
- 1 oz. brown sugar /30g
- 2 oz. butter, melted /60ml
- 2 tsp cinnamon /10g
- ¼ tsp salt /1.25g

Directions:

1. Whisk the white sugar, brown sugar, cinnamon, salt, and butter together. Place the apples in a baking dish and coat them with the mixture.
2. Slide the dish into the Foodi and cook for 10 minutes on Roast at 350 °F or 175°C.
3. Meanwhile, roll out the pastry on a floured flat surface, and cut each sheet into 6 equal pieces. Divide the apple filling between the parts.
4. Brush the edges of the pastry squares with the egg. Fold and seal the edges with a fork. Place on a lined baking sheet and cook in the fryer at 350 °F or 175°C for 8 minutes on Roast. Flip over, increase the temperature to 390 °F or 200°C, and cook for 2 more minutes.

Pineapple Cake

Servings: 4
Cooking Time: 50 Min

Ingredients:

- 2 oz. dark chocolate, grated /60g
- 4 oz. butter /120g
- 7 oz. pineapple chunks /210g
- 8 oz. self-rising flour /240g
- ½ cup sugar /65g
- 1 egg
- ½ cup pineapple juice /125ml
- 2 tbsp milk /30ml

Directions:

1. Preheat the Foodi to 390 °F or 200°C. Place the butter and flour into a bowl and rub the mixture with your fingers until crumbed. Stir in the pineapple, sugar, chocolate, and juice. Beat the eggs and milk separately, and then add them to the batter.
2. Transfer the batter to a previously prepared (greased or lined) cake pan, and cook for 40 minutes on Roast mode. Let cool for at least 10 minutes before serving.

Coconut Cream "custard" Bars

Servings:8
Cooking Time: 20 Minutes

Ingredients:

- 1¼ cups all-purpose flour
- 6 tablespoons unsalted butter, melted
- 2 tablespoons granulated sugar
- ½ cup unsweetened shredded coconut, divided
- ½ cup chopped almonds, divided
- Cooking spray
- 1 package instant vanilla pudding
- 1 cup milk
- 1 cup heavy (whipping) cream
- 4 tablespoons finely chopped dark chocolate, divided

Directions:

1. Select BAKE/ROAST, set temperature to 375°F or 190°C, and set time to 15 minutes. Select START/STOP to begin. Let preheat for 5 minutes.
2. To make the crust, combine the flour, butter, sugar, ¼ cup of coconut, and ¼ cup of almonds in a large bowl and stir until a crumbly dough forms.
3. Grease the Ninja Multi-Purpose Pan or an 8-inch round baking dish with cooking spray. Place the dough in the pan and press it into an even layer covering the bottom.
4. Once unit has preheated, place pan on Reversible Rack, making sure the rack is in the lower position. Open lid and place rack in pot. Close crisping lid. Reduce temperature to 325°F or 1675°C.
5. Place remaining ¼ cup each of almonds and coconut in a Ninja Loaf Pan or any small loaf pan and set aside.
6. When cooking is complete, remove rack with pan and let cool for 10 minutes.
7. Quickly place the loaf pan with coconut and almonds in the bottom of the pot. Close crisping lid.
8. Select AIR CRISP, set temperature to 350°F or 175°C, and set time to 10 minutes. Select START/STOP to begin.
9. While the nuts and coconut toast, whisk together the instant pudding with the milk, cream, and 3 tablespoons of chocolate.
10. After 5 minutes, open lid and stir the coconut and almonds. Close lid and continue cooking for another 5 minutes.
11. When cooking is complete, open lid and remove pan from pot. Add the almonds and coconut to the pudding. Stir until fully incorporated. Pour this in a smooth, even layer on top of the crust.
12. Refrigerate for about 10 minutes. Garnish with the remaining 1 tablespoon of chocolate, cut into wedges, and serve.

Nutrition:

- InfoCalories: 476,Total Fat: 33g,Sodium: 215mg,Carbohydrates: 39g,Protein: 6g.

Coffee Cake

Servings:8
Cooking Time: 30 Minutes

Ingredients:

- Cooking spray
- 1 box yellow cake mix
- 1 cup water
- ⅓ cup vegetable oil
- 3 large eggs
- 4 cups all-purpose flour
- 1 cup granulated sugar
- 3 tablespoons cinnamon
- 2 cups unsalted butter, melted
- Confectioners' sugar, for garnish

Directions:

1. Grease a Ninja Tube Pan or a 7-inch Bundt pan with cooking spray.
2. Close crisping lid. Select BAKE/ROAST, set temperature to 325°F or 165°C, and set time to 5 minutes. Select START/STOP to begin preheating.
3. In a large bowl, mix together the cake mix, water, oil, and eggs until combined. Pour the batter into the prepared pan.
4. When unit has preheated, place pan on Reversible Rack, making sure the rack is in the lower position. Open lid and place rack with pan in pot. Close crisping lid.
5. Select BAKE/ROAST, set temperature to 325°F or 165°C, and set time to 30 minutes. Select START/STOP to begin.
6. In another large bowl, combine the flour, sugar, and cinnamon. Add the butter and mix until well combined and the mixture is a crumble.
7. After 25 minutes, open lid and check for doneness. If a toothpick inserted into the cake comes out clean, the cake is done. If necessary, close lid and continue baking.
8. Open lid and spread the crumble topping on top of the cakes. Close lid and bake for an additional 4 to 5 minutes.
9. When cooking is complete, carefully remove pan from pot and place it on a cooling rack. Let cool. Using a fine mesh sieve, garnish the coffee cake with confectioners' sugar.

Nutrition:

- InfoCalories: 1152,Total Fat: 65g,Sodium: 464mg,Carbohydrates: 132g,Protein: 13g.

Caramel Apple Bread Pudding

Servings: 6
Cooking Time: 35 Minutes
Ingredients:
- 2 cups water
- Butter flavored cooking spray
- ½ cup applesauce, unsweetened
- ½ cup almond milk, unsweetened
- ¼ cup molasses
- 2 eggs
- ½ tsp vanilla
- ½ tsp cinnamon
- 1/8 tsp nutmeg
- 2 ½ cups whole wheat bread, cut in 1-inch cubes
- ½ cup apple, peeled & cut in 1-inch cubes

Directions:
1. Place rack in the cooking pot and pour the water in. Spray an 8x8-inch baking dish with cooking spray.
2. In a large bowl, whisk together everything except the bread and apples.
3. Lay the bread cubes in the prepared dish and top with apples. Pour applesauce mixture, ¼ at a time, over apples. Let sit 5 minutes, then pour another ¼ liquid mixture. Repeat process until liquid and bread are 1/4-inch from top of the dish.
4. Place the dish on the rack and add the tender-crisp lid. Set to bake on 325°F or 165°C. Bake 30-35 minutes or until the bread pudding passes the toothpick test and top is golden brown.
5. Transfer to wire rack and let cool 10 minutes before serving.

Nutrition:
- InfoCalories 199,Total Fat 3g,Total Carbs 33g,Protein 8g,Sodium 233mg.

Nutty Baked Pears

Servings: 2
Cooking Time: 25 Minutes
Ingredients:
- 2 pears, halved
- 1 tsp cinnamon
- ¼ cup walnuts, chopped
- 2 tsp maple syrup

Directions:
1. Place the rack in the cooking pot. Line a small baking sheet with parchment paper.
2. Cut a small slice off the back of the pears so they lie flat. Use a teaspoon or melon baller to scoop out the seeds. Place the pears, cut side up, on prepared baking sheet.
3. Sprinkle pears evenly with cinnamon and fill the middles with walnuts. Drizzle with maple syrup.
4. Place the pears on the rack and add the tender crisp lid. Set to bake on 375°F or 190°C. Bake 20-25 minutes until pears are tender and the tops are lightly browned. Serve immediately.

Nutrition:
- InfoCalories 228,Total Fat 10g,Total Carbs 34g,Protein 3g,Sodium 3mg.

Buttery Cranberry Cake

Servings: 8
Cooking Time: 40 Minutes
Ingredients:
- Butter flavored cooking spray
- 2 eggs
- 1 cup sugar
- 3/8 cup butter, softened
- ½ tsp vanilla
- 1 cup flour
- 6 oz. fresh cranberries

Directions:
1. Set cooker to bake on 350°F or 175°C. Spray an 8-inch baking pan with cooking spray.
2. In a large bowl, beat eggs and sugar until light in color and slightly thickened, about 5-7 minutes.
3. Add butter and vanilla and continue beating another 2 minutes.
4. Stir in flour just until combined. Gently fold in cranberries.
5. Spread batter in prepared pan and place in the cooking pot. Add the tender-crisp lid and bake 35-40 minutes or until the cake passes the toothpick test.
6. Remove from cooker and let cool in pan 10 minutes before transferring to a wire rack to cool completely.

Nutrition:
- InfoCalories 259,Total Fat 10g,Total Carbs 40g,Protein 3g,Sodium 88mg.

Coconut Cake

Servings: 4
Cooking Time: 55 Min
Ingredients:
- 3 Eggs, Yolks and Whites separated
- ½ cup Coconut Sugar /65g
- ¾ cup Coconut Flour /98g
- 1 ½ cups warm Coconut Milk /375ml
- 1 cup Water /250ml
- 2 tbsp Coconut Oil, melted /30ml
- ½ tsp Coconut Extract /2.5

Directions:
1. In a bowl, beat in the egg yolks along with the coconut sugar. In a separate bowl, beat the whites until soft form peaks.
2. Stir in coconut extract and coconut oil. Gently fold in the coconut flour. Line a baking dish and pour the batter inside. Cover with aluminum foil.
3. Pour the water in your Foodi and add a reversible rack. Lower the dish onto the rack.
4. Seal the pressure lid, choose Pressure, set to High, and set the time to 35 minutes. Press Start. Do a quick pressure release, and serve.

Rustic Strawberry Rhubarb Tart

Servings: 8
Cooking Time: 25 Minutes
Ingredients:
- 1 ¼ cups white whole wheat flour
- 3 tbsp. + 2 tsp Stevia
- ¼ tsp salt
- ½ cup coconut oil
- 2- 3 tablespoons ice cold water
- 2 cups strawberries, hulled & halved
- 1 cup rhubarb, chopped
- 2 tbsp. water

Directions:
1. In a medium bowl, stir together, flour and 1 tablespoon Stevia. Add coconut oil and use a fork, or your hands, to mix in until mixture resembles pea-sized crumbs.

2. Two teaspoons at a time, mix in ice water until mixture forms a dough. Form into a ball, wrap in plastic wrap and refrigerate 30 minutes.
3. Set the cooker to sauté on med-low heat. Add strawberries, rhubarb, 2 tablespoons water, and 2 tablespoons Stevia to the pot. Cook 15 minutes, stirring frequently, until rhubarb is soft. Transfer to a bowl to cool slightly.
4. Unwrap the dough and flatten slightly. Place between sheets of wax paper and roll out to about an 8-inch circle that is ½-inch thick.
5. Wipe out the cooking pot and add the rack. Transfer the crust to a sheet of parchment paper.
6. Place the fruit filling in the center of the crust, leave a 2-inch border. Fold the edges over the fruit and sprinkle the crust with remaining 2 teaspoons Stevia.
7. Carefully place the galette on the rack and add the tender-crisp lid. Set to bake on 350°F or 175°C. Bake 20-25 minutes until filling is bubbling and crust is golden brown.

Nutrition:
- InfoCalories 196,Total Fat 14g,Total Carbs 17g,Protein 3g,Sodium 75mg.

Coconut Lime Snack Cake

Servings: 8
Cooking Time: 20 Minutes
Ingredients:
- Butter flavored cooking spray
- 2 eggs
- ½ cup coconut milk
- 3 tbsp. honey
- 1 tsp vanilla
- ¼ cup + 1 tbsp. fresh lime juice, divided
- 1 tbsp. + 1 tsp lime zest, divided
- 2 ¼ cup almond flour, sifted
- 1 tsp baking soda
- ½ cup coconut, unsweetened & shredded
- ½ cup powdered Stevia

Directions:
1. Place the rack in the cooking pot. Spray an 8-inch baking pan with cooking spray.
2. In a large bowl, beat eggs, milk, honey, vanilla, ¼ cup lime juice and tablespoon zest until thick and frothy, about 6-8 minutes.
3. Fold in flour, baking soda, and coconut just until combined. Pour into prepared pan.
4. Place the cake on the rack and add the tender-crisp lid. Set to bake on 350°F or 175°C. Bake 15-20 minutes or until cake passes the toothpick test.
5. Let cool in the pan for 10 minutes, then invert onto a serving plate.
6. In a small bowl, whisk together powdered sugar, remaining tablespoon lime juice, and remaining teaspoon lime zest. Drizzle over the top of cooled cake. Serve.

Nutrition:
- InfoCalories 183,Total Fat 13g,Total Carbs 28g,Protein 5g,Sodium 35mg.

Chocolate Chip Cheesecake

Servings: 12
Cooking Time: 50 Minutes
Ingredients:
- Butter flavored cooking spray
- 16 oz. cream cheese, fat free, soft
- ½ cup + 1 tbsp. Stevia, divided
- 3 eggs

- 1 tsp vanilla, divided
- ½ tsp fresh lemon juice, divided
- ½ cup mini chocolate chips
- 1 cup sour cream, fat free

Directions:
1. Spray an 8-inch baking pan with cooking spray.
2. In a large bowl, beat cream cheese and ½ cup Stevia until smooth.
3. Beat in eggs, one at a time, beat well after each addition.
4. Add ½ teaspoon vanilla, and ¼ teaspoon lemon juice and stir until combined. Stir in chocolate chips and spoon into prepared pan.
5. Place the pan in the cooking pot and add the tender-crisp lid. Set to bake on 325°F or 165°C. Bake 40 minutes, or until top starts to brown.
6. In a small bowl, combine sour cream, remaining Stevia, vanilla, and lemon juice, mix well. Spread over top of cheesecake and bake another 10 minutes.
7. Transfer to a wire rack to cool. Cover with plastic wrap and refrigerate at least 4 hours before serving.

Nutrition:
- InfoCalories 127,Total Fat 5g,Total Carbs 22g,Protein 8g,Sodium 312mg.

Carrot Cake

Servings: 8
Cooking Time: 40 Minutes
Ingredients:
- Butter flavored cooking spray
- 3 eggs
- 1 cup almond flour, sifted
- 1/3 cup Stevia
- 1 tsp baking powder
- 1 tsp apple pie spice
- ¼ cup coconut oil, melted
- ½ cup + 1 tbsp. heavy cream
- 1 cup carrots, grated
- ½ cup walnuts, chopped
- 4 oz. cream cheese, soft
- ¼ cup butter, soft
- ½ tsp vanilla
- ½ - 1 cup powdered Stevia

Directions:
1. Lightly spray a 6x3-inch cake pan with cooking spray.
2. In a large bowl, beat eggs, flour, Stevia, baking powder, apple pie spice, oil, and ½ cup cream until fluffy.
3. Fold in carrots and nuts and pour into prepared pan.
4. Place in cooking pot and add tender-crisp lid. Set to bake on 350 °F or 175°C. Bake 30-35 minutes or until cake passes the toothpick test. Transfer to wire rack and let cool 10 minutes in pan, then invert onto serving plate.
5. In a large bowl, beat cream cheese, butter, and remaining cream until smooth and creamy.
6. Stir in vanilla and enough powdered Stevia until frosting is thick enough to spread. Cut cake in half horizontally and spread with 1/3 of the frosting in the middle, then frost outside. Serve.

Nutrition:
- InfoCalories 345,Total Fat 34g,Total Carbs 25g,Protein 8g,Sodium 137mg.

Pumpkin Spice Bread Pudding

Servings: 8
Cooking Time: 5 Hours
Ingredients:

* Butter flavored cooking spray
* 1 ¼ cups almond milk, unsweetened
* ¾ cups pumpkin puree, sugar free
* ½ cup honey
* 1 egg
* 4 egg whites
* ½ tsp cinnamon
* ¼ tsp ginger
* 1/8 tsp allspice
* 1/8 tsp cloves
* 5 cups whole grain bread, cubed

Directions:

1. Lightly spray the cooking pot with cooking spray.
2. In a large bowl, whisk all ingredients, except bread, until smooth and combined.
3. Place the bread in the cooking pot and pour the liquid mixture over it, stir gently.
4. Add the lid and set to slow cooking on low. Cook 4-5 hours or until bread pudding passes the toothpick test. Let cool slightly before serving.

Nutrition:

* InfoCalories 155,Total Fat 2g,Total Carbs 30g,Protein 6g,Sodium 162mg.

Delicious Almond And Apple

Servings: 4
Cooking Time: 14 Min
Ingredients:

* 3 Apples, peeled and diced
* ½ cup Milk /125ml
* ½ cup Almonds; chopped or slivered /65g
* ¼ tsp Cinnamon /1.25g

Directions:

1. Place all ingredients in the Foodi. Stir well to combine and seal the pressure lid. Cook on Pressure for 4 minutes at High. Release the pressure quickly. Divide the mixture among 4 serving bowls.

Cinnamon Mulled Red Wine

Servings: 6
Cooking Time: 30 Min
Ingredients:

* 2 cardamom pods
* 8 cinnamon sticks
* 3 cups red wine /750ml
* 1/4 cup honey /62.5ml
* 6 whole cloves
* 6 whole black peppercorns
* 6 tangerine wedges
* 2 tangerines; sliced
* 1 tsp fresh ginger; sliced /5g
* 1 tsp ground cinnamon /5g

Directions:

1. In the Foodi, combine red wine, honey, cardamom pods, 2 cinnamon sticks, cloves, tangerines slices, ginger, and peppercorns.

Seal the pressure lid, choose Pressure, set to High, and set the timer to 5 minutes. Press Start.
2. Release pressure naturally for 20 minutes. Press Start. Using a fine mesh strainer, strain your wine. Discard spices.
3. Divide the warm wine into glasses and add tangerine wedges and a cinnamon stick for garnishing before serving.

Spiced Poached Pears

Servings: 4
Cooking Time: 4 Hours
Ingredients:

* 4 ripe pears, peeled
* 2 cups fresh orange juice
* ¼ cup maple syrup
* 5 cardamom pods
* 1 cinnamon stick, broke in 2
* 1-inch piece ginger, peeled & sliced

Directions:

1. Slice off the bottom of the pears so they stand upright. Carefully remove the core with a paring knife. Stand in the cooking pot.
2. In a small bowl, whisk together orange juice and syrup. Pour over pears and add the spices.
3. Add the lid and set to slow cooking on low. Cook 3-4 hours or until pears are soft. Baste the pears every hour or so.
4. Serve garnished with whipped cream and chopped walnuts if you like, or just serve them as they are sprinkled with a little cinnamon.

Nutrition:

* InfoCalories 219,Total Fat 1g,Total Carbs 53g,Protein 2g,Sodium 6mg.

Cherry Almond Bar Cookies

Servings: 9
Cooking Time: 15 Minutes
Ingredients:

* Butter flavored cooking spray
* ¼ cup dates
* 2 bananas
* 1 cup oats
* ½ cup cherries, dried, chopped
* ½ cup almond flour
* ½ cup almonds, chopped

Directions:

1. Place the rack in the cooking pot. Spray an 8x8-inch baking pan with cooking spray.
2. Place the dates in a food processor and pulse until they form a paste.
3. In a large bowl, mash the bananas with a fork.
4. Mix in remaining ingredients. Spread evenly in prepared pan.
5. Place the pan on the rack and add the tender-crisp lid. Set to bake on 325°F or 165°C. Bake 15 minutes or until top is golden brown. Remove to wire rack to cool before cutting.

Nutrition:

* InfoCalories 177,Total Fat 5g,Total Carbs 30g,Protein 5g,Sodium 2mg.

Chocolate Brownie Cake

Servings: 6

Cooking Time: 35 Minutes.

Ingredients:

- ½ cup 70% dark chocolate chips
- ½ cup butter
- 3 eggs
- ¼ cup Erythritol
- 1 teaspoon vanilla extract

Directions:

1. In a microwave-safe bowl, stir in the chocolate chips and butter and microwave for about 1 minute, stirring after every 20 seconds.
2. Remove from the microwave and stir well.
3. Set a "Reversible Rack" in the pot of the Ninja Foodi.
4. Close the Ninja Foodi's lid with a crisping lid and select "Air Crisp".
5. Set its cooking temperature to 350 °F or 175°C for 5 minutes.
6. Press the "Start/Stop" button to initiate preheating.
7. In a suitable, add the eggs, Erythritol and vanilla extract and blend until light and frothy.
8. Slowly add in the chocolate mixture and beat again until well combined.
9. Add the mixture into a lightly greased springform pan.
10. After preheating, Open the Ninja Foodi's lid.
11. Place the springform pan into the "Air Crisp Basket".
12. Close the Ninja Foodi's lid with a crisping lid and select "Air Crisp".
13. Set its cooking temperature to 350 °F or 175°C for 35 minutes.
14. Press the "Start/Stop" button to initiate cooking.
15. Place the hot pan onto a wire rack to cool for about 10 minutes.
16. Flip the baked and cooled cake onto the wire rack to cool completely.
17. Cut into desired-sized slices and serve.

Nutrition:

- InfoCalories: 302; Fats: 28.2g; Carbohydrates: 5.6g; Proteins: 5.6g

Apple Crisp

Servings:8

Cooking Time: 20 Minutes

Ingredients:

- 4 to 5 Granny Smith apples, peeled and cut into 1-inch cubes
- 1 tablespoon cornstarch
- ½ cup, plus 1 tablespoon water
- 2 teaspoons cinnamon, divided
- 1 teaspoon freshly squeezed lemon juice
- 5 tablespoons granulated sugar, divided
- ½ cup all-purpose flour
- ½ cup rolled oats
- ⅔ cup brown sugar
- ⅓ cup unsalted butter, melted

Directions:

1. Place the apples in the Ninja Multi-Purpose Pan or a 1½-quart round ceramic baking dish.
2. In a small bowl, stir together the cornstarch, 1 tablespoon of water, 1 teaspoon of cinnamon, lemon juice, and 3 tablespoons of granulated sugar. Pour this mixture over the apples.
3. Place pan on Reversible Rack, making sure the rack is in the lower position. Cover the pan with aluminum foil. Pour the remaining ½ cup of water into the pot. Insert rack with pan in pot.

Assemble pressure lid, making sure the pressure release valve is in the SEAL position.

4. Select PRESSURE and set to HI. Set time to 0 minutes. Select START/STOP to begin.
5. In a medium bowl, combine the flour, oats, brown sugar, butter, remaining 1 teaspoon of cinnamon, and remaining 2 tablespoons of granulated sugar until a crumble forms.
6. When pressure cooking is complete, allow the pressure to naturally release for 10 minutes. After 10 minutes, quick release remaining pressure by moving the pressure release valve to the VENT position. Carefully remove lid when pressure has finished releasing.
7. Remove the foil and stir the fruit mixture. Evenly spread the crumble topping over the apples. Close crisping lid.
8. Select AIR CRISP, set temperature to 375°F or 190°C, and set time to 10 minutes. Select START/STOP to begin.
9. Cooking is complete when the top is browned and the fruit is bubbling. Remove rack with the pan from the pot and serve.

Nutrition:

- InfoCalories: 261,Total Fat: 9g,Sodium: 6mg,Carbohydrates: 46g,Protein: 2g.

Strawberry Cheesecake

Servings: 8

Cooking Time: 20 Minutes

Ingredients:

- Butter flavored cooking spray
- 16 oz. cream cheese, soft
- 2/3 cup powdered Stevia
- 1 tsp vanilla
- 2 eggs, room temperature
- 1 cup strawberries, chopped

Directions:

1. Place the trivet in the cooking pot and add enough water to cover bottom by 1 inch. Spray an 8-inch springform pan with cooking spray.
2. In a large bowl, beat cream cheese until smooth.
3. Beat in Stevia and vanilla until combined.
4. Beat in eggs, one at a time and beat until thoroughly combined.
5. Pour into prepared pan. Cover bottom and sides of pan with foil to prevent any water from leaking in. Place the pan on the trivet.
6. Add the lid and select pressure cooking on high. Set timer for 20 minutes.
7. When the timer goes off, use natural release to remove the lid. Transfer cheesecake to wire rack to cool completely.
8. Cover and refrigerate 8 hours or overnight. Top with chopped strawberries before serving.

Nutrition:

- InfoCalories 219,Total Fat 21g,Total Carbs 20g,Protein 5g,Sodium 225mg.

Egg Custard

Servings: 4
Cooking Time: 20 Min
Ingredients:

- 1 Egg plus 2 Egg yolks
- ½ cups Milk /125ml
- 2 cups Heavy Cream /500ml
- 2 cups Water /500ml
- ½ cup Sugar /65g
- ½ tsp pure rum extract /2.5ml

Directions:

1. Beat the egg and the egg yolks in a bowl. Gently add pure rum extract. Mix in the milk and heavy cream. Give it a good, and add the sugar. Pour this mixture into 4 ramekins.
2. Add 2 cups or 500ml of water, insert the reversible rack, and lay the ramekins on the reversible rack. Choose Pressure, set to High, and set the time to 10 minutes. Press Start. Do a quick pressure release. Wait a bit before removing from ramekins.

Simple Cheesecake

Servings: 12
Cooking Time: 1 Hour 10 Minutes

Ingredients:

- 1 cup almond flour
- 4 tbsp. butter, unsalted, melted
- ½ tsp cinnamon
- 16 oz. cream cheese, soft
- ½ cup Stevia
- 1 tsp vanilla
- 1 tsp fresh lemon juice
- 2 eggs, room temperature
- 1 cup water

Directions:

1. In a large bowl, combine almond flour, butter and cinnamon and stir just until combined. Press on the bottom of a 7-inch springform pan. Refrigerate.
2. In a separate large bowl, beat cream cheese, Stevia, and vanilla until smooth. Slowly beat in lemon juice.
3. Beat in eggs, one at a time, beat well after each addition. Pour into chilled crust.
4. Cover tightly with foil and wrap another piece of foil around the sides and bottom.
5. Add 1 cup of water to the cooking pot and add the trivet. Place the cheesecake on the trivet. Add the lid and set to pressure cook on high. Set the timer for 40 minutes.
6. When the timer goes off, use natural release to remove the pressure. Remove from the cooking pot and let cool completely. Once it has reached room temperature, refrigerate overnight.

Nutrition:

- InfoCalories 232,Total Fat 22g,Total Carbs 5g,Protein 5g,Sodium 154mg.

Double Chocolate Cake

Servings: 12
Cooking Time: 1 Hour

Ingredients:

- ½ cup coconut flour
- 1½ cups Erythritol
- 5 tablespoons cacao powder
- 1 teaspoon baking powder
- ½ teaspoon salt
- 3 eggs
- 3 egg yolks
- ½ cup butter, melted and cooled
- 1 teaspoon vanilla extract
- ½ teaspoon liquid stevia
- 4 ounces 70% dark chocolate chips
- 2 cups hot water

Directions:

1. Grease the Ninja Foodi's insert.
2. In a large bowl, stir in the flour, 1¼ cups of Erythritol, 3 tablespoons of cacao powder, baking powder and salt.
3. In a suitable bowl, add the eggs, egg yolks, butter, vanilla extract and liquid stevia and beat until well combined.
4. Stir in the egg mixture into the flour mixture and mix until just combined.
5. In a small bowl, add hot water, remaining cacao powder and Erythritol and beat until well combined.
6. In the prepared Ninja Foodi's insert, stir in the mixture evenly and top with chocolate chips, followed by the water mixture.
7. Close the Ninja Foodi's lid with a crisping lid and select "Slow Cooker".
8. Set on "Low" for 3 hours.
9. Press the "Start/Stop" button to initiate cooking.
10. Transfer the pan onto a wire rack for about 10 minutes.
11. Flip the baked and cooled cake onto the wire rack to cool completely.
12. Cut into desired-sized slices and serve.

Nutrition:

- InfoCalories: 169; Fats: 15.4g; Carbohydrates: 4.4g; Proteins: 3.9g

Blueberry Peach Crisp

Servings: 8
Cooking Time: 40 Minutes
Ingredients:

- 1 cup blueberries
- 6 peaches, peeled, cored & cut in ½-inch pieces
- ½ cup + 3 tbsp. flour
- ¾ cups Stevia, divided
- ½ tsp cinnamon
- ¼ tsp salt, divided
- Zest & juice of 1 lemon
- 1 cup oats
- 1/3 cup coconut oil, melted

Directions:

1. Place the rack in the cooking pot.
2. In a large bowl, combine blueberries, peaches, 3 tablespoons flour, ¼ cup Stevia, cinnamon, and 1/8 teaspoon salt, toss to coat fruit. Stir in lemon zest and juice just until combined. Pour into an 8-inch baking dish.
3. In a medium bowl, combine oats, ½ cup Stevia, coconut oil, remaining flour and salt and mix with a fork until crumbly. Sprinkle over the top of the fruit.
4. Place the dish on the rack and add the tender-crisp lid. Set to bake on 350 °F or 175°C. Bake 35-40 minutes until filling is bubbly and top is golden brown. Serve warm.

Nutrition:

- InfoCalories 265,Total Fat 11g,Total Carbs 44g,Protein 6g,Sodium 74mg.

Steamed Lemon Pudding

Servings: 6

Cooking Time: 90 Minutes

Ingredients:

- Nonstick cooking spray
- ¾ cup butter, unsalted, soft
- 1 cup caster sugar
- 2 eggs
- 2 cups flour
- 1 tsp baking powder
- Zest & juice from 2 lemons

Directions:

1. Lightly spray a 1 liter oven-safe bowl with cooking spray.
2. Add the butter and sugar to the bowl and beat until light and fluffy.
3. Add the eggs, one at a time, beating well after each addition.
4. Stir in the flour and baking powder until combined.
5. Fold in the lemon zest and juice and mix until smooth. Cover lightly with foil.
6. Pour 1 ½ cups water into the cooking pot and add steamer rack.
7. Place the bowl on the rack, secure the lid. Set to steam on 212°F or 100°C. Cook 90 minutes, or until pudding is cooked through.
8. Remove the pudding from the cooker and let sit 5 minutes before inverting onto serving plate.

Nutrition:

- InfoCalories 446,Total Fat 17g,Total Carbs 66g,Protein 7g,Sodium 33mg.

Steamed Blackberry Pudding

Servings: 6

Cooking Time: 50 Minutes

Ingredients:

- Butter flavored cooking spray
- 1 ½ cups water
- 5 ¼ tbsp. butter, soft
- 8 tbsp. caster sugar
- Zest of 1 lemon
- 2 eggs
- 1 cup flour
- 4 tbsp. milk
- 4 tbsp. honey
- 1 ½ cups blackberries

Directions:

1. Spray 6 ramekins with cooking spray. Pour the water in the cooking pot and add the steamer rack.
2. In a large bowl, beat butter, sugar, and lemon zest until light and fluffy.
3. Beat in eggs, flour, and milk until combined. Stir in 2 tablespoons honey.
4. Drizzle the remaining honey in the bottoms of the ramekins. Add blackberries and pour the pudding mixture over them.
5. Tent the ramekins with foil, leave some space for puddings to rise while cooking. Place the ramekins on the steamer rack.
6. Add the lid and select steam function. Cook 40-50 minutes, or until puddings pass the toothpick test. Transfer to wire rack to cool slightly.
7. To serve, invert onto serving plates and top with whipped cream if desired, or just eat them plain.

Nutrition:

- InfoCalories 318,Total Fat 12g,Total Carbs 48g,Protein 5g,Sodium 109mg.

Pecan Apple Crisp

Servings: 6

Cooking Time: 35 Minutes

Ingredients:

- Butter flavored cooking spray
- 3 apples, peeled & diced
- 1 tbsp. sugar
- 1 3/8 tsp cinnamon, divided
- ¼ cup + ½ tbsp. almond flour, divided
- ½ cup oats
- ¼ cup pecans, chopped
- 1/8 tsp salt
- 1/8 cup coconut oil, melted
- 1/8 cup honey

Directions:

1. Place the rack in the cooking pot. Spray an 8x8-inch baking pan with cooking spray.
2. In a large bowl, combine apples, sugar, 1 teaspoon cinnamon, and ½ tablespoon almond flour, toss to coat the apples. Pour into prepared pan.
3. In a medium bowl, combine oats, remaining flour, pecans, remaining cinnamon, salt, oil, and honey. Use a fork to mix until mixture resembles fine crumbs. Pour over apples.
4. Place on the rack and add the tender-crisp lid. Set to bake on 350°F or 175°C. Bake 30-35 minutes, or until apples are tender and topping is golden brown.
5. Transfer to a wire rack to cool slightly before serving.

Nutrition:

- InfoCalories 293,Total Fat 18g,Total Carbs 30g,Protein 7g,Sodium 62mg.

Lemon Cheesecake

Servings: 12

Cooking Time: 4 Hours

Ingredients:

- For Crust:
- 1½ cups almond flour
- 4 tablespoons butter, melted
- 3 tablespoons sugar-free peanut butter
- 3 tablespoons Erythritol
- 1 large egg, beaten
- For Filling:
- 1 cup ricotta cheese
- 24 ounces cream cheese, softened
- 1½ cups Erythritol
- 2 teaspoons liquid stevia
- 1/3 cup heavy cream
- 2 large eggs
- 3 large egg yolks
- 1 tablespoon fresh lemon juice
- 1 tablespoon vanilla extract

Directions:

1. Grease the Ninja Foodi's insert.
2. For crust: in a suitable, add all the ingredients and mix until well combined.
3. In the pot of prepared of Ninja Foodi, place the crust mixture and press to smooth the top surface.

4. With a fork, prick the crust at many places.
5. For filling: in a food processor, stir in the ricotta cheese and pulse until smooth.
6. In a large bowl, add the ricotta, cream cheese, Erythritol and stevia and with an electric mixer, beat over medium speed until smooth.
7. In another bowl, stir in the heavy cream, eggs, egg yolks, lemon juice and vanilla extract and beat until well combined.
8. Stir in the egg mixture into cream cheese mixture and beat over medium speed until just combined.
9. Place the prepared filling mixture over the crust evenly.
10. Close the Ninja Foodi's lid with a crisping lid and select "Slow Cooker".
11. Set on "Low" for 3-4 hours.
12. Press the "Start/Stop" button to initiate cooking.
13. Place the pan onto a wire rack to cool.
14. Refrigerate to chill for at least 6-8 hours before serving.

Nutrition:
- InfoCalories: 410; Fats: 37.9g; Carbohydrates: 6.9g; Proteins: 13g

Bacon Blondies

Servings:6
Cooking Time: 35 Minutes

Ingredients:
- 6 slices uncooked bacon, cut into ¼ slices
- 1½ cups unsalted butter, at room temperature, plus additional for greasing
- 1 cup dark brown sugar
- 2 cups all-purpose flour
- Ice cream, for serving

Directions:
1. Grease the Ninja Multi-Purpose Pan with butter.
2. Select SEAR/SAUTÉ and set to HI. Select START/STOP to begin. Let preheat for 5 minutes.
3. Place the bacon in the pot. Cook, stirring frequently, for about 5 minutes, or until the fat is rendered and bacon starts to brown. Transfer the bacon to a paper towel-lined plate to drain. Wipe the pot clean of any remaining fat and return to unit.
4. In a medium bowl, beat the butter and brown sugar with a hand mixer until well incorporated. Slowly add in the flour and continue to beat until the flour is fully combined and a soft dough forms. Next, fold the cooked bacon into the dough.
5. Press the dough into the prepared pan. Place pan on Reversible Rack, ensuring it is in the lower position. Lower rack into pot. Close crisping lid.
6. Select BAKE/ROAST, set temperature to 350°F or 175°C, and set time to 25 minutes. Select START/STOP to begin.
7. After 20 minutes, open lid and check for doneness by sticking a toothpick through the center of the dough. If it comes out clean, remove rack and pan from unit. If not, close lid and continue cooking.
8. When cooking is complete, remove rack and pan from unit. Let the blondies cool for about 30 minutes before serving with ice cream, if desired.

Nutrition:
- InfoCalories: 771,Total Fat: 54g,Sodium: 453mg,Carbohydrates: 60g,Protein: 12g.

Citrus Steamed Pudding

Servings: 8
Cooking Time: 1 Hour

Ingredients:
- Butter flavored cooking spray
- 3 ½ cups water, divided
- 3 tbsp. + 1 tsp butter, soft
- 1 cup sugar, divided
- 2 tsp orange zest, finely grated
- 1 tbsp. + 2 tsp lemon zest, finely grated
- 2 eggs
- ¼ cup milk
- ¼ cup + 1 tbsp. orange juice, unsweetened, divided
- 2 cups self-rising flour, sifted
- 1 orange, peel & pith removed, chopped
- 1 ½ tbsp. cornstarch

Directions:
1. Spray a 6-cup oven-safe bowl with cooking spray. Pour 2 cups water in the cooking pot and add the steamer rack.
2. In a large bowl, beat 3 tablespoons butter, ½ cup sugar, and 4 teaspoons orange and lemon zest until smooth.
3. Beat in eggs, one at a time, and beating well after each addition.
4. In a small bowl, stir together milk and ¼ cup orange juice.
5. Fold flour, orange pieces, and milk mixture into butter mixture, alternating between ingredients, begin and end with flour.
6. Pour into prepared bowl and tent with foil. Tie with kitchen string and place on the steamer rack. Add the lid and set to steam. Cook 1 hour or until the pudding passes the toothpick test. Transfer to wire rack.
7. Drain any remaining water from the cooking pot. Set cooker to saute on medium heat.
8. Add remaining sugar and cornstarch to the pot. Slowly pour in 1 ½ cups water, stirring constantly until combined. Cook 5 minutes, or until thickened.
9. Stir in tablespoon of lemon juice, tablespoon orange juice, tablespoon lemon zest, and teaspoon butter and cook until butter has melted and mixture is smooth.
10. To serve: invert pudding onto serving plate and drizzle sauce over the top. Slice and serve.

Nutrition:
- InfoCalories 305,Total Fat 8g,Total Carbs 54g,Protein 5g,Sodium 68mg.

Orange Banana Bread

Servings: 12
Cooking Time: 45 Min

Ingredients:
- 3 ripe Bananas, mashed
- 1 cup Milk /250ml
- 1 ¼ cups Sugar /162.5g
- 2 cups all-purpose Flour /260g
- 1 stick Butter, room temperature
- 1 tbsp Orange Juice /15ml
- 1 tsp Baking Soda /5g
- 1 tsp Baking Powder /5g
- ¼ tsp Cinnamon /1.25g
- ½ tsp Pure Vanilla Extract /2.5ml
- A pinch of Salt

Directions:

1.   In a bowl, mix together the flour, baking powder, baking soda, sugar, vanilla, and salt. Add in the bananas, cinnamon, and orange juice. Slowly stir in the butter and milk. Give it a good stir until everything is well combined. Pour the batter into a medium-sized round pan.
2.   Place the reversible rack at the bottom of the Foodi and fill with 2 cups of water. Place the pan on the reversible rack. Seal the pressure lid, select Pressure and and set the time to 40 minutes at High. Press Start. Do a quick pressure release.

Chocolate Fondue

Servings: 12
Cooking Time: 5 Min
Ingredients:

- 10 ounces Milk Chocolate; chopped into small pieces /300g
- 1 ½ cups Lukewarm Water /375ml
- 8 ounces Heavy Whipping Cream /240ml
- 2 tsp Coconut Liqueur /60ml
- ¼ tsp Cinnamon Powder /1.25g
- A pinch of Salt

Directions:
1.   Melt the chocolate in a heat-proof recipient. Add the remaining ingredients, except for the liqueur. Transfer this recipient to the metal reversible rack. Pour 1 ½ cups or 375ml of water into the cooker, and place a reversible rack inside.
2.   Seal the pressure lid, choose Pressure, set to High, and set the time to 5 minutes. Press Start. Once the cooking is complete, do a quick pressure release. Pull out the container with tongs. Mix in the coconut liqueur and serve right now. Enjoy!

Apple Vanilla Hand Pies

Servings: 8
Cooking Time: 40 Min
Ingredients:

- 2 apples, peeled, cored, and diced
- 1 package refrigerated piecrusts, at room temperature
- 1 lemon, juiced
- 3 tbsps sugar /45g
- ¼ tsp salt /1.25g
- 1 tsp vanilla extract /5ml
- 1 tsp corn-starch /5g
- Cooking spray

Directions:
1.   In a large mixing bowl, combine the apples, sugar, lemon juice, salt, and vanilla. Allow the mixture to stand for 10 minutes, then drain, and reserve 1 tbsp of the liquid. In a small bowl, whisk the corn-starch into the reserved liquid and then, mix with the apple mixture. Put the crisping basket in the pot and close the crisping lid. Choose Air Crisp, set the temperature to 350°F or 175°C, and the time to 5 minutes. Press Start/Stop to preheat.
2.   Put the piecrusts on a lightly floured surface and cut into 8 circles. Spoon a tbsp of apple mixture in the center of the circle, with ½ an inch's border around the dough. Brush the edges with water and fold the dough over the filling. Press the edges with a fork to seal.
3.   Cut 3 small slits on top of each pie and oil with cooking spray. Arrange the pies in a single layer in the preheated basket. Close the crisping lid. Choose Air Crisp, set the temperature to 350°F or 175°C, and set the time to 12 minutes. Press Start/Stop to begin baking. Once done baking, remove, and place the pies on a wire rack to cool. Repeat with the remaining hand pies.

Cranberry Pie

Servings: 8
Cooking Time: 35 Minutes
Ingredients:

- Nonstick cooking spray
- ¾ cup flour
- ½ cup sugar
- ¼ tsp salt
- 2 cups cranberries
- 1/3 cup walnuts, chopped
- ½ stick butter, melted
- ½ cup liquid egg substitute
- 1 tsp almond extract

Directions:
1.   Place the rack in the cooking pot. Spray an 8-inch pie plate with cooking spray.
2.   In a large bowl, stir together flour, sugar, and salt.
3.   Add cranberries and walnuts and toss to coat.
4.   Add butter, egg substitute, and almond extract and mix well. Spread in prepared pan and place on the rack.
5.   Add the tender-crisp lid and set to bake on 350°F or 175°C. Bake 30-35 minutes or until pie passes the toothpick test. Transfer to wire rack to cool.

Nutrition:
- InfoCalories 145,Total Fat 9g,Total Carbs 27g,Protein 4g,Sodium 149mg.

Apricots With Honey Sauce

Servings: 4
Cooking Time: 15 Min
Ingredients:

- 8 Apricots, pitted and halved
- ¼ cup Honey /62.5ml
- 2 cups Blueberries /260g
- ½ Cinnamon stick
- 1 ¼ cups Water /312.5ml
- ½ Vanilla Bean; sliced lengthwise
- 1 ½ tbsp Cornstarch /22.5g
- ¼ tsp ground Cardamom /1.25g

Directions:
1.   Add all ingredients, except for the honey and the cornstarch, to your Foodi. Seal the pressure lid, choose Pressure, set to High, and set the time to s 8 minutes. Press Start. Do a quick pressure release and open the pressure lid.
2.   Remove the apricots with a slotted spoon. Choose Sear/Sauté, add the honey and cornstarch, then let simmer until the sauce thickens, for about 5 minutes. Split up the apricots among serving plates and top with the blueberry sauce, to serve.

Mexican Chocolate Walnut Cake

Servings: 8
Cooking Time: 2 ½ Hours
Ingredients:

- Butter flavored cooking spray
- 1½ cups flour
- ½ cup cocoa powder, unsweetened
- 2 tsp baking powder
- 2 tsp ground cinnamon
- ¼ tsp cayenne pepper

- 1/8 tsp salt
- 1 cup sugar
- 3 eggs, beaten
- ¾ cup coconut oil melted
- 2 tsp vanilla
- 2 cups zucchini, grated
- ¾ cup walnuts, chopped, divided

Directions:

1. Spray the cooking pot with cooking spray and line the bottom with parchment paper.
2. In a medium bowl, combine dry ingredients and mix well.
3. In a large bowl, beat sugar and eggs until creamy.
4. Stir in oil, vanilla, zucchini, and ½ cup walnuts until combined. Fold in dry ingredients just until combined.
5. Pour batter into cooking pot and sprinkle remaining nuts over the top. Add the lid and set to slow cooking on high. Cook 2 ½ hours or until cake passes the toothpick test. Transfer cake to a wire rack to cool before serving.

Nutrition:

- InfoCalories 452,Total Fat 28g,Total Carbs 48g,Protein 7g,Sodium 189mg.

Almond Cheesecake

Servings: 8

Cooking Time: 25 Minutes

Ingredients:

- Butter flavored cooking spray
- 16 oz. cream cheese, fat free, soft
- ½ cup + 1 tbsp. sugar
- 3 eggs
- 1 tsp almond extract, divided
- ½ tsp fresh lemon juice, divided
- 1 cup sour cream, low fat
- ¼ cup almonds, sliced

Directions:

1. Spray an 8-inch springform pan with cooking spray.
2. In a large bowl, beat cream cheese and ½ cup sugar until smooth.
3. Beat in eggs, one at a time. Then add ½ teaspoon almond extract and ¼ teaspoon lemon juice and beat until mixed. Pour in prepared pan.
4. Place the pan in the cooking pot and add the tender-crisp lid. Set to bake on 325°F or 165°C. Bake 15 minutes, center will still be slightly soft.
5. In a small bowl, combine sour cream, remaining sugar, extract, and lemon juice until smooth. Spread over the top of the cheesecake and sprinkle with almonds. Bake another 10 minutes.
6. Let cool completely, cover and refrigerate at least 4 hours before serving.

Nutrition:

- InfoCalories 115,Total Fat 2g,Total Carbs 25g,Protein 12g,Sodium 465mg.

Irish Cream Flan

Servings: 3

Cooking Time: 10 Minutes

Ingredients:

- ¼ cup + 2 tbsp. sugar, divided
- 1 tbsp. water
- 1 cup half and half
- ¼ cup Irish cream flavored coffee creamer

- ¼ cup Irish cream liqueur
- 2 eggs

Directions:

1. In a small saucepan over medium heat, heat ¼ cup sugar until melted and a deep amber color. Swirl the pan occasionally to distribute the heat.
2. When the sugar reaches the right color remove from heat and carefully stir in the water until combined. Drizzle over the bottoms of 3 ramekins.
3. In a small oven-safe bowl, whisk the eggs.
4. In a small saucepan over medium heat, stir together half and half, creamer, Irish cream, and remaining sugar. Heat to simmering.
5. Gradually whisk the warm liquids into the eggs 2 tablespoons at a time, whisking constantly. After a 1/3 of the cream mixture has been added, slowly pour the remaining mixture into the eggs, whisking constantly until combined.
6. Pour 1 cup water into the cooking pot and add the trivet.
7. Pour the egg mixture into the ramekins and cover tightly with foil. Place them on the trivet.
8. Secure the lid and set to pressure cooking on high. Set the timer for 5 minutes. When the timer goes off, use natural release to remove the lid. Transfer custards to a wire rack and uncover to cool.
9. Cover with plastic wrap and refrigerate at least 4 hours before serving. To serve, use a small knife to loosen the custards from the sides of the ramekin and invert onto serving plate.

Nutrition:

- InfoCalories 215,Total Fat 9g,Total Carbs 25g,Protein 7g,Sodium 134mg.

Chocolate Bread Pudding With Caramel Sauce

Servings: 14

Cooking Time: 3 Hours

Ingredients:

- Butter flavored cooking spray
- 8 cups whole wheat bread, cubed
- 1 cup dark chocolate chips
- ¼ cup cocoa powder, unsweetened
- ½ cup + 1/3 cup Stevia
- 1 cup pecans, chopped, divided
- 1/8 tsp salt
- 2 eggs
- 4 egg whites
- 1 2/3 cup skim milk, divided
- 1 cup almond milk, unsweetened
- 3 tsp vanilla, divided
- 1 tbsp. cornstarch

Directions:

1. Spray cooking pot with cooking spray. Add the bread cubes.
2. In a medium bowl, combine chocolate chips, cocoa, ½ cup Stevia, ¾ cup nuts, and salt, mix well.
3. Whisk in eggs, egg whites, 1 cup milk, coconut milk, and 1 teaspoon vanilla until smooth. Pour over bread and stir to make sure all of the bread cubes are covered. Sprinkle remaining nuts over the top.

4. Add the lid and set to slow cooking on low. Cook 3 hours or until bread pudding passes the toothpick test.
5. In a medium saucepan, combine remaining Stevia and cornstarch. Stir in remaining milk and cook over med-low heat until sauce has thickened.
6. Remove from heat and stir in remaining 2 teaspoons vanilla. Drizzle over bread pudding and serve.

Nutrition:

- InfoCalories 269,Total Fat 14g,Total Carbs 27g,Protein 8g,Sodium 60mg.

Chocolate Rice Pudding

Servings: 8
Cooking Time: 20 Minutes

Ingredients:

- 2/3 cup brown rice, cooked
- 2 cans coconut milk
- ½ cup Stevia
- ½ tsp cinnamon
- 1/8 tsp salt
- 1 tsp vanilla
- ½ cup dark chocolate chips

Directions:

1. Set cooker to sauté on medium. Add milk, Stevia, cinnamon, and salt and bring to a simmer, stirring frequently.
2. Stir in rice and reduce heat to low. Cook 15 minutes, stirring occasionally, until pudding has thickened.
3. Turn off cooker and stir in vanilla and chocolate chips until chocolate has melted. Serve warm or refrigerate at least one hour and serve it cold.

Nutrition:

- InfoCalories 325,Total Fat 22g,Total Carbs 35g,Protein 3g,Sodium 62mg.

Fried Oreos

Servings:9
Cooking Time: 8 Minutes

Ingredients:

- ½ cup complete pancake mix
- ⅓ cup water
- Cooking spray
- 9 Oreo cookies
- 1 tablespoon confectioners' sugar

Directions:

1. Close crisping lid. Select AIR CRISP, set temperature to 400°F or 205°C, and set time to 5 minutes. Select START/STOP to begin preheating.
2. In a medium bowl, combine the pancake mix and water until combined.
3. Spray the Cook & Crisp Basket with cooking spray.
4. Dip each cookie into the pancake batter and then arrange them in the basket in a single layer so they are not touching each other. Cook in batches if needed.
5. When unit has preheated, open lid and insert basket into pot. Close crisping lid.
6. Select AIR CRISP, set temperature to 400°F or 205°C, and set time to 8 minutes. Select START/STOP to begin.
7. After 4 minutes, open lid and flip the cookies. Close lid and continue cooking.

8. When cooking is complete, check for desired crispness. Remove basket and sprinkle the cookies with confectioners' sugar. Serve.

Nutrition:

- InfoCalories: 83,Total Fat: 2g,Sodium: 158mg,Carbohydrates: 14g,Protein: 1g.

Cherry Clafoutti

Servings: 6
Cooking Time: 20 Minutes

Ingredients:

- 2 cups water
- Butter flavored cooking spray
- 2 cups cherries, pitted
- ¾ cup sour cream, low fat
- 4 egg yolks, at room temperature
- 1/3 cup honey
- ¼ cup milk
- 1 tbsp. vanilla
- ½ cup flour

Directions:

1. Place the rack in the cooking pot. Pour in the water. Spray a 2-quart baking dish with cooking spray.
2. Place the cherries in the prepared dish.
3. In a large bowl, whisk together sour cream, egg yolks, honey, milk, and vanilla, mix well.
4. Stir in flour until combined. Pour over cherries. Place the dish on the rack.
5. Secure the lid and set to pressure cooking on low. Set timer for 25 minutes. When timer goes off, use quick release to remove the lid.
6. Transfer dish to wire rack to cool 10 minutes. Slice and serve warm.

Nutrition:

- InfoCalories 184,Total Fat 6g,Total Carbs 27g,Protein 4g,Sodium 35mg.

Chocolate Walnut Cake

Servings: 6
Cooking Time: 20 Minutes

Ingredients:

- 3 eggs
- 1 cup almond flour
- 2/3 cup Erythritol
- 1/3 cup heavy whipping cream
- ¼ cup butter softened
- ¼ cup cacao powder
- ¼ cup walnuts, chopped
- 1 teaspoon baking powder

Directions:

1. In a suitable bowl, mix all the ingredients and with a mixer, beat until fluffy.
2. Add the mixture into a greased Bundt pan.
3. With a piece of foil, cover the pan.
4. In the Ninja Foodi's insert, place 2 cups of water.
5. Set a "Reversible Rack" in the Ninja Foodi's insert.
6. Place the Bundt pan over the "Reversible Rack".
7. Close the Ninja Foodi's lid with a pressure lid and place the pressure valve to the "Seal" position.
8. Select "Pressure" mode and set it to "High" for 20 minutes.

9. Press the "Start/Stop" button to initiate cooking.
10. Switch the pressure valve to "Vent" and do a "Quick" release.
11. Place the pan onto a wire rack to cool for about 10 minutes.
12. Flip the baked and cooled cake onto the wire rack to cool completely.
13. Cut into desired-sized slices and serve.

Nutrition:

- InfoCalories: 270; Fats: 25.4g; Carbohydrates: 7g; Proteins: 8.9g

Strawberry And Lemon Ricotta Cheesecake

Servings: 6
Cooking Time: 35 Min

Ingredients:

- 10 strawberries, halved to decorate
- 10 oz. cream cheese /300g
- 1 ½ cups water /375ml
- ¼ cup sugar /32.5f
- ½ cup Ricotta cheese /65f
- One lemon, zested and juiced
- 2 eggs, cracked into a bowl
- 3 tbsp sour cream /45ml
- 1 tsp lemon extract /5g

Directions:

1. In the electric mixer, add the cream cheese, quarter cup of sugar, ricotta cheese, lemon zest, lemon juice, and lemon extract. Turn on the mixer and mix the ingredients until a smooth consistency is formed. Adjust the sweet taste to liking with more sugar.
2. Reduce the speed of the mixer and add the eggs. Fold it in at low speed until it is fully incorporated. Make sure not to fold the eggs in high speed to prevent a cracker crust. Grease the spring form pan with cooking spray and use a spatula to spoon the mixture into the pan. Level the top with the spatula and cover it with foil.
3. Open the Foodi, fit in the reversible rack, and pour in the water. Place the cake pan on the rack. Close the lid, secure the pressure valve, and select Pressure mode on High pressure for 15 minutes. Press Start/Stop.
4. Meanwhile, mix the sour cream and one tbsp of sugar. Set aside. Once the timer has gone off, do a natural pressure release for 10 minutes, then a quick pressure release to let out any extra steam, and open the lid.
5. Remove the rack with pan, place the spring form pan on a flat surface, and open it. Use a spatula to spread the sour cream mixture on the warm cake. Refrigerate the cake for 8 hours. Top with strawberries; slice it into 6 pieces and serve while firming.

Blackberry Crisp

Servings: 6
Cooking Time: 45 Minutes

Ingredients:

- 6 cups blackberries
- 2 tbsp. sugar, divided
- 1 tbsp. cornstarch
- 1 cup oats
- ½ cup almond flour
- ½ cup almonds, chopped
- 1 tsp cinnamon
- ¼ tsp salt
- ¼ cup coconut oil, melted

Directions:

1. Add the rack to the cooking pot. Spray an 8-inch baking dish with cooking spray.

2. In a large bowl, add the blackberries, 1 tablespoon sugar, and cornstarch, toss to coat. Pour into prepared dish.
3. In the same bowl, combine oats, flour, nuts, cinnamon, salt, coconut oil, and remaining sugar, mix well. Pour over berries.
4. Place the dish on the rack. Add the tender-crisp lid and set to bake on 350°F or 175°C. Bake 30-35 minutes or until top is golden brown. Transfer to wire rack to cool before serving.

Nutrition:

- InfoCalories 282,Total Fat 13g,Total Carbs 38g,Protein 6g,Sodium 100mg.

Chocolate Cheesecake

Servings: 10
Cooking Time: 20 Minutes

Ingredients:

- For Crust
- ¼ cup coconut flour
- ¼ cup almond flour
- 2½ tablespoons cacao powder
- 1½ tablespoons Erythritol
- 2 tablespoons butter, melted
- For Filling
- 16 ounces cream cheese, softened
- 1/3 cup cacao powder
- ½ teaspoon powdered Erythritol
- ½ teaspoon stevia powder
- 1 large egg
- 2 large egg yolks
- 6 ounces unsweetened dark chocolate, melted
- ¾ cup heavy cream
- ¼ cup sour cream
- 1 teaspoon vanilla extract

Directions:

1. For the crust: in a suitable, mix together flours, cacao powder and Erythritol.
2. Stir in the melted butter and mix until well combined.
3. Stir in the mixture into a parchment paper-lined 7-inch springform pan evenly, and with your fingers, press evenly.
4. For filling: in a food processor, add the cream cheese, cacao powder, monk fruit powder and stevia and pulse until smooth.
5. Stir in the egg and egg yolks and pulse until well combined.
6. Add the rest of the ingredients and pulse until well combined.
7. Place the prepared filling mixture on top of the crust evenly and with a rubber spatula, smooth the surface.
8. With a piece of foil, cover the springform pan loosely.
9. In the Ninja Foodi's insert, place 2 cups of water.
10. Set a "Reversible Rack" in the Ninja Foodi's insert.
11. Place the springform pan over the "Reversible Rack".
12. Close the Ninja Foodi's lid with a pressure lid and place the pressure valve in the "Seal" position.
13. Select "Pressure" mode and set it to "High" for 20 minutes.
14. Press the "Start/Stop" button to initiate cooking.
15. Switch the pressure valve to "Vent" and do a "Natural" release.
16. Place the pan onto a wire rack to cool completely.
17. Refrigerate for about 6-8 hours before serving.

Nutrition:

- InfoCalories: 385; Fats: 35.6g; Carbohydrates: 9.8g; Proteins: 8.9g

Yogurt Cheesecake

Servings: 8
Cooking Time: 40 Minutes
Ingredients:
- 4 cups plain Greek Yogurt
- 1 cup Erythritol
- ½ teaspoon vanilla extract

Directions:
1. Line a cake pans with Parchment paper.
2. In a suitable, stir in the yogurt and Erythritol and with a hand mixer, mix well.
3. Stir in vanilla extract and mix to combine.
4. Add the mixture into the prepared pan and cover with a paper kitchen towel.
5. Then with a piece of foil, cover the pan tightly.
6. In the Ninja Foodi's insert, place 1 cup of water.
7. Set a "Reversible Rack" in the Ninja Foodi's insert.
8. Place the ramekins over the "Reversible Rack".
9. Close the Ninja Foodi's lid with a pressure lid and place the pressure valve to the "Seal" position.
10. Select "Pressure" mode and set it to "High" for 40 minutes.
11. Press the "Start/Stop" button to initiate cooking.
12. Switch the pressure valve to "Vent" and do a "Quick" release.
13. Place the pan onto a wire rack and remove the foil and paper towel.
14. Again, cover the pan with a new paper towel and refrigerate to cool overnight.

Nutrition:
- InfoCalories: 88; Fats: 1.5g; Carbohydrates: 8.7g; Proteins: 7g

Raspberry Crumble

Servings: 6
Cooking Time: 40 Min
Ingredients:
- 1 package frozen raspberries /480g
- ½ cup rolled oats /65g
- ⅓ cup cold unsalted butter; cut into pieces /44g
- ½ cup all-purpose flour /65g
- ⅔ cup brown sugar /88g
- ½ cup water, plus 1 tbsp /265ml
- 2 tbsps arrowroot starch /30g
- 5 tbsps sugar; divided /75g
- 1 tsp freshly squeezed lemon juice /5ml
- 1 tsp cinnamon powder /5g

Directions:
1. Place the raspberries in the baking pan. In a small mixing bowl, combine the arrowroot starch, 1 tbsp or 15ml of water, lemon juice, and 3 tbsps or 45g of sugar. Pour the mixture all over the raspberries.
2. Put the reversible rack in the lower position of the pot. Cover the pan with foil and pour the remaining water into the pot. Put the pan on the rack in the pot. Put the pressure lid together, and lock in the Seal position. Choose Pressure, set to High, and set the time to 10 minutes, then Choose Start/Stop to begin.
3. In a bowl, mix the flour, brown sugar, oats, butter, cinnamon, and remaining sugar until crumble forms. When done pressure-cooking, do a quick release and carefully open the lid.
4. Remove the foil and stir the fruit mixture. After, spread the crumble evenly on the berries. Close the crisping lid; choose Air Crisp, set the temperature to 400°F or 205°C, and the time to 10 minutes. Choose Start/Stop to begin crisping. Cook until the top has browned and the fruit is bubbling. When done baking, remove the rack with the pan from the pot, and serve.

Coconut Rice Pudding

Servings:6
Cooking Time: 8 Minutes
Ingredients:
- ¾ cup arborio rice
- 1 can unsweetened full-fat coconut milk
- 1 cup milk
- 1 cup water
- ¾ cup granulated sugar
- ½ teaspoon vanilla extract

Directions:
1. Rinse the rice under cold running water in a fine-mesh strainer.
2. Place the rice, coconut milk, milk, water, sugar, and vanilla in the pot and stir. Assemble pressure lid, making sure the pressure release valve is in the SEAL position.
3. Select PRESSURE and set to HI. Set time to 8 minutes. Select START/STOP to begin.
4. When pressure cooking is complete, allow pressure to naturally release for 10 minutes. After 10 minutes, quick release remaining pressure by moving the pressure release valve to the VENT position. Carefully remove lid when unit has finished releasing pressure.
5. Press a layer of plastic wrap directly on top of the rice (it should be touching) to prevent a skin from forming on top of the pudding. Let pudding cool to room temperature, then refrigerate overnight to set.

Nutrition:
- InfoCalories: 363,Total Fat: 18g,Sodium: 31mg,Carbohydrates: 50g,Protein: 5g.

Churro Bites

Servings:7
Cooking Time: 12 Minutes
Ingredients:
- Cooking spray
- 1 box cinnamon swirl crumb cake and muffin mix, brown sugar mix packet removed and reserved
- 2 large eggs
- 1 cup buttermilk
- 1 teaspoon ground cinnamon, divided
- ¼ cup packed light brown sugar
- 1½ cups water
- 1 tablespoon granulated sugar
- Chocolate sauce, for serving (optional)
- Caramel sauce, for serving (optional)
- Strawberry sauce, for serving (optional)
- Whipped topping, for serving (optional)
- Peanut butter, for serving (optional)

Directions:
1. Lightly coat 2 egg bite molds with cooking spray and set aside.
2. In a large bowl, combine the cake mix, brown sugar mix packet, eggs, buttermilk, and ½ teaspoon of cinnamon. Mix until evenly combined.
3. Using a cookie scoop, transfer the batter to the prepared mold, filling each three-quarters full. Tightly cover the molds with aluminum foil, or with the silicone cover that came with the egg molds.
4. Pour the water into the cooking pot. Place the egg molds onto the Reversible Rack in the lower steam position and lower into the pot.

5. If using a foil sling (see TIP), ensure the foil cover is tight enough to support the egg mold that will sit on top. Rotate the top egg mold slightly to ensure that the molds do not press into one another.

6. Assemble the pressure lid, making sure the pressure release valve is in the SEAL position.

7. Select PRESSURE and set to HI. Set the time to 12 minutes. Select START/STOP to begin.

8. When pressure cooking is complete, allow the pressure to naturally release for 10 minutes. After 10 minutes, quick release any remaining pressure by moving the pressure release valve to the VENT position. Carefully remove the lid when the unit has finished releasing pressure.

9. In a small bowl, stir together the brown sugar, granulated sugar, and remaining ½ teaspoon of cinnamon. Set aside.

10. Using the sling, remove the egg molds from the pot and let cool for 5 minutes.

11. One at a time, place a plate over the egg mold and flip the mold over. Gently press on the mold to release the churro bites.

12. Roll the warm churro bites in the brown sugar mixture, and sprinkle any remaining brown sugar on top. Serve with your favorite dipping sauce.

Nutrition:
- Info.

Almond Milk

Servings: 4
Cooking Time: 20 Min

Ingredients:
- 1 cup raw almonds; soaked overnight, rinsed and peeled /130g
- 2 dried apricots; chopped
- 1 cup cold water /250ml
- 4 cups water /1000ml
- 1 vanilla bean
- 2 tbsp honey /30ml

Directions:
1. In the pot, mix a cup of cold water with almonds and apricots. Seal the pressure lid, choose Pressure, set to High, and set the timer to 1 minute.

2. When ready, release the pressure quickly. Open the lid. The almonds should be soft and plump, and the water should be brown and murky. Use a strainer to drain almonds; rinse with cold water for 1 minute.

3. To a high-speed blender, add the rinsed almonds, vanilla bean, honey, and 4 cups or 1000ml water. Blend for 2 minutes until well combined and frothy. Line a cheesecloth to the strainer.

4. Place the strainer over a bowl and strain the milk. Use a wooden spoon to press milk through the cheesecloth and get rid of solids. Place almond milk in an airtight container and refrigerate.

Crispy Coconut Pie

Servings: 8
Cooking Time: 1 Hour

Ingredients:
- 3 eggs
- 1 ½ cup Stevia
- 1 cup coconut, grated
- ½ cup butter, melted
- 1 tbsp. vinegar
- 1 tsp vanilla
- 1/8 tsp salt
- 1 9" pie crust, raw

Directions:

1. In a large bowl, beat the eggs.
2. Add remaining ingredients and mix well. Pour into pie crust.
3. Use a foil sling to carefully place the pie in the cooking pot. Add the tender-crisp lid and set to bake on 350°F or 175°C. Bake 1 hour or until top is nicely browned and crisp.
4. Transfer to a wire rack to cool before serving.

Nutrition:
- InfoCalories 427, Total Fat 22g, Total Carbs 45g, Protein 3g, Sodium 304mg.

Rhubarb, Raspberry, And Peach Cobbler

Servings: 6
Cooking Time: 40 Minutes

Ingredients:
- 1 cup all-purpose flour, divided
- ¾ cup granulated sugar
- ½ teaspoon kosher salt, divided
- 2½ cups diced fresh rhubarb
- 2½ cups fresh raspberries
- 2½ cups fresh peaches, peeled and sliced into ¾-inch pieces
- Cooking spray
- ¾ cup brown sugar
- ½ cup oat flakes (oatmeal)
- 1 teaspoon cinnamon
- Pinch ground nutmeg
- 6 tablespoons unsalted butter, sliced, at room temperature
- ½ cup chopped pecans or walnuts

Directions:
1. Select BAKE/ROAST, set temperature to 400°F or 205°C, and set time to 30 minutes. Select START/STOP to begin. Let preheat for 5 minutes.

2. In a large bowl, whisk together ¼ cup of flour, granulated sugar, and ¼ teaspoon of salt. Add the rhubarb, raspberries, and peach and mix until evenly coated.

3. Grease a Ninja Multi-Purpose Pan or a 1½-quart round ceramic baking dish with cooking spray. Add the fruit mixture to the pan.

4. Place pan on Reversible Rack, making sure the rack is in the lower position. Cover pan with aluminum foil.

5. Once unit has preheated, place rack in pot. Close crisping lid and adjust temperature to 375°F or 190°C. Cook for 25 minutes.

6. In a medium bowl, combine the remaining ¾ cup of flour, brown sugar, oat flakes, cinnamon, remaining ¼ teaspoon of salt, nutmeg, butter, and pecans. Mix well.

7. When cooking is complete, open lid. Remove the foil and stir the fruit. Spread the topping evenly over the fruit. Close crisping lid.

8. Select BAKE/ROAST, set temperature to 400°F or 205°C, and set time to 15 minutes. Select START/STOP to begin. Cook until the topping is browned and the fruit is bubbling.

9. When cooking is complete, remove rack with pan from pot and serve.

Nutrition:
- InfoCalories: 476, Total Fat: 19g, Sodium: 204mg, Carbohydrates: 76g, Protein: 6g.

RECIPE INDEX

Printed in Great Britain
by Amazon